THE CAMBRIDGE COMPANION TO
COMMON-SENSE PHILOSOPHY

Common-sense philosophy is important because it maintains
that we can know many things about the world, about
ourselves, about morality, and even about things of a
metaphysical nature. The tenets of common-sense
philosophy, while in some sense obvious and unsurprising,
give rise to powerful arguments that can shed light on
fundamental philosophical issues, including the perennial
problem of scepticism and the emerging challenge of
scientism. This *Companion* offers an exploration of common-
sense philosophy in its many forms, tracing its development as a
concept and considering the roles it has been assigned to play
throughout the history of philosophy. Containing fifteen newly
commissioned chapters from leading experts in the history of
philosophy, epistemology, the philosophy of science, moral
philosophy, and metaphysics, the volume will be an essential
guide for students and scholars hoping to gain a greater
understanding of the value and enduring appeal of common-
sense philosophy.

RIK PEELS is Associate Professor of Philosophy, Theology and
Religion at Vrije Universiteit Amsterdam. He is the author of
many books on epistemology and ethics, including
Responsible Belief: A Theory in Ethics and Epistemology
(2017), and is the editor of *Perspectives on Ignorance from
Moral and Social Philosophy* (2017) and *The Epistemic
Dimensions of Ignorance* (with Martijn Blaauw, 2017).

RENÉ VAN WOUDENBERG is Professor of Philosophy at Vrije
Universiteit Amsterdam and Director of the university's
Abraham Kuyper Center for Science and the Big Questions. He
is the co-editor, with Rik Peels and Jeroen de Ridder, of
Scientism: Prospects and Problems (2018) and *Scientific
Challenges to Common Sense Philosophy* (2020).

T0381538

Continued at the back of the book

The Cambridge Companion to

COMMON-SENSE PHILOSOPHY

Edited by

Rik Peels
Vrije Universiteit Amsterdam

René van Woudenberg
Vrije Universiteit Amsterdam

CAMBRIDGE
UNIVERSITY PRESS

University Printing House, Cambridge CB2 8BS, United Kingdom

One Liberty Plaza, 20th Floor, New York, NY 10006, USA

477 Williamstown Road, Port Melbourne, VIC 3207, Australia

314–321, 3rd Floor, Plot 3, Splendor Forum, Jasola District Centre, New Delhi – 110025, India

79 Anson Road, #06–04/06, Singapore 079906

Cambridge University Press is part of the University of Cambridge.

It furthers the University's mission by disseminating knowledge in the pursuit of education, learning, and research at the highest international levels of excellence.

www.cambridge.org
Information on this title: www.cambridge.org/9781108476003
DOI: 10.1017/9781108598163

First published 2021

A catalogue record for this publication is available from the British Library.

ISBN 978-1-108-47600-3 Hardback
ISBN 978-1-108-46936-4 Paperback

Contents

PART II

Contributors

Thomas Baldwin is Professor of Philosophy at the University of York. His publications include *G. E. Moore* (1990), and he has edited some of Moore's works, including *Principia Ethica* (1993) and his *Early Philosophical Writings* (2011).

Richard Bett is Professor of Philosophy and Classics at Johns Hopkins University. He is the author of *Pyrrho, His Antecedents, and His Legacy* (2000) and has translated several works by Sextus Empiricus. He edited *The Cambridge Companion to Ancient Scepticism* (2010), and Cambridge University Press has published a collection of his essays, *How to Be a Pyrrhonist* (2019).

Jeroen de Ridder is Associate Professor of Philosophy at Vrije Universiteit Amsterdam and Professor of Christian Philosophy by special appointment at the University of Groningen. He is co-editor of *Scientism: Prospects and Problems* (2018), *The Routledge Handbook of Political Epistemology* (forthcoming), and *Social Virtue Epistemology* (forthcoming).

Nicolas de Warren is Associate Professor of Philosophy at Pennsylvania State University. He is the author of *A Momentary Breathlessness in the Sadness of Time* (2018), and co-edited a volume of source materials on phenomenology and the First World War, *Philosophers at the Front* (2018).

Krista Lawlor is Professor of Philosophy at Stanford University. She is the author of *New Thoughts about Old Things* (2001), *Assurance: An Austinian View of Knowledge and Knowledge Claims* (2013), and various articles, especially on self-knowledge, knowledge attribution, and J. L. Austin.

Joanna Lawson is a graduate student in philosophy at Yale University. She has an MPhil in philosophical theology from Oxford, and an MA in philosophy from UNC, Chapel Hill.

Noah Lemos is the Legum Professor of Philosophy at The College of William and Mary. He is the author of *Intrinsic Value* (1994), *Common Sense* (2004), and *An Introduction to the Theory of Knowledge* (2007).

Rik Peels is Associate Professor in Philosophy and Religion & Theology at Vrije Universiteit Amsterdam. He has published *Responsible Belief: A Theory in Ethics and Epistemology* (2017), edited *Moral and Social Perspectives on Ignorance* (2017), and co-edited *The Epistemic Dimensions of Ignorance* (2016) with Martijn Blaauw, *Scientism: Prospects and Problems* (2018) with Jeroen de Ridder and René van Woudenberg, and *Scientific Challenges to Common Sense Philosophy* (2020) with Jeroen de Ridder and René van Woudenberg.

Massimo Pigliucci is the K. D. Irani Professor of Philosophy at the City College of New York. His books include *Nonsense on Stilts: How to Tell Science from Bunk* (2010), *How to Be a Stoic: Using Ancient Philosophy to Live a Modern Life* (2017), and *A Handbook for New Stoics: How to Thrive in a World Out of Your Control* (2019) with Greg Lopez.

Duncan Pritchard is Distinguished Professor of Philosophy at the University of California, Irvine. His publications include *Epistemic Luck* (2005), *The Nature and Value of Knowledge* (co-authored, 2010), *Epistemological Disjunctivism* (2012), and *Epistemic Angst* (2015).

Chris Ranalli is a postdoctoral researcher at Vrije Universiteit Amsterdam. He has held fellowships at the Universität zu Köln and the Universidad Nacional Autónoma de México.

Nicholas Rescher is Professor of Philosophy at the University of Pittsburgh. He has published many books, including, most recently,

Philosophical Progress, and Other Philosophical Studies (2014), and *Pragmatism in Philosophical Inquiry* (2016).

Orly Shenker is Associate Professor at the programme for history and philosophy of science at the Hebrew University of Jerusalem, holds the Eleanor Roosevelt Chair in History and Philosophy of Science, and is the director of the Sidney M. Edelstein Centre for History and Philosophy of Science, Technology and Medicine. She has co-authored (with Meir Hemmo) *The Road to Maxwell's Demon: Conceptual Foundations of Statistical Mechanics* (2012).

René van Woudenberg is Professor of Philosophy at Vrije Universiteit Amsterdam and the director of the Abraham Kuyper Center for Science and the Big Questions at the same university. His recent publications include *The Epistemology of Reading and Interpretation* (Cambridge, forthcoming).

Stephen I. Wagner is Emeritus Professor of Philosophy at St. John's University/College of St. Benedict in Minnesota. He is the author of *Squaring the Circle in Descartes' Meditations: The Strong Validation of Reason* (Cambridge 2014).

Paul Wood is Emeritus Professor of Philosophy at the University of Victoria, Canada. He has published widely on science and philosophy in the Scottish Enlightenment.

Introduction: Why Common Sense Matters

René van Woudenberg and Rik Peels

'Common sense' is a notion that philosophers seem unable to work without. They have used it for a variety of purposes. Some use it merely as a more or less neutral term to refer to truisms and platitudes that are widely held, such as that there is a material world external to our minds or that nature can be known by human beings. Others have gone further and used the term in order to make certain claims about it. Immanuel Kant, for example, urged that when we attempt to settle a philosophical dispute, we should never appeal to common sense. Thomas Reid and G. E. Moore, by contrast, held that common sense provides legitimate points of reference for settling philosophical debates. Other claims involving common sense concern its relation to science. Some philosophers have claimed that common sense is at odds with science – that the flipside of scientific progress is the undoing of common sense.[1] But others have argued that science, in Gustav Bergmann's memorable phrase, is 'the long arm of common sense' (Bergmann 1957: 20). In one way or another, philosophers had a need to speak of common sense.

This introduction shows why and how common sense matters to philosophy, thus lightening up the terrain that subsequent chapters explore in much greater detail. First, we explain briefly what *common sense* is and, next, what common-sense *philosophy* is. Then we consider whether, and if so how, common sense should *matter* to philosophy; can we not do without common sense? Subsequently, we turn to criticisms of the idea that common sense matters to philosophy and criticisms of the very idea of common-sense philosophy. We conclude with a short note on the organization of this book.

WHAT IS COMMON SENSE?

When one tries to pinpoint the referent of 'common sense' as the notion is used in the philosophical literature, one will be struck by the fact that it is used to refer to rather different kinds of things: to a particular group of beliefs, to a set of intuitions, to a number of principles, to a belief-forming faculty, and to a loose array of methodological rules.

The Greeks used the notion to refer to beliefs that are widely held. That Zeus is the highest god in the pantheon was widely believed in ancient Greece and hence qualifies as a common-sense belief (see Chapter 1 by Richard Bett in this volume).

In later times, philosophers wielded a much more restricted notion of common-sense belief. Thomas Reid, for instance, delineated common-sense beliefs as beliefs that are widely held and that have, in addition, such properties as that their denials are absurd, that they are not believed on the basis of some kind of scientific investigation, and that they are foundational to practices that humans are ineluctably engaged in.[2] Take the belief that there is life and intelligence in the people we converse with. This belief is widely shared, its denial is absurd, it is not based on some form of scientific investigation, and it is foundational to such practices as buying and selling, education, and leading a social life. Hence, this notion of common sense is much more restricted than the notion that the Greeks used. That Zeus is the highest god of the pantheon was once widely believed. But its denial is not absurd, nor is it foundational to a practice that humans are ineluctably engaged in. Therefore, it is not a common-sense belief in Reid's sense.

'Common sense' is also used to refer to certain intuitions that we have. If we think of intuitions as intellectual seemings, then the following sentences state intellectual intuitions: there presently is a body which is *your* body (to use an example from G. E. Moore); and no proposition can be true and false at the same time. An intellectual seeming is not necessarily a belief, nor does it necessarily lead to one.

It may intellectually seem to you that velocities are additive, but you do not believe it – at least, not if you are aware of the fact that Einstein's theory of special relativity entails that velocities are not strictly additive. But no doubt often there is nothing wrong with believing what intellectually seems to be the case; for instance, that the thoughts we are conscious of must have a subject. Here, then, is a common-sense intuition of a proposition, an intuition that leads us to believe it as well.

The phrase 'common sense' is also used to refer to principles of reasoning and inquiry widely held to be utterly plausible and wholly unproblematic. Examples include:

- in *epistemology*: the principle of credulity ('It is probable that what seems to be the case actually is the case') and the principle of epistemic conservatism ('It is unreasonable to revise or alter a belief one has without good reason to do so');
- in *metaphysics*: the principle of parsimony (Occam's razor: 'Entities should not be multiplied beyond necessity'), the principle that 'every change has a cause', and the principle that 'everything that begins to exist must have a cause';
- in *ethics*: the principle of double effect ('There is a morally relevant difference between those consequences of our actions that we intend and those we do not intend but still foresee'), as well as the principle that 'like cases should be treated equally';
- in the *philosophy of science*: the principle of parsimony (Occam's razor).

Occasionally (but the idea never had many adherents), Thomas Reid spoke of a 'faculty' of common sense – a faculty operating in humans alongside perception, memory, and reason (see Reid (1785) 2002).

Finally, 'common sense' is also used to refer to what could *very* loosely be called a method for doing philosophy (see Daley 2010: chapter 1). If that method is used or applied, what we then have – the activity as well as the results thereof – could be called 'common-sense philosophy'.

WHAT IS COMMON-SENSE PHILOSOPHY?

In broad strokes, *common-sense philosophy* is philosophy that is roughly characterized by three methodological features.[3]

First, it accords common-sense beliefs, intuitions, and principles a strong and privileged epistemic status: roughly speaking, they have authority with default status and should only be given up, if that is possible at all, in the face of extraordinarily strong reasons. (We note that Moore held that no reason is strong enough to force us to give up a common-sense belief: 'the common sense view of the world', he said, 'is in certain fundamental features wholly true' (Moore (1925) 1993: 110). Other common-sense philosophers, however, have adopted the idea that common-sense beliefs and intuitions are potentially defeasible; they are innocent until proven guilty.)

Second, common-sense philosophy evaluates extant philosophical positions by how well they square with common-sense beliefs, common-sense intuitions, and common-sense principles; if the positions deny, or entail the denial of, common-sense beliefs, intuitions, or principles, then that is decidedly a strike against them.

Third and finally, when not engaged in philosophical critique but in constructive philosophy, common-sense philosophy takes common-sense beliefs, intuitions, and principles as *data points* that should be given their rightful place. In Thomas Reid's view, common sense is the soil on which the flower of philosophy should bloom: 'Philosophy … has no other root but the principles of Common Sense: it grows out of them, and draws its nourishment from them: severed from this root, its honours wither, its sap is dried up, it dies and rots' (Reid (1764) 1997: 19). Moore, Chisholm, and other common-sense philosophers concurred: common-sense beliefs and intuitions are data points to be reckoned with, or even starting points for philosophical theorizing.

WHY COMMON SENSE MATTERS TO PHILOSOPHY

Common sense and appeals to common sense play an important role in various subfields of philosophy, even if they are not named or presented as 'appeals to common sense'. Epistemologists, for example, have offered many proposals as to how the concept of knowledge should be analysed. In the course of these discussions, counterexamples to proposed analyses have been presented, and these counterexamples usually triggered common-sense intuitions about knowledge. Edmund Gettier's counterexamples to the justified-true-belief account of knowledge, for example, triggered common-sense intuitions about knowledge – even if Gettier himself did not use the expression 'common-sense intuition' (see Gettier 1963). The intuition that Gettier appealed to can be described by means of Bertrand Russell's case of the man who looks at a clock that indicates that it is twelve o'clock; the man forms the belief that it is twelve o'clock, and it actually *is* twelve o'clock. Now suppose that the clock served the man well over many years; then his belief seems justified as well. He has a justified true belief. However, unbeknownst to him, the clock came to a halt exactly twenty-four hours ago. Then, although he has a justified true belief, so the Gettier argument goes (thereby relying on a common-sense intuition), it would seem that he has no knowledge. (Between brackets we note that appeals to common sense are often made by means of such locutions as 'It seems (to me) that ... ', 'It would appear that ... ', 'It is intuitive that ... ', 'It would be utterly strange to say that ... ', 'Thinking that ... would be absurd', and 'The person in the street holds that ... '.)

Appeals to common sense are by no means restricted to epistemology. Think, for example, about the discussion in meta-ethics about the claim that moral responsibility requires the ability to do otherwise. This claim, or one very close to it, is one of Reid's common-sense 'first principles': 'No man can be blamed for what it was not in his power to hinder' (Reid (1785) 2002: 494). Harry Frankfurt famously presented the case of a 'counterfactual intervener' who would have made Jones do deed D if Jones were to decide 'on his own steam' not to do D – but the intervener need not come into action as Jones does D 'on his own steam' (Frankfurt 1969). In this case, says Frankfurt, it is intuitive that Jones *is* morally responsible for doing D, and hence it would seem that the principle that moral responsibility requires the ability to do otherwise is false. Our point is not to take a stance on Frankfurt's example, but to flag the fact that the Jones case that Frankfurt presents is meant to trigger common-sense intuitions (although, again, not under that description). This case is interesting because Frankfurt brings a common-sense intuition (about the Jones case) to bear against another common-sense intuition (about a general principle concerning responsibility). This illustrates – admittedly in a somewhat backhanded way – that common sense really matters to philosophy. Common-sense intuitions compare to the bumpers in a pinball machine: they move our thoughts in a way somewhat analogous to the way the bumpers move the pinball. In this example, two common-sense intuitions set our thoughts in motion: the intuition behind Reid's first principle, and our intuition that Jones is responsible.

In ethics we find appeals to common sense in, for example, the discussion of utilitarianism – roughly, the view that the morality of an action exclusively depends on its results. If abusive teachers, corrupt politicians, or slave owners get some utility from their actions, this should be as much thrown in the balance of reasons as the welfare (or rather, the absence thereof) of their victims. If no other action would produce as much overall benefit, then the abuse is, by the utilitarian's light, morally justified. And this, Shafer-Landau suggests, just seems plain wrong, for it is intuitively obvious that some actions are intrinsically wrong (Shafer-Landau 2012: 143). Here we see an appeal to common sense, albeit, again, not under that name.

The same holds in metaphysics, although there the dialectical situation seems to be rather different than in epistemology and ethics. Whereas in the latter fields common sense (common-sense beliefs, intuitions, principles) functions as a court of appeal, in metaphysics that seems far less the case. One area of metaphysical discussion of which this is true concerns material objects, their parts, and their identity across time. As Peter van Inwagen (1997: x) has said, common sense tells us (1) that the world contains numerous material objects,

(2) that many of these objects have parts that are themselves material objects, (3) that these objects endure through time, (4) that these objects can sometimes gain or lose parts, (5) that no two material objects can occupy the same space at the same time, and (6) that we humans are able to identify and know these material objects. Common sense tells us a lot!

However, it has been argued, there is a problem: the common-sense propositions are inconsistent with each other.[4] And if they are, this means that common sense cannot be fully relied upon, for in that case at least one of the propositions of common sense should be rejected. But what this shows is *not* that common sense *plays no role* in metaphysics, nor does it show that it *should play no role* in metaphysics. Rather, what it shows is that common sense does in fact play a *very* important role in metaphysical theorizing: the six common-sense propositions function somewhat analogously to the bumpers of the pinball machine – they move metaphysical thinking processes. The alleged inconsistency of the six propositions does not show that common sense should play no role in metaphysical theorizing either. It shows, at best, that we may have to give up something that *seemed* plain common sense, but was not. But that we may have to discard some common-sense beliefs does not entail that *none* of them can be a court of appeal. In fact, this example shows that alleged common-sense intuitions or beliefs may lose their innocence and be found guilty.

It is not only in epistemology, meta-ethics, ethics, and metaphysics that common sense and appeals to it matter. We should expect common sense to matter in *all* fields of philosophy. Let us illustrate this by reference to the field of philosophical reflection on the writing and reading of texts – which can be thought of as a subfield of what is often called 'hermeneutics'. There is a general heuristic for how to spot common-sense assumptions in a field, namely, by reflecting on the question 'what would obviously be absurd to assert in this field?' A related heuristic is to concentrate on a practice in the field and reflect on the question 'which statement *s* is such that it is obvious that you cannot consistently engage in the practice and deny *s*?' We note that the inclusion of the element of 'obviousness' is motivated by the idea that common-sense propositions don't require, for their identification, scientific research or protracted and technical forms of reasoning.

If we apply this heuristic to the field of writing and reading texts, the following three propositions would seem to be common-sense propositions:

1. Texts have authors.
2. Authors mean to communicate things by means of their texts.
3. People can often come to know what authors mean to communicate by means of reading their texts.

After all, the denials of these propositions are obviously absurd. Moreover, it is obvious that you cannot consistently engage in the practice of writing texts and deny (1). It is also obvious that you cannot consistently engage in the practice of reading letters and messages directed to you and deny (2). Finally, it is obvious that you cannot consistently engage in the practice of higher education (which involves lots of reading) and deny (3). The point about identifying these common-sense propositions is not, of course, to startle ourselves and others with them. They are truisms, platitudes, not worth stating – that is to say, until people start thinking and saying things that entail their denial. And in the area of hermeneutics and literary theory, many statements are made that at the very least *seem* to entail their denial.[5] This has triggered a fundamental discussion – with common-sense intuitions once again functioning not wholly unlike the buffers on a pinball machine.[6]

All of this goes to show that common sense does indeed matter to philosophy: common sense, in one way or another, needs to be, and in fact usually is, reckoned with. The purpose of this book is, first, to register this fact and, second, to stimulate reflection and discussion on *why* it matters to philosophy and *how* exactly, and on which role and what sort of authority common sense has been and should be given in philosophical thinking.

CRITICISMS OF APPEALS TO COMMON SENSE

Common sense and appeals to it in philosophical discussions have been frowned upon. Immanuel Kant, for instance, in the Introduction to his *Prolegomena to Any Future Metaphysics*, says:

> It is indeed a great gift of God to possess ... plain common sense. But this common sense must be shown in action by well-considered and reasonable thoughts and words, not by appealing to it as an oracle when no rational justification for one's position can be advanced. To appeal to common sense when science and insight fail, and no sooner – this is one of the subtle discoveries of modern times, by means of which the most superficial ranter can safely enter the lists with the most thorough thinker and hold his own. But as long as a particle of insight remains, no one would think of having recourse to this subterfuge. Seen clearly, it is but an appeal to the opinion of the multitude, of whose applause the philosopher is ashamed, while the popular charlatan glories and boasts in it.
> (Kant (1783) 1950: 7)

Although not everything Kant says here is fully clear, what *is* clear is that he is less than enthusiastic about appeals to common sense in philosophy. Appeals to common sense, he holds, are appeals to the opinions of the multitude. And although he does not say *why* it is wrong to make such an appeal, we may perhaps assume that it is because he relies on some principle like 'If the multitude thinks that *p*, *p* is false or unreasonable'.

What Kant says is, for a number of reasons, at the very least puzzling, if not problematic. First, as indicated earlier on, the common-sense philosopher does not hold that each and every proposition believed by the multitude is a common-sense proposition. For, in addition to being widely believed (or assumed), common-sense propositions have such properties as that their denials are absurd, that they are not believed on the basis of some kind of scientific investigation, and that they are foundational to practices that humans are ineluctably engaged in. Many beliefs held by the multitude lack these properties – such as the belief that reading poetry is worthless and useless, or that travelling the world (never mind one's ecological footprint) is a really fine thing to wish for and to do. So common-sense beliefs are, at best, a subset of beliefs held by the multitude.

Second, Kant does say that having common sense is a gift of God. But he immediately adds that it 'must be shown in action by well-considered and reasonable thoughts and words, not by appealing to it as an oracle when no rational justification for one's position can be advanced'. This is puzzling. For it looks as if Kant says that God offers us a gift that we should reject! Or rather, it looks as if he says: 'Now see here, common sense is something that is really important, and we can get it (if we can get it), in two ways: as a gift from God, or through our own rational activity. But we should not want to get it in the former way, only in the latter.' The question is why this should be so.

Third, it is puzzling, and in a subtle way also in tension with the idea that common sense is a gift from God, that Kant relies on some principle like: 'If the multitude thinks that p, p is false or unreasonable'. In the philosophical tradition, principles like this have often been considered implausible. *Consensus gentium* arguments keep making their appearance, be it under the name of 'wisdom of the crowds', 'common sense', or 'folk philosophy'. Saying that 'p is believed by the multitude and therefore p is false or unreasonable' just is not convincing. For a basic idea behind *consensus gentium* arguments is that the universality of a belief is taken to be evidence that it is instinctive – and that the best explanation of its being instinctive is that it is true.[7]

Fourth, as Noah Lemos has suggested, Kant may have wanted to bring against appeals to common sense that common-sense beliefs *lack justification*, and that therefore appeals to them are no better than appeals to oracles. And he may have thought that such beliefs lack justification because the common-sense philosopher does not adduce arguments that buttress those beliefs. But if that is what motivates Kant's complaint, it cannot, again, be taken very seriously. For why should we assume that the only way in which a belief can be justified is by adducing reasons in favour of it? 'Why', Lemos urges, 'must we think that the only way in which one can be justified in believing ... that there are other people who have bodies and talk, is on the basis of an argument?' (Lemos 2004: 68). And he next suggests that there *are* sources of justification in addition to argument – such as a belief's originating in perception, or memory – and that common-sense philosophers acknowledge the justificatory potential of these sources.

Therefore, we should not assume that Kant has made a serious case against common-sense philosophy. Let us see whether Bertrand Russell's case fares any better:

> The man who has no tincture of philosophy goes through life imprisoned in the prejudices derived from common sense, from the habitual beliefs of his age or his nation, and from convictions which have grown up in his mind without the co-operation or consent of his deliberate reason. To such a man the world tends to become definite, finite, obvious; common objects rouse no questions, and unfamiliar possibilities are contemptuously rejected.
>
> Philosophy, though unable to tell us with certainty what is the true answer to the doubts which it raises, is able to suggest many possibilities which enlarge our thoughts and free them from the tyranny of custom.
>
> Thus, while diminishing our feeling of certainty as to what things are, it greatly increases our knowledge as to what they may be; it removes the somewhat arrogant dogmatism of those who have never travelled into the region of liberating doubt, and it keeps alive our sense of wonder by showing familiar things in an unfamiliar aspect. (Russell 1912: chapter 15)

What Russell is opposed to is, in a way, unremarkable: he is opposed to prejudice, contemptuous rejections of unfamiliar possibilities, and arrogant dogmatism. What he is in favour of is, in a way, unremarkable as well: he is in favour of beliefs and convictions that are reasonable, of admitting liberating doubt, and of keeping alive a sense of wonder. Are these aversions and allegiances such that anyone having them should be opposed to common sense and to common-sense philosophy, as Russell's words may seem to suggest?

It should be clear that common-sense beliefs as Reid, Moore, and Chisholm think of them aren't mere prejudices, at least not when we think of a prejudice as 'an unfair or unreasonable opinion or feeling formed beforehand without knowledge or thought'. After all, what is unfair or unreasonable about the belief that there is a material world external to our minds or about the belief that there is a body that is *your* body? Also, common-sense philosophers who believe these propositions give their beliefs a great deal of thought. Nor should we think that common-sense beliefs as Reid, Moore, and Chisholm think of them are merely dogmatically held beliefs, at least not when we think of dogmatic beliefs as 'beliefs that are held more strongly than the evidence warrants' or as 'beliefs that are held uncritically, i.e., without paying sufficient heed to objections and alternatives'. After all, there would seem to be a lot of evidence for such strongly held beliefs as that humans have identity over time and that no proposition can be true and false at the same time. Nor are these beliefs held uncritically, at least not by common-sense philosophers – in fact, Reid, Moore, and Chisholm pay a lot of attention to objections and alternatives. Also, there is no reason to think that common-sense beliefs crowd out a sense of wonder. It would rather seem to work in the other direction: acknowledging the common-sense beliefs that we find we have induces a sense of wonder about the complexity of cognitive abilities, about how they interact, and about how difficult it is to chart them properly. As to the suggestion that common sense does not suggest 'possibilities which enlarge our thoughts and free them from the tyranny of custom', we note that Reid engaged in meta-reflections on the very topic of possibility itself and explicitly engaged Hume's claim that conceivability is a guide to possibility (see Van Woudenberg 2006).

If we read the words of Russell that we quoted as a critique of (appeals to) common sense, then Russell's criticism fares no better than Kant's. A third kind of critique of (appeals to) common sense is exemplified by what have come to be called 'debunking arguments'. Debunking arguments have been launched against so-called folk psychology and against certain common-sense ideas concerning ethics. We briefly provide two illustrations.

First, 'folk psychology' is a (somewhat pejorative) term that is used to refer to a network of common-sense principles that supposedly jointly constitute a 'theory' that we use when we try to explain the behaviour of our fellow humans. The theory gives pride of place to beliefs, desires, and intentions – these are the terms in which we explain the behaviour of others, if not of ourselves. Espousing what they call 'eliminativism', Paul and Patricia Churchland have offered debunking arguments against such explanations (see Churchland 1986; 2002). They presume that mature neuroscience will show that folk psychology is radically false, that there really are no such things as beliefs, desires, and intentions, and that these labels don't latch on to anything real. They also argue that we cannot know through introspection the reasons for which we act, because there are no such reasons as common sense conceives of them, and so on. Eliminativism thus aims to debunk common-sense folk psychology.

Second, as Sharon Street (2006) and others have argued, there are good reasons from biology to think that common-sense moral beliefs are misguided. The basic idea here is that common sense embraces moral realism, that is, the view that there are objective moral truths that exist independently from us, such as that promises ought to be kept and that killing is wrong, and that we can *know* such truths. Street, however, argues that there are debunking defeaters for such common-sense beliefs, because biology should lead us into thinking that our moral beliefs have been selected for the survival value they afford, *not* because they are true. These arguments thus counter common-sense beliefs about morality.

Other debunking arguments target common-sense beliefs about the material world, about free will, and about purpose. We bring this out only to note that this volume contains no chapters that discuss such science-based debunking arguments of common-sense beliefs. A separate volume is dedicated to such arguments (see Peels et al. 2020). The crucial question here is whether it really is *science* (when well executed) that debunks common sense or whether it is a particular philosophical *view about science* that does the trick – such as scientism (roughly, the view that only the natural sciences deliver rational belief, knowledge, and understanding).[8]

ORGANIZATION OF THE BOOK

The first part of the book is concerned with the history of common-sense philosophy. The second part of the book discusses various critical issues for common-sense philosophy from a contemporary and broadly analytic perspective.[9]

NOTES

1 For various examples of this, see De Ridder et al. (2018); Peels et al. (2020).

2 Reid ((1785) 2002: 433). For a fuller delineation, see Chapter 7 by René van Woudenberg in this volume.

3 Somewhat different characterizations of common-sense philosophy are offered by Campbell (1988); Coady (2007); Kelly (2008).

4 See the chapters by Wiggins, Geach, and Heller in Rae (1997).

5 For instance, Fish (1980). A response to Fish that in a way appeals to common-sense intuitions about texts and meanings and authorial intentions, although not under that label, is Gaskin (2013: chapter 5).

6 Van Woudenberg (2018) offers an analysis of reading that refers to common-sense intuitions of the sort mentioned in the body of the text. The subject is extensively treated in Van Woudenberg (2021).

7 *Consensus gentium* arguments thus usually take the form of an inference to the best explanation. Zagzebski (2012: 69–74), however, develops a *consensus gentium* argument that does *not* aim to explain the generality of some beliefs. Zagzebski's argument links trust in the beliefs of others with self-trust.

8 'Scientism' is a term that is no longer used in a pejorative sense. See, for example, Rosenberg (2011); Ross et al. (2007). Volumes entirely devoted to a discussion of scientism are De Ridder et al. (2018); Boudry and Pigliucci (2017).

9 We thank Hilary Gaskin for her kind encouragement throughout the entire process. We thank Elisa Matse for helpful assistance in various organizational matters pertaining to the book. We also thank Mathanja Berger for her splendid and meticulous work on this volume as a research assistant. This publication was made possible through the support of a grant from the Templeton World Charity Foundation. The opinions expressed in this publication are those of the authors and do not necessarily reflect the views of the Templeton World Charity Foundation.

Part I

I Attitudes towards Common Sense in Ancient Greek Philosophy

Richard Bett

Broadly speaking there are two contrasting attitudes towards common sense prevalent in ancient Greek philosophy. On the one hand, there is a dismissive attitude: common sense, understood as what people in general routinely think, is regarded as simply misguided and out of touch with the way things really are. On the other hand, there is a tendency to regard human beings as such as having cognitive capacities that can afford them correct insights – if only they will let these capacities operate as they could or should, without being distracted or misled by various factors that throw them off course. Although these two attitudes are in a clear tension with one another, we frequently find them together in the same philosophers. Indeed, it is not too much to say that we find both strands present, to varying degrees, almost throughout the history of Greek philosophy. Perhaps this is not surprising, at least as regards the early period. Inasmuch as philosophers claimed to be doing something new and distinctive, they inevitably defined themselves to some extent in opposition to what they took to be the ordinary views of the people around them. Yet as long as they wanted to be heard and understood, there was a limit to how far the rejection of common sense could go without becoming self-defeating.

In the course of Greek philosophy, we also see the emergence of theorizing about common sense – that is, theories explaining how human beings come to have the (at least roughly correct) picture of the world that they attain by adulthood. Such theorizing is not fully explicit until the post-Aristotelian period, but there are hints of it in both Plato and Aristotle; and it fits more naturally with the second of the two attitudes I have sketched than with the first. Less common – although we see elements of this as well – are explanations for why, as the first of these two attitudes presumes, human beings are so likely to develop mistaken ideas about the world.

In what follows, I pursue these themes chronologically. Given the space available, I confine myself to major philosophers who give these matters substantial and explicit attention. These include a selection of thinkers from the Presocratic period, as it is usually called, Plato, Aristotle, the Stoics and the Epicureans, and the Pyrrhonian sceptic Sextus Empiricus. As already suggested, by 'common sense' I shall mean simply the views commonly and unreflectively held by people in general, without regard to their source or subject. This is no doubt a somewhat broader and less precise conception of common sense than those discussed in many essays in this volume. But this is what a wide variety of Greek philosophers have something to say about, and this, if anything, is what gives them a place in a volume about philosophical treatments of common sense.

EARLY GREEK PHILOSOPHY

In the earliest period of Greek philosophy it is clearly the first of the two attitudes I have distinguished, the dismissive one, that is the more visible. As early as Xenophanes (c.570–c.478 BCE) we find ordinary people's views about the gods subjected to withering criticism. The ordinary view, ascribed to Homer and Hesiod but also to 'mortals' (brotoi) in general, is stigmatized for its anthropomorphism, as well as for the immorality (by humans' own standards) that the gods are depicted as displaying (DK 21B11–17[1]). The correct view, according to Xenophanes, is quite different: god[2] is quite unlike humans, either physically or mentally, ordering the world not by moving around – that would not befit a being of this stature – but by a kind of telekinesis. We only have a few lines (DK 21B23–6), and the details are not explained, but the contrast is clear: there is the mistaken, everyday view of the divine, and then there is the correct view, and the two are more or less diametrically opposed to one another.

There is much more of this kind of attitude as the tradition develops; the singling out of the views of 'mortals' for criticism or ridicule becomes a familiar trope. The very first sentence of Heraclitus' book lambasted human beings in general (*anthrôpoi*) for failing to comprehend the central principle of the universe – what he calls the *logos* – even when he explains it to them (DK 22B1); another remark a little later[3] expands on this by saying that although this *logos* is 'common' (*xunos*) to everyone, 'most people live as if they had private insight' (*hôs idian echontes phronêsin*, DK 22B2). At least ten further fragments continue this theme of the cluelessness of almost everyone,[4] especially for their failure to grasp the *logos* (DK 22B72) – including, again, Homer and Hesiod (DK 22B40, 42, 57). The closest we come to an explanation of their lack of understanding is a fragment where we are told that 'they trust the people's singers and take the crowd as their teacher, not knowing that most people are bad and few are good' (DK 22B104); but if this is meant as an explanation (assuming that, as commonly in Greek philosophy, goodness and badness have a cognitive as well as an ethical dimension), it scarcely advances beyond tautology.

Parmenides, too, makes the mistaken views of 'mortals knowing nothing' (DK 28B6.4) a central focus of his work. There is the true path of wisdom, leading to insights concerning the unchanging character of what truly is; and then there are 'the opinions of mortals, in which there is no true trust' (DK 28B1.30). One of the most baffling aspects of the work is that it seems to advance *both* of these, even while emphasizing that the second is not to be trusted. While the interpretation of Parmenides' thought is deeply controversial, for this and other reasons, I think we can venture to say that the mistake of mortals consists in their taking the everyday world of changing objects at face value and as being without qualification real. And in Parmenides' case we do have something of an explanation of this error: it stems from an uncritical reliance on the senses as opposed to reason (DK 28B7).

Xenophanes, Heraclitus, and Parmenides are probably the most outspoken among the early Greek thinkers in their denunciations of common sense, although they are not the only ones.[5] But at least in the case of Heraclitus and Parmenides, and perhaps in Xenophanes' case too, one can also find signs of the second, more conciliatory attitude I identified at the outset. In addition to all the disparaging remarks, the fragments of Heraclitus include the following: 'thinking (*to phronein*) is common to all' (DK 22B113) and 'All humans have a share in knowing themselves and thinking soundly (*sôphronein*)' (DK 22B116). At least in the second of these, the emphasis seems to be more on how to act than on the nature of the world; *sôphronein*, 'thinking soundly', is the verb corresponding to *sôphrosunê*, the word for one of the central Greek virtues, which is usually translated as 'moderation' or 'temperance', and the reference to 'knowing themselves' supports the idea of a mainly practical orientation. Nonetheless, we have here a much more positive estimation of the shared intellectual capacities of humans in general than we might have expected from the dismissive fragments. It is purely a matter of guesswork how these and the dismissive fragments might have been combined in Heraclitus' thinking. Nonetheless, it does look as if the condition of being out of touch with how things are – the normal human condition, according to the two opening fragments and others like them – is not necessarily the whole story concerning common sense, and is perhaps not even inevitable or permanent.

In Parmenides, too, there is at least a serious question of how deep the error of ordinary people is supposed to go. While many scholars have taken Parmenides to be arguing that the everyday world perceived by the senses is simply an illusion, and ordinary thinking therefore mistaken through and through, this is by no means the only possibility. On one alternative view, the mistake of 'mortals' is to suppose that the world as shown us by the senses is the only reality there is, and that it can be understood on its own terms. In fact, there is a deeper level of explanation afforded by true reflection about what is, and this is what one would need to employ for a proper understanding of the world as we perceive it. If this is the case, mortal beliefs are not irretrievably misguided; they could in principle be corrected.[6] On another reading, ordinary thinking is indeed misguided, but it is not *wholly* misguided; to the extent that the world shown us by the senses can be understood as a *likeness* of what truly is – and to some extent it can – ordinary thinking has some degree of closeness to the truth.[7] Generally speaking, the more positive the role one can find for the second half of Parmenides' poem, the one expounding 'the opinions of mortals', the more one will be able to rescue common sense, which treats the world revealed by the senses as unproblematically real, from the complete obloquy to which it initially seemed to be consigned.

Even in Xenophanes' case, there is perhaps a hint of a more positive conception of common sense. It is not on the specific subject of divinity (the subject of his critical comments) but has to do with inquiry quite generally. A two-line fragment reads, 'Not from the beginning did gods reveal all things to mortals, but in time by investigating they discover better' (DK 21B18). The fragment has often been read as celebrating the progress of knowledge from one generation to another. But that would be reading a lot into the word 'in time' (*chronôi*), and I prefer to read Xenophanes as endorsing individual *investigation*, which has to be patient and time-consuming – the contrast being with instant ('from the beginning') divine revelation, which is impossible.[8] And the actual or potential recipients of truth are given simply as 'mortals' (*thnêtoi*), not some limited group possessed of special insight. There seems to be at least a suggestion that all of us have the capability for some level of understanding – at any rate (and here is maybe a connection with the negative strand we looked at earlier), if we can let go of misguided notions about the gods.[9]

PLATO

Contempt for the views of 'the many' is a recurring theme in the dialogues of Plato. In the *Crito*, probably one of Plato's earliest works, Crito worries that he will look bad in most people's eyes if he does not help Socrates to escape from prison; it will seem as if he was not willing to bribe the officials to let him go. Socrates' response is, who cares what most people will think? An obvious response, which Crito delivers, is that Socrates of all people should care, seeing that a jury of ordinary people has convicted him and sentenced him to death. But Socrates replies that 'the many' are in fact without any genuine power either for good or for bad, since they are incapable of making someone wise or foolish (44b–d). And this introduces a point that will be central to the dialogue: that what matters most – perhaps the only thing that truly matters – is the state of one's soul. Later, in constructing his argument against escaping, Socrates says that we should not concern ourselves with the opinions of people in general, but only of those with understanding (46d–47a); who these people are (or whether they even exist) is not made clear, but ordinary people are clearly assumed to lack such understanding. Since just actions benefit, and unjust actions harm, the agent, this means that the opinions of the many concerning what one should do are of no consequence; what is important is the opinion of the person who understands justice and injustice (47c–48a). And this is so even though the decision of the many can lead to one's death, because it is not living that is most important, but living well (48a–b). The view cries out for elaboration and support, which in this dialogue it does not receive; we have to wait until the *Republic* for that. But it is both extreme in itself and explicitly developed by way of a rejection of ordinary opinion as a source of insight.

Socrates propounds similar views in the *Gorgias* and again draws attention to their conflict with common sense. Reacting to Socrates' argument that one is worse off doing injustice than suffering it, Polus says, 'Don't you think you have been refuted, Socrates, when no human being would say the kind of things you are saying?' (473e4–5). Socrates replies that he is uninterested in putting the matter to a majority vote; the only 'witness' who matters is the person with whom he is having a discussion (474a–b). But the *Gorgias* emphasizes how Socrates' extraordinary ideas fail to win people over at a gut level, despite the arguments; Polus' final reaction to Socrates' position is that it is absurd, despite apparently being consistent with things said earlier (480e1–2),[10] and Callicles, entering the conversation just afterwards, observes that if Socrates is right, 'our whole human life will be turned upside down' (481c3–4) – an outcome that he is never willing to accept over the many twists and turns of argument that follow.

The *Republic*, too, takes up the challenge of arguing that one is better off being just rather than unjust, for reasons that have to do purely with the state of one's soul rather than because of the rewards and punishments usually bestowed by society. And here too the view is presented as plainly contrary to common sense, which would hold that justice is a regrettable, though necessary, constraint on our behaviour (358a). In the *Republic*, as I said, we get some real argument for the position that is maintained without support in the *Crito*. And in the *Republic* we get some indication of what a truly knowledgeable person would be like; it would be a philosopher who has penetrated far beyond ordinary thinking to a grasp of the ultimate nature of things, as embodied in the Forms, and who is therefore equipped to rule a community the likes of which has never existed and quite possibly never will exist. These are the only people who can appropriately be put in charge, and the rest must be content to follow their directives.

I have picked three dialogues treating related topics, in which the dismissal of common sense is particularly obvious; much more could be said along these lines with reference to other topics and other dialogues. But in Plato, as in the early thinkers we considered in the previous section, rejection of common sense is not the whole story. For another prominent idea in several of Plato's works is that 'learning is recollection'; that is, that we are all possessed at birth of a stock of knowledge, and that what we call learning is really the retrieval of the knowledge that is already inside us. In the *Meno* this idea is invoked to explain how a young boy, a slave in Meno's household who has never been taught geometry, is nonetheless able to grasp the truth of a certain geometrical result (82b–86b). In the *Phaedo* it is used as part of an argument for the soul's existence before birth: we have concepts such as perfect equality, and we can be reminded of these concepts by encountering approximations to them (such as sticks or stones that are in a rough-and-ready way equal, but not perfectly so), but we never encountered pure instances of them in this life – so we must already have had them prior to this life (72e–77a).

Here we seem to have a powerful affirmation of a kind of common knowledge – a range of general concepts and/or reasoning abilities – that is shared by all of us.[11] How widely this knowledge is supposed to extend is not clear; in the *Meno* Socrates says the soul has learned 'everything' (81c6–7), but this is hardly informative without further specification. Another question is what it will take to bring this knowledge to a fully explicit state. The *Meno* and the *Phaedo* pick cases where it is successful. But in the *Meno* the process is explicitly said to be incomplete; by the end of the scene the boy only has (correct) opinions, not knowledge, although Socrates adds that he would be able to reach full knowledge through further iterations of the same kind of questioning (85c9–d1).[12] More importantly, this whole episode in the *Meno* is designed to reassure Meno that inquiring into the nature of virtue is indeed worthwhile, despite the lack of (explicit) knowledge on either his or Socrates' part; the knowledge is in us, if only we can dig it out. But while in the geometry case Socrates can lead the boy with appropriate questions, there is no such helpful interlocutor showing the path in the case of virtue. In ethics, as opposed to mathematics, Socrates is very good at exposing problems in ideas offered by others, but he insists (in the *Meno* and in many other dialogues) that he does not himself have anything positive to offer; nor does he ever identify anyone else who does.

Thus we arrive at a picture of a common sense with a curious status. It is buried within all of us, and seems to offer us the prospect of coming to understand a great many important subjects, if only we can achieve access to it. But there is a serious question as to whether we can do this. This duality seems to be reflected in the way many of the dialogues are framed. Socrates' discussions are frequently with figures who, while no doubt educated as one would expect of an upper-class Greek of the time, are not, as we might say, full-time intellectuals. The search is frequently for the nature of some virtue or other characteristic that is of special interest or relevance for the person or persons concerned (courage for Laches, friendship for Lysis, piety for Euthyphro, etc.). And unless one thinks that the purpose of these dialogues is purely destructive, showing these characters that they do not know what they are talking about, the assumption behind asking them about these qualities seems to be that they (and by extension a good many other people) have something of value to contribute on topics of importance. And yet many of these dialogues lead to no firm conclusions, and certainly not to a grasp of the nature of the quality under examination. The knowledge buried inside us thus seems destined to stay wholly inactive, at least on the topics Socrates cares most about.

The idea that we unknowingly have a higher level of understanding (if that is what we should call it) that may sometimes be at odds with what we presently think is alluded to periodically in the *Gorgias* – although here 'learning is recollection' is not an explicit theme. Socrates claims that tyrants have the least power of anyone and do not do what they want; when Polus protests, Socrates replies that this is what 'Polus says' too (466d6–e4). That is, if Polus will properly consider the consequences of his deepest commitments, he will see that this is what he must say, despite its being absolutely antithetical to what he now says. And equally, if the tyrant will consider the consequences of his deepest commitments, he will see that, contrary to his usual self-conception, the things he really wants are not available to him in his current condition. Later, too, Socrates says that Callicles equates the pleasant and the good, while he himself does not, and adds, 'And I think Callicles doesn't either, when he sees himself correctly' (495e1–2). However, as we saw, neither Polus nor Callicles is brought to a genuine acknowledgement of what, according to Socrates, they 'really think'.

We can therefore distinguish two types or levels of common sense in Plato. There is what most people normally say and think, and this is frequently treated with the greatest suspicion. And then there is a deeper level of common sense gestured at in some of Plato's works, a common sense that (leaving aside the more fanciful elements) we can call innate, and that is shared by all of us. The trouble is that these two levels are frequently at odds with one another, and the deeper common sense, which is the one that would deserve our trust, is difficult if not impossible to bring to the surface, at least on the ethical questions that Socrates devoted his life to. The *Gorgias*, which I have relied on in considering both levels, is perhaps the dialogue where this tension is most apparent. As for why the misguided common sense should so regularly win out, this is not clear; to point to the pernicious influence of society is hardly helpful, seeing that society is composed of human beings all of whom, according to the 'learning is recollection' story, have the deeper common sense within them. But the fact is that the dialogues as a whole do not seem to be optimistic about the deeper common sense gaining a hold on our thinking and action; 'learning is recollection' is only mentioned in three dialogues, and never in ways that point to significant progress in our (surface-level, explicit) understanding.

ARISTOTLE

Aristotle's orientation on this matter is rather different; if we wanted to name the major Greek philosopher who came closest to deserving the label 'philosopher of common sense', Aristotle would be the winner. He clearly thinks that there is such a thing as the collective wisdom of humanity; we frequently see an assumption on his part that what people generally think must be more or less on the right lines. This is most explicit when it comes to ethical questions. Having offered an initial specification of the good for human beings in Book 1 of the *Nicomachean Ethics*, he immediately adds: 'But we must examine it not only from our conclusion and the points from which our argument takes off, but also from the things that are said about it; for with a true account the realities are in harmony, while with a false one the truth is quickly in conflict' (1098b9–12). The 'things said' – that is, the things commonly said in the wider society – are therefore taken as a check on the correctness of his argument; and the second half of the sentence is especially remarkable in its unstated assumption that 'the realities' (ta huparchonta) and 'the truth' of the situation are reliably captured in these 'things said'. The next several chapters then consider the issue in light of a number of commonly held views; for example, that the fortunes of one's descendants would make no difference at all to how one's life is rated is dismissed because it is 'contrary to the opinions' – that is, again, commonly held opinions (1101a24). Similarly, in his discussion of pleasure in Book 10 of the same work he rejects the suggestion that pleasure is not a good on the basis that it conflicts with a universally shared view. 'What seems so to everyone, that we say *is* so', he declares; 'there is no way the person who does away with trust in this will have anything *more* trustworthy to say' (1172b36–1173a2).

But this tendency in Aristotle is not confined to ethics. In the first chapter of the *Rhetoric*, while introducing the topic of methods of persuasion and who is likely to be best at spotting them, he asserts quite generally that 'human beings are naturally oriented well enough [hikanôs] towards what is true and mostly hit upon the truth' (1355a15–17). And the same assumption seems to be behind the famous sentence that opens the *Metaphysics*: 'All human beings by nature desire to know' (980a21). For it is plain from the following discussion that he takes this desire to be one that is regularly satisfied, at least at a basic level. It is not just that we *want* to know; the world cooperates, and we are the kind of beings equipped for it to do so. The everyday mindset of people in general, including their ability to learn from experience, has a natural orientation towards seeing the world as it actually is.

All this is very different from the ridiculing of ordinary views that was so prominent in Plato or Parmenides; clearly Aristotle has a kind of respect for common sense that is not matched even on the most conciliatory readings of their views on this subject. Still, we should be careful not to exaggerate the point; here too some important qualifications must be made. First, despite the seeming universality of several of the passages quoted just now, it is far from clear that the common sense to which Aristotle gives credit is the common sense of everyone whatever. At least on some topics – or perhaps in some frames of mind[13] – it looks as if he rather envisages the views of a restricted group of people: not necessarily philosophers or other theorists, but at least people who have been well brought up and have received a good general education. Again in Book 1 of the *Nicomachean Ethics*, he says that 'the person who is going to be a good enough listener about fine and just things, and generally about political matters, must have been raised in fine habits' (1095b3–5). The reason is that in studying these questions, one has to begin with an adequate sense of *what* things are in fact fine, just, etc. That is the starting point towards understanding *why* they are so; and the person who has been well brought up (but not, it is suggested, anyone else) will occupy that necessary starting point. And this is immediately reinforced when Aristotle gives an initial review of views concerning the good. One of these, that the good life is the life of enjoyment (*apolaustikon*) – which seems to mean the life devoted to various forms of physical gratification – is ascribed to 'the many', and is immediately dismissed as slavish and subhuman (1095b19–20). Another view, ascribed to 'the refined' (*charientes*, 1095b22), is treated with much more respect, even though it too is said to be in need of some modification. Thus, when a few chapters later Aristotle turns to the question of 'the things that are said' about the good, we may well suspect that the people by whom these things are 'said' are a relatively restricted sector of society. Similarly, in his discussion in Book 3 of what kinds of things are appropriately wished, he asserts that it is the excellent person (*spoudaios*) who is the criterion in these matters; 'for the excellent person judges everything correctly, and in each case what is true is apparent to him' (1113a29–31). By contrast, people who are less than excellent do not see things straight. So if Aristotle does endorse a kind of common sense, it is considerably less expansive than one might have expected from the remarks we considered at the start of this section. And the dismissive kind of attitude that I identified at the outset is by no means absent in his case.

The other caveat about Aristotle and common sense is this. It has sometimes been held that Aristotle's philosophical method involves starting with ordinary opinions. These opinions may be refined in the course of the inquiry, and some may even be rejected, but the idea is that one begins by collecting the ordinarily held views on some topic, on the assumption that this will be a good initial pointer to the correct theory that one aims to develop. One will also collect the views of those who have previously studied the topic and those whose views are for any other reason thought to be especially authoritative; so it is not as if ordinary opinions are the only starting point. But they are, according to this reading, at least among the ideas that one should begin by reviewing. This method has sometimes been called the 'endoxic' method, and it has been thought to be especially clearly on display in a much-discussed passage at the start of *Nicomachean Ethics* Book 7; here Aristotle says that, on the subject of *akrasia* or weakness of will, we must begin by reviewing how things appear, the goal being as far as possible to vindicate the *endoxa*, the 'reputable opinions', on the subject (1145b2–7). Now, a thorough discussion of Aristotle's methodology is far beyond the scope of this chapter. I will simply point out that this kind of interpretation of his method has recently been subjected to extensive and well-reasoned criticism (Frede 2012; Davia 2017). According to the critics, the passage in the *akrasia* discussion is nowhere near as representative as it has sometimes been taken to be, and even the discussion of *akrasia* itself by no means conforms to the large-scale endorsement of widely held, or even reputable, opinions on the topic that the opening methodological remarks might have led one to expect. Thus, to return to a phrase that I floated at the beginning of this section, if by 'philosopher of common sense' one means a philosopher whose methods in some way involve building on common sense, there are real limits to how far it is applicable even to Aristotle.

STOICS AND EPICUREANS

The Stoics had a theory of concept formation that bears importantly on our topic. According to one of the fullest reports of this theory, in a passage of Aetius, a newborn human being 'has the leading part of the soul like a papyrus all ready for writing on' and 'on this writes each one of the concepts [*ennoiôn*]'. This naturally reminds us of the *tabula rasa* in Locke (1997: Books 1 and 2), and the theory certainly has an empiricist side; the 'writing' of the concepts on the soul occurs by means of the clustering of many similar perceptual impressions (*phantasiai*). Thus the concept of the horse develops from our seeing and remembering many different horses; and concepts in general are regarded as generic impressions imprinted in the memory (Plutarch, *On Common Conceptions* 1084F–1085B). However, it is not accidental, and not *merely* a matter of experience, which concepts do in fact develop. Human nature, which, like everything else in the Stoic universe, is teleologically designed, plays a part in this too. Now, Aetius also says that some concepts develop by nature alone, while others need human instruction; the term *ennoia* includes both categories, but the former are also called *prolêpseis*, usually translated 'preconceptions'. He also says that, according to the Stoics, our rationality is 'completed from our preconceptions'; exactly what this amounts to is perhaps not quite clear, but evidently these preconceptions are a crucial component in what it is for us to be rational. According to Diogenes Laertius (7.54), Chrysippus actually named preconceptions as one of the criteria of truth. But even if this was not a standard Stoic claim, it is clear that preconceptions play an indispensable role in our ability to discern the truth. For it is our rationality that puts us in a position to distinguish true from false, in particular by the special type of impression that they call 'apprehensive' (*kataléptikê*), which is most commonly cited as the Stoic criterion of truth – that is, an impression that is in some sense guaranteed to be correct. Not all our impressions are apprehensive, but it is clear from the way the Stoics present this idea that apprehensive impressions are supposed to be a regular feature of everyone's orientation to the world.[14]

In their notion of *prolêpsis* or preconception, the Stoics are close to the Epicureans; indeed, the term first seems to appear in Epicurus (e.g., *Kuriai Doxai* 37, 38). According to the Epicureans, as Diogenes Laertius tells us, *prolêpsis* is 'a sort of apprehension or correct opinion or concept [*ennoian*] or universal thought stored away inside, that is, a memory of what has often been revealed externally, for example "This is a human being"; for as soon as "human being" is said, its shape is thought of in virtue of preconception' (10.33; cf. 31). Diogenes also attributes to Epicurus the view that *prolêpsis* is one of the criteria of truth (10.31); and Epicurus appears to expand upon this point when he says that one must have a clear conception of what one is talking about before one can successfully pursue any inquiry (*Letter to Herodotus*, Diogenes Laertius 10.37; cf. Sextus Empiricus, *M* 11.21).

The Stoics and Epicureans certainly do not agree on everything. The Epicureans think that sense perception is, as such, inerrant, and that error is introduced by the interpretations we make of what we are perceiving,[15] whereas the Stoics certainly do allow that there are mistaken sense impressions. And the Epicureans do not believe in a teleologically ordered universe. But the two schools seem to be at one in their admission of preconceptions as built up through experience and as a source of correct insight. And to that extent, they seem both to be representative of the second and more positive of the two attitudes I identified at the outset. Collectively these preconceptions seem to add up to something we could well call common sense; they are shared by all rational beings, and they are capable of playing an important role in revealing to us how things are.

Once again, though, as with Aristotle, we find that this seemingly optimistic outlook is tempered by other considerations. The Stoics pose as an ideal the sage (*sophos*), the person who never assents to any impressions other than 'apprehensive' ones, and who therefore never makes a mistake. Such a person would be a paragon of both virtue and wisdom, and these two things are scarcely distinguishable in the Stoic outlook. Not surprisingly, the sage is at best extremely rare, and perhaps even non-existent. But while this by itself might seem unproblematic – of course perfection is not likely to be actually achieved – the Stoics also adopt a rigid either/or mentality; those of us who are not sages (that is to say, all of us) are instead gripped by vice and ignorance. One might respond that surely there are degrees of vice and ignorance, but the Stoics will not accept this; anything less than (complete) virtue or wisdom is vice or ignorance, pure and simple. As Plutarch (*On Common Conceptions* 1063A–B) explains the view, someone just below the surface of the ocean is just as drowned as someone hundreds of fathoms down; and similarly, you remain an unqualified fool and sinner right up to the point of attaining the opposite states. Of course, this way of putting it does allow that some people may be closer to attaining success than others; and there is reason to think that the Stoics had more to say about progress towards virtue than our sources make it seem.[16] All the same, the kind of common sense recognized by the Stoics, consisting in the natural ability to grasp a great many truths, turns out to be regarded as, in itself, a wholly unimpressive achievement; so long as one is still subject to error, either epistemological or ethical, one is a fool or a sinner. To get beyond this state, one needs to achieve an absolutely unshakeable understanding of the nature of the world, the nature of the good, and one's own place in the teleological order of things. Although no Stoic pretended to have reached that pinnacle, their exposition of this ideal, and their all-or-nothing attitude towards it, seem to give them a place (alongside everyone else we have considered) among the detractors of common sense; despite the apparently optimistic picture of concept development that we saw just a moment ago, this is quite inadequate to lead us to the condition that is the true fulfilment of human nature.

The Epicureans are not as extreme in their demarcation of wisdom and folly. But it is clear that for them, too, the common sense embodied in the concepts we acquire and the truths they allow us to grasp do not suffice to rescue us from disastrous error. According to Epicurus, if you recognize that the world consists of atoms and void, and that we ourselves are composed of atoms and void, you will understand that the many natural phenomena, such as earthquakes or thunderstorms, that are commonly regarded as divine punishments are no such thing, and that you yourself have nothing to fear from death. Almost no one besides the Epicureans themselves understands these things (or many other important points connected with them). And so the Epicureans too qualify as detractors of common sense as well as exponents of a kind of common sense; despite being able to grasp much that is true, ordinary thinking is off track in crucial respects.

In neither the Stoic nor the Epicurean case is there much explanation of why there is so much error. (And given that for the Stoics, this is, by divine design, the best of all possible worlds, the phenomenon may seem especially troubling in their case.) But one interesting indication in Epicurus comes in his discussion of the nature of the divine in the *Letter to Menoeceus* (Diogenes Laertius 10.123–4). 'Believe that god is an immortal and blessed animal', he says, 'as the common conception [*noêsis*] indicates; and do not attach to him anything alien to his immortality or unsuitable to his blessedness.' Most ordinary opinions about the gods utterly fail in this respect, he continues; 'For the declarations of the many about the gods are not preconceptions [*prolêpseis*] but false suppositions.' Hence the pernicious ideas current in society, such as that gods care about human beings and punish them for wrongdoing, etc. Thus it looks as if one source of error, at any rate, is that people do not appreciate what their preconceptions actually entail and what they do not; in this particular case, if they properly followed out the true implications of the preconception of god as immortal and blessed, as the Epicureans themselves have done, there would be no problem. Of course, that still leaves the question why these preconceptions, which seem to put us in a position to discern the truth, should also be open to such radical misinterpretation.

SEXTUS EMPIRICUS

I close with a word on Sextus Empiricus, the only Greek sceptic of whom we have substantial surviving writings.[17] Sextus not infrequently expresses a preference for the everyday ideas of ordinary people over the theoretical abstractions of non-sceptical philosophers (or dogmatists, in his terminology). For example, in his discussion of signs – that is, means of inferring from the observed to the unobserved – Sextus expresses suspicion of signs of the kind employed by the dogmatists, which allegedly give them an insight into the underlying (and never directly observable) nature of things, but happily accepts signs of the kind employed by ordinary people, where something observed serves as a sign of something currently unobservable, and where there has been a regular observed connection between objects of the two types – for example, smoke as a sign of fire. Commenting on this, Sextus proclaims himself on the side of ordinary life and against the dogmatists' dubious theorizing (*PH* 2.102; cf. *M* 8.156-8[18]). Similarly, in his work on the specialized sciences (*Adversus Mathematicos* 1–6), he several times contrasts an everyday activity (reading and writing, observation of the sky for predicting the weather, or the playing of musical instruments) with theoretical counterparts of these (grammatical theory, astrology, and music theory) (*M* 1.49–56, 5.1–2, 6.1–3); he has no problem with the former and his scrutiny will be directed to the latter. In addition, in explaining how a sceptic can act, Sextus says that among the kinds of appearances the sceptic can use to guide decisions and actions are 'the handing down of laws and customs' (*PH* 1.23–4). Without endorsing them as the naturally right way to behave, the sceptic treats the everyday practices of his society as a guide to what to do.[19]

In a variety of ways, then, Sextus presents himself as in tune with common sense, unlike philosophers of a non-sceptical persuasion. But in Sextus too there are other indications that point in a different direction. His usual procedure is to create oppositions among opinions and impressions on any given subject, leading to suspension of judgment about the truth of the matter. Much of the time the items placed in opposition are philosophical theories. But often they are everyday impressions of things; this is particularly obvious in the case of the Ten Modes, or standardized sets of oppositions, that he ascribes to the earlier sceptics (*PH* 1.35–163). And in several cases the views of ordinary people on some topic are explicitly included among these oppositions. This is true, for example, of the existence of the gods (common sense says yes, *M* 9.50), the reality of motion (common sense affirms it, *PH* 3.65; *M* 10.45), and the reality of place, where part of the case in favour of this consists in everyday observations (*PH* 3.120; cf. 3.135). But if this is so, then Sextus' attitude towards common sense is not, or not always, one of uncritical acceptance; instead, he suspends judgment about these matters. One might suggest that he can distinguish between an everyday kind of belief in these things and the assertion that they really exist in nature, and that his suspension of judgment applies only to the latter; and indeed, in the case of place, he does distinguish between a rough-and-ready sense of place and a philosophically precise sense (*PH* 3.119; *M* 10.15). But if he is going to invoke ordinary views among the opposing considerations that lead to suspension of judgment, it is not clear that this distinction can be sustained; if ordinary views are among the mass of opposing views whose juxtaposition contributes to suspension of judgment, they must also be among the views on which judgment is suspended. And this is quite explicit in the case of ordinary views about what things are good or bad; it is not only philosophers but also ordinary people who believe that certain things are really, or by nature, good and others bad, whereas the sceptic suspends judgment about this (*PH* 1.30).

So in Sextus, too, we find a duality of attitude about common sense. Much of the time he appears to be sympathetic to common sense; but on several occasions he treats it as one more element, alongside philosophical theories, to be placed in opposition with a view to suspension of judgment. The latter attitude is not exactly the same as the outright rejection of common sense that we have seen, in certain contexts and to varying degrees, among all the other philosophers considered here. But it suggests just as high a level of suspicion of common sense as he shows towards any of the theories of the dogmatists. And for a sceptic, that is as close to dismissal as one is going to get.

CONCLUSION

So the verdict seems clear, across a wide range of thinkers: when it comes to common sense, Greek philosophy is deeply ambivalent. Aristotle may be the most sympathetic to common sense, and some of the Presocratics perhaps the most dismissive; but in their combination of some level of sympathy and some level of dismissiveness, the Greek philosophers are remarkably consistent.[20]

NOTES

1 DK is a standard abbreviation for Diels and Kranz 1951.

2 Xenophanes says 'one god, greatest among gods and humans' (DK 21B23.1). The first two words sound monotheistic, which would heighten still further the contrast with ordinary views of the time. But the rest of the line seems to contradict this. For brief discussion see Lesher (1992: 96–102).

3 Our information on the placing of these two fragments comes from Sextus Empiricus, *Adversus Mathematicos* 7.132–3; except for these two, we have no reliable information about the order of the surviving fragments in Heraclitus' book.

4 The only named persons receiving his praise are Bias of Priene (DK 22B39), generally included as one of the Seven Sages, and a certain Hermodorus, apparently of his own town of Ephesus (DK 22B121).

5 Empedocles and Anaxagoras both criticize ordinary people for speaking as if things come into being and perish. In reality, what looks like the coming into being and perishing of ordinary objects is the mixing and separation of elements that themselves enjoy permanent existence (DK 31B8–12, 59B17). But the error involved here does not appear to be particularly deep, and correcting it does not seem to require wholesale revision of everyday views.

6 So Curd (1998: especially chapter 3). Curd also provides a useful summary of previous interpretations.

7 So Johansen (2016). As Johansen points out, this reading brings Parmenides into a certain proximity with Plato's picture of cosmology in the *Timaeus*.

8 For this reading see Lesher (1991).

9 The mistake implied in this fragment is the idea that gods speak directly to humans. But that might easily connect with the anthropomorphism that was central to Xenophanes' critique of ordinary views about gods.

10 The Greek here, *tois mentoi emprosthen isôs soi homologeitai*, is difficult; it is not quite clear whether Polus is agreeing about the consistency with earlier points or is only observing that the position no doubt strikes *Socrates* as consistent. The *soi* ('to you') seems to point towards the latter, but it is an unusual construction.

11 'Learning is recollection' also appears in the *Phaedrus*. The picture here is not incompatible with what I have just suggested, but the emphasis in the *Phaedrus* is much more on a distinctive philosophical use of recollection. For this reason I do not focus on this dialogue.

12 Plausibly, by coming to understand the principles of geometry and becoming able to apply these principles without leading questions from someone else.

13 The project of attempting to render everything in Aristotle consistent can, I think, be taken too far. The works of Aristotle that we have are not finished treatises and were surely composed over a considerable period of time; it would be by no means surprising if they revealed conflicting inclinations concerning how much credit to give the views of the average person.

14 The nature and source of the guarantee of correctness is controversial. For relevant texts and basic discussion, see Long and Sedley (1987: sections 39 and 40). See also Hankinson (2003).

15 For relevant texts and discussion, see Long and Sedley (1987: section 16).

16 On progress in Stoicism, see Inwood and Donini (1999: especially section 10).

17 With one exception noted below, I do not attempt to reconstruct the attitudes towards common sense of either the earlier Pyrrhonians or the sceptical thinkers of the Academy; the evidence is just too sketchy.

18 These are standard abbreviations for Sextus' works. *PH* (based on the title in Greek) stands for *Outlines of Pyrrhonism*; *M* stands for *Adversus Mathematicos*.

19 In this respect Sextus may be at odds with the supposed founder of Pyrrhonian scepticism, Pyrrho of Elis; while much of what we hear about Pyrrho may be invention or embellishment, many of the anecdotes passed

down about him do suggest a radically unconventional lifestyle
(e.g., Diogenes Laertius 9.62–9).

20 Thanks to the editors, Rik Peels and René van Woudenberg, for some very
helpful comments on a previous version of this chapter.

2 Common Sense, Science, and Scepticism in the Early Modern World

Stephen I. Wagner

The philosophical thought of the early modern world offers us instructive lessons regarding the relationship between common sense and philosophical thought. Concern with this relationship was inaugurated primarily by philosophers confronting the new Galilean-Copernican science of the sixteenth and seventeenth centuries. This scientific world view challenged the views of Aristotle and the Scholastic philosophers, which accorded more with common sense, particularly regarding the nature of sensory objects and our perception of them.

The early modern world is, most often, seen as the period from Descartes to Hume. The progress of thought within this period is part of a bigger context of development. We see a precursor of the concern with common-sense beliefs in Bacon's 'idols of the mind', which challenged the role of common sense as it was embedded in popular beliefs. And there is a clear path from the work of the early modern thinkers to the common-sense tradition of the Scottish Enlightenment and beyond.

I will focus on views about common sense, science, and scepticism in the work of Descartes, Locke, and Berkeley. I will urge that Descartes and Locke inaugurated a doubt of the common-sense world view and, as those who followed saw it, ended with a scepticism about central common-sense beliefs. Seen in this light, Berkeley attempts to overcome their scepticism, primarily regarding the existence of objects and their qualities in the world. I will highlight Berkeley's claim that he was defending common sense. Finally, I will look at these philosophers' thoughts about mind in a way which offers a revealing perspective towards Berkeley's view of common sense.

Descartes set the agenda of attempting to reconcile the claims of science, scepticism, and common sense. Locke made progress in this attempt, while Berkeley offered a more thorough, but incomplete, reconciliation. Their work led to the continuation of this reconciling project in the early modern work of Hume, Reid, and others. In some respects this project still informs contemporary work in epistemology.

THE CLAIMS OF COMMON SENSE

The claims of common sense can be characterized in several ways. I will focus on considerations which are prominent in contemporary discussions and are helpful in spelling out the relationship between philosophy, science, and scepticism in the early modern period.

Lynd Forguson suggests that, rather than focusing on a list of 'common-sense propositions', we should

> enunciate the most fundamental, ground-floor, components of common sense; those to which we are so deeply and fundamentally committed that an elucidation of them throws explanatory light on the most intimate and pervasive features of our every day thought and action. (Forguson 1989: 3–4)

Forguson claims there are two such components: common-sense realism (CSR) and rational psychology. The first of these 'has as its domain what philosophers would call the ontological and epistemological relations between oneself and everything else'; the second 'has as its focus the explanation of behavior' (Forguson 1989: 4). CSR makes two claims:

> First ... there is a single physical world common to myself and all other people and sentient beings who are now alive or who have ever lived ... Secondly, common-sense realism is the view that the world is made up of objects, events and states of affairs that are independent of the thoughts and experiences I and others have of it.[1]

Rational psychology holds that

> We describe and account for our own and others' actions by
> reference to a framework of explanation and a set of concepts that
> we do not use in connection with the behavior of inanimate things
> and primitive organisms.[2]

Forguson adds that 'Central to both components', and linking them to
one another, is a 'common sense concept of mind' which 'figures in
the other two components' (Forguson 1989: 4). CSR will be my focus
in the next three sections. In the final section I will consider the
concept of mind in Descartes, Locke, and Berkeley as it relates to
rational psychology.

Noah Lemos offers a similar twofold model of 'propositions that
one cannot reject and still be a member of the common sense tradition': 'one cannot deny the existence of material objects' and 'one
cannot deny that there are other people who know a lot about the
world around them' (Lemos 2004: 11). Lemos sees several epistemological claims as central to the common-sense tradition:

> First, it holds that we do know pretty much what we think we
> know. Second, it holds that there are some propositions that almost
> everyone knows, that are matters of common knowledge. Third, it
> holds that we may take these propositions as data for assessing
> various philosophical theories ... Fourth, it assigns a great deal of
> weight to these propositions, holding it to be more reasonable to
> accept them than any philosophical theory or premise that implies
> that they are false. (Lemos 2004: 5)

And Marek Tomeček suggests that we must distinguish between
implicit and *explicit* common sense. Forguson and Lemos describe
common sense as explicit, by specifying its foundational beliefs and
the role of common-sense beliefs within a philosophical system. But,
as implicit, 'common sense [is] outside of philosophical systems – that
is why it can function as their measure' (Tomeček 2015: 35). Implicit
common sense serves a methodological role as a criterion, perhaps an

ultimate decision-maker, in deciding between theories which are, otherwise, equally plausible. Nicholas Rescher, too, sees the 'dicta of common sense' not as philosophy, but as imposing 'limiting restrictions on viable philosophizing' (Rescher 2005: 207).

These characterizations of common sense provide the framework for my discussion.

SCIENCE, SCEPTICISM, AND CSR

René Descartes

Descartes's central goals were to develop and ground his scientific views, which he hoped would replace the Aristotelian/Scholastic view of the world. Descartes's metaphysics would be the roots of his tree of knowledge, grounding the epistemological certainty of his scientific claims.[3] In order to develop those metaphysical beliefs about God, human nature, and the physical world, Descartes had to challenge many common-sense claims that were central to the Aristotelian world view. These claims, Descartes thought, were primarily an inheritance from our early upbringing, when we were embedded in the world of the senses. To ground his science, scepticism opposing common sense had an essential role to play by eliminating our 'prejudices' and providing a solid foundation to his new scientific world view.

Indeed, Descartes utilized scepticism in a unique way. His intent was not to argue for sceptical conclusions about human knowledge. Rather, his scepticism would rid the meditator of her sense-based beliefs and lead her to the epistemological tool – her faculty of clear and distinct perception – which could provide metaphysical and scientific knowledge. Descartes's doubts in his first meditation are a first step towards putting in place his epistemological foundation. His approach made the relationship between science, common sense, and scepticism a central concern within the period that followed.

We must understand the opening line of Descartes's *Discourse on the Method* in a way that is often not made clear. Descartes (1964:

VI, 1; 1984–5: I, 111) says: 'Good sense is the best distributed thing in the world.' Commentators have often read this claim as supporting common sense (for instance, Tomeček 2015: 36). But Descartes continues:

> [T]he power of judging well and of distinguishing the true from the false – which is properly what we call 'good sense' or 'reason' – is naturally equal in all men, and consequently ... the diversity of our opinions does not arise because some of us are more reasonable than others but solely because we direct our thoughts along different paths and do not attend to the same things. (Descartes 1964: VI, 1–2; 1984–5: I, 111)

Our power to distinguish 'the true from the false' is our mind's activity of clear and distinct perception. Although this power is common to us all and provides beliefs that all of us *can* know, our ability to use this faculty requires discipline and training, and is often unrecognized by most people.

Some who defend our need to rely on common sense argue that we cannot carry out the wholesale doubt of our early beliefs which, for Descartes, is needed to give us access to this faculty. If common-sense views are impossible to avoid, we must start our philosophizing with those beliefs. Descartes insisted that doubting these views could, and should, be done through training:

> I should like my readers not just to take the short time needed to go through [the first meditation], but to devote several months, or at least weeks, to considering the topics dealt with, before going on to the rest of the book. If they do this they will undoubtedly be able to derive much greater benefit from what follows. (Descartes 1964: VII, 130; 1984–5: II, 94)

This work is needed to discover the resources of our reason and to free the meditator from ordinary word usage, which embodies our prejudices:

> Descartes' scientific programme aiming to supplant the defects and prejudices of our common-sense view of the world inherited from childhood is expressed in technical terms which, not surprisingly, depart from ordinary usage. For example the word *idea* is much broader than was usual at the time ... and includes basically everything mental and conscious. (Tomeček 2015: 14)

Descartes knew he was challenging common-sense beliefs:

> I do not expect any popular approval, or indeed any wide audience. On the contrary I would not urge anyone to read this book except those who are willing to meditate seriously with me, and to withdraw their minds from the senses and from all preconceived opinions. (Descartes 1964: VII, 9; 1984–5: II, 8)

Indeed, Descartes separated the epistemological demands of science from those of everyday affairs. The latter required 'moral certainty' about our beliefs, that is, 'having sufficient certainty for application to ordinary life, even though they may be uncertain in relation to the absolute power of God' (Descartes 1964: VIIIA, 327; 1984–5: I, 290). But metaphysical and scientific beliefs demanded 'absolute certainty', which arises 'when we believe that it is wholly impossible that something should be otherwise than we judge it to be' (Descartes 1964: VIIIA, 328; 1984–5: I, 290). As we will see, Locke and Berkeley recognized the need to relax this latter demand.

CSR can serve as our focus since it is a view which Forguson, among others, has offered us as an essential component of common sense. The force of Descartes's initial scepticism is to cast doubt on CSR. George Pappas offers a helpful fourfold account of CSR:

> *CSR existential part.* There are ordinary macro physical objects. They and some of their non-relational qualities exist independently of, and unaffected by, perceivers and perceptions.
> *CSR metaphysical part.* Each of these objects has the sensible qualities it is typically perceived to have, and none has phenomenal individuals (ideas, sensa) as constituents.

CSR perceptual part. These objects and their qualities are typically immediately and publicly perceived as they are.

CSR epistemic part. We typically gain immediate, non-inferential and certain knowledge of these objects and of some of their sensible qualities.[4]

Descartes's initial doubts question all four parts of this view, stemming from his doubt of the existential part of CSR. Descartes's first meditation accomplishes this doubt by insisting that we might be dreaming or there might be an evil demon deceiving us about the existence of physical objects. But Descartes claims that the meditator can resolve this doubt by using clear and distinct perception, after this faculty has been validated by his proofs of God's existence and non-deception.

If he can resolve this doubt of the first part of CSR, Descartes's epistemological and metaphysical views still conflict with central elements of CSR. First, he sets up a three-term model of sensation of external objects, interposing 'ideas' between the mind and external objects. This 'veil of ideas' model maintains that objects are not *immediately* perceived or known. Thus, Descartes replaces CSR with a 'representative realism', challenging the claims of the perceptual and epistemic parts of CSR.

Second, the meditator's clear and distinct perceptions of bodies will show that their essence is extension. This entails that physical objects in themselves are characterized only by qualities that are mathematically definable, and do not possess what Locke will call 'secondary qualities', such as colour. For Descartes, the ideas of these secondary qualities are 'confused ideas of sensation', resulting from the union of mind and body. Nor do bodies possess or transmit to us Aristotelian substantial forms, such as coldness. So, Descartes ultimately rejects the naïve elements of the metaphysical and perceptual parts of CSR, which assert that we perceive sensible qualities as they are in the objects.

Finally, while Descartes believed his sceptical doubts could be answered, Forguson is right to say that 'virtually all of his contemporaries and successors have thought [that his answer to scepticism is] a failure' (Forguson 1989: 91), most notably because of circularity in his proofs of God's existence. Many have seen scepticism about the existence of physical objects – thus, about realism in general – as the result of Descartes's inquiry. For them, a philosophy more sympathetic to the beliefs of common sense must serve as the antidote to this unsettling result.

Whether Descartes's response to scepticism succeeds or not, he challenges a central component of common sense – doubts about CSR have been raised.

John Locke

In his *Essay concerning Human Understanding*, Locke explains that his goals, too, are to support the new science of his day:

> in an age that produces such masters, as ... the incomparable
> Mr. Newton, with some others of that strain; 'tis ambition enough
> to be employed as an under-labourer in clearing ground a little, and
> removing some of the rubbish, that lies in the way to knowledge.
> (Locke 1975: 10)

This 'rubbish' involves central elements of CSR.

Locke says that parts of his work are 'somewhat out of the common road' (Locke 1975: 3). Nevertheless, he is often described as a common-sense philosopher. John Jenkins explains how to understand Locke's claim:

> Locke was pre-eminently a philosopher of common sense. This
> does not mean that he simply mirrored views about the world held
> by the man in the street. It would rarely occur to the ordinary man
> to suppose, for example, that we never see the world directly,
> though Locke did appear to hold such a view ...
>
> What it does mean to call him a philosopher of common
> sense is that his thought was prudent and cautious, and restricted
> by basic presuppositions about the world. He was never prepared to

allow his arguments to carry him further than what he could naturally believe in. There are many places in the *Essay* ... when the logic of his own argument demanded that he adopt a certain position which, by ordinary standards, would seem absurd. That is the point at which Locke throws logic to the wind and makes for a compromise position in which he can feel comfortable, even at the expense of consistency. (Jenkins 1983: xii–xiii)

Like Descartes, Locke was sceptical about the accuracy and helpfulness of common usage and 'ordinarily received' ideas. He tells us we need rules 'to remedy the defects of speech',

> because common use has not so visibly annexed any signification to words, as to make men know always certainly what they precisely stand for: and because men in the improvement of their knowledge come to have ideas different from the vulgar and ordinarily received ones, for which they must either make new words ... or else must use old ones, in a new signification. (Locke 1975: III, XI, § 12, 514–15)

So, for example, Locke used a new term, 'secondary qualities', to 'improve our knowledge' about physical objects by denying the common-sense belief that colours are intrinsic properties of those objects.

But Tipton explains that we should balance Locke's scepticism about some common-sense beliefs with an allegiance to others:

> Locke did not set out to affront common sense and ... he certainly did not see the tendency of his thought as skeptical. It is true that he was very conscious that there were areas in which finite human beings could not expect to have knowledge, but in general his concern was to emphasize how much we can be assured of and the extent to which our ordinary and scientific beliefs about the world are justifiable ... [W]here a line of thought seems to run counter to common sense, the author's tendency is to fail to follow the line of thought through or to write as if the difficulty has been, or at least quite certainly could be, solved. (Tipton 1974: 19)

To understand how Locke reaches his conclusions, we should see him as accepting the central model of Descartes's epistemology and attempting to offer a solid empiricist answer to Descartes's sceptical doubts. Locke's introduction of the term 'idea' illustrates his agreement with Descartes's three-part model of perception:

> I must here in the entrance beg pardon of my reader, for the frequent use of the word *idea*, which he will find in the following treatise ... it being that term which, I think, serves best to stand for whatever is the object of the understanding when a man thinks. (Locke 1975: I, I, § 8, 47)

Like Descartes, the perception of this intermediary between the mind and external things sets up a representative theory of perception, in which objects and their qualities are not immediately perceived. Thus, Locke rejects the direct realism in the perceptual part of Pappas's outline of CSR.[5]

For Descartes, this epistemological model raised a doubt about the existential part of CSR – the view that physical objects exist independently of us. Locke's answer to this doubt shows the limitations of his scepticism:

> The notice we have by our senses of the existence of things without us, though it be not altogether so certain as our intuitive knowledge, or the deductions of our reason about the clear abstract ideas of our own minds; yet it is an assurance that deserves the name of knowledge. If we persuade ourselves that our faculties act and inform us right concerning the existence of those objects that affect them, it cannot pass for an ill-grounded confidence: for I think nobody can be so skeptical as to be uncertain of the existence of the things which he sees and feels. (Locke 1975: IV, XI, § 3, 631)

We can see here Locke's different vision of the role that scepticism should play in the 'improvement of our knowledge'. While we do need to correct some beliefs of the 'vulgar', Locke refuses to extend his doubts as far as Descartes – he was unwilling to raise Descartes's doubt of our cognitive faculties. Thus, Locke did not have to confront the challenge of Descartes's validation project. Indeed, Locke was not committed to achieving the metaphysical certainty that Descartes demanded. Rather, he asked only for what Descartes called 'moral certainty':

> this evidence is as great as we can desire, being as certain to us as our pleasure or pain, i.e., happiness or misery; beyond which we have no concernment, either of knowing or being. Such an assurance of the existence of things without us is sufficient to direct us in attaining the good and avoiding the evil which is caused by them, which is the important concernment we have of being made acquainted with them. (Locke 1975: IV, XI, § 8, 635)

With Descartes, Locke also rejects a central element of the metaphysical part of CSR. Objects do not have many of the sensible qualities they are perceived to have, namely, their secondary qualities. It is necessary

> to distinguish the primary and real qualities of bodies, which are always in them (viz., solidity extension, figure, number, and motion or rest ...), from those secondary and imputed qualities, which are but the powers of several combinations of those primary ones, when they operate without being distinctly discerned. (Locke 1975: II, VIII, § 22, 140)

Locke's explanation of how these powers operate is in line with the atomistic science of his day: 'it is evident that some singly imperceptible bodies must come from [the objects] to the eyes, and thereby convey to the brain some motion which produces these ideas which we have of them in us' (Locke 1975: II, VIII, § 12, 136). While Locke does offer arguments about the relativity of perception which are consistent with this view, he seems to accept the perspective of the new science in order to defend realism about primary qualities, rather than seeking to solidly derive this realism. As Tipton says, although

'Locke does talk about proving that the distinction between qualities must be made as it was made by the scientists of his day, it seems more natural to interpret him as in general assuming that the scientific account is the right one' (Tipton 1974: 35–6).

To understand Berkeley's reactions, we must recognize that Locke was sceptical about our knowledge of both corporeal and spiritual substances, since we cannot understand their natures. Locke resisted the empiricist view that our perception of an object is exhausted by a grasp of its qualities. Rather, he argued that these qualities need a 'common subject' to 'support' them:

> when we talk or think of any particular sort of corporeal
> substances, as horse, stone, etc., though the idea we have of either
> of them be but the complication or collection of those several
> simple ideas of sensible qualities which we use to find united in
> the thing called horse or stone; yet *because we cannot conceive
> how they should subsist alone, nor one in another*, we suppose
> them existing in, and supported by, some common subject; which
> support we denote by the name substance, though it be certain
> we have no clear or distinct idea of that thing we suppose
> a support. (Locke 1975: II, XXIII, § 4, 297)

Notoriously, Locke referred to this substance as a 'something, he knew not what' (Locke 1975: II, XXIII, § 2, 296). In part, Berkeley built his own denial of corporeal substance on Locke's struggle to ground solid knowledge of such a substance. Locke also asserted an ignorance of our idea of mental substance – here he differs from Berkeley, as we will see.

Finally, Locke is sceptical about what he envisions as a central goal of science – the discovery of the true nature, or 'real essences', of objects. Locke saw the formation of ideas of essences as a process of abstraction, not as an insight of a Cartesian pure intellect. For him, abstraction can provide us with ideas of the nominal essences of things, but cannot reveal 'the real internal, but generally … unknown constitution of things' (Locke 1975: III, III,

§ 15, 417). Berkeley overcame this scepticism by assigning a different role to scientific inquiry.

George Berkeley

Berkeley's role in the development of these issues is best seen by looking at his answer to scepticism about the existence of objects in the world, which he saw as the inevitable result of his predecessors' work. As with Descartes, scepticism plays a unique role in Berkeley's thinking. He believed that pushing the sceptical arguments of his predecessors to their limit would provide an answer to them. This answer, he claimed, was in line with common sense.

Tipton (1974: 52, 19) explains that 'Berkeley was fully aware of the sceptical tendency implicit in the Cartesian as in the empiricist approach to philosophy, as well as in the thinking of the scientists ... [T]he mistakes in it were rooted in the account of what it is to perceive a physical object'. This account 'takes the root of skepticism to be the opening of a gap between experience and the world, forced by theories of ideas, like Locke's' (Grayling 2005: 167). Berkeley explains, in his *Principles of Human Knowledge*, that because of these theories

> we have been led into very dangerous errors, by supposing a twofold existence of the objects of sense – the one, *intelligible* or in the mind, the other *real* or without the mind ... This ... is the very root of Scepticism; for so long as men thought that real things subsisted without the mind and that their knowledge was only so far forth *real* as it was conformable to *real things*, it follows that they could not be certain they had any real knowledge at all. For how can it be known, that the things which are perceived, are conformable to those which are not perceived, or exist without the mind? (Berkeley 1964: 86, 78)

In his *Philosophical Commentaries*, Berkeley formulates the issue in a succinct way:

> The supposition that things are distinct from Ideas takes away all real Truth, & consequently brings in a Universal Scepticism, since all our knowledge & contemplation is confin'd barely to our own Ideas.[6]

Descartes's and Locke's acceptance of scientific accounts of perception led, in large part, to their sceptical conclusions. For Berkeley, their scientific causal account attempts to explain our ordinary awareness of external objects, but ends by concluding that we are not directly aware of these objects at all, and cannot even be sure they exist. Tipton describes the 'paradoxical position' (Tipton 1974: 19) that Descartes and Locke are led to in their three-step analysis of sensory experience. They start with the common-sense view that we are aware of public objects and their properties in the world. But science then describes a process of perception in which the object conveys into the mind impulses that cause representations of the table, namely, ideas or mental objects. Finally, this representative model of perception leads them to question whether we can be sure that those objects or their properties exist, ending with a scepticism about their initial commitment. So, paradoxically, seeing an object is explained as the result of a process which starts with the object and ends without the perception of the object.

Berkeley answers this scepticism by pushing it to its limit:

> Berkeley's solution to the problem is in essence staggeringly simple. He holds that if the root cause of scepticism is to be found in the supposition that real things are distinct from ideas, opposition to scepticism must rest on the contrary supposition, viz. that ideas and things are to be identified. The tactic involves pushing the sceptic's case to the limit and denying that there is a material world lying behind what we actually experience when we perceive. But having done this Berkeley can turn the tables on the sceptic by claiming that there is no longer any case for scepticism. The truth as he sees it is that there is only one world, a world which our senses inform us of and which is made up of

ideas, and that this world is the real world. It has been thought unreal only by those who have made the mistake of supposing that there is *another* world beyond the limit of experience and of which the world as we know it in immediate experience can be only a shadow. (Tipton 1974: 53)

Berkeley sided with a central aspect of common sense, grounded in 'a proposition that almost everyone knows', as Lemos (2004: 5) puts it. For Berkeley, trusting the senses is a basic tenet of common sense; as he says, 'We must with the Mob place certainty in the senses'.[7] And Berkeley was satisfied with the same moral certainty about his conclusions that Locke embraced. He insisted that philosophical terms and analyses must remain 'anchored in everyday situations':

> [Berkeley] explicitly claims the word *real*, and at the same time *know* back to ordinary language from the Cartesian theoretical attempt to ward off skepticism ... He refuses even to be drawn into the Cartesian doubt, suspecting that [Descartes's] attempt to solve the skeptical question fails ... The words *real* and *know* must have application in our everyday life to stay justified and the vulgar are justified in their usage. (Tomeček 2015: 24)

Moreover, Berkeley overcomes Locke's scepticism within the sciences, since his world view provides a role for science that differs from Locke's search for 'real essences'. Since Berkeley's world is as we perceive it to be, the work of science is, instead, to uncover relations between phenomena. These discoveries of natural correlations avoid any concerns about the existence of causal connections between objects. In the *Principles*, 'any simple inductive generalization counts as a law of nature, and phenomena are explained by inclusion in such generalizations' (Downing 2005: 249). But, as Lisa Downing (2005: 249–50) explains,

> In *De Motu*, Berkeley develops a specialized sense of 'law of nature' according to which the laws of nature are the most general principles from which observed regularities in the phenomena can

be deduced. A phenomenon is explained scientifically, then, when it is shown to follow from these most general principles.

This view allows scientists to use experiments and reasoning to develop universal laws. For these reasons, Berkeley was convinced that he had answered the sceptics:

> That what I see, hear and feel doth exist, that is to say, is perceived by me, I no more doubt than I do of my own being. But I do not see how the testimony of sense can be alleged, as a proof for the existence of any thing, which is not perceived by sense. We are not for having any man turn sceptic, and disbelieve his senses; on the contrary we give them all the stress and assurance imaginable; nor are there any principles more opposite to skepticism, than those we have laid down.[8]

The second issue central to Berkeley's reaction to his predecessors is his claim that his immaterialism is compatible with common sense. He focuses on this issue in *Three Dialogues between Hylas and Philonous*. His defender, Philonous, asks the materialist, Hylas: '[A]re you content to admit that opinion for true, which upon examination shall appear the most agreeable to common sense, and remote from skepticism?'[9] Philonous adds: 'I am content, Hylas, to appeal to the common sense of the world for the truth of my notion' and 'I endeavor to vindicate common sense.'[10] Famously, in the *Philosophical Commentaries*, Berkeley writes: 'I side in all things with the Mob.'[11] The precise significance of these claims has been extensively debated; I will not attempt to definitively resolve that debate. Rather, I will try to shed light on Berkeley's claims by looking at two issues: whether these claims should be read as defending an implicit view of common sense and whether they support a commitment to CSR.

The above claims do seem to support an implicit use of common sense. Tomeček explains that, while Berkeley offers some examples of common sense, he 'conspicuously fails to generalize on what common sense consists in' (Tomeček 2015: 25), and

> By refusing to define a commonsensical position positively,
> Berkeley is espousing ... implicit common sense. His consistent
> strategy is to exclude certain propositions as non-commonsensical
> but never to make positive statements of the type 'common sense is
> to believe in the existence of external physical objects' or such.
> That would be an attempt to accommodate common sense to
> a philosophical scheme of things, or an attempt at an *explicit*
> version of common sense. Instead, Berkeley's common sense forms
> the ultimate limit of meaning, its truths so well known and obvious
> that they can not even be formulated. (Tomeček 2015: 38–9)

A. David Kline (1987: 21–31) pursues this perspective and asks a helpful question: why does Berkeley care about conformity to common sense? To answer this question, Kline distinguishes between such conformity as an 'epistemic virtue' and as a 'practical virtue'. On the former view, the role of common sense is much the same as criteria which are used to decide between competing scientific theories, like 'explanatory power, simplicity, consistency with background scientific, religious and philosophical frameworks, and avoidance of new problems', or as a 'tie-breaking criterion' when other criteria are equally balanced (Kline 1987: 21). But Kline argues that this model does not adequately explain *why* common sense is an epistemic virtue, and he attempts to explain what makes it so.

The implicit view focuses on non-commonsensical opinions and Kline explains that, for Berkeley, these opinions are '*extravagant* and *paradoxical*' (Kline 1987: 25). They also have absurd consequences 'which are jarring to common sense [and] take three forms: contradictions, violations of simple perceptual judgments, and violations of simple introspective judgments' (Kline 1987: 29). Since these consequences may be harmful, Kline finds a bridge between Berkeley's 'practical and epistemic pronouncements':

> When philosophers go about uttering noncommonsensical views
> they may do considerable harm. They run a serious risk of turning
> people into skeptics and misologists. (Kline 1987: 24)

> Common sense has no epistemic force *qua* common sense. But
> once it is clear what particular forms realize the shock to the
> vulgar's consciousness, the epistemic kick is transparent. (Kline
> 1987: 29)

As such, 'Common sense far from being a tie breaker is rather the
touchstone of acceptability' (Kline 1987: 23).

This commitment to implicit common sense must be aug-
mented by recognizing that Berkeley uses common sense explicitly
in his opposition to Descartes and Locke's representative realism. So,
it seems that Berkeley does not offer us a single-sided view. Rather,
his view can be described as a 'Janus-faced defense of common sense
and ordinary language' (Tipton 1974: 17), reflected in his claim that 'in
such things we ought to *think with the learned and speak with the
vulgar*'.[12]

George Pitcher clarifies this by distinguishing between
a 'conciliatory' and 'non-conciliatory' attitude towards common
sense. The former 'regards all, or most, of the common sense view of
the world as true and as known to be true'. The latter 'supposes that if
there are metaphysical principles which are either self-evidently true
or demonstrably true, and that if a metaphysical system based on such
principles should happen to conflict with the deliverances of common
sense, then so much the worse for common sense' (Pitcher 1984: 141).
Pitcher specifies a principle which Berkeley saw as 'absolutely certain
and, indeed almost self-evidently true':

> (I) In sense perception, what the perceiver in every case is directly
> (or immediately) aware of ... is just one or more ideas of sense.
> (Pitcher 1984: 95)

But this principle would not be accepted as a tenet of common sense:

> ordinary, commonsense people would not recognize (I) as one of
> their own convictions: it ... seems to have consequences that
> directly conflict with certain aspects of the commonsense view of
> the world. Berkeley, then, finds himself in the awkward position of

having to adopt both a conciliatory and a non-conciliatory attitude. Principle (I), for him, is more certain than any belief of common sense; so for its sake he has to be non-conciliatory. But he is eager to defend any feature of the commonsense view of the world that can live happily with principle (I); to that extent, he is conciliatory. (Pitcher 1984: 143)

Berkeley's Janus-faced posture towards common sense is made clearer by his relationship to CSR. A. A. Luce (1963) and T. E. Jessop (1953) have emphatically interpreted Berkeley as a common-sense realist. And George Pappas argues that Berkeley 'explicitly accepted' several claims of Pappas's four-part view of CSR (Pappas 1991, 30–40). For Berkeley, there are ordinary macro objects and they have the sensible qualities they are typically perceived to have. So, objects are immediately and publicly perceived, and we typically gain immediate and certain knowledge of them and of some of their sensible qualities.

But we can also see that Berkeley cannot qualify as a CSRist for the following reason:

> Berkeley emphatically did not accept a claim common to all realisms, namely, that physical objects do not have sensa as constituents. Or, put another way, all realists reject something Berkeley certainly accepted, viz. the phenomenalist view that physical objects are collections of sensible ideas. It would be more acceptable to label Berkeley a common sense phenomenalist or ... a *common sense idealist*. Berkeley is not a realist, and so he is not a CSRist, and this despite the fact that he accepts [a number of] claims that help to constitute CSR. (Pappas 1991: 40)

So, we can find 'two Berkeleys in the texts' (Pappas 1991: 40), in relation to common sense. As Berkeley says:

> I do not pretend to be a setter-up of *new notions*. My endeavours tend only to unite and place in a clearer light that truth, which was before shared between the vulgar and the philosophers: the former

> being of the opinion, that *those things they immediately perceive*
> *are the real things;* and the latter that *the things immediately*
> *perceived are ideas which exist only in the mind.* Which two
> notions put together do in effect constitute the substance of what
> I advance.[13]

And we can agree with Tipton's analysis of Berkeley's Janus-faced
position:

> There are two supposed truths here. By putting the emphasis on his
> acceptance of the first proposition Berkeley can present himself as
> the champion of common sense. But by putting the emphasis on the
> latter the critics can without *ignoratio elenchi,* see him as the most
> outrageous affronter of it. (Tipton 1974: 56)

Berkeley, then, can be seen as leaving us with a philosophical
view that accords more with the claims of CSR than do the views of
Descartes or Locke. But, strictly, his view does not satisfy the elements of Pappas's description. It does not accord with the 'existential
part', which claims that 'There are ordinary macro physical objects.
They and some of their non-relational qualities exist independently
of, and unaffected by, perceivers and perceptions.' His work provides
an impetus for Hume and others to complete the reconciliation of
science, scepticism, and common sense.

MIND, SPIRITS, AND COMMON SENSE

The second element in the conception of common sense which I have
adopted is Forguson's 'rational psychology'. This refers to 'a framework of explanation and a set of concepts' we use to 'describe and
account for our own and others' actions' but which we 'do not use in
connection with the behavior of inanimate things and primitive
organisms' (Forguson 1989: 4). At the basis of these explanations are
desiderative and epistemic states:

> There are two broad categories of mental states which constitute
> the reasons, the rational causal elements, we appeal to in our

explanations of human behavior. On the one hand are *desiderative*
states: states of wanting, desiring, craving, wishing for, [etc.] ...
People's *epistemic states*, on the other hand, are constituted by
their beliefs ... concerning what is or was the case and their
expectations, convictions, conjectures and hypotheses concerning
what will or would or might be the case if certain things were to
happen or be done ... Rational psychology is the ... view that
actions are a function of relevant epistemic states and the net
desiderative state. (Forguson 1989: 5–8)

This model of human mind, action, and nature is common to
Descartes's and Locke's views of our behaviour in the world. While
both were metaphysical dualists, this model depicts the functioning
of the mind insofar as it motivates our action. The understanding and
will together capture Forguson's epistemic and desiderative elements.
Descartes tells us that his nature, as a combination of mind and body,
'does indeed teach me to avoid what induces a feeling of pain and to
seek out what induces feelings of pleasure' (Descartes 1964: VII, 82;
1984–5: II, 57). And these actions are based on epistemic states which
need only be morally certain.

Locke explains the interaction of desiderative and epistemic
states in a comparable way, which we 'do not use in connection
with the behavior of inanimate things and primitive organisms':

Desire is always moved by evil, to fly it ... For all that we desire, is
only to be happy. But, though this general desire of happiness
operates constantly and invariably, yet the satisfaction of any
desire can be suspended ... till we have maturely examined
whether the particular apparent good which we then desire makes
a part of our real happiness. (Locke 1975: II, XXI, § 71, 283)

Forguson seems correct to claim that this view of ourselves is so
fundamental to common sense that 'It is difficult to overestimate
the extent to which our commitment to rational psychology is impli-
cated in our everyday lives' (Forguson 1989: 8).

Despite the ubiquity of this view, Berkeley offers a different view of ourselves which is, for him, an element of common sense. John Russell Roberts (2007) explains that Berkeley's view differs in a fundamental way from what rational psychology entails since Berkeley adds a crucial consideration.

The initial context for Roberts's discussion is Wilfrid Sellars's 'Philosophy and the Scientific Image of Man' (Sellars 1963: 1–40). Roberts explains that Berkeley privileges what Sellars calls the 'manifest' over the 'scientific image':

> 'the manifest image' has come to name our view of the world as consisting of the sorts of items which we meet in sense perception . . . [T]here is an important sense in which the manifest image takes those things to *be* as they *appear* to perception . . . [T]his image of the world then competes with 'the scientific image' of man-in-the-world, and vice versa. The latter is our picture of reality as consisting, at most, of only a few kinds of things, and these things are the postulated entities of physical theory . . . [I]t will be tempting to identify Berkeley as one of the defenders of the manifest image over the scientific image. (Roberts 2007: 125–6)

And, 'by identifying Berkeley as a philosopher of the manifest image, we would have what we sought: an account of the connection between his metaphysics and his claim to be defending common sense' (Roberts 2007: 126).

But Roberts asserts that this perspective does not go deep enough in explaining Berkeley's or Sellars's 'basic entities' of the manifest image. That more basic ground has 'persons' rather than 'varied kinds of objects of perception' as its 'primary objects' (Roberts 2007: 127). To reach that level, we must have a conception of ourselves that incorporates 'the peculiar activity of man, conceptual activity' (Roberts 2007: 128). And, if Berkeley stopped at this conception, we would find close points of comparison between his view and the agents described by rational psychology. Berkeley's manifest image would accord with common sense regarding objects in the world and persons engaged in evaluative epistemic and desiderative activity.

Nevertheless, Roberts insists that this analysis would still miss Berkeley's fundamental view. That view goes beyond Sellars's framework and offers us the 'religious image' of man-in the-world, which sees *persons* as *spirits*:

> The most important distinguishing feature of this image is that it regards *spirit* as the basic category of being. (Roberts 2007: 142)

> We are finite spirits, made in [God's] image. (Roberts 2007: 136)

> In the religious image, the existence of the natural is distinct from, and fully dependent upon, the existence of the non-natural, i.e., the spiritual. (Roberts 2007: 129–30)

We might claim that 'while the manifest image is intimately connected to common sense, the religious image is not' (Roberts 2007: 142). But Berkeley's *complete* statement about siding with the mob suggests that he saw the religious image as reflecting common sense: 'All things in the Scripture which side with the Vulgar against the Learned side with me also. I side in all things with the Mob.'[14] So Roberts claims that 'Berkeley is only interested in defending his view as common sense insofar as a commitment to a traditional Judeo-Christian monotheism is considered a part of common sense' (Roberts 2007: 142). Berkeley's common-sense view replaces rational psychology with a view that elevates 'reverence and embrace [of] the salutary truths of the Gospel, which to know and to practice is the highest perfection of human nature'.[15]

Seeing Berkeley in this way shows that his immaterialism 'has a natural, even an inevitable place in the development of the religious image':

> There is nothing at all strange about adopting an eliminative attitude toward material substance from within the religious image because that view of reality can make no sense of the idea of

material substance, i.e., of an independently existing, absolutely nonspiritual being. Any attempt to introduce such a thing into the ontology undermines the image's conception of the fundamental nature of being and thereby destabilizes the religious image's very conception of reality and humanity's place in it.[16]

The religious image supports the elimination of material substance because that image is centred on the concept of power. For Berkeley, since the non-spiritual must be identified with the absence of active power, it would have no place in an ontology of spirit.

The strength of Roberts's suggestions is that they offer us a view of Berkeley which unifies his religious and immaterialist commitments by making them both central, intimately connected elements of a common-sense view. Berkeley's focus on the active power of mind deserves further investigation in the modern period.[17] This perspective can, I believe, shed new light on the work of his predecessors and on the tradition of thought which grew out of his work.

We see, then, that the work of Descartes, Locke, and Berkeley exhibits a progression in which the claims of science, scepticism, and common sense were continually, but not conclusively, reconciled. The work of these philosophers put in place the foundations upon which later thinkers, in the early modern period and beyond, would tackle this reconciliation challenge.[18]

NOTES

1 Forguson (1989: 14–15). Forguson's claim is true of *most* states of affairs; some *do* depend on what we think about them (e.g., the value of money). We will see that George Pappas expands this description of CSR in a crucial way.

2 Forguson (1989: 4). We not only do this but *are correct* in doing so.

3 As Descartes explains in the French edition of the *Principles of Philosophy* (1964: IXB, 14; 1984–5: I, 186).

4 Pappas offers two different versions of this four-part analysis in Pappas (1991: 27–9) and in Pappas (2000: 184–5). I include elements of both versions, incorporating the naïve formulations of the metaphysical and

perceptual parts. This formulation fits the common-sense view that Forguson intends and helps us focus on the elements of CSR which are central for us.

5　There has been debate about whether Locke held a representative theory of perception. But Berkeley read him that way, so I will adopt that view to explicate this period's progression of thought.

6　Berkeley (1964), *Philosophical Commentaries*, Notebook A 606, 75.

7　Berkeley (1964), *Philosophical Commentaries*, Notebook A 740, 90.

8　Berkeley (1964), *The Principles of Human Knowledge*, 40, 57.

9　Berkeley (1964), *Three Dialogues between Hylas and Philonous*, 172.

10　Berkeley (1964), *Three Dialogues between Hylas and Philonous*, 234, 244.

11　Berkeley (1964), *Philosophical Commentaries*, Notebook A 405, 51.

12　Berkeley (1964), *The Principles of Human Knowledge*, 51, 62.

13　Berkeley (1964), *Three Dialogues between Hylas and Philonous*, 262.

14　Berkeley (1964), *Philosophical Commentaries*, Notebook A 405, 51.

15　Berkeley (1964), *The Principles of Human Knowledge*, 156, 113.

16　Berkeley (1964), *The Principles of Human Knowledge*, 156, 113.

17　In Wagner (2014) I provide a reading of the *Meditations* in which the active power of the human mind is central to Descartes's response to scepticism.

18　I would like to thank Rik Peels and René van Woudenberg for their helpful comments and suggestions on this chapter.

3   The Scottish School of Common-Sense Philosophy

Paul Wood

INTRODUCTION

During the eighteenth century the appeal to common sense as an answer to scepticism received two influential formulations: one by Claude Buffier and the other by Thomas Reid and the Scottish 'school'[1] of common-sense philosophy. Whereas Buffier was primarily concerned to curb the sceptical implications of Descartes's philosophy and Locke's way of ideas, the members of the Scottish school attacked the scepticism they believed manifested itself more broadly in the writings of Descartes, Locke, Berkeley, and, especially, David Hume.[2] While Hume admitted that *A Treatise of Human Nature* (1739–40) was a 'very sceptical' book, he differentiated his position from Pyrrhonism, stating that 'Philosophy wou'd render us entirely *Pyrrhonian*, were not nature too strong for it' (Hume (1740) 2007: Vol. 1, 413–14). Hume dismissed Pyrrhonian scepticism on the grounds that it was an irrefutable but nevertheless untenable *'Jeux d'esprit'* which was invariably subverted by our natural instincts and beliefs and of no 'durable good or benefit to society'.[3] Instead, Hume defended a 'Moderate' or 'Academic' form of scepticism which mitigated 'the force of ... Pyrrhonian doubt' by relying on 'common sense and reflection'. For him, Academic scepticism was 'useful' because it teaches us that 'there is a degree of doubt, and caution, and modesty' which befits the 'just reasoner', and that 'philosophical decisions are nothing but the reflections of common life, methodized and corrected' (Hume (1748) 2000: 120–1). Hume's attempt to distance himself from Pyrrhonian scepticism failed, however, for he was widely denounced in Scotland and elsewhere as a Pyrrhonist and atheist.

This chapter explores the responses of the Scottish school of common-sense philosophy to Hume's supposed Pyrrhonism and irreligion. We shall see that Reid's answer to Hume differed significantly from those advanced by the two figures said to be fellow members of the Scottish school: James Beattie and James Oswald. This chapter also discusses Hume's reply to his Scottish critics, as well as the debate in Britain in the 1770s and 1780s sparked by the writings of Reid, Beattie, and Oswald. The chapter concludes with an examination of Dugald Stewart's reformulation of the appeal to common sense and a brief account of the rapid decline of the Scottish school.

THOMAS REID

Thomas Reid probably first learned about ancient and early modern scepticism from his regent George Turnbull at Marischal College Aberdeen.[4] After graduating in 1726, Reid read many of the prominent philosophers of the day including George Berkeley, whose works were said by Turnbull's colleague Patrick Hardie to contain a 'train of paradoxes' which promoted 'pure scepticism' and undermined religious belief (Hardie 1719: 6–7). In the 1740s, Reid encountered Hume's *A Treatise of Human Nature*. We do not know when he initially read the *Treatise* or what he made of the book on reading it. He later claimed: 'Ever since the treatise of human Nature was published I respected Mr Hume as the greatest Metaphysician of the Age ... I read that treatise over and over with great care, made an abstract of it and wrote my observations upon it' (Reid (1764) 1997: 257). Neither his 'abstract' nor his 'observations' survive. The only evidence of his engagement with Hume in the 1740s is a manuscript dated 22 October 1748 wherein he addressed Hume's sceptical deconstruction of the idea of the self in terms which foreshadowed his argument in the *Inquiry* and elsewhere that our notion of the self was a 'first principle' of common sense which was 'immediately inspired by our constitution' through a natural 'suggestion' of the mind.[5]

During the 1750s Reid articulated his common-sense philosophy in three overlapping contexts: his Aberdeen circle's response to Hume, his teaching at King's College Aberdeen, and his participation in the Aberdeen Philosophical Society. One of Reid's earliest Aberdonian associates was David Fordyce. Before his death in 1751, Fordyce had read the publications of 'the great Metaphysician' Hume (Fordyce 1748). Fordyce's correspondence suggests that he may have inspired Reid's use of *the principle of credulity* to counter Humean scepticism.[6] Reid's understanding of Hume was also shaped by his friends Alexander Gerard, George Campbell, and Robert Traill, who all attacked Hume's irreligion while acknowledging that he was a gifted writer and an accomplished anatomist of human nature (Traill 1755: 17; Gerard 1760: 6, 39, 48; Campbell 1762: v–vii). Reid's view of Hume displays the same mix of censure and praise. He maintained that Humean scepticism was 'destructive of the faith of a Christian, ... the science of a philosopher, and ... the prudence of a man of common understanding'. Nevertheless, he regarded Hume as 'undoubtedly one of the most acute metaphysicians that this or any age hath produced'.[7] The ambivalent attitude of Reid and his associates towards Hume resembles that of the Moderate clergymen in Edinburgh who admired (and publicly defended) Hume's person but who nevertheless sharply disagreed with his philosophical doctrines.[8]

The second context was Reid's lecturing at King's College (Reid (1764) 1997: 5). A set of student notes from his logic lectures, along with the four orations he delivered at graduation ceremonies held at King's, allow us to track the development of his teaching while he was in Old Aberdeen. These sources tell us that by 1756, Reid appealed to the principles of common sense in his classes in order to neutralize what he took to be Hume's Pyrrhonism. Initially, his response to Hume was primarily methodological, based on what he called his five 'laws of practicing philosophy'.[9] By 1759 he had also formulated his critique of the theory of ideas to undermine Humean scepticism.

According to Reid, this theory affirmed that 'the human mind does not immediately perceive objects that are external and absent but perceives them through certain images or likenesses depicted in the mind that are called ideas'. Ideas were thus a sceptical wedge separating the mind from its objects.[10] He now taught that this theory had given birth to the system of philosophy found in Hume's *Treatise* and *Philosophical Essays*, which had served as 'an arrogant bulwark of the scepticism of today'. Yet Hume's system had an Achilles heel: it rested 'its whole weight on the hypothesis of ideas'. Consequently, once the theory of ideas was shown to be baseless, Hume's Pyrrhonism 'instantly collapse[d]'.[11]

The third context in which Reid's common-sense philosophy evolved was the Aberdeen Philosophical Society (also known as the Wise Club), which was founded by Reid and his closest associates (Ulman 1990). The proceedings of the society thus reflected the intellectual preoccupations of Reid's circle and, especially, their engagement with Hume's writings.[12] Beginning in 1758, Reid gave a series of seven formal discourses devoted to his critique of Hume and the theory of ideas which partly overlapped with material in his lectures and orations at King's and which later appeared in revised form in the *Inquiry* (Reid (1764) 1997: 5, 267–315; Ulman 1990: 111). In January 1758 he also proposed a question targeting Hume's distinction between impressions and ideas which was discussed at length at two meetings held the following July (Ulman 1990: 85–6, 190). Although the responses of his fellow members to his contributions to the club are undocumented, his discourses and question probably generated lively debate because Hume had both detractors and supporters within the society (compare Suderman 2001: 28–9). Nevertheless, the club members all shared Reid's worries about the irreligious implications of Humean scepticism and were sympathetic to the apologetic dimension of his attack on Hume and the ideal system. Reid's contributions to the society define a pivotal phase in the formulation of his common-sense philosophy, for they mark the moment at which his doctrines began to circulate beyond the institutional confines of King's College. When his philosophy finally emerged in print, it registered the three different contexts in which it took shape and gave voice to the complex response of Reid and his circle to Hume's writings.

In making the transition from the private to the public sphere, Reid's common-sense philosophy was also scrutinized by David Hume. By mid-1762, Reid had drafted the *Inquiry*'s chapters on smell, taste, hearing, and touch. He then sent them to the Moderate clergyman Hugh Blair, who in turn lent the chapters to Hume. Hume queried Reid's lack of method in presenting the book's basic argument, his treatment of secondary qualities and the distinction between our visual and tactile ideas of extension, and his apparent revival of the doctrine of innate ideas. He also bridled at 'one particular Insinuation' which likely questioned his religious orthodoxy and which Reid seems to have subsequently deleted.[13] Blair informed Reid of Hume's comments, to which Reid responded in a detailed summary of the leading themes and core argument of the book.[14] During the period in which Reid composed this 'Abstract', he also drafted the *Inquiry*'s lengthy chapter on sight. He sent copies of both manuscripts via Blair to Hume in late 1762 or early 1763. Having read the 'Abstract' and the further instalment of the *Inquiry*, Hume wrote to Reid congratulating him on the entertaining style of his forthcoming book, while studiously avoiding any substantive comments on Reid's critique of the *Treatise*.[15] Reid replied, thanking Hume for his 'Candor and Generosity' and stating that in the *Inquiry* he had attempted to 'preserve [a] due mean betwixt Confidence and Despair' in criticizing his adversary's sceptical 'System'. He also said that Hume deserved praise for making the sceptical implications of the theory of ideas explicit and for having 'furnished [the] proper artillery' for attacking Humean scepticism itself. Furthermore, he invited Hume to comment on the complete text of the *Inquiry*, writing that he would 'take it as a very great favour to have your opinion upon [the complete text], from which I make no doubt of receiving light, whether I receive conviction or not'.[16] There is no evidence to suggest that Hume did so. This episode is puzzling because Hume passed over the opportunity to correct any of Reid's misreadings of his philosophy. He neither questioned Reid's characterization of his philosophy as leading to 'absolute' scepticism nor clarified for Reid the sense in which he considered himself a sceptic.

Notwithstanding the deep philosophical differences between Hume and Reid, Reid's *Inquiry* shows that his common-sense philosophy was rooted in Hume's *Treatise*. The narrative arc of Reid's history of the theory of ideas in the *Inquiry* pivots on Hume's exposure of the sceptical implications of the ideal system (Reid (1764) 1997: 3–4). The Pyrrhonism of the *Treatise* was, as Reid had earlier stated in his orations, an unintended consequence of the ideal system created by Descartes. It took a consummate metaphysician such as Hume to bring the inherent scepticism of that system to light. Reid's task was thus to scrutinize the philosophical assumptions upon which the *Treatise* rested in order to counter Hume's Pyrrhonism.[17]

Hume's sceptical solution to sceptical doubt in the *Treatise* was the starting point for Reid's answer to Hume. In the conclusion to Book 1 of the *Treatise*, Hume maintained that 'total scepticism' was irrefutable but also untenable. 'Nature', he observed, 'breaks the force of all sceptical arguments . . . and keeps them from having any considerable influence on the understanding'. Nature had furnished the mind with original principles such as our senses and understanding, which despite their fallibility must be 'implicitly followed'. Nature had also endowed us with natural beliefs (e.g., in the existence of body), which 'we must take for granted in all our reasonings'.[18] Reid agreed with these claims, but reframed them to serve as the basis for his own common-sense solution to sceptical doubt.

To counter Pyrrhonism, Reid followed Hume in appealing to nature, our natural beliefs, and the original principles of the human mind. But Reid's theism gave the term 'nature' and its cognates a different meaning from what it had in Hume's lexicon. Unlike Hume, Reid saw both nature and human nature as God's creation. As such, they exhibit design and attest to the governance of a providential deity (Reid (1764) 1997: 11). The anatomy of the human body and mind thus reveal a structure or system (what he called our 'constitution') instituted by God. In appealing to human nature, therefore, Reid's answer to Pyrrhonism differed profoundly from Hume's. Whereas Hume could give no reason why we should trust the senses or our understanding to arrive at true beliefs, Reid contended that such trust is grounded on the fact that our 'constitution' is divinely created (see especially Reid (1764) 1997: 168–71). The biblical text from Job 32:8 quoted on the title page of the *Inquiry*, 'The inspiration of the Almighty giveth them understanding', illustrates this point. The principles of common sense are, for Reid, 'a part of that furniture which nature hath given to the human understanding'. These principles, he declared, 'are the inspiration of the Almighty' and 'serve to direct us in the common affairs of life', even though we are unable to 'give a reason for them' (Reid (1764) 1997: 33, 215). Moreover, since God is no deceiver, we can rely on human nature (of which the principles of common sense are a component) to provide us with true, if limited, knowledge about ourselves, the natural order, and our creator.[19] Reid's common-sense reply to Humean scepticism was thus a reformulation of the providential naturalism he was taught by George Turnbull.[20]

Moreover, Reid's delineation of the relationship between philosophy and common sense was founded on his providential naturalism. Whereas Hume depicted philosophy to be at odds with 'nature' and suggested that in common life we simply ignore or learn to manage the contradiction between the two, Reid maintained that the triad of philosophy, common sense (his equivalent for 'nature'), and common life can function together harmoniously once we recognize that philosophy and common life are rooted in common sense.[21] Because he believed that nature and human nature exhibit the same 'consistency, uniformity, and beauty' that characterize God's works, it followed that 'there must ... be some order and consistency in the human faculties'. Since 'common sense and reason have both one author', there could be no inherent conflict between the two, or between common life and philosophy. Because the theory of ideas occasioned a clash between reason and common sense and led to philosophical conclusions which contradicted the basic assumptions of common life, he maintained that the theory had to be abandoned since it subverted the proper relations that ought to subsist among the constituent parts of human nature as well as the harmony between common life and philosophy. Furthermore, in his view the disjunction between nature and philosophy that Hume spoke of could only end in disillusionment and despair. Humean scepticism, Reid observed, 'tend[s] to slacken every nerve of the soul, to put every noble purpose and sentiment out of countenance, and spread a melancholy gloom over the whole face of things' (Reid (1764) 1997: 19, 68–9, 201–2). But he was confident that knowledge and virtue would flourish, once the harmony between our faculties and between common sense and philosophy was restored, and sceptical doubt nullified.

CREATING THE SCOTTISH SCHOOL OF COMMON-SENSE PHILOSOPHY

Reid's *Inquiry* met with a muted reception following its appearance in early 1764. In the mid-1770s, however, common-sense philosophy became a matter of intense public debate, sparked by the publication of James Oswald's *An Appeal to Common Sense in Behalf of Religion* (1766–72) and, especially, James Beattie's widely read *An Essay on the Nature and Immutability of Truth* (1770) (Wood 2018). Oswald's variant of the philosophy of common sense was not a product of the cultural milieu shared by the members of Reid's circle in the northeast of Scotland, even though Oswald may have studied at King's College. Instead, he developed his philosophical views largely in isolation while serving as a parish minister in the Highlands and later at Methven in Perthshire. Although Oswald met and corresponded with Reid and cited the *Inquiry* in the *Appeal*, there is little evidence to suggest that Oswald was influenced by the technical details of Reid's anatomy of the mind.[22] Rather, what he valued most about Reid's work was that it was a riposte to irreligion. He therefore enlisted Reid as an ally in his polemical campaign against sceptics, infidels, and misguided religious apologists who relied on reason to defend the truth of Christianity. There was also a wide conceptual gulf between their respective appeals to common sense. Whereas Reid formulated his conception of common sense primarily as an antidote to Humean scepticism, Oswald addressed the broader, and more diffuse, phenomenon of the erosion of religious belief. Furthermore, Oswald's invocation of common sense owed far more to the French Jesuit, Claude Buffier, than it did to Reid (Oswald 1766–72: Vol. 1, 64, 77).

James Beattie, on the other hand, was a product of the cultural milieu of Reid's circle. Educated at Marischal College, Beattie succeeded his teacher Alexander Gerard as the Marischal professor of moral philosophy and logic in 1760.[23] Shortly thereafter he was elected a member of the Wise Club. At club meetings in 1765–7 he introduced the question, 'What is the difference between Common Sense and Reason?', and then answered this question in two discourses which formed the basis for his *Essay* (Ulman 1990: 134–5, 139, 142, 195). Although Beattie's version of common-sense philosophy resembles Reid's, there are nevertheless important differences between their appeals to common sense. Even though both Reid and Beattie characterized the principles of common sense as 'instincts', Beattie associated these principles with our feelings, sentiments, and 'the heart', whereas Reid saw them as bound up with our natural judgments.[24] Moreover, unlike Reid, Beattie was highly critical of the study of metaphysics. Writing to Thomas Blacklock about the agenda of the *Essay*, he affirmed that the 'metaphysical spirit' found in the writings of Hume, Reid, and George Campbell was 'the bane of true learning, true taste, and true science' because it gave rise to 'modern scepticism and atheism'. Furthermore, he complained that this spirit had 'a bad effect upon the human faculties, and tends not a little to sour the temper, to subvert good principles, and to disqualify men for the business of life'. Consequently, Beattie emphasized that the *Essay* was intended to counter the pernicious 'metaphysical spirit' that infected the thinking of Hume, Reid, and Campbell.[25] While he accepted that there was a legitimate form of metaphysics dealing with a '[plain] account of the faculties of the mind, and of the principles of morals and natural religion', he nevertheless devoted much of the *Essay* to denouncing the 'metaphysical spirit' he had complained of to Blacklock (Beattie 1774: 402–4, 483, and also 432–4). In attacking this 'metaphysical spirit', he explicitly distanced himself from Hume. But he also implicitly dissociated himself from Reid's brand of the science of the mind. In doing so, Beattie hinted at a notable difference between their versions of common-sense philosophy.[26]

Beattie's condemnation of metaphysics also coloured his perception of the cordial relations that subsisted between Hume and his critics Reid, Campbell, and Gerard.[27] Following the lead of Reid's Aberdeen circle, Beattie portrayed Hume as a sceptic whose *Treatise* inculcated a universal doubt 'sufficient to overturn all belief, science, religion, virtue, and society, from the very foundation' (Beattie 1774: 242). Although he echoed his fellow Aberdonians in denouncing Hume as an 'extravagant' sceptic, Beattie's polemic against his adversary was more nuanced historically.[28] For he did not regard Hume as simply reformulating the tenets of Pyrrhonism. Rather, he saw Hume as the most extreme example of what he labelled 'modern scepticism'.[29] 'Modern scepticism', according to Beattie, originated in 'the first part of the *Principia* of Des Cartes' and was later taken up by Malebranche, Locke, and Berkeley. In the writings of these philosophers, scepticism had challenged the dictates of common sense but it had not been used to subvert the truth of Christianity. The uneasy truce between scepticism and religion was, however, broken by the appearance of Hume's *Treatise*, which, Beattie maintained, was an unashamedly atheistical book (Beattie 1774: 303, 470–71 n). Moreover, the character of Hume's scepticism was different from that of other ancient and modern sceptics because Hume self-consciously marshalled his battery of sceptical arguments to destroy the foundations of truth, virtue, and human happiness (Beattie 1774:

especially 475–83). Hence Beattie felt justified in attacking Hume with the ad hominem arguments that feature prominently in the *Essay*, given that his adversary's unmitigated scepticism threatened to undermine religion and morality.[30]

The threat of Humean scepticism made him question the 'extraordinary adulation' of Hume found in the writings of Reid and Campbell. Beattie remarked to Blacklock that he 'could not conceive the propriety of paying compliments to a man's *heart*, at the very time one is proving that his aim is to subvert the principles of truth, virtue, and religion; nor to his *understanding*, when we are charging him with publishing the grossest and most contemptible nonsense'. Whereas Reid and Campbell regarded Hume as a gifted philosopher and shared his taste for metaphysics, Beattie differed from them on both counts. Because he viewed Hume as a cold-hearted subverter of religion and morality, he maintained that Reid and Campbell were wrong to treat Hume with politeness and to engage him in metaphysical combat. Instead, he wished that the pair had 'expressed themselves with a little more firmness and spirit' rather than indulging in inconsequential disputes over the finer points of Humean metaphysics. Since he had no desire to join Reid and Campbell as fellow travellers with Hume and the modern sceptics, he sought to counter Humean scepticism by 'speaking from the heart, and speaking ... with warmth' in defending 'the cause of truth, religion, virtue, and mankind'.[31] His rebuttal of Hume consequently displayed a personal animus that was absent from the criticisms published earlier by his fellow Aberdonians. In both style and substance, therefore, Beattie's formulation of common-sense philosophy differed from those of Reid, Campbell, and Gerard.

Hume was irked by Beattie's vitriol. He affixed to the second volume of the posthumous edition of his *Essays and Treatises on Several Subjects* an 'Advertisement' which served as 'a compleat Answer to Dr Reid and to that bigotted silly Fellow, Beattie'.[32] Hume used the 'Advertisement' to define the canon of the works he had authored. Significantly, he excluded the *Treatise* from his canon because it had been 'projected before he left College' and 'published not long after'. Targeting Reid and Beattie, he observed that those 'who have honoured the Author's Philosophy with answers, have taken care to direct all their batteries against that juvenile work ... and have affected to triumph in any advantages, which, they imagined, they had obtained over it'. This, he said, was a 'practice very contrary to all rules of candour and fair-dealing, and a strong instance of those polemical artifices, which a bigotted zeal thinks itself authorised to employ'. He therefore stipulated that it was not the *Treatise* but rather the two *Enquiries* which 'contain[ed] his philosophical sentiments and principles' (Hume 1777: Vol. 2, iii).

In publishing the 'Advertisement', Hume disowned the Pyrrhonian scepticism that Reid, Beattie, and many others had read into the *Treatise*. He also undermined the narrative arc of Reid's history of the ideal system as well as Beattie's genealogy of modern scepticism, thereby drawing the sting out of their criticisms. The message of the 'Advertisement' was clear: the duo had laboured to discredit a work and a philosophical system that Hume did not acknowledge as his own. Moreover, the 'Advertisement' registered his strong disapproval of the rhetorical weapons they had employed against him. Beattie took note of Hume's comments in the preface to the sixth edition of his *Essay*. While he now acknowledged that his adversary had 'many good as well as great qualities' as a person, he insisted that he saw no reason to 'make any material change in the reasoning or in the plan' of the *Essay* because the *Treatise* remained in circulation (Beattie 1777: xi–xvi). No trace survives of Reid's immediate reaction to Hume's 'Advertisement'.[33]

The publication in 1774 of *An Examination of Dr. Reid's Inquiry ... Dr. Beattie's Essay ... and Dr. Oswald's Appeal to Common Sense* by Joseph Priestley initiated a protracted debate over the merits of the common-sense philosophy advanced by Reid, Oswald, and Beattie. As a devoted follower of Locke and David Hartley and a defender of the rational character of Christianity, Priestley was highly critical not only of his opponents' appeal to an 'unknown something' called *'common sense'* but also of the view he ascribed to them that religion is founded on instincts, feelings, and sentiments rather than reason. While the hostile tone of Priestley's critique drew widespread censure, the *Examination* nevertheless set the terms of the debate that ensued, for he fostered the perception that despite their differences the three Scots constituted a 'triumvirate' who subscribed to the same philosophical principles (Priestley 1774: 153, 200, 222; Wood 2018: 171–9, 180). One of Priestley's critics, Joseph Berington, was the first to claim that Reid, Beattie, and Oswald ought to be regarded as members of a school of common-sense philosophy. Although it remains unclear how familiar Berington was with the trio's works, he maintained that the three Scottish writers formed a 'Scotch school' and that their appeal to common sense constituted 'the philosophy of Scotland' (Berington 1776: 116, 122). Hence it was not Immanuel Kant who initially created the concept of a Scottish school of common-sense philosophy, as is often said (Kant (1783) 1971: 5–10). Nor was the phrase coined by a Scottish author celebrating or criticizing the ideas of his or her fellow countrymen. Rather, the notion of a Scottish school was originally invented in the context of a philosophical and religious dispute between two English clergymen of different denominations. It was only much later that Dugald Stewart domesticated the idea of a school of Scottish philosophy in Scotland (Stewart (1815–21) 1854–60: Vol. 1, 427–74).

Priestley solicited responses to his criticisms from the 'triumvirate', but none of them issued a public reply immediately after the appearance of the *Examination*.[34] Reid and Beattie privately fumed about Priestley's abuse and both wrote rebuttals of his critique of their appeals to common sense (see especially Reid (1775?) and Beattie (1775–6)). Reid published an anonymous review of Priestley's *Hartley's Theory of the Human Mind* (1775) which attacked Priestley's necessitarianism and materialism as well as his reliance on unsubstantiated hypotheses to explain mental phenomena. But in the review he said nothing about the philosophical issues raised in

Priestley's *Examination* (Reid 1775; 1776). Meanwhile, he had read a pair of discourses to the Glasgow Literary Society in 1769 and 1770 wherein he attempted to clarify the meaning of the term 'common sense' and to elucidate his conception of the operations of this power of the mind.[35] His subsequent treatment of common sense in the *Essays on the Intellectual Powers of Man* was thus as much a product of his own recognition of the need to spell out what he meant by the term as it was a belated answer to Priestley.

Although Reid said little about common sense in the *Essays* that he had not uttered before in either his lectures at King's College and Glasgow or his discourses for the Glasgow Literary Society, he finally addressed Priestley's denial of the philosophical legitimacy of the appeal to common sense. Whereas Priestley had dismissed this appeal as an unjustifiable innovation in the science of the mind based on the dangerously ambiguous notion of common sense, Reid insisted that, far from being novel, his use of the term followed the precedents set by ordinary language and the writings of earlier philosophers. Furthermore, he affirmed that his claim that common sense was a form of judgment accurately reflected the popular meaning of the word 'sense'.[36] Implicitly, he here distanced himself from Beattie and Oswald, who both characterized common sense primarily in terms of instinct, feeling, and sentiment. Elsewhere in the *Essays*, Reid explicitly stated that each of them had developed their versions of common-sense philosophy independently. Moreover, in countering Priestley's accusation that the trio had plagiarized Buffier's *Traité des premières véritez et de la source de nos jugements* (1724), he suggested that such an accusation illustrated his critic's 'superficial knowledge' of the recent history of metaphysics.[37] He therefore questioned the validity of Priestley's account of the intellectual genealogy of their appeal to common sense as well as Priestley's depiction of Beattie and Oswald as his philosophical disciples. Reid would thus have probably denied that the three of them constituted a school of Scottish common-sense philosophy in any meaningful sense.

DUGALD STEWART AND THE DECLINE OF THE SCOTTISH SCHOOL OF COMMON-SENSE PHILOSOPHY

Despite the enormous popularity of the *Essay*, Beattie failed to attract any notable philosophical disciples. By contrast, Reid gained a number of followers in Scotland, including the highly influential Edinburgh professor of moral philosophy, Dugald Stewart. Having studied under Reid at Glasgow in the winter of 1771–2, Stewart became a close associate and the guardian of his mentor's philosophical legacy. Prompted by Priestley and other critics of the writings of Reid, Beattie, and Oswald, Stewart began to rethink the triumvirate's appeal to common sense. By 1793 he acknowledged in his lectures that their appeal was irremediably ambiguous. Drawing on the writings of Adam Ferguson and George Campbell, he reformulated Reid's appeal to common sense. Stewart taught that there were three distinctive types of 'intuitive evidence': that of axioms, that of the consciousness of ourselves, and that of the 'fundamental laws of human belief, which form an essential part of our constitution'. According to Stewart, this third type of evidence encompassed 'our own personal identity ... the existence of the material world [and] the continuance of those laws which have been found, in the course of our past experience, to regulate the succession of phenomena' and he emphasized the importance of this kind of evidence, stating that 'all our conduct, and all our reasonings' are founded upon it. Furthermore, he affirmed that our belief in these truths was 'coeval with the first operations of the intellect' and was 'necessary for the preservation of our animal existence'. It was this set of 'intuitive truths' that had been targeted by 'modern sceptics', whose criticisms had gained credence because 'some late writers' used the term 'common sense' ambiguously in vindicating the *'Principles of Common Sense'*. Stewart wanted to preserve the basics of the appeal to common sense, but the cost of doing so was to eliminate the problematic term 'common sense' from the vocabulary of philosophy.[38]

Stewart identified Beattie as the main culprit in using the term in a confusing manner. While he acknowledged that Reid's 'phraseology' in delineating the nature of common sense was not 'so precise & distinct as might have been wished', he also observed that 'Dr. Beattie's language' was 'far more loose & exceptionable than that of Dr. Reid'. He indicated that this was because Beattie lacked the acuity to make the 'Pneumatological distinctions' required to elucidate the proper philosophical meaning of the term 'common sense'. Moreover, he regretted the 'very unlucky consequence [that] has unquestionably resulted from the coincidence of so many Writers [i.e., Reid, Beattie, and Oswald] ... in adopting the same phrase about the same period', because even though 'their views differ widely in various respects, they have in general been classed together as partizans of a new Sect, & as mutually responsible for the doctrines of each other'.[39] Stewart therefore questioned whether a coherent Scottish school of common-sense philosophy existed.

By the time Stewart came to write his *Dissertation* on the history of early modern philosophy, however, he had come to accept that a school of Scottish philosophy flourished in the eighteenth century. While he dated the beginnings of the school to Francis Hutcheson's Glasgow lectures, Hume was the pivotal figure in his narrative of the rise of the school. In his estimation, Hume's *Treatise* 'contributed, either directly or indirectly, more than any other single work, to the subsequent progress of the Philosophy of the Human Mind'.[40] Echoing Reid and Beattie, he maintained that the primary aim of the *Treatise* was 'to establish a universal scepticism, and to produce in the reader a complete distrust in his own faculties' (Stewart (1815–21) 1854–60: Vol. 1, 437). Hume's 'universal scepticism' was, for Stewart, the catalyst for the investigations of Reid and the other members of the Scottish school. Reid's *Inquiry* was 'the first direct attack which appeared in Scotland upon the sceptical conclusions of Mr Hume's philosophy' as well as the work which, in his view, propounded the philosophical principles to which all of Hume's Scottish critics subscribed (Stewart (1815–21) 1854–60: Vol. 1, 456,

460). Hume and Reid were, therefore, cast as the two patriarchs of the Scottish school. Stewart's silence about Beattie was deafening.[41]

At the turn of the nineteenth century, Stewart's influence spread across the Atlantic world. When he died in 1827, he was widely celebrated as the pre-eminent moral philosopher of his day. His students greatly admired his classroom eloquence, yet they were divided over the merits of his philosophical principles. One ex-pupil who embraced Stewart's reformulation of Reid's common-sense philosophy was Robert Eden Scott, who dedicated his *Inquiry into the Limits and Peculiar Objects of Physical and Metaphysical Science* to his mentor and declared that 'in the philosophy of the human mind, I shall always be proud to acknowledge myself your disciple' (Scott 1810: iii). Before his premature death in 1811, Scott did much to revive the teaching of the different branches of philosophy at King's College Aberdeen and, in so doing, he turned King's into one of the last bastions of the Scottish school of common-sense philosophy (Wood 1993: 138–43).

Other former students were unreceptive to the doctrines of Stewart and those of his mentor Reid. Francis Jeffrey's critique of Stewart's delineation of the science of the mind, for example, signalled the growing disenchantment with Reid's philosophical legacy among Stewart's ex-pupils (Jeffrey 1803–4). More importantly, Stewart's hand-picked successor, Thomas Brown, rejected outright the principles of Reid's philosophy. He granted that Reid had displayed 'great caution', 'considerable acuteness', and a 'great power of patient investigation' in defending 'the primary and essential interests of religion and morality', but he maintained that Reid's philosophical achievements had been greatly overrated in Scotland, largely because of the eloquent exposition of Reid's views in Stewart's lectures and writings (Brown 1824: Vol. 1, 258–75, 525–6). Brown struck out on his own divergent path philosophically, as did the next occupant of the Edinburgh moral-philosophy chair, John Wilson. Even in Glasgow, the propagation of Reid's philosophy effectively ceased after the death in 1797 of Reid's protégé and successor, Archibald Arthur.

Arthur's replacement, James Mylne, was a vigorous critic of both Reid and Stewart, and distanced himself from their philosophical doctrines (Cowley 2015: chapters 7–10). The collapse of what Joseph Priestley had called 'the new empire of common sense' in the Scottish universities was thus precipitous (Priestley 1774: 201). By 1827, the Scottish school of common-sense philosophy had vanished in northern Britain, even though the idea that such a school existed flourished well into the twentieth century in histories of philosophy and in university classrooms across the globe.

NOTES

1 Although the term 'school' is problematic when applied to the group of Scottish common-sense philosophers discussed in this chapter, I will use the term for want of a better word.

2 On Buffier, see Marcil-Lacoste (1982).

3 Hume ((1745) 2007: vol. 1, 425); Hume ((1748) 2000: 119–20).

4 Turnbull set a disputation question on the criterion of truth for Reid's class in 1726; see Turnbull ((1726) 2014: 74).

5 Reid ((1764) 1997: 36–8, 316–17); compare Reid ((1785) 2002: 42–4, 472–4).

6 Although the principle of credulity applied primarily to human testimony, Reid's characterization of the principle had significant ramifications philosophically insofar as he saw testimony as an analogue of perception; Reid ((1764) 1997: 171, 190–202). For Fordyce on trust as the ground of common life, see Fordyce (1735).

7 Reid ((1764) 1997: 4, 32). Writing to Hume, Reid avowed himself Hume's 'Disciple in Metaphysicks'; Thomas Reid to David Hume, 18 March 1763, in Reid (2002: 31).

8 On Hume and the Moderates, see Harris (2015: especially 354–66).

9 Reid (1989: 31, 41, 49–50); compare Reid ((1764) 1997: 21).

10 Reid (1989: 57–8); compare Reid ((1764) 1997: 4).

11 Reid (1989: 59, 66–7). Reid drew an explicit link between the scepticism engendered by the theory of ideas and that of the Pyrrhonists in stating that the hypothesis of ideas 'leads us straight to the acatalepsy [ataraxia] of the Sceptics'; Reid (1989: 74).

12 Reid to David Hume, 18 March 1763, in Reid (2002: 31).

13 Hume to Hugh Blair, 4 July 1762, in Reid (2002: 18–19); Wright (1987).

14 Reid's 'Abstract' is transcribed in Reid ([1764] 1997: 257–62).

15 Hume to Reid, 25 February 1763, in Reid (2002: 29–30).

16 Reid to Hume, 18 March 1763, in Reid (2002: 31). Reid identified Hume's 'system' with scepticism in the 'Abstract'; Reid ([1764] 1997: 258).

17 Reid ([1764] 1997: 16–24). For Hume as a Pyrrhonist see Reid ([1764] 1997: 20–1), where Reid's language echoes passages in Part IV, Book 1 of the *Treatise*, 'Of the Sceptical and other Systems of Philosophy'. Although Reid saw Hume as a Pyrrhonist, he also maintained that neither Pyrrho nor Hume were consistent in their scepticism because their behaviour contradicted their sceptical principles. Furthermore, he claimed that Hume and his fellow sceptics did not push their scepticism far enough because they did not question the reliability of reason in formulating their arguments against the trustworthiness of the senses. Pyrrhonian scepticism was, for Reid, ultimately self-defeating; Reid ([1764] 1997: 20–1, 24), and Reid ([1785] 2002: 571–2).

18 Hume ([1739–40] 2007: vol. 1, 125 (1.4.1.12 and 1.4.2.1)).

19 Compare John Locke; see Locke ([1690] 1990: 44–6; 1.i.4–6).

20 Norton (1982: 153–73). Reid also argued that the trustworthiness of our mental faculties is a principle of common sense; Reid ([1785] 2002: 480–2). Since Reid held that these principles are implanted in human nature by God, his argument was rooted in his providential naturalism.

21 Hume ([1739–40] 2007: vol. 1, 123–5 (1.4.1.7–12), 143 (1.4.2.53), 171–7 (1.4.7.1–14)); Reid ([1764] 1997: 12, 19, 21). Even though Reid maintained that there was no *necessary* conflict between the common life and philosophy, he recognized that some beliefs appropriate to common life were at variance with the conclusions of philosophy; Reid ([1764] 1997: 12, 24, 57, 167, 188, 203, 208).

22 Oswald to Reid, 16 October 1766, in Reid (2002: 56); Oswald (1766–72: vol. 1, 38, 167–8, and vol. 2, 329).

23 Alexander Gerard first introduced Beattie to elements of Reid's common-sense philosophy; Wood (1993: 112, 116).

24 Compare Reid ([1764] 1997: 193–4, 198) with Beattie (1774: especially 45, 51–2).

25 Beattie to Blacklock, 9 January 1769, in Forbes (1807: vol. 1, 171).

26 Beattie (1774: 407–17). These issues were also at play in Beattie's lectures; Wood (1993: 119–29).

27 Hume to Reid, 25 February 1763, in Reid (2002: 30).

28 Beattie to Blacklock, 9 January 1769, in Forbes (1807: vol. 1, 168). Beattie
was even more critical of Hume's scepticism in private than he was in
print; see Mossner (1948).

29 Beattie turned Reid's account of the history of the ideal system into
a narrative of the rise of 'modern scepticism'. Beattie may also have taken
the term 'modern scepticism' from Reid; see Reid ((1764) 1997: 31, 77,
210), and Reid ((1785) 2002: 461–2).

30 Beattie (1774: 347–9); Beattie to Blacklock, 9 January 1769, in Forbes (1807:
vol. 1, 171–4).

31 Beattie to Blacklock, 9 January 1769, in Forbes (1807: vol. 1, 169–70,
172–3); Beattie (1774: 447).

32 Hume to William Strahan, 26 October 1775, in Hume (1932: vol. 2, 301).

33 Circumstantial evidence suggests that Reid knew Hume's
'Advertisement'. One of his page references in the *Intellectual Powers* is
to the 1777 edition of Hume's *Essays and Treatises*; see Reid ((1785)
2002: 32).

34 Beattie and Oswald exchanged letters with Priestley; see Priestley (1774:
346–71).

35 Glasgow Literary Society (1764–79: 29, 34), Glasgow University Library;
Reid (1769) and Reid (1770).

36 Priestley (1774: 119–27, 197–203, 213–31); Reid ((1785) 2002: 423–34).

37 Reid ((1785) 2002: 526); compare Beattie (1777: xi).

38 Stewart (1793: 53–4). Compare Ferguson (1785: 84–8); Campbell (1776: vol.
1, 103–20).

39 Wood (2012: 113–15); compare Stewart's assessment of Reid's appeal to
common sense in Stewart (1803: 152–64).

40 Stewart ((1815–21) 1854–60: vol. 1, 431). Stewart noted that Hume had
disowned the *Treatise* in the 'Advertisement' to the 1777 edition of the
Essays and Treatises but nevertheless discounted Hume's comments;
Stewart ((1815–21) 1854–60: vol. 1, 432n).

41 Stewart did acknowledge that Beattie had made a contribution to the
study of 'the metaphysical principles of the fine arts'; Stewart ((1815–21)
1854–60: vol. 1, 463).

4 Husserl, Common Sense, and the Natural Attitude

Nicolas de Warren

INTRODUCTION

The aim of this chapter is to understand how the themes of 'ordinary experience' and 'common sense' form a central vein in Husserl's thinking, albeit in a way that cannot be directly identified with a philosophy of common sense, given the transcendental orientation of Husserl's thinking and its distinctively descriptive method of phenomenological understanding. Characterized from various vantage points and marked with a variegated terminology ('natural', 'naïve', 'pre-given', and 'obvious'/'taken for granted') the celebrated phenomenological call 'Back to the things themselves!' can sensibly be translated into the call 'Back to the obvious!' – to what is common and ordinary – without, however, taking the sense of the obvious as a theme of philosophical reflection for granted. Unlike notions of common sense as either a class of trivially true propositions, or as intuitive self-evident truths, or as uncultivated understanding, the plural ways in which what goes without saying in its obviousness becomes significant for Husserl delineates and motivates the phenomenological description of the world as 'lived through' and structured according to the many ways of intentionality.

As explored in this chapter (without claiming any exhaustiveness), the main claim here is to demonstrate how Husserl's thinking eschews any monolithic or one-dimensional account of ordinary experience as well as any conventional account of common sense, and that it does not venture a definition of common sense, to the annoyance, perhaps, of what is commonly expected of philosophical analysis. As Husserl insists, one does not in phenomenology *begin* with a definition. Rather, one pursues a definition through variations of descriptions and analytic reflections, or circumscriptions, that progressively conceptually map, as it were, structures of intentionality. Maps, however, are not territories, such that as an 'infinite task', phenomenological analysis guards against any premature arrival at a definition, especially for what remains elusive in its makeup, namely, the many senses in which we take for granted what is commonplace about experience. As argued in this chapter, it belongs to the obviousness of commonsensical experiencing that we understand it without it having to be defined and, moreover, that any proposed definition runs the risk of both falling short of and presupposing what is already understood. To mitigate against this elusiveness, *how* we speak about common sense and ordinary experience, and what we take for granted, we must not just look for 'definitions' but engage and draw upon the richness of the obvious, allowing it to be descriptively shown, or seen, and not just said.

The chapter is divided into the following sections: after an overview of the connection between intentionality, the concept of the life-world, and the theme of common sense, it turns to Husserl's source of inspiration for his phenomenological attentiveness to the 'taken-for-granted' character of our structured experience of the world in the writings of Richard Avenarius. Looking at this muted influence on the formation of Husserl's thinking allows us to recognize the sense in which Husserl takes up the problem of common sense and ordinary experience, while it at the same time allows us to discern the originality of Husserl's own phenomenological approach. On this basis, the chapter next considers how Husserl fashions his own conception of the 'natural world' in its delineation of the 'a priori structures of common sense'. The novelty of Husserl's approach, as highlighted in this discussion, is his contention that ordinary experience exhibits the taken-for-granted structured contours of any *possible* human experience. Common sense functions as an a priori pre-understanding of the many senses in which experience of the world is possible. With this insight in hand, the chapter follows Husserl's detailed descriptions of the various commonsensical ways in which we ordinarily experience the world. Such descriptions are meant to showcase the richness of ordinary experience, but they also delineate the contours of the structures of intentionality that will become the explicit theme, or field of exploration, for a phenomenological examination of consciousness. Husserl's phenomenology, it is here argued, can profitably be seen as a philosophical exploration of the empire of the obvious. The chapter brings its discussion to a close with a set of reflections on the commonsensical understanding of what might be called the 'thereness' or 'presentness' of the world which underlies and conditions any possible experience. By way of some concluding remarks, this chapter suggests how Husserl's understanding of common sense, ordinary experience, and the natural attitude, as developed here, sets the ground for his later conception of the life-world.

IN SEARCH OF THE OBVIOUS

Husserl's phenomenological philosophy is commonly credited with discovering, through an indefatigable exploration across research manuscripts, lecture courses, and publications, the manifold structures of intentionality as the essential fixture of experience. Although Husserl received a decisive impulse from Brentano's descriptive psychological account of 'intentional relation' – the defining characteristic of consciousness that Brentano traced back through ancient and Scholastic commentaries to Aristotle – Husserl never failed to proclaim his own phenomenological analyses of intentionality as historically unprecedented and philosophically original; in fact, as providing the means for establishing a rigorous transcendental foundation for our knowledge of the world and ourselves as conscious and rational beings. But, even as Husserl repeatedly touted the novelty of his discovery of intentionality, it is significant that he likewise claimed that the central thought of intentionality – that consciousness is consciousness of something, that is, an object of possible experience – represents what was most obvious and taken for granted in ordinary experience. It would, indeed, appear commonsensical to claim that consciousness is, to give but a few examples from its varied manifestations, being directed at something, attending to something, remembering something, perceiving something, or imagining something. As Husserl (1950b: 217) writes in *Ideen I*: '"Consciousness of something" is something eminently obvious and taken for granted [*ein sehr Selbstverständliches*].'[1] Without having to turn to philosophy, let alone phenomenology, we already commonly understand that 'to be conscious' is 'to be conscious of something', much as you are presently conscious of reading these words, wondering, perhaps, what *more* could be said about what goes without saying in everyday experience.

Husserl's expression *ein sehr Selbstverständliches* can be taken to mean 'something taken for granted' as well as 'something entirely commonplace', and, in these combined senses, it represents a phenomenological invocation of 'common sense' in terms of what 'naturally' goes without saying in our ordinary experience of ourselves in the world. For Husserl, what seems clear with 'maximal obviousness' (*absolute Selbstverständlichkeit*) in ordinary experience is that any 'seeing, grasping what is self-evident' – for example, that I am sitting here writing these words, that you are presently reading these very same words – is 'something ultimate', where the meaning of 'ultimate' is to be taken as basic to ordinary experience, as par for the course (Husserl 1950a: 51). It goes without saying that 'intentionality' – that consciousness is always consciousness of something – is what is most evidently taken for granted about how we experience the world. Nobody needs it to be explained that to be conscious is to be conscious of something (perceiving something, thinking something, etc.). Everyone would readily understand (i.e., take it to be self-evident) what 'intentionality' says about experience, with or without having such a formulated and explicit notion in mind. Yet, even as such a fact about consciousness would appear to be trivially true, it is just as much, as Husserl states, something 'extremely obscure' (*und doch zugleich höchst Unverständliches*). For what proves philosophically puzzling is *how* consciousness, in common and ordinary experience, is so constituted as to 'transcend' itself in its encounter with objects of the world; that is, how consciousness is 'about' something, directed towards an object imbued with sense, as being thus and so, within a world of ongoing experience.

In Husserl's parlance, this 'puzzle of transcendence' (*das Rätsel der Transzendenz*) does not mean to suggest any metaphysical dualism between 'mind' and 'world', the myth of the given, or an inner space of representation (the so-called Cartesian Theatre), but, on the contrary, frames the question of under what sense, and how, consciousness is intrinsically 'about' something: it belongs to the essential makeup of conscious beings like ourselves that we relate to objects ('are conscious of') in the world under a determinate form of sense, as being thus and so. 'Transcendence' is Husserl's technical term for the 'aboutness' character of consciousness, but also that consciousness is always *someone's* consciousness and hence inseparable from self-awareness as the individual *who* is conscious of something. Intentionality, in this frame of thinking, is *both* what is most commonly understood about experience, so ubiquitous as to be trivial and left unsaid, indeed, unconceptualized, *and* what is most incomprehensible, so opaque upon further reflection as to have led generations of philosophers down 'labyrinths of false paths'. Such false paths (on Husserl's reckoning: based on an uncritical acceptance of some type of dualism or a psychological reduction of our knowledge of the world) leads either to scepticism with regard to the possibility of securing, in a theoretical form of knowledge, what we obviously in some sense already know – that consciousness is about something – or to dogmatism with regard to how such an experience, and hence knowledge, of the world is possible.

This emphasis on intentionality as 'at once' (*zugleich*) *ein sehr Selbstverständliches* and *höchst Unverständliches*, as very banal and highly puzzling, runs throughout Husserl's thinking and becomes centrally expressed in Husserl's notion of the life-world, by which Husserl understands the embedded character of intentionality within an openness to and experience of being-in-the-world.

What goes without saying in the course of any experience of something is that something is experienced in the world, and hence that the world is present to us, much as we are present to the world, through experience. This presentness of the world, as the backdrop for any possible experience, represents a further dimension of what ordinarily remains taken for granted; namely, that we find ourselves in the world – a world that *itself* is not *something* that we perceive in the same manner as we perceive something in the world. What is more commonsensical than that, whatever it is that we experience, we do so in the world, and hence that the world is in some sense always and enduringly *there*, that we always stand in the presence of the world?

Husserl's notion of the life-world, as designating the world as taken for granted, would at first glance seem to represent an exemplary case of recognizing the philosophical significance of 'ordinary experience' or 'common sense', on the basis of which any knowledge, and especially theoretical knowledge of the natural sciences, is grounded. In the words of Stanley Rosen (2002: 54), Husserl's life-world represents 'one of the most thorough attempts in the past hundred years to ground philosophy in everyday or pre-theoretical life', or what Rosen terms 'ordinary experience'. Explicit references to the obviousness of the world in its structuring of intentionality notwithstanding, the theme of 'ordinary experience' or 'common sense' never became an organized and explicit theme in Husserl's writings; even the term 'common sense' (*der gesunde* or *der gemeine Menschenverstand*) does not figure in Husserl's writings. Unlike Heidegger, Husserl never developed a phenomenology of everyday experience – for which Heidegger takes Husserl to task with his accusation of 'jumping over' the everydayness of being-in-the-world (*Alltäglichkeit*). As noted by Barry Smith (1995: 395): 'It must be pointed out immediately that Husserl himself does not use the expression "common sense" as a technical term of his philosophy.' Where, then, and how, can we identify the theme of 'common sense' in Husserlian phenomenology?

THE NATURAL CONCEPT OF THE WORLD IN AVENARIUS

Refracted through different terms (*naïve*, *natürliche*, *Vorgefundenheiten*, *Selbstverständlichkeit*), the general theme of the 'obviousness of ordinary experience' is a salient feature of Husserl's phenomenological thinking. In comparison with other philosophical approaches to 'common sense', 'ordinary experience', or 'pre-theoretical experience' (not to suggest that these terms are entirely interchangeable), what distinguishes Husserl's approach can be at first assessed by turning to what Husserl himself acknowledged as its initial catalyst. As he remarks: 'The first attempt at a pure description of what is already given, found' (i.e., what is taken for granted) was made by Avenarius.[2] Along with others who contributed to Husserl's thinking (Brentano, James, Meinong, Natorp), Avenarius's pivotal role can be tracked through Husserl's manu-scripts and lecture courses (most prominently, in the 1910–11 lecture course 'The Basic Problems of Phenomenology'). Avenarius's turn to 'pure experience', by which he understands a basic and common experience of the world, intelligible on its own terms, even as it passes for obvious (*anschaulich* in this combined sense), first called Husserl's attention to the philosophical significance of ordinary experience. Before any theory, as Husserl comments in his notes on Avenarius, the world is already there, or pre-given; prior to any theor-etical formulations, what is given in experience (*das Gegebene*) must be described as the necessary anchorage for any consequent philo-sophical reflection or form of knowledge. In terms that anticipate the direction of Husserl's own thinking, Avenarius proposed to 'suspend any metaphysical encroachments upon the concept of the world and saw in the restitution of the "natural" concept of the world of pure experience the task of a theory and critique of experience' (Husserl 1992: 35). This givenness of the world should not be 'violated' by theoretical thinking.[3] This appeal to the originality of the world in pure experience offers a critical point of leverage *against* philosoph-ical 'violations' and its falsifications of experience: philosophical definitions and theories that would obscure or countermand what is commonly experienced. In this regard, the notion of 'pure experience' stands opposed to the Kantian meaning given to that term. For Avenarius, 'pure experience' is *not* the transcendental form of experience as abstracted and removed from actual ('empirical') experience. Pure experience is rather intrinsically intelligible (*selbstverständlich*) on its own terms, without any supervening (and obscuring) metaphysical conceptions or philosophical theories.

Avenarius's appeal to 'pure experience' is meant to dispel the false problem of the world. It is not that philosophical reflection needs to 'explain' or 'deduce' the world (whether there is a so-called external reality, or why there is a world rather than not), but rather that philosophy must suspend itself in calling into question how it historically has propounded metaphysical views of the world that have obscured the natural (i.e., ordinary and taken-for-granted) apprehension of the world in ordinary experience. The anchorage of knowledge in pre-theoretical experience, without any metaphysical suppositions, serves a critical function to delimit and expose the pretensions of reason.[4] For Husserl, Avenarius's discovery of the empire of the obvious allows for a novel reformulation of the question: 'Was ist die Welt?' (Husserl 1992: 100). But, unlike Avenarius's own appeal to 'pure experience' and the natural concept of the world against the pretensions of transcendental thought as well as other types of idealism, Husserl's challenge will reside in demonstrating how a philosophical recuperation of ordinary experience – the world as it is primordially given – provides the necessary point of departure for a *transcendental* form of thinking. The common and ordinary givenness of the world becomes leveraged as an entryway into the 'new dimension' of transcendental phenomenology.

In order to rediscover the primordial experience of the world, philosophical thinking must begin by suspending itself, that is, by bracketing its constructed theories, in order to uncover and recover its own presupposition in the commonsensical apprehension of the world. As Avenarius remarks: 'What was at the beginning of my "spiritual", or "intellectual", development is what philosophy tries to teach me about by means of special theories; what was at the beginning of my philosophizing, however, I myself can give direct information about.'[5] In a compelling stylistic move, Avenarius adopts a first-person mode of speaking, bereft of technical terminology, in order to underline his suspension of philosophical theories and return to the obvious. As Avenarius states: 'I, with all my thoughts and feelings, found myself within an environment. This environment was composed of manifold components, which stood in manifold relationships of dependency among each other. The surroundings also included fellow human beings with manifold statements; and what they said was usually again in a relationship of dependence on the surroundings.'[6] This original – without prior deliberation or explicit acknowledgement – situatedness underpins what is most characteristic of experience, namely, that every experience is an experience of something determinate, that is, experienced in a particular fashion. Human experience testifies to the variability of how things are experienced; things are experienced in many ways, but throughout the manifold ways in which things of the world are experienced, or, to draw on a more contemporary idiom, ways in which the world 'shows up', there remains a constant assumption of the world, not as a particular object of experience, but as the common sense of perpetually finding oneself surrounded by a world pervading any determinate experience whatsoever.

This default, or natural, assumption entails a threefold obviousness: we take it for granted that there is a world composed of things linked together in causal relation, that the world is populated by other persons, and that we are able to make sense of the world through language, or, in other words, that we encounter the world as meaningful through speaking about the world and addressing each other. Things, other persons, and language form the basic components of the natural concept of the world, here characterized by Avenarius as *Vorgefundenes* ('something already found' or 'something there already to be found'). On this description, the world is intuitively (*anschaulich*) experienced as a world in which I find myself within a proximate surrounding, or environment (*Umgebung*), populated by things – chairs, tables, plants, etc. – within a nexus of causal relations.[7] Other persons are also encountered in the world as primarily manifest to me in speech and embodied action.

Expressed in Avenarius's terms of art, the natural concept, or commonplace understanding, of the world entails two different kinds of values: experiences (*Erfahrungen*) and hypothesis (*Hypothese*).[8] The term 'experience' designates what is encountered or discovered (*das Vorgefundene*) in the world: things and other persons. Such things as I encounter in the world hang together in a holistic way. Things of the world 'fit together' (*zusammengesetzt*) within a whole – the world; hence Avenarius's admittedly misleading use of the term 'concept' (*Begriff*), when, in fact, he does not mean 'concept' in a cognitive or conceptual manner. This embeddedness of things within the world as a whole is structured in the most commonplace of settings according to different relations of dependency, of which causality is the most salient. In addition, our common understanding of world operates on the 'hypothesis', or supposition, that sounds emitted from other persons express meaning and, in turn, are expressions of intent and volition. It is commonsensical to presume that words spoken to me bear some kind of meaning (*Sinn*), much as my own spoken words are infused with a meaning expressing my own intent and volition. These two forms of values, however, do not represent any kind of dualism 'in the philosophical sense of the term', but represent an integral 'plurality'.[9]

What is taken for granted in ordinary experience is not only the relationships among things in the world as well as the presence of others, but also what we might term the 'speakability' of the world; the commonplace assumption, in other words, that we relate to the world and others in the world through acts of speaking (and hearing). This assumption of the 'speakability' of the world – that others can be addressed in speech – does not appear to presuppose any shared language but merely that recognized other persons are assumed to be speaking beings and, by the same token, that I recognize a person insofar as I recognize a *speaking* being. When I encounter a stranger without knowing which language she might speak, I – on this conception – nonetheless spontaneously address the other as a speaking being. The general assumption is not that others speak the same language (as me), but that 'others will answer questions asked of them'. This 'hypothesis' that the sounds emitted by others are meaningful and hence manifest the other as a speaking person with her own intentions and volitions, assumes nonetheless in an unspoken way (never reflected upon by Avenarius himself) a common familiarity with the kinds of sounds that would even count as a linguistic expression. Sounds (clicking sounds, for example) that might not fit into such a common assumption of what counts as a meaningful combination of sounds would, on this account, fall outside the bounds of common intelligibility, and hence common sense. Despite Avenarius's contention that the natural concept of the world is not culturally or historically conditioned, this assumption of the recognizability of what counts as a linguistic utterance introduces a significant complication in his argument. Along with the 'hypothesis' of others as speaking persons, Avenarius advances that we commonly assume that others in our environing world behave and move their bodies much as we do. The assumption of common behaviour, although not explicitly stated as such, finds its locus in the assumption of analogous bodily movement and gestures. Bodily gestures, much as linguistic utterances, are commonsensically assumed to express intention and volition.

Rather than speak of the 'problem of the world', by which Avenarius references traditional questions concerning the reality of the external world, Avenarius proposes that we should more meaningfully speak of 'the puzzle of the world'. The natural concept of the world does not secure the certainty of 'external reality' against the presumptions of philosophical speculation nor demarcate a set of unassailable and indemonstrable propositions. The appeal to the natural concept of the world disabuses philosophical thinking of the false problem of the external world (or problem of reality) with its underlying dualism between 'mind' and 'world'. The natural concept of the world – the commonplace sense in which the world is always there – cannot be conflated with 'reality' if by the latter we understand a philosophical image of an external reality beyond perceptible experiences, or the 'world' as it is in itself, independently of experience. Traditional scepticism with regard to the 'external world' hangs on a constructed image of 'reality', as ontologically different from the mind. While such metaphysical theories, as with any activity of human consciousness, presuppose the natural concept of the world, they obscure it by replacing it with an *image* of the world as constructed or fabricated by theory. Every form of theoretical thinking rests on the intuitive and pre-theoretical assumption of the world which cannot be logically or metaphysically demonstrated. Although Avenarius speaks of the world as 'the general content of what is already found' (*der allgenmeine Inhalt des Vorgefundenen*), he is keen to disabuse any suggestion of a monolithic 'thing' or 'substance' called the world. Crucially, idealism must tacitly assume the givenness of the world, but by the same token Avenarius rejects naïve realism, since he eschews any primordial characterization of the intuitive apprehension of the world as 'real' or 'actual'. Such determinations of the world – appearance as distinct from reality – only come to mind upon reflection. The environing world is given in ordinary experience as neither 'reality' nor 'appearance'. As Avenarius states, the presentness of the world is continually and repeatedly given, as the one and the same world, throughout experience; it is given in the form of a 'vivid intuition' (*lebendige Anschauung*), not as a 'logical normal form of a concept'. The common sense with which we find ourselves 'in the world' cannot be equated with the universality of a concept or pure form of intuition. As Avenarius writes:

> That is the world, as I already found it at the beginning of my philosophical thinking, as something existing, stable, familiar, with which I am acquainted, understood; how the world continues to live on as a thought, how it always, renewed again and again,

returns to me as a fact and in all these repetitions remains the same. In a word: it is the content of my primary, or beginning, concept of the world, which, evidently, coincides with the form of a living intuition, or presentness, and cannot be brought into the normal form of a concept.'[10]

In the same vein, Avenarius understands the natural concept of the world as more primordial, and hence 'universal' in this sense, than particular world views (*Weltanschauungen*) or theoretical images of the world. The commonsensical apprehension of the world provides the basis from which the world becomes constituted and experienced in greater specification and sophistication. The argument is *not* that, with this primordial presentness of the world, which we naturally presuppose, we already have the world fully constituted before us. The commonsensical apprehension of the world is underdetermined vis-à-vis supervening variations in world view. It is thus 'incipient' (*anfänglich*) in two senses: it is that from which we engage and reflect on the world; it is the minimal form of the world's presentness on which variations of the world (what Avenarius terms 'variation-appearances') are anchored. Although the primordial concept of the world can neither be meaningfully doubted (since any doubt already presupposes this givenness of the world) nor logically or theoretically demonstrated (the quest for a 'proof' for the world's givenness is superfluous), Avenarius notes that 'the primordial concept of the world is also the general concept of the world that any capable human being would express – as long as one is not a psychotic or, in fact, a philosopher who changes [*variierten*] it'.[11]

THE A PRIORI OF COMMON SENSE IN HUSSERL

Avenarius provided a decisive catalyst for the development of Husserl's conception of the 'natural attitude', his understanding of the significance of ordinary experience for a phenomenological critique of knowledge, and the formation of the concept of the 'life-world' in his later writings.[12] Husserl mobilizes this guiding insight into the presentness of the world in a transcendentally inflected direction, thus breaking with Avenarius's own critique of pure experience. Husserl refashions the concept of the natural world into an argument for the anchorage of knowledge in what he terms 'a real ontology'. As he writes, 'every science of nature, insofar as they presuppose the thesis of the natural view of the world [*Weltansicht*] and in this frame and in this sense investigate being [*das Sein*], is bound in an a priori manner to a real ontology' (Husserl 1992: 38). Husserl in this manner validates on his own terms the insight proposed by Avenarius that the natural concept of the world is not to be equated with a subjective view of the world, which 'every human being strangely and factually brought themselves to the world', or as a historical world view, or as an empirical representation of the world (anthropological, cultural, etc.). The natural concept of the world couches an *ontological* understanding of the sense of being as manifest in our commonplace encounter with things (natural objects and fabricated objects) as well as other persons in the world. This basic ontological understanding is pre-theoretical and woven into the common sense of how we find ourselves in the world. Ordinary experience is, on this Husserlian understanding, an ontologically pre-structuring of theoretical knowledge. The basic ontological regions of being are presupposed as given in ordinary experience by any theoretical knowledge. What is taken for granted in its obviousness are different senses of being: that there are things, that there are animals, that there are other persons, etc. Such ontological contours of ordinary experience are not arbitrary as they underpin variations in our experience as well as the possibility of error and illusion. Even when I am mistaken or deceived about any given experience, it is still commonsensical that things must have certain properties, for example, that visible objects must be coloured and that physical things must be causally interconnected. Although I might come to doubt whether this particular perception of a coloured object is veridical, for example, I do not doubt that perceptual objects as such must have, among other properties, colour.

These ontological contours of ordinary experience suggest to Husserl the idea that the natural concept of the world harbours an a priori and eidetic structure of experience, given that things of the world are not experienced, as the condition for their intelligibility, in random and arbitrary ways. We take it for granted that things still unknown to us shall, when discovered, be coloured things, have spatial configuration, etc. – such are the commonplace assumptions that compose 'common sense'. It would, indeed, be odd if one were to expect that an as yet unknown thing would have no colour, would not possess a recognizable, three-dimensional spatial configuration, etc. As Husserl writes:

> However actual experiences emerge in which human beings have the concept of the world as a unified content, as long as the talk of one world, in which human beings exist, which they have as consciousness of the world, and have as experienced and along with this, posit empirical existence [Dasein] in perceptions, experiences, etc., as long as this kind of talk makes sense, the natural concept of the world remains absolute and a priori. (Husserl 1992: 41)

Husserl's novel contention here is that ordinary experience, described under the heading of 'natural concept of the world', exhibits 'an a priori of nature'. Husserl understands here under the term 'nature' the realm of all psychical objects of *possible* human experience. The natural concept of the world is itself an a priori structure that is commonly lived through in an anonymous manner. As Husserl writes: 'We look in this attitude to the natural world, nature in the broadest sense; this look is the natural attitude. That delivers the a priori of nature, unfolded in a real ontology' (Husserl 1992: 43). Importantly, Husserl contends that the 'a priori' of the natural concept of the world, or, in other words, the a priori of the 'facticity of the world' (*Weltfaktum*), does not preclude another 'thesis' than the natural. Although the 'fact' that there is a world is absolutely self-evident and, in this sense, an obvious commonplace assumption underlying experience, this does not exclude the possibility of adopting other attitudes towards the world in taking distance from this default common sense. Such a possibility of another attitude does not mean that the self-evident presentness of the world is questionable in the sense of dubitable or deniable. In fact, although ordinary experience presents us with countless occasions in which we are mistaken or deceived by what we perceive, or experience otherwise than expected, there is no possible circumstance in which the world *as such* could be meaningfully called into question. The assumption that there is a world – in other words, that we must be in a world to even doubt something of the world – remains indemonstrable: there is no possible proof that the world exists, since any proposed proof already presupposes that there is a world in which such a proof could at all be stated. That I am deceived with any given particular perception (whether, for example, I correctly perceive this object in front of me) cannot be generalized or extrapolated into a doubt about whether the world *as such* is there. Although particular cases of deception, illusion, and hallucination are common enough, the sense in which the world is there in common cannot be called into question; for, in fact, it is only on the basis of this common sense (that there is a world) that it makes any sense to call into question anything in the world. It is, as Husserl contends, the basic significance of 'ordinary experience' that it forecloses as *ein Unsinn* (nonsense) that there would be any reasonable motivation to claim that there could be another world, or a different world, or no world at all. As Husserl writes: 'There cannot be anything in the world that cancels the sense of talking about, or referring to, the world, since everything presupposes the world as sense (as being).'[13] This is not, however, to advance the claim that it is nonsense to imagine another possible world or that the world could become otherwise. It is *ein Unsinn* that the actual world (*wirkliche Welt*) would not be actual, but not *ein Unsinn* that there could possibly be another kind of world, or that from this actual world another kind of world might evolve or be configured in the future. Any imaginable world or the world as the future might discover it must nonetheless not violate the common-sensical apprehension of *this* world as actually there and presently experienced.

The articulations of ordinary experience are moulded along the contours of an a priori ontology of nature: the spatiotemporal spread of physical objects in causal relations, including, importantly, the structure of objects as objects of possible experience – that is, as manifestations of the world. The a priori ontological structures har-boured within ordinary experience and, in this regard, underpinning the texture of common sense do not stem from concepts of the pure understanding in synthetic combination with pure forms of intuition (as with Kant) nor represent arbitrary concepts formed through abstraction. The topographic landscape of ordinary experience delin-eates ontological patterns of the many senses in which we experience things. Such patterns, the recognizable style of the coursing of ordin-ary experience, are rendered into an explicit and theoretical theme of reflection through Husserl's phenomenological method of reduction and eidetic variation. Husserl's theory of essences is distilled, as it were, from ordinary experience; such essential ('eidetic') structures are not, strictly speaking, 'concepts' but are instead the underlying *gestalts* or schemas within experience on the basis of which concepts gain traction.

THE EMPIRE OF THE OBVIOUS

Husserl launches his phenomenological undertaking of a transcen-dental critique of knowledge with a direct and pre-theoretical descrip-tion of the world in the natural attitude. Husserl speaks of the world in the natural *attitude*, having abandoned Avenarius's characteriza-tion of a natural concept of the world (a term which Husserl continues to use in his earlier 1910–11 lectures). Husserl nonetheless retains Avenarius's stylistic device of adopting a first-person point of view (*Ichrede*), unencumbered with technical philosophical terms of art, in his description. Unlike Avenarius's descriptions, Husserl's descrip-tion of ordinary experience (or what he also calls 'natural life') delineates in advance the contours of intentionality that will become the central and explicit theme of phenomenological inquiry. This delineation of ordinary experience anticipates the phenomenological 'discovery' of intentionality – namely, the fundamental structures of intentionality in their transcendental significance, that is, as the condition of possibility for experience. If, in this regard, phenomenological analysis of intentionality, in its manifest and multiplanar forms, seeks to uncover the *conditions* under which experience is at all possible, this fixture of intentionality is, on the other hand, already delineated and 'lived', that is, experienced, within ordinary experience. Once we have broached the domain (methodologically by way of the suspension of the natural attitude, transcendental reduction, and eidetic variation) of phenomenological analysis, ordinary experience retrospectively appears as already having been constituted by the functions of intentionality, which, as it were, operated within ordinary experience 'behind our backs' and 'beneath' the threshold of our default awareness in the natural attitude.

Husserl's description of ordinary experience maps the contours of what commonly passes as self-evident, obvious, and trivial – as going without saying. Consciousness – by which Husserl implicitly means wakeful consciousness – is always a consciousness of myself in the world as extending spatially around me and unfolding temporally about me. Consciousness is always someone's consciousness; to be conscious of something is at the same time to be conscious of *oneself* as being conscious of something. Consciousness always bears the stamp of 'my consciousness'; i.e., self-consciousness of an experiencing I. What it evidently *is* to be conscious – the sense in which consciousness occurs – is to be conscious from a first-person point of view in some determinate and directed way; it is to perceive something, to think about something, to imagine something, etc. In perceptual experience – sight, hearing, etc. – things are given to me in an intuitive (*anschaulich*) manner, that is, as present to me without any theoretical kind of knowing. One does not need a theory of knowledge in order to know, that is, perceive, that this glass is on the table;

one does not need an explicit theory of language in order to know how to speak a language. One might say that things in ordinary experience are there for me in an obvious and banal way, and hence, *anschaulich* in this sense as 'self-evident'. Such things that are there for me in an evident way – the books on my table, the furniture in my room – are things that I perceive as 'existing' (*als daseiende*). The commonplace sense in which we encounter things as evidently there (*anschaulich*) is in the sense of things 'existing' presently in front of me, as present at hand (*vorhanden*). For things to be present at hand is for things to occupy a determinate spatial location vis-à-vis my own spatial location (and, hence, my body) as well as for things to be present at hand in time, as encountered, or manifest, in the now in which I also am now myself. Things are present for me when I am attending to them, with my attention fixed on them, but also, in a more implicit way, when I am *not* directly attending to them or doing anything with them; in such instances, things are commonly understood to still exist, even if I am not in any direct perceptual contact with such things. The vast majority of things in the world that are commonly known to me as existing, in fact, are obviously still there for me, even if I am not there myself, but here. My commonsensical understanding of how things exist for me is, in other words, not hemmed by the restricted horizon of what I actually perceive in the here and now. Commonsensically, the horizon of what I take to be there in the world extends along horizons of *possible* perceptions, of what I could perceive, thus encompassing things that I 'know' to exist even if I am not directly there to perceive them. We move about our daily lives in the surety that all those things we have left behind or are about to see again still exist despite our absence.

Consciousness of things in the world does not only occur in perceptual experiences, actual or possible. I am likewise conscious of things in the manner of feeling, valuing, acting, and thinking. In short, what commonly runs through the varieties of experience is that consciousness is always conscious in a determinate or particular manner – there is no experience of consciousness as such, but an experience of consciousness as perceiving, attending, etc. – along with a determinate and familiar way in which things are 'present for me' (*vorhanden*) or there before me, or *could* be there for me, and hence as discoverable as not there for me. As Husserl (1950b: 63) writes: 'I of course "know" or "understand" [*ich gerade "weiss"*] that the unseen parts of an object and unseen objects in my environment are still there, and this knowledge [*Wissen*] of the layout of my house, the arrangement of objects in my office, etc., is not a conceptual knowing [*vom begrifflichen Denken*].' This 'knowing' that unseen parts of an object are not missing, or that my home is still standing (unless, to my horror, I discover that it has been destroyed in sudden disaster), forms the backbone of the commonsensical confidence without which I would not be able to operate in the world. It is the commonsensical form of 'knowing' in the sense of being taken for granted, not called into question unless motivated from some determinate circumstance (e.g., I see my house in ruins). Much of this commonsensical confidence in how the world is rests on a developed nexus of habits that structure and orient this implicit knowing. There would be, in these terms, no common sense without habits and habitualities, in terms of which knowledge of the world is given a determinate and stable content. The unfolding of my present experience, however, is situated within a 'horizon of indeterminate reality [*Wirklichkeit*], of which I am dimly conscious' (Husserl 1950b: 68). On Husserl's description, temporality forms an essential dimension of how we 'live through' our ordinary experience of the world, and hence, in this sense, of how we commonsensically understand our place in the world. We take for granted that when we go to sleep, we shall awake at some point in the future; and even if we were afflicted by a certain dread of not surviving our own sleep, it would seem commonsensical to us that the world would not therefore disappear with our own feared condition of remaining forever asleep.

Throughout such descriptions of ordinary experience in the natural attitude, Husserl consistently and deliberately employs quotation marks to indicate an inflected sense of a given term. We 'know' that our house is still standing even when we are not at home; the world is 'present' or 'exists' (*vorhanden*) even though no one can perceive the world as such as an object; we 'know' that the unseen sides of an object are not missing; we 'know' that there stands another person, conscious of herself, in front of me. Such quotations mark the elusiveness of describing that commonplace mode of 'knowing' and way of 'being' that defines ordinary experience and, in this sense, sculpts the contours of common sense. The 'knowing' of ordinary experience is structured, vast, and articulated, and cannot be reduced to any one sense of such obvious 'knowing'. It is remarkable, in fact, that our ordinary language, not to mention our theoretical concepts, are mostly overdetermined vis-à-vis the sense in which common sense operates. 'Knowing', 'cognition', 'intuition', and kindred terms tend to overintellectualize the operative sense of our commonplace understanding of the world, speaking, as it were, from a reflective standpoint. For Husserl, as he develops through his analysis of the 'lived-body' and 'kinaesthetic intentionality' in his *Ding und Raum* lectures and *Ideen II*, our 'knowing' of the location of objects in the room and 'knowledge' of what such objects are is first and foremost *articulated* in our knowing how to handle them, move around them, etc. Under the broad heading of 'passive synthesis', Husserl charts the various ways in which much of our dealings in the world occur at a pre-reflective level of 'knowing'. Such 'knowing' is, however, not conceptual (*begrifflich*), yet it is 'intuitive' (*anschaulich*); it is not reflective, and yet presupposes wakeful consciousness and, mostly, attentiveness. Concepts are not 'used' or 'applied' to ordinary experi- ence; on the contrary, we can only use or apply concepts on the basis of already 'knowing' how to do things with words, with things, how to take in in one glance an object's features, etc. And yet, although common sense is not a cognitive form of knowing, its lived articula- tion unfolds along recognizable and familiar patterns. This suggests that ordinary experience and the forms of our experiencing are struc- tured in non-arbitrary ways; not by concepts of the mind, but in terms of what Husserl, once he's excavated them through the method of reduction and eidetic variation, will discover as 'essential structures'. The invisible (from the vantage point of ordinary experience) structure of the visible (ordinary experience) is not structured in terms of concepts that are 'applied' or 'projected' on to the world by the mind. Along with the temporal configuration of what is taken for granted of experience, we take for granted that we can use our bodies to move about and act in and on the world. Husserl, in this regard, speaks of our 'lived-body' (*Leib-Körper*) as centred on the 'I can' (*Ich kann*), as the embodied sense of *being able* to move my body, produce sounds with my vocal cords, etc. (see Husserl 1952: §§ 59–60). This embodied sense of 'I can' represents the obviousness that this body is *mine to move*, as spontaneously enacted when, for instance, I get up from a chair. In this regard, to be sure, noted here in brief, the temporal and spatial configuration of the world is anchored in the common experience of my own existence as temporal and embodied in relation to the world.

Our ordinary experience of the world is equally populated with the lives of other creatures and, most significantly, other human beings, whom we commonly assume to perceive the world in very much the same terms as we do. Although it belongs to common sense to affirm that other persons experience the world from their own individual point of view – the 'first-person point of view' – it is likewise a commonplace that I implicitly understand that other persons experience the world in the same *forms* of experience as I do: through perception, emotions, thinking, etc. I may not see the world as you do, nor know what is it like for you to perceive the world from your first-person point of view, and yet I have no doubt that you do *perceive* the world, much as I am also able to perceive. Acknowledging that there is a 'first-person point of view' only makes sense on the assumption that, despite our individual perspectives, it is the same world that we perceive in ways that are structurally common. It would be uncommon, indeed, to think that another person might have X-ray vision rather than visual organs that take in

the same spectrum of light as I do. Manifestly, other persons are there
for me in different ways: in physical proximity, in addressing and
being addressed in speech, in memories, etc. What underpins the
different ways in which I encounter others is that I have no cause, or
reason, to doubt the existence of those who speak to me and engage
with me even as I am barred from any direct access to their thoughts,
intentions, etc. Although it belongs to common sense to regard other
persons as having lives and first-person perspectives of their own, *how*
such a consciousness of others is constituted is not as obvious. This
question formed a central theme in Husserl's thinking; however, he
never arrived at a conclusive analysis.[14]

THE PRESENCE OF THE WORLD

What distinguishes Husserl's phenomenological descriptions of what
we might term the 'obviousness of the world' in its many forms of
being taken for granted, or 'common sense' in this phenomenological
sense, gravitates around the fundamental sense in which it goes without saying that the world is 'there'. This enduring presentness of the
world is not identified with a determinate way in which the world is
structured through our actions, symbolic systems, and bodily engage-
ments. The presentness of the world is textured with different 'environments', or 'worlds' in this plural and determinate sense. As Husserl
writes: 'This world is not only there [*für mich da*] as merely a world of
things [*Sachenwelt*], but also immediately as a world of values,
a world of goods, [and] a practical world' (Husserl 1950b: 59). Things
of the world not only bear properties such as colour, smell, and shape;
they also have values, aesthetic qualities, etc. I perceive a glass on the
table with the characteristic of 'to drink with', 'ugly', and 'next to
the books'. Objects are not just present (*vorhanden*), but their presentness is imbued with practical and aesthetic values. Such values
texture and shape the appearance of things: the glass *looks* brittle; the
wooden table *sounds* solid. Moreover, things and, most saliently,
other persons are likewise imbued with social characteristics and
symbolic coding which structures their manner, or style, of

manifestation, the legibility of which textures ordinary experience, building its social or cultural common sense. As Husserl outlines, we exist among a plurality of environments (*Umwelten*), surroundings (*Umgebungen*), and worlds (*Welten*): the world of sports, the environment of the office and 'office culture', etc. This plurality of worlds, as different orientations within the world, are each structured in our ordinary experience through different fixtures of intentionality, the constitutive significance of which phenomenology understands as its challenge to map and render thematic through its descriptive and 'eidetic' (i.e., descriptions of essential patterns or structures) analyses.

What underlies different forms of ordinary experience, as we toggle back and forth in our daily lives among our different worlds and environments, is a common experience of the presentness of the world – that we find ourselves nested within the presentness of the world as such. For Husserl, this presentness of the world cannot be doubted or called into question; it can, however, become temporarily 'suspended' in its obviousness such that the empire of the obvious can become an explicit theme of phenomenological investigation. Through such a 'suspension' of what he terms the 'natural attitude' – that is, our taken-for-granted orientation towards the world as there – phenomenological reflection undertakes its mapping of ordinary experience, as resting upon and constituted through fixtures of intentionality: the manifold ways in which we are conscious of ourselves in being conscious of things in the world. Throughout these manifold ways of experiencing, the world obtains in its obviousness. As Husserl comments: 'In this manner, I find myself in waking consciousness, always and within being able to change it, in relation to the one and the same world, even as the content of the world is always changing.' The world is always 'existing' for me (*immerfort für mich 'vorhanden'*) or, as Husserl likewise expresses himself, always 'here' (*da*).[15] Indeed, if there is anything that seems most obvious and always going without saying, it is that what is most commonsensical about how we experience the world is this commonplace that the world remains 'here', whether or not we ourselves are still there.[16]

NOTES

1 Unless otherwise noted, all translations are my own.

2 Husserl (1992: 35): 'Der erste Versuch einer reinen Beschreibung des "Vorgefundenen".'

3 'Keine Theoretisierung kann diesen Sinn verletzten' (Husserl 1992: 35).

4 Ultimately, Avenarius's concern is both to disabuse metaphysical falsifications of experience while at the same time reconciling our natural and 'human' experience of the world with the image of the world advanced by modern physiology and physics.

5 'Was am Anfang meiner "geistigen" Entwickelung war, darüber sucht die Philosophie mir vermittelst spezieller Theorien Belehrung zu verschaffen; was aber am Anfang meines Philosophierens war, darüber kann ich selbst unmittelbare Auskunft geben.'

6 Avenarius (1891: 1). 'Ich mit all meinen Gedanken und Gefühlen fand mich inmitten einer Umgebung. Diese Umgebung war aus mannigfaltigen Bestandteilen zusammengesetzt, welche untereinander in mannigfaltigen Verhältnissen der Abhängigkeit standen. Der Umgebung gehörten auch Mitmenschen an mit mannigfaltigen Aussagen; und was sie sagten, stand zumeist wieder in einem Abhängigkeitsverhältnis zur Umgebung.' For similarities with the views of G. E. Moore, see Baldwin's chapter in this volume.

7 Avenarius notes in passing that he has omitted from consideration animals and animal worlds.

8 It goes without saying that Avenarius's use of the terms 'values' and 'hypothesis' is not aligned with their contemporary understanding. He most likely understands the term 'hypothesis' in its original Greek meaning: as that which stands under; i.e., as an assumption, not in any theoretical sense, but as a commonplace stance towards others.

9 Avenarius fashions what he terms the 'empirico-critical principle of coordination' (empirico-kritische Prinzipialkoordination) as regulating the interactions and 'homogeneity' of the two values (experiences and hypothesis) so as to account for the inseparability yet distinctness of the experiencing self and its environments.

10 Avenarius (1891: 9). 'Das war die Welt, wie ich sie am Anfang meines Philosophierens als ein Seiendes, Sicheres, Bekanntes, Vertrautes, Begriffenes vorfand – wie sie als Gedanke mit mir weiterlebte – wie sie mir als Tatsache stetsfort von neuem wiederkehrte und in allen

Wiederholungen dieselbe blieb. Mit einem Wort: es war der Inhalt meines anfänglichen Weltbegriffs, der sich freilich noch in der Form mit der lebendigen Anschauung deckte und noch nicht in eine "logische" Normalform des Begriffs gebracht war.' Note the deliberate use of the past tense *war* (here translated as 'is' for a cleaner English sentence) to indicate that our explicit statements, such as these, about what is already given, or found, are always based on how the world has already been found.

11 Avenarius (1891: 14). The loss of the 'natural obviousness' or 'self-understanding' of the world in the condition of simple schizophrenia is the object of an important study in phenomenological psychiatry by Wolfgang Blankenburg (2012).

12 See Sommer (1985); Bermes (2004: 114–27); Soldinger (2010: 189–217); and Perkins (2016).

13 Husserl (1992: 41). 'In der Welt kann nicht etwas sein, was den Sinn der Rede von Welt aufhebt, weil es ihn eben als Sinn (als Wesen) voraussetzt.'

14 See Husserl's influential analysis in his *Cartesian Meditations*.

15 Husserl (1950b: 64). The German expression *da* could also be rendered as 'there'.

16 My thanks to the editors of this volume for their insightful suggestions and helpful remarks on earlier drafts of this chapter.

Moore and Common Sense

Thomas Baldwin

INTRODUCTION

G. E. Moore (1873–1958) was an important and influential British philosopher during the first half of the twentieth century. He spent much of his life in Cambridge; he was appointed a lecturer at the university in 1911, and from 1925 until he retired in 1939 he was professor of mental philosophy and logic. He first came to prominence through his criticisms of idealist philosophy and his influential book on ethics, *Principia Ethica* (Moore 1903). Moore then published several important papers on metaphysics, epistemology, and the philosophy of perception, many of which were gathered together in two collections: *Philosophical Studies* (Moore 1922) and *Philosophical Papers* (Moore 1959d). Among these was his paper 'A Defence of Common Sense' (Moore 1925), which is central to an account of his conception of common sense. There are two other works to mention now. The first is an early series of lectures entitled 'Some Main Problems of Philosophy' which he delivered in 1910–11 but which were not published until 1953 (Moore 1953c). Moore begins these lectures by setting out a conception of philosophy as one in which what he calls 'the views of Common Sense' have a central role. The second is his late paper 'Proof of an External World' (Moore 1939) in which he attempts to meet the Kantian challenge of proving the existence of an external world by employing his common-sense method of argument.

THE COMMON-SENSE VIEW OF THE WORLD

'A Defence of Common Sense' was first published in a volume of 'personal statements' by British philosophers which the editor J. H. Muirhead intended would 'give the contributors an opportunity of stating authentically what they regard as the main problem of philosophy and what they have endeavoured to make central in their own speculation upon it' (Muirhead 1924: 10). As his title indicates, Moore (1959d: 44) used this opportunity to identify himself as a defender of common sense: 'I am one of those philosophers who have held that the "Common Sense view of the world" is, in certain fundamental features, *wholly* true.' Moore's approach was nonetheless idiosyncratic. He starts by simply setting out a series of 'truisms, every one of which (in my own opinion) I *know*, with certainty, to be true' beginning with some truths concerning his body:

> There exists at present a living human body, which is *my* body. This body was born at a certain time in the past ... Ever since it was born, it has been either in contact with or not far from the surface of the earth. (Moore 1959d: 33)

Moore continues by mentioning further obvious facts concerning the situation of his body, including such facts as that the earth 'had existed also for many years before my body was born' (Moore 1959d: 33). Moore now turns to himself:

> I am a human being, and I have, at different times since my body was born, had many different experiences ... e.g. I have often perceived both my own body and other things which formed part of its environment, including other human bodies; I have not only perceived things of this kind, but have also observed facts about them, such as, for instance, the fact which I am now observing, that that mantelpiece is at present nearer to my body than that bookcase. (Moore 1959d: 33)

Thus the list of truisms concerns not only his body and its spatiotemporal environment, but also his mind and its environment. And since, as we shall see below, Moore attaches a good deal of importance to the analysis of simple 'judgments of perception' such as 'This is a hand', it is worth noting that Moore includes judgments of this kind among his truisms.

Concerning this list, Moore makes three claims. First, it is a list of propositions which he himself knows with certainty to be true (Moore 1959d: 32). Second, a similar list of propositions can be constructed for 'very many (I do not say all)' other people, and each such person knows with certainty, concerning the list which concerns himself, that these propositions are true. Third, he, Moore, knows with certainty this last point, namely, that each person knows the truth of the propositions which concern him (Moore 1959d: 34). Moore does not add explicitly that in this respect his position is not special, that is, that each person also knows that everyone knows the truth of the truisms which concern them, so that knowledge concerning this knowledge of truisms is common knowledge. But I think it is plausible to include this point in Moore's conception of common sense.

It is hard at first to see how this list of truisms and our knowledge of them can be a point of great philosophical importance. It might be thought to be a point of some significance for human psychology and sociology, as a norm for the mutual understanding that most people have of themselves and each other; but Moore takes it that his common-sense view of the world provides a central contribution to philosophy. He begins by setting out two ways of challenging his view: there are some philosophers, he suggests, who will want to dispute the truth of the truisms in his list; and there are others who will want to dispute his claim that these truisms are things that are known. This distinction is, in effect, one between 'metaphysical' debates concerning the truth of some of Moore's supposed truisms and epistemological debates concerning knowledge of them, although the debates are connected by a link which Moore himself emphasizes in 'A Defence of Common Sense', namely, that assertion brings with it a claim to knowledge (Moore 1959d: 43). We shall see later that the connections here are especially important and difficult to disentangle when assessing Moore's position in his 'Proof of an External World'. But for the moment I shall start from Moore's distinction, and discuss his response to challenges to the truth of his truisms.

COMMON SENSE AND METAPHYSICS

Moore identifies four implications from his truisms which enable him to frame debates which concern the truth of his truisms. He expresses these implications as 'Material things are real', 'Space is real', 'Time is real', and 'The Self is real' (Moore 1959d: 38–9), with the human body as a paradigm material thing with a spatial location and temporal existence, and the person whose body this is as a persisting self. So he sets up his discussion as a response to the denial of these four propositions, mainly the denial of 'Material things are real'. His response consists primarily of an argument to the effect that the denial of 'Material things are real' is incoherent. Moore argues that philosophers who deny that material things are real typically write of what 'we' believe or not, and thereby indicate that they know of the existence of other people, who of course have material bodies. So in denying the reality of material things, 'they have, therefore, been holding views inconsistent with propositions which they themselves *knew* to be true' (Moore 1959d: 41).

This argument is much too brisk to be persuasive; but what is most unsatisfactory about Moore's discussion is the way in which he fails to engage with philosophical debates concerning the nature of reality. While he allows that the term 'real' is ambiguous, so that it can be used to express propositions whose denial is compatible with his truisms, he holds that in 'the most natural and proper usage' of the term, this is not correct (Moore 1959d: 39). For, as he explains else-where (see Moore 1917), he takes it that the term 'real' is to be understood by means of a contrast with the term 'imaginary', and in this sense 'Material things are real' just means 'There exist material things' (Moore 1922: 211). When 'real' is understood in this way, however, Moore's claims are of little philosophical significance. For the metaphysician (such as Berkeley) or natural scientist (such as Eddington – see Eddington 1928) who disputes the reality of matter will not regard himself as challenging Moore's truisms. Their aim is to identify the basic structure of the world, and it is just this basic structure which they take to be real. From this point of view the thesis of the unreality of matter amounts to the claim that matter is not an element of the basic structure, which is instead composed of spirits and ideas (for Berkeley) or electromagnetic fields (for Eddington); and the familiar characteristics of material objects are taken to be properties which supervene upon features of the basic structure. When the debate is expressed in this way, the metaphysician and the scientist can accept Moore's truisms about the existence of his body and similar things but maintain that nothing follows from this concerning the reality of matter.

This conclusion is, in effect, supported by Moore's discussion of the significance of analysis in 'A Defence of Common Sense'. He maintains that while he is not at all doubtful about the truth of propositions such as 'This is a hand', he remains doubtful about the 'correct *analysis* of such propositions' (Moore 1959d: 53). Moore begins by saying that there are two points concerning this case about which he is certain. First, the 'subject (and, in a certain sense, the principal or ultimate subject) of the proposition' (Moore 1959d: 54) is a sense-datum; that is, the perceptual demonstrative 'This' is here used to refer to a sense-datum. Second, the judgment in question is not the judgment that this sense-datum is a hand. Just what the structure and content of the judgment amount to is then a task to be settled by 'analysis', concerning which Moore expresses his doubt. But since the question of the correct analysis is, in some degree, metaphysical – as Moore's description of the sense-datum as the 'subject (and, in a certain sense, the principal or ultimate subject) of the proposition' indicates – the way in which Moore separates this question from his common-sense affirmation that 'This is a hand' supports the previous conclusion that Moore's defence of common sense has no significant metaphysical implications.

If one looks back to Moore's early (1910–11) lectures, 'Some Main Problems of Philosophy', however, it appears that he holds a different opinion. The first lecture is entitled 'What is Philosophy?' and Moore's answer is that the aim of philosophy is

'To give a general description of the *whole* of the Universe' (Moore 1953c: 1). Moore now introduces common sense as a major resource for arriving at a description of the universe:

> Starting, therefore, from the view of Common Sense that there certainly are in the Universe (1) material objects in space and (2) the acts of consciousness of men and animals upon the earth, we might most simply get a general description of the Universe in one of two ways: Either by saying, these two kinds of things *are* the only kinds in the Universe; or by saying: they are the only kinds we *know* to be in it, *but* there may possibly be others. (Moore 1953c: 15)

This passage indicates that, in this first lecture, Moore's conception of common sense and its role in philosophy is different from that in 'A Defence of Common Sense'. For although Moore does not use the term 'metaphysics' in the lectures, it seems appropriate to think of his conception of philosophy as one which includes metaphysics, since the aim of philosophy is to specify 'all the most important kinds of things which we *know* to be in [the Universe]' (Moore 1953c: 1), and the passage quoted above shows that 'the view of Common Sense' is to guide the fulfilment of this goal. As the lectures continue, however, and Moore enters into detailed debates concerning reality, belief, and truth, the role of common sense diminishes. A particularly striking example concerns the status of propositions. In his third lecture, Moore introduces propositions as the things expressed by indicative sentences which we may then come to believe or disbelieve. Moore does not suggest that he is here simply expounding common sense, but he does present his position as a straightforward development of the primitive ontology of common sense which enables him to identify this new kind of thing – propositions – as a fundamental kind within the universe (Moore 1953c: 56). But later on, as Moore struggles to give an account of false belief, he finds that he is led to repudiate this conception of propositions as objects of belief, and he now writes, concerning this new position: 'it may be expressed by saying that there simply are no such things as propositions' (Moore 1953c:

265). Yet he adds that 'we can, and must, still continue to talk *as if* there were such things as propositions' (Moore 1953c: 265). So the commonsensical language of propositions is to be retained as a way of describing what we say and think, despite the fact that a deeper level of analysis will dispense with reference to propositions. The result is a dialectical situation similar to that which obtains in 'A Defence of Common Sense': we can retain the commonsensical idiom of propositions when we describe our statements, beliefs, and so on, while allowing that analysis reveals that in fact 'there simply are no such things as propositions'.

There is, however, one qualification to be introduced at this point concerning the role of common sense. One of Moore's earliest statements of his sense-datum theory of perception is his 1914 paper 'The Status of Sense-Data' (Moore 1914). Moore here introduces the trio of positions concerning the relationship between sense-data and material objects which dominate his discussions of perception thereafter. One of these is the phenomenalist hypothesis to the effect that propositions concerning material objects are to be analysed in terms of hypotheticals concerning possible sense-data one would apprehend. Moore expresses some support for this hypothesis, but adds that the great objection to it is that it implies that ordinary descriptions of material objects will have to be understood 'in a Pickwickian sense' in that straightforward indicative descriptions of the shape and size of a coin are to be understood as expressing complex hypothetical propositions concerning possible sense-data one might apprehend. Although Moore does not describe this objection as one to the effect that the phenomenalist analysis is an offence to our common-sense understanding of judgments concerning material objects, it is natural to interpret it this way, and in lectures on perception given as part of a course of lectures on metaphysics in 1928–9, Moore himself does use this language. In the long passage which follows, Moore is discussing the relevance of common sense to his usual trio of positions, where 'Type I' is direct realism, 'Type II' is indirect realism, and 'Type III' is phenomenalism (I leave the abbreviations Moore used in his lecture notes unchanged):

> It seems to me that there's an ambiguity wh. it's very important to clear up in the way in wh. 'Comm. Sense' is used.
>
> I don't think it's true that 'we' all do in fact take any view at all on the question to which Type I, II & III are answers: 'Comm. Sense' in one, & the most important of its senses, takes no view at all on this subject; it simply doesn't raise the question …
>
> It's only in quite another sense that we can say that C.S. takes or implies any view on the question to wh. these Types of view are answers.
>
> All we can say is, I think, that some of these views *would* appear more natural – less paradoxical than others – to any plain man who could understand the question …
>
> In this sense, I think, C.S. is against Type III … & I think a certain weight is to be attached to the fact that it is. But the position is a *totally* different one to that of Common Sense to the assertion that there are material objects etc.: i.e. to what is presupposed in saying that Common Sense exists. (Moore 1966: 88–9)

This passage confirms that common sense as expressed by the truisms of 'A Defence of Common Sense' has no implications for the choice between Moore's three accounts of perception. But Moore adds that there is a different kind of common-sense attitude to this choice, concerning which position '*would* appear more natural – less para-doxical than others – to any plain man who could understand the question'. And when the question is put in this way, common sense finds the phenomenalist analysis difficult to swallow. Thus Moore in effect introduces here his complaint concerning the Pickwickian aspect of phenomenalism. This is a type of appeal to common sense which many contemporary philosophers would endorse. For example, David Lewis famously described the response of many philosophers to his modal realism as 'an incredulous stare' (see Lewis 1986: 133), whose legitimacy as an expression of common-sense beliefs and attitudes he acknowledged. But he went on to write that this response should not be regarded as decisive:

> Common sense has no absolute authority in philosophy. It's not that the folk know in their blood what the highfalutin' philosophers may forget. And it's not that common sense speaks with the voice of some infallible faculty of 'intuition'. It's just that theoretical conservatism is the only sensible policy for theorists of limited powers … Part of this conservatism is reluctance to accept theories that fly in the face of common sense. But it's a matter of balance and judgment. (Lewis 1986: 134)

Lewis captures very well here the substance of Moore's incredulous stare at the Pickwickian aspect of the phenomenalist analysis. But it is important to recognize that although this aspect of the appeal to common sense in philosophical debate is affirmed by Moore in the notes cited above, it is not one that Moore seeks to defend in 'A Defence of Common Sense'.

COMMON SENSE AND EPISTEMOLOGY

The second type of critical response to his truisms which Moore mentions in 'A Defence of Common Sense' is that of philosophers who, without disputing the truth of those truisms which do not involve a claim to knowledge, hold that we lack knowledge of some of these truisms, typically those which involve the existence of material objects or the existence of persons other than oneself. In his reply Moore begins by accusing these critics of self-contradiction. For, he says, these critics do not simply deny that they themselves know that other people exist; they also deny that anyone has knowledge of this kind, and in doing so they imply not only that there have been other people who lack this knowledge, but also that they know that there have been such people – which contradicts their sceptical claim (Moore 1959d: 42–3). This argument is not one of Moore's happiest constructions: the general sceptical denial does not bring with it an implication that there actually are any other people; the sceptic can simply assert that if there are any other people, then they too would lack knowledge of the existence of others, and there is no incoherence in combining this assertion with an implied claim to knowledge of it.[1]

What Moore goes on to say to elucidate further his claims to common-sense knowledge, however, includes a potentially more interesting line of thought. First, he acknowledges that most of his truisms are things that he does not know '*directly*', that is, he knows them only because he has had evidence for them; for example, he knows that the earth existed for many years before he was born only because he has known other things which were evidence for it. But, he continues, 'I certainly do not know exactly what the evidence was' (Moore 1959d: 44), and he adds:

> We are all, I think, in this strange position that we do *know* many things, with regard to which we *know* further that we must have had evidence for them, and yet we do not know *how* we know them, i.e. we do not know what the evidence was. If there is any 'we', and if we know that there is, this must be so: for that there is a 'we' is one of the things in question. (Moore 1959d: 44)

Moore's suggestion seems to be that this is a typical mark of our general common-sense knowledge – that our knowledge of things such as that the earth existed for many years before one was born and that there are many other people besides ourselves is so deeply embedded in the background structure of our ordinary knowledge that although we must have had evidence for them, we cannot say what the evidence is, especially where it is non-circular evidence that is sought. At this point, therefore, Moore's defence of common-sense knowledge brings to the surface an important question as to how we know these things. In 'A Defence of Common Sense', Moore himself seems to think that there is nothing much that one can say about this: he writes, 'I think I have nothing better to say than that it seems to me that I *do* know them, with certainty' – that is, we must just learn to live with this 'strange' feature of the human condition.[2]

In the 1910–11 lectures 'Some Main Problems of Philosophy' (Moore 1953c), Moore introduces a different dialectical strategy. The context in which he sets it out is one in which he has been discussing what he calls 'Hume's theory' concerning the way in which knowledge of the existence of material objects might be obtained;[3] and the conclusion which he has reached by combining 'Hume's principles' with a subjectivist version of the sense-datum theory of perception according to which sense-data are essentially 'dependent on the mind' (Moore 1953c: 43) is that '*If* 'Hume's principles are true, nobody can ever *know* of the existence of any material object' (Moore 1953c: 119). One response to this might be to replace the subjectivist sense-datum theory with a realist theory, but although Moore considers this option in these lectures, he does not pursue it. The reason for this decision is that he believes that he has a better option. He begins his statement of the new argument in the following passage, in which he is considering whether or not he knows the existence of a pencil which he is then holding up:

> It seems to me, in fact, there is really no stronger and better
> argument than the following. I *do* know that this pencil exists; but
> I could not know this, if Hume's principles were true; *therefore*,
> Hume's principles, one or both of them, are false. (Moore 1953c:
> 119–20)

He recognizes that this argument 'seems like begging the question' (Moore 1953c: 120); but, he observes, his argument is on a par with that of his sceptical opponent in that both arguments rely on the conditional 'if Hume's principles are true, nobody can ever *know* of the existence of any material object'. The difference is just that where the sceptic affirms Hume's principles and infers that Moore does not know that this pencil exists, Moore affirms that he does know that the pencil exists and infers by contraposition that the conjunction of Hume's principles and the subjectivist sense-datum theory are not true. Moore now observes that the premises of any argument which is to provide persuasive knowledge of its conclusion must themselves be known, and he suggests that this point can be used to assess the relative merits of his position and that of the sceptic by deciding which argument has premises which are better known, or at least more certain, than those of the other (Moore 1953c: 122). Moore therefore sets out to show that the premise of his argument is the better known. The first way in which he argues for this is by maintaining that the premise that he knows that this pencil exists is itself something which he knows 'immediately' (Moore 1953c: 125). Moore does not offer any argument for this questionable claim, which is reminiscent of the notorious KK principle: $Kp \rightarrow KKp$ (if a knows p then a knows that a knows p).[4] But in a later lecture he provides a different argument for his central thesis that any sceptical argument is 'sure to depend upon some premiss which is, in fact, less certain than the premiss that I do know of the existence of this pencil' (Moore 1953c: 126). His new argument is that any such sceptical argument is bound to rely on general claims about the limits of knowledge (such as Hume's principles), and that such principles must be based upon 'empirical induction' –

> upon observation of the cases in which we obviously do know propositions of the kind in question, and of those in which we obviously do not, and of the circumstances which distinguish the one class from the other. But, this being so, it follows that no such general principle can have greater certainty than the particular instances upon the observation of which it is based. (Moore 1953c: 143)

This is a much more powerful argument. It draws its strength from Moore's insistence that in thinking about issues of this kind, one needs to start by considering particular cases where one's judgments about what is involved are well entrenched in ordinary thought and practice (Moore 1953c: 126). This does not mean that Moore was right to hold that philosophical debates about the limits of knowledge are matters of 'empirical induction' as if there were some hard empirical facts concerning knowledge to be 'observed'. But he was surely right to hold that there is a strong presumption in favour of constructing general principles in this area which respect well-entrenched judgments concerning particular cases. In some cases, we may come to modify our judgments in the light of persuasive general considerations so that we reach a new 'reflective equilibrium'.[5] But it is very hard to accept that such modification would involve overturning our strong conviction that in normal circumstances we know such things as 'This is a pencil'.

In his lectures Moore is somewhat cautious in his statement of the conclusion of this new line of argument:

> All this, I am aware, is only strictly an argument in favour of the position that we do not know that we do not know of the existence of material objects. But there is, I think, a real and important difference between this position and the dogmatic position that we *certainly do not* know of their existence. And, in practice, if not in logic, it is, I think, an important step towards the conviction that we *do* know of their existence. (Moore 1953c: 144)

Moore's practice does in fact show him stepping well beyond the thesis that 'we do not know that we do not know of the existence of material objects'. When he returns to this issue in his 1918 paper 'Some Judgments of Perception', he lays out this new argument very briskly, taking as his example the question whether we know such things as 'This is a finger':

> we may safely challenge any philosopher to bring forward any argument in favour either of the proposition that we do not know it, or of the proposition that it is not true, which does not rest upon some premiss which is, beyond comparison, less certain than is the proposition which it is designed to attack. (Moore 1922: 228)

Surprisingly, Moore does not use this argument when discussing sceptical challenges to common sense in 'A Defence of Common

Sense'; instead he just relies on the unsatisfactory argument, discussed above, that sceptics have contradicted themselves. Nonetheless, it is obvious that the conclusion of this argument is central to common sense as Moore expounds it in 'A Defence of Common Sense'. As I have indicated, more has to be said to vindicate the argument, for the issue of how one achieves reflective equilibrium in philosophical debates is itself a philosophical issue and not simply a matter of common sense. But since the key consideration in this argument is, for Moore, a matter of common sense, it seems legitimate to regard his argument not just as a defence of common sense but as an argument from common sense.

MOORE'S PROOF

In his 1939 British Academy lecture 'Proof of an External World' (Moore 1939), Moore combines themes from his earlier discussions of common sense (although without ever using the expression 'common sense') in a way which makes discussion of this famous paper a good way of concluding a discussion of his conception of common sense and its significance.

Moore starts the paper by saying that he wants to provide a 'proof of an external world' of a kind which would dispel Kant's complaint that no such proof has yet been given. He then spends most of the paper discussing the way in which Kant's phrase 'things outside of us', which is central to his conception of an external world, is to be interpreted. The interpretation Moore ends up with is that something is 'outside of us' when it is 'external to our mind' in the sense that its existence is *logically independent* (Moore 1959d: 144) of experience.

Having prepared the ground, Moore delivers his proof:

I can prove now, for instance, that two human hands exist. How? By holding up my two hands, and saying, as I make a certain gesture with the right hand, 'Here is one hand', and adding, as I make a certain gesture with the left, 'and here is another'. And if, by doing

> this, I have proved *ipso facto* the existence of external things, you
> will all see that I can also do it now in numbers of other ways.
> (Moore 1959d: 145–6)

Moore now proceeds to claim that 'the proof which I gave was a perfectly rigorous one' (Moore 1959d: 146). For, he says, his proof satisfies the basic requirements (1) that the premises be different from the conclusion, (2) that he know the truth of the premises, and (3) that the conclusion follow from the premises. Moore takes it that it is obvious that requirements (1) and (3) are satisfied, and this is indeed the case with respect to requirement (1). Requirement (3) is, however, more problematic, and I shall return to it. But what of requirement (2)? Moore is very brisk in his treatment of this; he declares:

> How absurd it would be to suggest that I did not know it, but only
> believed it, and that perhaps it was not the case! You might as well
> suggest that I do not know that I am now standing up and talking –
> that perhaps after all I'm not, and that it's not quite certain that
> I am. (Moore 1959d: 146–7)

Having defended his proof in this way, Moore acknowledges that 'many philosophers will still feel that I have not given any satisfactory proof of the point in question'. The main objection he considers is that he has not proved his premise. Moore's response is that this is indeed the case, but that to do so he would need to prove that he is not now dreaming, which he cannot do (Moore 1959d: 149). Moore has his critic reply that, in that case, he does not know his premise; to which Moore responds by denying that what we cannot prove we do not know. But he gives no argument for this, beyond asserting the very point which the objection calls into question – that he does know the premise of his proof despite the fact that he cannot prove it. And with this unsatisfactory argument Moore ends his lecture.

Moore's 'proof' has attracted more attention than any other aspect of his philosophy, except for the 'naturalistic fallacy' debates in ethics. The main reason for this attention is, I think, the proof's apparent simplicity and the challenge it raises for more complex approaches to philosophical debates about scepticism and knowledge of the external world.[6] I want to start an assessment of the proof by returning to the distinction which I took from Moore's 'Defence' concerning the distinction between metaphysical debates about the nature of reality and epistemological debates about the limits of knowledge. For a central question concerning Moore's 'Proof' is whether it is intended to be a proof of the existence of an external world or a proof that we can have knowledge of the existence of an external world. The title of the lecture certainly suggests the first aim; but given the emphasis on knowledge in the latter part of the paper, the lecture has often been understood to have the second aim as well. Moore (1942) himself addressed this issue in his reply to his critics:

> I have sometimes distinguished between two different propositions, each of which has been made by some philosophers, namely (1) the proposition 'There are no material things' and (2) the proposition 'Nobody knows for certain that there are any material things'. And in my latest published writing, my British Academy lecture called 'Proof of an External World', ... I implied with regard to the first of these propositions that it could be *proved* to be false in such a way as this; namely, by holding up one of your hands and saying '*This* hand is a material thing; therefore there is at least one material thing'. But with regard to the second of these two propositions, which has, I think, been far more commonly asserted than the first, I do not think I have ever implied that *it* could be *proved* to be false in any such simple way; e.g., by holding up one of your hands and saying 'I know that this hand is a material thing; therefore at least one person knows that there is at least one material thing'. (Moore 1942: 668)

Moore's testimony here is unequivocal. Although Moore's 'Proof' itself shows that epistemological considerations have an important role in the construction of his proof, it is clear that his intention was to establish metaphysical claims such as that there really are external things and not to refute sceptical doubts about our knowledge that there are such things.

Moore's test for something's being 'external' was that it is something whose existence is logically independent of experience; so a key question is whether the premise of Moore's proof – 'Here is one hand and here is another' – establishes that the existence of his hands is logically independent of experience. It is very hard to see that it does, and the problem here is particularly salient for someone like Moore, who holds a sense-datum theory of perception according to which the 'real and ultimate subject' of judgments of perception such as 'Here is a hand' is a sense-datum. For whatever sense-data are, they are not things whose independence from experience could be established simply by demonstrating 'Here is a hand' or anything similar. A further problem, which is independent of the complications of the sense-datum theory, affects Moore's requirement (3) that the conclusion of the proof follow from the premises: this concerns the identity of the proof's conclusion. Is it just that there are human hands? In that case requirement (3) is satisfied, but the proof is not a proof that there are external things. Or is the conclusion that there are external things, things whose existence is independent of experience? In that case it is not clear how requirement (3) is satisfied. Whichever option one takes, Moore's proof seems to require the assumption that hands are external things, things whose existence is logically independent of experience. But this can certainly be challenged.

Moore was indeed challenged on this point by John Wisdom in his paper 'Moore's Technique' (Wisdom 1942). Wisdom suggested that there is something sophistical about Moore's proof in that his assumption of an unquestionable connection between 'Here is a hand' and 'Matter exists' is exactly what those philosophers who have denied the existence of matter have called into question (Wisdom 1942: 433). In his reply to Wisdom (Moore 1942: 669–70), Moore accepts that there is indeed a sense of the expression 'material thing' such that 'There are material things' does not follow from 'This is a human hand'. But, Moore insists, that sense of 'material thing' just concerns the *analysis* of a proposition such as 'This is a human hand', to the effect that a position such as phenomenalism is true; and, he continues, there is another sense of 'material thing' such that from 'There are no material things' there does follow 'There are no human hands'. Thus, as before, Moore's claim is that questions of analysis do not contribute to questions concerning the reality of an external world, which can be settled at the level of common-sense demonstrations of one's hands. But in the light of Moore's careful analysis of what it is for something to be an external thing, something whose existence is logically independent of experience, this is not persuasive. For that is not a point to be settled by a common-sense demonstration, but requires a persuasive analysis of judgments of perception. I argued earlier that Moore's appeals to common sense in his 'Defence' and elsewhere do not provide a basis for claims about the reality of material objects. I am afraid that this conclusion is confirmed by this assessment of the significance of Moore's 'Proof'.

However, I also suggested that Moore's discussions of common sense include two constructive contributions to epistemological debates. First, Moore's claims in his early lectures to knowledge of particular facts such as 'This is a pencil' are examples of a type of prima facie certainty to which more abstract general principles about the limits of knowledge are answerable. They are not unchallengeable, but there is a presumption in their favour. The second point, which Moore notes in his 'Defence', is that some of our general common-sense knowledge of the world – for example that the earth has existed for years – is so deeply embedded in the structure of our understanding that it is very hard to identify evidence for it; we are in 'this strange position' that we do know many things without knowing how we know them. Both of these points are relevant to the final pages of Moore's 'Proof' where he turns from his statement of his proof to a defence of it focused around his claims to knowledge.

Moore's defence of his claim to know the premise of his proof ('Here is one hand', etc.) is just the affirmation of his certainty concerning this knowledge which I cited earlier (Moore 1959d: 146–7). As I have mentioned, Moore does acknowledge that there are those who will think that this defence of his claim to know the premise of his proof is not enough to vindicate his proof: they hold that he needs to prove the premise. Moore's response was that this challenge is misconceived; for although, he says, he cannot prove the premise, he does not need to do so. I think that Moore's discussion of this challenge is itself misconceived. First, by the standards of Moore's own proof, it seems reasonable to hold that the premise, 'Here is one hand', can be proved. Moore himself suggests a way of doing so:

> If one of you suspected that one of my hands was artificial he might be said to get a proof of my proposition 'Here's one hand, and here's another', by coming up and examining the suspected hand close up, perhaps touching and pressing it, and so establishing that it really was a human hand. (Moore 1959d: 149)

Moore says that this procedure is not really a proof; but it could be easily developed into a proof comparable to his own 'perfectly rigorous' proof in which the conclusion follows logically from a definition of a hand and premises expressing the content of the examination of the suspected hand. What one can say, however, is that this new proof would not add decisively to anyone's certainty concerning the truth of 'Here's a hand'; for it would rely on similar empirical evidence concerning its premises. This point connects with the reason Moore himself gives for rejecting his suggestion, namely, that he thinks that to prove 'Here's a hand' he would need to prove that he is not dreaming, which, he thinks, he cannot do; for if Moore's proof is vulnerable to doubts of this kind, they will not be alleviated by the new proof. Yet Moore's approach here seems to me to be a mistake. The question of whether Moore is dreaming is not relevant to the question whether the proof he has offered is a proof of the proposition 'Here is a hand'. If one wants to challenge a putative mathematical proof, one has to identify a fault in the proof itself. It would show a strange misunderstanding to demand of a mathematician who has offered a complex proof that she prove that she was not dreaming when she advanced her proof, and to reject her proof just because she could not prove that she was not then dreaming.

The way to legitimate Moore's concern with the question of whether he was dreaming is to modify the issue raised by his imagined critic. Where Moore has the critic demand that Moore prove the premise he claimed to know, which Moore says he cannot do (mistakenly, in my opinion), one can imagine the critic asking Moore to prove that he knows this premise. For if Moore were to be dreaming, he would not then know such things as 'Here is one hand'; hence it seems that if Moore is to prove that he knows this premise, he does need to demonstrate that he is not dreaming, which, Moore says, he cannot do. Whether this is indeed a serious problem for Moore's proof, however, depends on whether the critic's demand that Moore prove that he is not dreaming is reasonable. Moore says, concerning the proposition that he is dreaming:

> I have conclusive evidence that I am awake: but that is a very
> different thing from being able to prove it. I could not tell you what
> all my evidence is; and I should require to do this at least, in order to
> give you a proof. (Moore 1959d: 149)

These comments are similar to his earlier remarks in his 'Defence' about the 'strange position' that we are in with respect to our common-sense knowledge, such as one's knowledge that the earth existed for many years before one was born; namely, that although we do know these things, we cannot say how we know them. And one suggestion to make, concerning both cases, is that precisely because we cannot say how we know these things, the familiar demand that we should be able to show that we can exclude all the possible ways in which it would turn out that we are mistaken is unreasonable. And one might defend this suggestion by introducing the other strand in Moore's defence of common-sense knowledge, namely, that general principles concerning the vindication of claims to knowledge are answerable to our convictions concerning what we know for certain in particular cases such as 'This is a hand'. Hence, where one confronts the objection that, because (for deep reasons) one cannot eliminate the hypothesis that one is dreaming, one does not know what appears to one to be absolutely certain (e.g., that 'This is a hand'), it is reasonable to reject the demand that one demonstrate that one is not dreaming and to maintain one's claim to knowledge. Thus, whereas Moore ends his 'Proof' in a rather unsatisfactory way in which he appears to be dogmatic in insisting, without argument, that he knows 'Here's a hand' (etc.) without being able to prove it, he could have reinforced his proof by adding that his knowledge of the premise of his proof is an instance of the kind of common-sense knowledge for which no further proof can be reasonably demanded.[7]

NOTES

1　This is not to deny that in advancing their sceptical claims sceptics sometimes contradict themselves. Russell (1948: 196) gives the classic example: 'I once received a letter from an eminent logician, Mrs. Christine Ladd Franklin, saying that she was a solipsist, and was surprised that there were no others. Coming from a logician, this surprise surprised me.'

2　Wittgenstein discusses cases of this kind in *On Certainty* (Wittgenstein 1969: see §§ 91–171). Unlike Moore, he distinguishes between our certainty concerning these things and the appropriateness of claims to knowledge of them. I have discussed the relationship between the positions advanced by Moore and Wittgenstein in 'Wittgenstein and Moore' (Baldwin 2011).

3　Since Hume actually says little about *knowledge* of the 'continued and distinct' existence of objects, the 'theory' Moore attributes to Hume is at best an adaptation of some of Hume's arguments concerning 'scepticism with regard to the senses' to his own purposes. But the fact that Moore misrepresents Hume's arguments in this way is not important here.

4　For critical discussion of this principle, see Williamson (2000: 114–19).

5　This phrase comes, of course, from John Rawls's discussion of moral theory; see Rawls (1999: 40–6).

6 See Stroud (1984) for a careful assessment of Moore's position and its relationship to traditional debates.

7 There is, of course, much more to be said on these issues. I myself think that the Moorean position sketched above needs to be supplemented by 'externalist' considerations. But this is not the place to enter into a discussion of these matters.

6 Common Sense and Ordinary Language: Wittgenstein and Austin

Krista Lawlor

Ludwig Wittgenstein (1889–1951) and J. L. Austin (1911–60) expend tremendous intellectual energy to defuse sceptical problems. What relation do we find in their work between 'ordinary-language' methods and the defence of common sense? Thinking through this question encourages fresh appreciation of Wittgenstein's and Austin's remarkable efforts on behalf of common sense against sceptical challenges.

WITTGENSTEIN AND AUSTIN: METAPHILOSOPHY AND ORDINARY LANGUAGE

Is Wittgenstein an 'ordinary-language philosopher'? The question is vexed (Avramides 2017). The difficulty of interpreting Wittgenstein's texts is widely recognized, but the difficulty of classification owes as much to the 'ordinary-language philosophy' side of the equation. What exactly is 'ordinary-language philosophy'? There is no simple answer. Rather than argue about the meaning of the term – not a very interesting or useful project here – I'll take Austin as a paradigm 'ordinary-language philosopher': his brief methodological remarks are the touchstone for other philosophers working in the same vein.

Because Austin's methods are rooted in a metaphilosophical outlook, it is illuminating to start by comparing Austin's and Wittgenstein's attitudes towards philosophy and its problems, liabilities, and prospects. When we make this comparison, we find Wittgenstein and Austin share many elements of their metaphilosophical outlook, and consequently they offer strikingly similar approaches to some perennial problems of philosophy.

The plan for the chapter: we'll start with Wittgenstein's meta-philosophy, and then compare it to Austin's. Next, we'll consider Austin's methods, and see how they are rooted in his metaphilosophy. We'll then briefly consider Austin's and Wittgenstein's responses to the philosophical 'problem of other minds' and, at somewhat greater length, their responses to the sceptical 'problem of the external world'. With a perspective on metaphilosophical commitments, we'll better appreciate the role of ordinary-language philosophy in defending common sense, as each of Austin and Wittgenstein defends it.

WITTGENSTEIN AND AUSTIN: METAPHILOSOPHY

Wittgenstein and Austin share important views about philosophical problems and how to approach them. They have their differences, too, at least on some interpretations, in their views about the final aim of philosophy.

Paul Horwich articulates Wittgenstein's metaphilosophy this way:

> To a *very* first approximation, [Wittgenstein] came to think that the paradigm philosophical problems have the form:
>
> How could there be such a thing as X?
>
> – where X is some perfectly familiar, ordinarily unproblematic phenomenon, but where *a priori* considerations have been advanced whose import is that, despite appearances, X is in fact impossible . . .
>
> However, according to Wittgenstein, philosophy is incapable of establishing such dramatic results: the arguments must somehow be wrong, and their initial plausibility must derive from some language-based confusion in our thinking about them. Consequently, our job is not to find out whether the phenomenon in question is possible, or to try to prove that it really is or really is not, or to discern, in light of the paradoxical considerations, what its true nature must be, but rather to remove the confusion that is responsible for the misguided philosophical argument. When this

has been done, we will not be left with any positive theory or new understanding. The net result will be simply that we have cured ourselves of a particular tendency to get mixed up.[1]

As Horwich notes, it's not that Wittgenstein thinks common-sense opinion is sacrosanct and never needs revision (Baker 2002: 301). Wittgenstein's point is rather the *defectiveness* of philosophical methods that yield such sceptical results as that there is no such thing as free and blameworthy action, knowledge of other minds, or of the world around us, no such thing as time, causation, or meaning. The philosopher's job is not to prove that the target phenomena (free will, other minds, the external world, meaning, time) really do exist, but to unravel the sceptical philosopher's arguments. This will not involve more argument, or a 'positive theory or new understanding'; nor will it involve brute insistence that these things do exist, and that we know as much (*pace* G. E. Moore – see 'Our Knowledge of the External World' below); rather it will involve discerning the picture or model that underlies the sceptical argument. Such misleading pictures or models arise from the philosopher's misapprehension of our language:

> Our investigation is therefore a grammatical one. Such an
> investigation sheds light on our problems by clearing
> misunderstandings away. Misunderstandings concerning the use of
> words, caused, among other things, by certain analogies between
> the forms of expression in different regions of language.
> (Wittgenstein 1953: 90)

> A *picture* held us captive. And we could not get outside it, for it lay
> in our language and language seemed to repeat it to us inexorably.
> (Wittgenstein 1953: 115)

The philosopher should dissolve sceptical problems by showing how alternative models make sense of our ordinary ways of talking or thinking about the target phenomena. Then we will see the optional character of sceptical reasoning.

Austin's metaphilosophy shares a great deal with Wittgenstein's. While Austin gives no connected statement of what is wrong with traditional philosophy, he gives the gist: philosophers are prone to oversimplifying – they're too ready to generalize from small samples or to force questionable dichotomies. For example (Austin 1962: 3, see also 82):

> My general opinion about this [sense-data] doctrine is that it is
> a typically scholastic view, attributable, first, to an obsession with
> a few particular words, the uses of which are over-simplified, not
> really understood or carefully studied or correctly described;
> and second, to an obsession with a few (and nearly always the same)
> half-studied 'facts'. (I say 'scholastic', but I might just as well have
> said 'philosophical'; over-simplification, schematization, and
> constant obsessive repetition of the same small range of jejune
> 'examples' are not only not peculiar to this case, but far too
> common to be dismissed as an occasional weakness of
> philosophers.) The fact is, as I shall try to make clear, that our
> ordinary words are much subtler in their uses, and mark many more
> distinctions, than philosophers have realized; and that the facts of
> perception, as discovered by, for instance, psychologists but also as
> noted by common mortals, are much more diverse and complicated
> than has been allowed for. It is essential, here as elsewhere, to
> abandon old habits of Gleichschaltung, the deeply ingrained
> worship of tidy-looking dichotomies.

Like Wittgenstein, Austin holds that tendencies to oversimplify and dichotomize lead philosophers to ill-posed questions and pseudo-problems. Austin agrees that the traditional philosopher's methods are scientistic, in seeking to construct generalizations that will explain the complexity of observed phenomena in simple terms and that will deny our pre-theoretic opinions, while stubbornly ignoring recalcitrant data. Targeting logical positivist A. J. Ayer, he writes (Austin 1962: 82): 'For consider some questions about "real" colour. Here there are many cases of a kind which Ayer, generalizing on the basis of one example, takes no account of.' Like Wittgenstein, Austin holds that philosophical problems are often generated by the philosopher's tendency to be misled by superficial features of our language. For instance, Austin's take on the 'problem of freedom' is that philosophers are misled by their own special use of 'free':

> While it has been the tradition to present this [i.e., 'free'] as the 'positive' term requiring elucidation, there is little doubt that to say we acted 'freely' (*in the philosopher's use, which is only faintly related to the everyday use*) is to say only that we acted *not* unfreely, in one or another of the many heterogeneous ways of so acting (under duress, or what not). (Austin 1961b: 128, my emphasis)

The philosopher's use of 'free' adds nothing to the characterization of an act beyond more specific ordinary characterizations. We do better as philosophers, Austin argues, to focus instead on the specific ordinary characterizations that do tell us something about our actions (Austin 1961b: 98):

> we [philosophers] become obsessed with 'freedom' when discussing conduct. So long as we think that what has always and alone to be decided is whether a certain action was done freely or was not, we get nowhere; but so soon as we turn instead to the numerous other adverbs used in the same connexion ('accidentally', 'unwillingly', 'inadvertently', &c), things become easier, and we come to see that no concluding inference of the form 'Ergo, it was done freely (or not freely)' is required.

Wittgenstein and Austin see traditional philosophy as rife with oversimplification that ignores recalcitrant facts, rife with disputes over ever-ramifying alternative theories that traditional philosophers have no rational criteria for preferring. ('Why should we prefer the positivist's language of "sense data" at all?' Austin asks – knowing that no answer is forthcoming.)

WITTGENSTEIN AND AUSTIN ON CONSTRUCTIVE PHILOSOPHY

Wittgenstein holds that philosophers should not persist in their traditional projects of attempting theoretical reductions of phenomena or resolving problems through positive explanatory claims. Instead philosophy should be 'therapeutic' and seek to dissolve the pseudo-problems and ill-posed questions by showing them for what they are:

> These are, of course, not empirical problems; they are solved, rather, by looking into the workings of our language, and in such a way as to make us recognize those workings; *in despite of* an urge to misunderstand them. The problems are solved, not by giving new information, but by arranging what we have already known. Philosophy is a battle against the bewitchment of our intelligence by means of language. (Wittgenstein 1953: 109)

After philosophers have completed their therapeutic work, what is left is a clearer view of our ordinary practices just as they were, and an appreciation of the fact that our language is fine as it is, as are our pre-theoretic opinions: 'Philosophy may in no way interfere with the actual use of language; it can in the end only describe it … It leaves everything as it is' (Wittgenstein 1953: 124).

Interpreters disagree about whether Wittgenstein holds that philosophy properly ends with the resolution of philosophical problems. Some argue that Wittgenstein would prohibit all further philosophical theorizing, beyond the work it takes to dissolve traditional philosophical problems. Others argue that Wittgenstein's metaphilosophical stance only prohibits *scientistic* theorizing (see Horwich 2011: 66n30).

Recently, interpreters of Austin have questioned the extent to which Austin shares Wittgenstein's views about philosophy properly ending with the resolution of philosophical problems. As some read him, Austin shares with Wittgenstein the view that the final goal of philosophy is therapeutic (Fischer 2005). Others read Austin as holding that philosophy goes beyond the dissolution of traditional philosophical problems, and instead read him as both demonstrating the form that a new philosophy should take (Gustafsson and Sorli 2011; Garvey 2014; Tsohatzidis 2018) and constructing some semantic tools to serve philosophers in this new work (Travis 2008; Lawlor 2017).

A strong case can be made that Austin believes the philosopher's job extends beyond the dissolution of pseudo-problems. Readers of *Sense and Sensibilia* will find Austin patiently dismantling sense-data theory and sounding a therapeutic tone about its task: 'unpicking, one by one, a mass of seductive (mainly verbal) fallacies, of exposing a wide variety of concealed motives – an operation which leaves us, in a sense, just where we began' (Austin 1962: 5).

But readers will also find Austin calling on philosophers to take ordinary epistemic commitments more seriously. As we have seen, Austin holds that 'common mortals' are already quite good at noticing 'the facts of perception'. Common or folk epistemology takes in the diversity and complexity of our epistemic access to the world around us, marking important distinctions (e.g., between *looking* and *seeming* a certain way). The job of philosophers is to attend to our ordinary epistemic commitments as they inquire into perception. Similarly, readers of 'A Plea for Excuses' (Austin 1961c) find not only the dissolution of the problem of freedom, which hinges on the problematic 'philosophical' use of the word 'free', but also a call to philosophers to work out a total account of action, and to investigate the relation of freedom and responsibility. And readers of 'Other Minds' (1961a) find not only the dissolution of the problem of other minds, but also a call to philosophers to theorize about the nature of knowledge: in this text, Austin offers the first articulation of a relevant alternatives account of knowledge, an interesting position on the incorrigibility of perceptual knowledge, and an argument against knowledge as a mental state.

On Austin's view, the work of philosophers does not end when we have a clearer view of our ordinary practices. We look into the workings of our language not only to resolve philosophical problems, but also to investigate and theorize about the worldly phenomena of interest to us. Austin's 'ordinary-language' methods are made to serve philosophers in their constructive tasks.

ORDINARY-LANGUAGE METHODS

What are Austin's methods? A familiar picture of Austin at work has him at his Saturday morning meetings with other Oxford philosophers, consulting the dictionary, and putting friends on the spot with tough questions (e.g., asking for the difference between playing golf *correctly* and playing it *properly*). He displays extraordinary attention to nuances of meaning, revealed in brilliantly imagined situations. What is the point of all this attention to 'what we should say, when'? Obviously, it's aimed at revealing subtle distinctions in the meanings of ordinary terms. Seeing only this much, some dismiss his work. C. D. Broad writes:

> To imagine that a careful study of the usages, the implications, the
> suggestions, and the nuances of the ordinary speech of
> contemporary Englishmen could be a substitute for, or a valuable
> contribution towards, the solution of the philosophical problems of
> sense-perception, seems to me one of the strangest delusions which
> has ever flourished in academic circles.[2]

A more synoptic and generous understanding sees Austin methodically dissolving traditional sceptical problems and assembling positive theories of important human phenomena.

H. P. Grice, a sometime proponent of ordinary-language philosophy, offers one such understanding, suggesting that Austin's methods are made for the purpose of unlocking the storehouse of common-sense belief through conceptual analysis (Grice 1989: 171ff.). First we botanize our language, surveying all the cases in which it is appropriate to deploy or withhold an expression; then we venture a general characterization of the types of case in which it is appropriate to apply a given expression and test it; this characterization is the foundation of an analysis of the concept expressed by the target expression (Grice 1989: 174, 376).

Grice sees one immediate challenge for the ordinary-language philosopher. While most anyone might be brought to admit that we need to start philosophical inquiry with ordinary language, or admit that specialized inquiry in philosophy and other sciences starts with problems and questions stated in ordinary terms, the question is, why should specialized forms of inquiry continue to respect ordinary language?

In answer, Grice starts by observing that, while Austin shares with Moore the idea that common-sense belief is valuable, Austin was more circumspect than Moore about the truth value of particular claims made by particular individuals. Moore's personal belief 'Here is a hand' has no special epistemic status for being 'commonsensical'. Rather Austin holds that the 'common man' is an impersonal figure – one who embodies competent use of a shared public language, and who consequently deserves the philosopher's attention. Language encodes knowledge the human species has acquired over many trials:

> our common stock of words embodies all the distinctions men have found worth drawing, and the connexions they have found worth marking, in the lifetimes of many generations: these surely are likely to be more numerous, more sound, since they have stood up to the long test of the survival of the fittest, and more subtle, at least in all ordinary and reasonably practical matters, than any that you or I are likely to think up in our arm-chairs of an afternoon – the most favoured alternative method.[3]

Grice suggests Austin's position is similar to Aristotle's: the answer to the question why we should pay continued respect to ordinary language is that epistemic progress is secured by a dialectical process. Dialectic is a progressive scrutiny of 'the ideas of the Many' with the aim of discerning 'the ideas of the Wise', where progress is ensured only so long as inquiry keeps in touch with what is said by the Wise, and before them, by the Many (Grice 1989: 379).

While Grice here offers an important defence of Austin's methods, he is incorrect that Austin aims for *analyses* of concepts (Austin 1961b: 8). What we aim for, Austin says, is to get clearer about what we mean by our talk so as to get clearer about phenomena:

> When we examine what we should say when, what words we should use in what situations, we are looking again not merely at words (or 'meanings', whatever they may be) but also at the realities we use the words to talk about: *we are using a sharpened awareness of words to sharpen our perception of, though not as the final arbiter of, the phenomena.* For this reason I think it might be better to use, for this way of doing philosophy, some less misleading name than those given above – for instance, 'linguistic phenomenology', only that is rather a mouthful. (Austin 1961b: 130, my emphasis)

Consequently, Austin acknowledges that there are limits to the use of his method (1961b: 130):

> Using, then, such a method, it is plainly preferable to investigate a field where ordinary language is rich and subtle, as it is in the pressingly practical matter of Excuses, but certainly is not in the matter, say, of Time. At the same time we should prefer a field which is not too much trodden into bogs or tracks by traditional philosophy, for in that case even 'ordinary' language will often have become infected with the jargon of extinct theories, and our own prejudices too, as the upholders or imbibers of theoretical views, will be too readily, and often insensibly, engaged.

Moreover, Austin emphasizes that we must recognize that language and concepts grow; sometimes our theoretical purposes require innovation:

> in the course of stressing that we must pay attention to the facts of actual language, what we can and cannot say, and precisely why, another and converse point takes shape. Although it will not do to force actual language to accord with some preconceived model: it

equally will not do, having discovered the facts about 'ordinary usage' to rest content with that, as though there were nothing more to be discussed and discovered. There may be plenty that might happen and does happen which would need new and better language to describe it in.[4]

Since words only get their sense in the circumstances in which they are used, we need to pay attention to a wide range of circumstances for subtle differences in usage. More, we need to go beyond ordinary usage and consult other sources that draw helpful distinctions about our target phenomena – Austin identifies two such sources: the law and psychology (1961b: 134).

Finally, philosophers also need to be quite clear about the way common commitments are expressed in natural language. This is just to say, philosophers need an account of natural-language semantics. While Grice seems to think that we can limn the use of an expression and discover its *application conditions*, Austin insists that expressions *apply or fail to apply* to given cases only *in given circumstances*. 'Plea for Excuses' is quite clear about this; there we also find Austin motivating the choice of 'situation semantics' as the best approach to natural-language semantics.[5] That the truth or falsity of what we say does not depend on sentence meaning alone, but is determined by sentence meaning in circumstances, is the heart of Austin's 'situation semantics'.[6]

In sum, for Austin, philosophy doesn't end with dissolving pseudo-problems. Austin would have philosophers go beyond the dissolution of traditional philosophical problems and investigate the phenomena; the investigation begins by examining our common-sense philosophical commitments. The picture Austin has is that ordinary people are already philosophers, asking and answering interesting philosophical questions, for instance about the possibility of knowing the world through the senses, or about when to take someone's word and when not, or about the relation between free action and responsibility. Over time, our language comes to encode important facts about such topics. Philosophers have a role in making our ordinary theoretical commitments on such matters explicit, and rationally reconstructing these commitments. To uncover these commitments, philosophers must attend to the ways ordinary people talk, and bear in mind the ways ordinary language can be deceptive (Austin 1961b: 40–2). For these reasons, they need a theory of natural-language meaning.

THE PROBLEM OF OTHER MINDS

When we compare Wittgenstein and Austin on the problem of other minds, we see their metaphilosophy in action, with some interesting differences in their use of ordinary-language tools.

The problem of other minds starts with a seeming asymmetry between the way one knows one's own mind and the way one knows another person's mind. One knows one's own experiences immediately, without inference. One needn't observe one's own pain behaviour to know one is in pain. But one doesn't know immediately what another person experiences; one has to see what state they're in, what impacts the world has on them, and perhaps ask them about what they're feeling, in order to gain knowledge. What explains this asymmetry in ways of knowing? A tempting answer: mental states or experiences, such as pain, are private, occurring in a 'private arena', the 'Cartesian Theatre', with only one person in the audience, ever.

This picture or model explains the epistemic asymmetry we noted, but it also leads to puzzles and problems. If in fact your experiences are events hidden from me, how do I come to know what you experience? Your report 'I see red' could be about experiences others would call 'green' – how could we rule this out? Your report could even be systematically not about experiences at all: you might be a zombie – and again how could we rule this out?

Very roughly, Wittgenstein's resolution of the problem centres on this diagnosis: the mistake we fall into is to exaggerate the parallel between two kinds of language game – *expressions* of experiences ('I am in pain') and *observation reports* ('That is red'). We tend to extrapolate from the grammatical likeness here, and consequently add to the Cartesian Theatre image the idea that 'I am in pain' is a report, or a description of a thing one is observing. And what a curious thing it must be then – something such that when one observes it, one's relation to it is immediate and provides one absolute certainty about its qualities. Once these thoughts settle, says Wittgenstein, we are firmly in the grip of the problem of other minds.

Wittgenstein suggests that the problem dissolves when we question the picture that guides our thinking. That picture rests on tendencies we have to exaggerate the likeness of distinct language games. Wittgenstein's prescription is for us to drop the picture of the Cartesian Theatre, by reminding ourselves of other compelling facts – such as facts about the differences between the language games of making observation reports and giving expression to experiences. We learn how to make the observation report 'That is red' as children, when our adult teachers can see what we see. In contrast, we learn to say 'I am in pain' as an alternative to whimpering or crying:

> words are connected with the primitive, the natural, expressions of the sensation and used in their place. A child has hurt himself and he cries; and then adults talk to him and teach him exclamations and, later, sentences. They teach the child new pain behaviour. (Wittgenstein 1953: 244)

Once we let go the Cartesian Theatre picture, and remind ourselves of such facts, we can imagine alternative accounts of the phenomena with which we started: one needn't observe one's own pain behaviour in order to produce more of the same, saying 'I am in pain'. And when we see another shrieking and writhing, we do not need to make an inference from a connection we know best in our own case, but instead we might immediately form a belief that the other person is in pain. An innate tendency to be moved by seeing another person in pain to the conviction that they are in pain would just as well explain all the phenomena – including the asymmetry phenomena and the fact that our beliefs about others' pains sometimes enjoy just as much certainty as beliefs in our own (Horwich 2011: 189).

Compare Austin's approach to the problem. In his symposium contribution 'Other Minds', Austin begins with a discussion of knowledge, doubt, relevant alternatives, and fallibilism. Throughout, he is on the lookout for the philosopher's typical missteps (Austin 1961b: 75): 'If we say that I only get at the symptoms of his anger, that carries an important implication. But *is* this the way we do talk?' Only in the last few pages does Austin turn to the problem of other minds, and he targets how the problem arises. He suggests that what starts as a question about believing a person's testimony becomes an altogether different question in the sceptic's hands. We start with a question: 'Why believe a person when they speak (about their mental states)?'

> There are answers that we can give to this question [why believe the man?], which is here to be taken in the general sense of 'Why believe him ever?' not simply as 'Why believe him this time?'
> (Austin 1961b: 82)

And to such questions, Austin remarks, there will be straight-faced answers:

> We may say that the man's statements on matters other than his own feelings have constantly been before us in the past, and have been regularly verified by our own observations.

But Austin notes:

> These answers are, however, dangerous and unhelpful. They are so obvious that they please nobody: while on the other hand they encourage the questioner to push his question to 'profounder' depths, encouraging us, in turn, to exaggerate these answers until they become distortions.
>
> The question, pushed further, becomes a challenge to the very possibility of 'believing another man', in its ordinarily

accepted sense, at all. What 'justification' is there for supposing that there is another mind communicating with you at all? How can you know what it would be like for another mind to feel anything, and so how can you understand it?

Our initial general question becomes a sceptical challenge: what 'justification' is there for supposing that others have minds at all? Austin replies (1961b: 83):

> This however, is distortion. It seems, rather, that believing in other persons, in authority and testimony, is an essential part of the act of communicating, an act which we all constantly perform. It is as much an irreducible part of our experience as, say, giving promises, or playing competitive games, or even sensing coloured patches. We can state certain advantages of such performances, and we can elaborate rules of a kind for their 'rational' conduct (as the Law Courts and historians and psychologists work out the rules for accepting testimony). But there is no 'justification' for our doing them as such.

Two ideas are suggested here: first, there is the idea, familiar to us from Wittgenstein, that justification comes to an end, and beyond justified beliefs lies a realm of action which is itself not subject to assessment in terms of justification. Some beliefs (believing another person) form an essential part of the actions 'we all constantly perform' and as such are not up for assessment in terms of justification. There are no reasoned grounds that make for the 'justification' for *believing another about what they experience*. We do not, and cannot, justify our doing so, but neither can we justify with reasoned grounds our practices of communicating, our playing competitive games, or using our senses to perceive the environment around us. Nonetheless, we can take responsibility for what we believe, in accord with our understanding of the rational conduct of such activities. (There are answers to the question 'Why believe him ever?')

Austin's dissolution of the problem of other minds has striking similarities with Wittgenstein's, for instance, in his rejection of 'profounder' questions that encourage us to answers that distort the facts as we ordinarily see them. Perhaps surprisingly, Austin does not go in for lengthy analysis of ordinary talk of experiences, pains and toothaches, on his way to a dissolution of the problem, as we might expect from an ordinary-language philosopher, but instead he appeals to the idea that some practices are simply part of our lives. Austin here sounds more like Wittgenstein in those parts of his work where he emphasizes the practices that underwrite our language. On the other hand, Wittgenstein's own approach to the problem of other minds sounds more like that of a paradigm ordinary-language philosopher, resting as it does on careful attention to features of our experience-talk and observation-talk.

OUR KNOWLEDGE OF THE EXTERNAL WORLD

How do we know about the world around us? Idealists doubt that there are objects independent of our minds, and sceptics, while accepting that there may be such objects, doubt that there is any knowledge to be had about them.

In both Austin's and Wittgenstein's writings we find the strands of *several* compelling responses to the problem of our knowledge of the external world. (Wittgenstein tackles this problem in late notes collected as *On Certainty*; Austin's approach must be extracted from his work on knowledge in 'Other Minds', and *Sense and Sensibilia*.)

To bring focus to our discussion, it's helpful to contrast Austin and Wittgenstein as against G. E. Moore on the problem of the external world. G. E. Moore strikes back at sceptical and idealist doubts by affirming what he takes to be common sense. In 'A Defence of Common Sense', published in 1925, Moore gives a 'list of truisms' he knows to be true:

> There exists at present a living human body, which is *my* body. This body was born at a certain time in the past, and has existed

continuously ever since, though not without undergoing changes; it was, for instance, much smaller when it was born, and for some time afterwards, than it is now. Ever since it was born, it has been either in contact with or not far from the surface of the earth; and, at every moment since it was born, there have also existed many other things, having shape and size in three dimensions (in the same familiar sense in which it has), from which it has been *at various distances*.[7]

Moorean certainties have several interesting features: they are universally accepted (the 'beliefs of Common Sense', Moore says (1959b: 43), are those 'commonly entertained by mankind') and cannot be denied without some kind of inconsistency. (Wittgenstein alternatively suggests that to deny them would seem mad.) They cannot be proved but are known with certainty. (Wittgenstein alternatively suggests that knowledge and certainty are different things, although at some places he suggests knowledge and certainty have similar features.)[8]

The Moorean certainty 'Here is a hand' becomes a central premise in Moore's later argument in 'Proof of an External World', published in 1939; in this argument, he goes one better and attempts to refute idealism by formulating a proof of the existence of objects to be met with in space – that is, of a world external to our minds. His proof begins with a demonstration, in which Moore holds up his hands and makes a gesture with one:

1. Here is one hand.

Then Moore repeats the gesture with his other hand:

2. Here is another hand.

And he concludes:

3. Two human hands exist.

Since human hands are objects to be met with in space, or 'external objects', it follows from the fact that two such objects exist that

4. External objects exist.

Moore anticipates resistance to his proof and seeks to pre-empt it, noting that the premises are known to be true (although he cannot prove them in turn), the conclusion follows, and that we often accept such proofs (Moore 1939). If someone were asked to prove there were three typographic errors on a page, he could point them out one by one and thereby prove the claim.

Moore's work captured Wittgenstein's attention, and it occupied him both in his *Philosophical Investigations* and at great length in the notes he made shortly before his death, later published as *On Certainty*.[9] Austin's attitude towards Moore's defence of our knowledge of the external world is harder to trace, but clearly he worked within a discussion whose terms were set by Moore.

Moore's proof fails, Wittgenstein is sure. But he is equally sure that following on from Moore's attempt, we can diagnose what goes wrong in sceptical thinking.

Beyond this point, there is dispute about his aims in *On Certainty*. As we have seen, some hold that Wittgenstein's metaphilosophical stance restricts the aims of philosophy to 'therapy' or dissolving problems. Consequently, any positive theorizing about the nature of knowledge in *On Certainty* is felt by some to be a lamentable departure from his metaphilosophical commitments (Fogelin 1996). Others find many resources within the pages of *On Certainty* for thinking afresh about knowledge, with several suggestive lines of response to scepticism, provoked by Moore's attempt. Crispin Wright explores one such line, very roughly summarized this way: Moore's proof fails because whatever evidence Moore uses to support premise (1) only supports it if the conclusion (4) is already reasonably believed: an experience as of a hand before one supports the belief that here is a hand, but only 'conditional on the prior reasonableness of accepting' the conclusion.[10] Without reasonably accepting the conclusion, the experience as of a hand is consistent with any number of alternatives to (1), such as that one is dreaming a hand or seeing an illusion of a hand. For this reason, Moore's proof begs the question and cannot be dialectically effective against the sceptic (Pryor 2004). Moreover, we see how difficult the sceptical challenge really is – without support for (4) of the kind Moore tries to give, we're left to wonder how experiences count in favour of ordinary beliefs. In the end, then, Moore's proof has the effect of putting a fine point on sceptical argument – how after all do we know premises such as (1)? (See Wright 2004a: 79–80.)

One might turn the tables on the sceptic here, Wright suggests, if we follow a suggestion in *On Certainty* and defend the conclusion (4) by other means. Then we'll be in a position to say how our perceptual experiences support ordinary beliefs of the sort that are Moore's premises. One possibility is to hold that propositions such as (4) are not fact-stating propositions at all. Then 'where non-fact-stating "propositions" are concerned, the lack of evidential warrant for accepting them need be no criticism of our doing so' (Wright 1985: 79–80). Another possibility, which Wright pursues in subsequent work (Wright 2014), is instead to hold that while (4) may have truth conditions, and so be apt for fact-stating, our epistemic relation to (4) is not that of knowing or being justified in believing it; rather, we are entitled to accept it because it is necessary for inquiry. Entitlement is 'a kind of rational warrant' not dependent on evidence (Wright 2004b: 167). Here Wright follows suggestions in *On Certainty* in such passages as these:

> 341. The questions that we raise and our doubts depend on the fact that some propositions are exempt from doubt, are as it were like hinges on which those turn.

> 342. That is to say, it belongs to the logic of our scientific investigations that certain things are indeed not doubted.

> 343. But it isn't that the situation is like this: We just can't investigate everything, and for that reason we are forced to rest content with assumption. If I want the door to turn, the hinges must stay put.

The idea is that (4) is a 'hinge proposition'; we cannot aspire to investigate it, but rather are entitled to accept it as a requirement of inquiry.

Wright's explorations here have generated a line of research known as 'hinge epistemology' (Coliva and Moyal-Sharrock 2016). A difficult question for hinge epistemology is why it marks any advance in the defence of common sense – why is it better than scepticism?[11] If we allow that hinge propositions are not knowable or justifiably believed, then isn't that simply to concede victory to the sceptic?

Michael Williams (2004) suggests a different reading of Wittgenstein's dissolution of Cartesian scepticism. Williams observes that the hinge epistemologist offers us a 'framework reading' of On Certainty: the simple answer to the problem of the external world is that sceptical doubt is illegitimate, in transgressing one or another rule of our ordinary epistemic practices. But Williams notes that while the framework reading gives a direct answer to the sceptic, Wittgenstein is not content to leave things there; true to his metaphilosophy, he also wants a diagnosis of why the sceptic succumbs to the illusion of doubt. Williams reads Wittgenstein as devoting the first sixty-five sections of On Certainty to wrestling with this question. Then, finally, it is in section 90 that we find Wittgenstein's ultimate diagnosis:

> 90. 'I know' has a primitive meaning similar to and related to 'I see' ('wissen', 'videre'). And 'I knew he was in the room, but he wasn't in the room' is like 'I saw him in the room, but he wasn't there'. 'I know' is meant to express a relation, not between me and the sense of a proposition (like 'I believe') but between me and a fact. So that the fact is taken into my consciousness. (Here is the reason why one wants to say that nothing that goes on in the outer world is really known, but only what happens in the domain of what are called sense-data.) This would give us a picture of knowing as the perception of an outer event through visual rays which project it as

it is into the eye and the consciousness. Only then the question at once arises whether one can be certain of the projection. And this picture does indeed show how our imagination presents knowledge, but not what lies at the bottom of this presentation.

The reason the sceptic thinks that 'There are physical objects' is a hypothesis is that the sceptic is in the grip of a picture: a 'picture of knowing as the perception of an outer event through visual rays which project it as it is into the eye and the consciousness'. What creates this picture is in the first place our commitment to the idea that knowledge is a factive mental state. While the factivity of knowledge is innocent enough, the idea that knowledge is a mental state is dangerous. When we accept it, we face the question, how can my consciousness stand in a relation to a fact? And then the following answer tempts us: the fact in question must be a sense-datum. This answer encapsulates the picture of knowing as 'projection into the eye of consciousness', and it sets us off on a sceptical path. We find it natural to accept the picture of knowing as apprehending sense-data, from which we only infer the existence of physical objects.

On Williams's reading, we find Wittgenstein's metaphilosophy at the forefront of his response to scepticism: the so-called problem of the external world rests on an illusion – the illusion of the intelligibility of sceptical doubt – which is removed once we see the optionality of the picture that helped to sustain the illusion.

Austin, like Wittgenstein, offers us a variety of tantalizing responses to the sceptic. One Austinian response directly targets the philosophers' tendency to overgeneralize and dichotomize: for instance, sense-data theorists collapse the various objects of perception into a single category, 'material objects', as opposed to 'sense-data', and allege that statements about such objects must in general rest epistemically on statements about sense-data. Austin questions such dichotomies, and he rejects the idea that statements as types fall into epistemologically interesting dependence relations (Austin 1962: 111ff.).

A different line of response in 'Other Minds' focuses on the ordinary rules for using the term 'I doubt' – an approach very similar to Wittgenstein's. Here Austin might be read as offering the simple framework answer canvassed above: namely, the sceptic has broken the rules of doubting, as revealed by attention to our ordinary linguistic practices. Our practices with 'doubt' and 'know' follow particular rules, and the sceptic flouts them, leaving us to wonder at the intelligibility of Cartesian doubts.

Yet another direct anti-sceptical position can also be found in Austin's 'Other Minds'. Here Austin spends a lot of energy on what knowledge is, and his ruminations give birth to the Relevant Alternatives Theory of knowledge. A simple Relevant Alternatives response to Cartesian scepticism targets hyperbolic sceptical hypotheses as simply not relevant (Kaplan 2000). Still further development of Austin's response to contemporary formulations of the sceptical problem makes use of Austinian views about semantics of knowledge ascription (Lawlor 2013; 2017; 2018).

Finally, Austin also suggests a still more aggressively anti-sceptical answer: not only can we have ordinary knowledge, and ignore sceptical hypotheses as irrelevant, we can actually know the hyperbolic sceptical hypotheses are false (Leite 2012). That is to say, we can know that we are not globally deceived, or Brains-in-Vats, or dreaming everything. This interpretation puts Austin in company with Moore, defending our ordinary usage as a direct guide to what is knowable.

CONCLUSION

Austin and Wittgenstein make mighty efforts to find a way out of the maze of traditional philosophical problems, and they consistently attend to ordinary usage as a guide. As we have seen, their similar methods and metaphilosophical inclinations are consistent with an array of approaches to particular sceptical problems.

Wittgenstein and Austin may differ over the aim of philosophical inquiry – whether the aim is seeing that ordinary language is fine as it is, or whether it is to further our philosophical understanding of human social, ethical, and epistemic life. For Austin, anyway, clearly ordinary language *isn't* always fine as it is – the philosopher will find it in need of some clarification, some 'tidying up', and even revision, when the aim of understanding the phenomena requires it. Contrary to many critics, for Austin understanding ordinary language is not an endpoint, but a starting point in our understanding of phenomena. In contrast, at least sometimes, Wittgenstein suggests that ordinary language is fine as it is, and that our goal as philosophers is to show how this is so. As we have seen, some hold a strict line here and say that Wittgenstein's metaphilosophical stance restricts the aims of philosophy to dissolving philosophical problems, while others suggest that Wittgenstein's metaphilosophical prohibition on theory only extends to scientistic theorizing. Setting aside this thorny debate, it may safely be said that for both Austin and Wittgenstein, ordinary-language methods play a central role in both the dissolution of problems and in disciplining philosophical work. Ordinary-language methods are crucial for the defence of common sense.

NOTES

1 Horwich (2011: 4–6). Throughout this section, I draw on Horwich's characterization. For another take on Wittgenstein's metaphilosophy see Fogelin (2009).
2 Broad, 'Philosophy', cited in Pomeroy (1974).
3 Austin (1961b: 130). See also Austin (1962: 63).
4 Austin (1961b: 37). See also Austin (1962: 63).
5 For dissenting views about whether Austin aims to develop an account of the semantics of natural language see Baz (2012) and Crary (2002).
6 Recanati (2004); Travis (2008); Longworth (2015). Austin works out his semantic proposal in more detail in his paper 'Truth' (Austin 1961b: 85–102).
7 Moore (1959b). Moore's identification of truisms of common sense echoes Thomas Reid, whom he admired. See Jensen (1979).
8 Wittgenstein (1969: 308, 8, 357, 386, 415). White (1986: 314–18).

9 Wittgenstein (1953: §§ 324–6 and §§ 466–86). My exposition here owes much to Child (2011).

10 Wright (1985: 58). What we have here is a failure of closure of evidential support, as Wright notes on page 59.

11 Hinge epistemologists are quite aware of this problem. See Wright (2004b: 203ff.).

Part II

7 The Delineation of Common Sense

René van Woudenberg

INTRODUCTION

Common-sense philosophy is philosophy in which common-sense propositions play a crucial role: they are (defeasible) data points with which we should work both when we construct and when we evaluate philosophical theories. This indicates that common-sense philosophy accords a rather high epistemic status to common-sense beliefs: they are rational, or justified, and should not be abandoned unless there are very good reasons for doing so. The attitude of believing – or something in the neighbourhood of this attitude – is the default attitude we should have vis-à-vis common-sense propositions. Or so the common-sense philosopher tells us.

The purpose of this chapter is to delineate common-sense beliefs, which is, in fact, a twofold purpose: (1) to delineate the class of common-sense propositions and (2) to delineate the attitudes we have, or should have, vis-à-vis those propositions. I will *not* discuss the epistemic status of common-sense beliefs, so I won't discuss why or even whether such beliefs should be deemed rational or justified or should be accorded some other exalted epistemic status. (But I have no doubt that many of the considerations I shall raise are relevant to that issue.)[1]

Generally speaking, things can be grouped, categorized, or classified in different ways, by different principles. Which of the groupings is the most helpful, useful, or relevant one depends on the purpose of the grouping. Take the grouping of books: this can be done by author, by year of publication, by subject matter, by weight, by colour, or by other principles. Which of these groupings is the most helpful, useful, or relevant one depends on one's purposes.

Beliefs, too, can be grouped or classified by a number of principles. They have been grouped on the basis of being true (as opposed to being false), of being justified or not, of being warranted or not, of being reliably produced or not, of being basic or non-basic, of being necessarily true or contingently true, of qualifying as knowledge or not, of being a priori or a posteriori knowable, and so on. Beliefs can also be grouped by the principle of being a common-sense belief or not. This chapter explores by what criterion or criteria this grouping can be made. Before taking up the criterion question, I present in the next section a number of propositions that proponents of common-sense philosophy have judged to fall in the extension of 'propositions of common sense'.

I said that the usefulness or relevance of a grouping depends on the purposes of the grouper. Is there a purpose for the common-sense grouping of beliefs? I suggest there is: the purpose is to delineate a group of beliefs that a rational person is *at least* justified in having; or, to identify a group of propositions that a rational person is *at a minimum* justified in believing.

This chapter is organized as follows. First, I will identify a number of propositions that have been presented as contents of common-sense beliefs. Next, I will discuss a number of properties that common-sense proposition have or have been claimed to have (i.e., their non-scientific character, their widespread take-up, the incoherence of their denials, their non-testimonial and non-inferential character, and, finally, their imprecision). At the end of the chapter I will discuss the question whether common-sense propositions are mostly *believed* or whether we often take up other attitudes towards them.

REID'S AND MOORE'S COMMON-SENSE PROPOSITIONS

Since both Thomas Reid and G. E. Moore are card-carrying common-sense philosophers, we can do no better than to turn to them if we want to acquaint ourselves with propositions that have been qualified as common-sense propositions. Since both have offered rather extensive lists of common-sense propositions, whereas others in the common-sense tradition have not, the selection of Reid and Moore is fully appropriate. As will emerge, the lists are interestingly different, but not so different that we must straightaway abandon the hope of finding a criterion or criteria that delineate propositions of common sense. I keep to the historical order, so I first turn to Reid.

Reid[2] divides the propositions of common sense, which he also calls 'first principles' or 'principles of common sense', into contingent and necessary ones. I quote Reid's description of them and provide explanatory comments. First, he says (Reid (1785) 2002: 470):

> (C1) I hold, as a first principle, the existence of every thing of which I am conscious.[3]

Reid was thinking here of being conscious of one's pains, of one's thoughts, and of the operations of one's mind. (C1) says that it is a principle of common sense that 'If one is conscious of one's thought T, then thought T exists'. But in its wake a host of further propositions qualify as common-sense propositions, such as 'The present pain in my ankle exists' and 'My current pleasure exists'. Since there are numerous mental operations we can be conscious of, there are also many propositions that state for each time I am in a particular state that 'I am in that particular state', and for each time you are in that state that 'You are in that state'. All such propositions are common-sense propositions.

The next item on Reid's list is this ((1785) 2002: 472):

> (C2) The thoughts of which I am conscious, are the thoughts of . . . *myself*.

(C2) goes further than (C1) in that it states something about one's thoughts – one of the mental operations one can be conscious of – namely, that they are *one's own* thoughts, not someone else's. The principle itself is a common-sense proposition, but this one, too, brings many other propositions in its wake, such as 'That the earth has one moon is a thought of myself' and 'That China is bigger than

Japan is a thought of myself'. Since other people have thoughts as well, (C2) entails that there are uncountably many other common-sense propositions of this sort.

The next principle says (Reid (1785) 2002: 474):

(C3) Those things did really happen which I distinctly remember.

This is, again, a common-sense proposition that generates a host of others; for instance, by (C3), 'I was in Barcelona' is something that really happened, because I distinctly remember being in Barcelona. And what holds for me holds mutatis mutandis for you as well: if you distinctly remember that you were in Berlin, then 'I was in Berlin' is a common-sense proposition – *for you*, that is, *not* for those who've never been in Berlin and accordingly can't remember having been there. So whereas (C3) is a common-sense proposition for everyone, the many propositions that follow in its wake are person-relative.

Next on Reid's list is this principle ((1785) 2002: 476):

(C4) Our own personal identity and ... existence [continues] as far back as we remember anything distinctly.

The common-sense proposition here is that I, the very same person who is now having memories of events taking place, say, five years back, *existed* five years back. (C4) tells us that when I remember doing some particular thing five years back, I existed five years back and am identical to the person doing that thing five years back. The same holds for you, of course.

The next proposition is an endorsement of the reliability of our five senses (Reid (1785) 2002: 476):

(C5) Those things do really exist which we distinctly perceive by our senses.

If this is a common-sense proposition, then so is (when I see a particular red rose) the proposition 'That is a red rose', or 'That rose is red'. So if (C5) is a common-sense proposition, then uncountably many other propositions of the sort 'This is an ... ' (or 'This X has property Y') are common-sense propositions as well.

(C1)–(C5) all have distinctively epistemological elements:[4] they are propositions that state something *about* cognition. Some of the other principles, such as the following, are like them in this respect (Reid (1785) 2002: 480, 482, 484, 487):

> (C7) The natural faculties, by which we distinguish truth from error, are not fallacious.
>
> (C8) There is life and intelligence in our fellow-men with whom we converse.
>
> (C9) Certain features of the countenance, sounds of the voice, and gestures of the body, indicate certain thoughts and dispositions of mind.
>
> (C10) There is a certain regard due to human testimony in matters of fact, and even to human authority in matters of opinion.

These propositions all state something about cognition: (C7) says that our natural faculties (perception, memory, introspection, reason) are reliable. (C9) is a principle about evidence: certain features of faces, voices, and gestures evidence thoughts and mental dispositions; this is a very general proposition, and we should suppose it to be a generalization over a great number of more specific principles of evidence that Reid doesn't mention, such as, perhaps, 'Speaking with a high-pitched voice evidences nervousness'; 'Fixed eyes evidence mental concentration'; or 'Not looking others in the eye evidences either uncertainty or respect'. (C8) could be taken as a principle about evidence as well: the fact that we converse with other people evidences that they are alive and endowed with intelligence. (C10) is also a principle about evidence in that it says that human testimony concerning facts should be given some evidential weight.

The remaining propositions on Reid's list are not epistemic (not about cognition) but have broadly metaphysical content (Reid (1785) 2002: 478):

(C6) We have some degree of power over our actions,
and the determinations of our will.

The thought here is that the actions we perform aren't events that just happen to us, but that we have a say in them – that they are, at least to some degree, 'up to us'. Likewise, what it is that we will is not just something that happens to us, something we find ourselves stuck with, but something on which we have some influence. The final first principles of contingent truth on Reid's list are the following (Reid (1785) 2002: 488, 489):

(C11) It may always be expected, that [people] will regard their own interest and reputation.
(C12) In the phaenomena of nature, what is to be, will probably be like to what has been in similar circumstances.

These propositions concern what we should expect of other humans and what we should expect of nature: we should expect people to regard their own interest and reputation, and nature to behave uniformly.

All of these propositions, Reid affirms, are *contingently* true. By this he means that they *could* be false: although they are true, they aren't *necessarily* true – that is, there is no contradiction in affirming their denials. The next series of propositions, Reid holds, are not only true but *necessarily* true. He groups these principles according to the sciences to which they belong:

- (N1) *Grammatical principles*; e.g., 'That every adjective in a sentence must belong to some substantive expressed or understood' and 'That every complete sentence must have a verb' (Reid (1785) 2002: 491).
- (N2) *Logical axioms*; e.g., 'That any contexture of words which does not make a proposition, is neither true nor false; that every proposition is either true or false; that no proposition can be both true and false at the same time; that reasoning in a circle proves nothing', and 'That whatever may be truly affirmed of a genus, may

be truly affirmed of all the species, and all the individuals belonging to that genus' (Reid (1785) 2002: 491).

- (N3) *Mathematical axioms*, such as Euclid's (Reid (1785) 2002: 491).
- (N4) *Axioms of the fine arts*; Reid doesn't describe any of them in detail, but he is sure they exist. 'The virtues, the graces, the muses, have a beauty that is intrinsic. It lies not in the feelings of the spectator, but in the real excellence of the object. If we do not perceive their beauty, it is owing to the defect or to the perversion of our faculties' (Reid (1785) 2002: 493).
- (N5) *First principles of morals*; e.g., 'That an unjust act has more demerit than an ungenerous one'; 'That a generous action has more merit than a merely just one'; 'That no man ought to be blamed for what it was not in his power to hinder'; and 'That we ought not to do to others what we would think unjust or unfair to be done to us in like circumstances' (Reid (1785) 2002: 494).
- (N6) *Metaphysical principles*; e.g., 'That the qualities which we perceive by our senses must have a subject, which we call body, and that the thoughts we are conscious of must have a subject, which we call mind'; 'That whatever begins to exist, must have a cause which produced it'; and 'That design, and intelligence in the cause, may be inferred, with certainty, from marks or signs of it in the effect' (Reid (1785) 2002: 495–512).[5]

I now move on to G. E. Moore's common-sense propositions as he lists them in his famous essay 'A Defence of Common Sense'. All of them are person-relative – relative to Moore, that is. Here they are (Moore (1925) 1993: 106–8):

> (M1) There exists at present a living human body, which is *my* body.
>
> (M2) This body was born at a certain time in the past, and has existed continuously ever since.
>
> (M3) It has been either in contact with or not far from the surface of the earth.

(M4) At every moment since [this body] was born, there have also existed many other things, having shape and size in three dimensions, from which it has been *at various distances* ... and with which it was *in contact.*

(M5) Among the[se] things ... there have ... been large numbers of other living human bodies.

(M6) The earth has existed ... for many years before my body was born; and for many of these years, ... large numbers of human bodies had, at every moment, been alive upon it; and many of these bodies had died and ceased to exist before it was born.

(M7) I am a human being, and I have ... had many different experiences, of each of many different kinds.

(M8) I have often perceived both my own body and ... its environment.

(M9) I have ... also observed facts about them.

(M10) I have had expectations with regard to the future.

(M11) I have had ... beliefs.

(M12) I have thought of imaginary things.

(M13) I have had dreams.

(M14) I have had feelings of many different kinds.

Moore added that other human beings have held beliefs similar to (M1)–(M6) and have had experiences similar to those referred to in (M7)–(M14). Statements of these, he insisted, are also propositions of common sense. Generalizing, Moore says that the following single truism is also a proposition of common sense: 'Each of *us* ... has frequently *known*, with regard to *him*self or *his* body ..., everything which, in writing down my list of propositions [i.e., (M1)–(M14)], I was claiming to know about *my*self or *my* body' (Moore (1925) 1993: 109).

Two remarks about these lists are in order. First, Reid nor Moore laid any claim to completeness. Reid hints at a number of broad classes of common-sense propositions, but within each class he specifies only a couple of them. He doesn't even claim completeness for the set of broad classes in which the common-sense propositions fall. The ones that Reid mentions seem to be mentioned because of the critical potential they have in his ongoing discussions with Berkeley's immaterialism and Hume's scepticism. Moore's concern isn't completeness either but highlighting the most important points in which his philosophical position differs from positions taken up by some other philosophers; notably, absolute idealists and sceptics.

Second, now that we have before us a rather rich menu of common-sense propositions, the question arises as to what, if anything, ties this heterogeneity of propositions together so as to constitute one group – the group of common-sense propositions. It surely is not their *content*, since their contents range from propositions about epistemology and perception to mathematics, morals, and metaphysics, as well as one's individual experiences and thoughts. As such this need not be a problem: other groupings of beliefs aren't content-based either and are still useful. Think, for instance, of the a priori/a posteriori grouping, or the necessary/contingent grouping. The former is based on two different ways in which propositions can be justified, while the latter is based on two different ways in which propositions can possess the truth property.[6] But on what is the common sense/not so distinction based? That is the question I address in the next few sections. Drawing on representatives of the common-sense tradition, I point to a number of rather different features that (have been used to) delineate propositions of common sense.

NOT SCIENTIFIC

The first delineation is that propositions of common sense contrast with propositions that are adopted for scientific or scholarly reasons – namely, for reasons that require experiment, scientific investigation, or scholarly research. In order to adopt common-sense propositions, no scientific or scholarly inquiry is needed. Common-sense propositions aren't based on science or scholarship. Common-sense propositions hence contrast with such propositions as 'The earth revolves around its axis', 'Objects attract each other with a force that is directly proportional to the product of their masses and inversely proportional to the square of their centre's distances', and 'The manuscripts that Gerd Heidemann bought in 1981 were not Hitler's personal diary'.[7]

Take, for instance, the proposition that our identity stretches back at least as far as our memories do; for example, that I really lived in Indiana ten years ago (as I clearly remember having lived there). This belief isn't based on anything that merits the title 'scientific investigation'. Or take the proposition that I have thoughts: I believe this proposition but not for reasons that science has brought to my attention. Or consider the proposition that our cognitive faculties are not fallacious – that they don't, in a fundamental way, deceive us: we accept or assume this, but not on the basis of reasons that scientific research has furnished us with.[8]

Yet the propositions of common sense should not be thought of as being *isolated* from science or other practices of inquiry. Many of the propositions on Reid's list are foundational to established practices of research: (N1) to linguistics, (N2) to logic, (N3) to mathematics, (N5) to morals, etc. And Reid's epistemological propositions (C2), (C7), and (C10) are foundational to *all* practices of inquiry – to inquiry *as such*. Gustav Bergmann's remark, repeated by Susan Haack, that science is the 'long arm of common sense' can be seen as an endorsement of this idea (Bergmann 1957: 20; Haack 2007: 93–119). Science starts with propositions that aren't believed on the basis of science.

Common-sense propositions, then, are propositions that are not based on some form of inquiry. But the two classes are not co-extensive, because there are many propositions that are not based on some form of inquiry and yet don't qualify as common-sense propositions – for example, unfounded prejudices like ageism, classism, ableism, and sizeism. Hence common-sense propositions must be delineated in a further way.

WIDESPREAD

The very name 'common-sense proposition' suggests a further delineation: such propositions are 'common' or 'popular' in the sense that they are widely believed across times and places. And this is indeed a characteristic that Reid mentions: they have 'the consent of ages and nations' (Reid (1785) 2002: 464). Although Moore doesn't discuss explicitly in virtue of what a proposition is commonsensical, what he says entails that belief in such propositions is very widespread (Moore (1925) 1993: 108–9). Given what I said in the previous section, this should not be surprising, since they don't concern arcane matters that require scientific or scholarly investigation or special expertise. Rather, they are unexciting truisms, trivial platitudes, propositions mostly not worth stating explicitly: they are so plain, so obvious, so unremarkable, so wholly acceptable that disagreement about them is not to be expected outside the band of philosophers.

Still, the class of common-sense propositions is not co-extensive with the class of widely believed propositions. There are many propositions that are widely believed but surely aren't propositions of common sense. I suggest that none of the following propositions are propositions of common sense, even if they are widespread:

a. One shouldn't go fishing after it has rained.
b. The stars foretell our destinies.
c. The earth revolves around its axis.
d. The common cold is due to draft.
e. Free markets are the best way to distribute goods.
f. Democracy is a failed system.
g. Classical music isn't worth listening to.

Some of these widely believed propositions aren't propositions of common sense because they are based on scientific inquiry – (c) is a case in point. Others, like (b) and (d), are not propositions of common sense because they are held for dubious reasons. Yet others, like (e) and (f), are endorsed for reasons that face strong counterarguments. And yet others are just sheer prejudices, like (g).

For a widely believed proposition that is not based on scientific or other inquiry to be a common-sense proposition, more is needed. In the next few sections I discuss the following criteria: first, denials of them are, in some sense, incoherent; second, they are not believed on the basis of testimony; third, they are not believed on the basis of reasoning. Fourth, I shall discuss their alleged vagueness. Finally, I shall discuss the attitudes that we have vis-à-vis common-sense propositions, and I will argue that it isn't only the believing attitude that we take towards them.

DENIALS ARE PRAGMATICALLY INCOHERENT

In a number of places Reid contrasts common sense with foolishness. Or, assuming that we take the believing attitude vis-à-vis common-sense propositions, common-sense belief contrasts with foolish belief. Reid explicitly compares someone who denies a common-sense proposition to a madman, an exemplar of which would be the person who believes that his head is made of glass. Although Moore doesn't talk about foolishness, he too holds that there is something fundamentally amiss with denials of common-sense propositions. Reid and Moore have similar reasons for their verdicts: denials of common-sense propositions are, in some sense, contradictory. Let me offer some illustrations.

In order to be able to present them, I first introduce the notion of 'pragmatic incoherence'. For this we need to take note of the fact that activities, or even whole practices, have *presuppositions*. Some statement p is a presupposition of an activity provided one cannot sensibly engage in the activity and deny p: denying p is in some sense incoherent with engaging in the activity – it is 'pragmatically incoherent' to do so. The activity of playing tennis, for instance, has as one of its presuppositions the proposition that balls can be hit by rackets. What this means is that it is incoherent to play tennis and yet explicitly deny that balls can be hit by rackets – it is *pragmatically* incoherent. What Reid suggests is that the propositions of common sense are, in effect, presuppositions of practices that we are widely and ineluctably engaged in. Now consider (C4) and (M2), roughly the common-sense proposition that humans have identity over time. This is a pragmatic presupposition of the widespread

practice of making and accepting promises. For it would be pragmatically inconsistent to promise that you will come to a meeting
and yet deny that, barring fatal accidents, you will exist at future
times. Or consider (C7), roughly the common-sense proposition that
our faculties aren't systematically deceiving us and can lead us to
truths. This is a pragmatic presupposition of practices of inquiry,
including scientific inquiry. For it is inconsistent to engage in
inquiry and deny the proposition that our faculties aren't systematically deceiving us. Or, finally, consider one of the common-sense
propositions in (N5), 'That no man ought to be blamed for what it
was not in his power to hinder'. This is a presupposition of the
widespread practice of holding each other responsible for things
we do. It is pragmatically inconsistent to refrain from holding the
FBI responsible for the earth's distance to the moon and yet deny the
common-sense proposition at hand.[9]

So, there are practices that presuppose common-sense propositions. But it cannot be taken for granted that *all* presuppositions of
practices are common-sense propositions. In many practices, it is
pragmatically incoherent to deny a particular proposition while that
proposition is *not* a proposition of common sense. For instance, there
is the practice of ice-making for the purpose of ice skating. It would be
incoherent for an ice-maker to make ice through method M and yet
deny that ice can be made through M – but that ice can be made
through M is not a proposition of common sense. So the criterion
that it is pragmatically incoherent to engage in a practice and yet deny
a presupposition of the practice doesn't exclusively pick out common-
sense propositions. Still, the following observation seems true: the
more widespread a practice is, and the less optional engagement in it
is, the more the presuppositions of that practice qualify as common-
sense propositions. This way of putting things suggests that commonsensicality is a gradable property; in other words, that one proposition
can be more commonsensical than another. Later on I shall suggest
there is a further reason why commonsensicality should be thought of
as graded.

NON-TESTIMONIAL

Further delineation of common-sense propositions can be obtained when we notice that such propositions, when they are believed, are normally *not* believed on the basis of testimony. By contrast, we learn geographical, historical, and scientific facts in school or through books and the internet; we don't find them out all by ourselves. In some sense we do 'find them out', of course, but we find them out by reverting to the testimony of others – testimony that we had no reason to discard or distrust. But that is not the way we find out about the propositions of common sense. We find them out for ourselves, because they are, Reid ((1785) 2002: 453) says, 'self-evident', or 'immediately evident' – they have 'the light of truth in themselves'.[10] In matters of common sense, everyone is one's own authority; one need not defer to the authority of others, as we do when we accept the testimony of others (Reid (1785) 2002: 231). Moore surely joins in here. He doesn't believe the propositions of common sense he mentions on the basis of testimony of others. He sees for himself that they are true.

This constitutes a further delineation of common-sense propositions. For, as indicated in the previous section, many practices will have presuppositions that are *not* propositions of common sense. Many of these non-common-sense propositions will be believed or accepted on the basis of the testimony of others. One cannot engage in the medical practice of treating diabetes patients and deny that insulin beats diabetes, which means that the latter proposition is a presupposition of the practice. Yet the presupposition is, at least for most medical doctors, based on the testimony of others.

NON-INFERENTIAL

But if the propositions of common sense are normally not based on testimony nor, as suggested before, on scientific inquiry, what then are the grounds for believing or accepting them? Are they then grounded in arguments that we have in favour of them? Both Reid and Moore would emphatically deny this. As noted earlier, Reid held that they are 'self-evident', or 'immediately evident', by which he meant that they are not believed or accepted on the basis of reasoning or inference. And G. E. Moore held that any argument for common-sense propositions will proceed from premises that are less certain than the common-sense proposition that is presented as its conclusion.

However, propositions of common sense can be *conclusions* even if they are not arrived at through *inference*. Some of the common-sense propositions on Reid's and Moore's lists will be propositions that require, if one aims to ascertain them, at least *some* effort. It takes some effort, for example, to ascertain the moral propositions in (N5) and the metaphysical propositions in (N6). But the effort it takes is not the effort it takes to see or show that a conclusion follows from certain premises. Rather, the effort at hand is the effort of *reflection*. And reflection, too, can lead to conclusions. The point is that we should distinguish between conclusions of inference and conclusions of reflection, as Robert Audi (1999: 281–2) has suggested. One can come to the conclusion that Mr X is a murderer on the basis of two premises: (1) that the priest's first confessant confessed to a murder, and (2) that Mr X testified that he was the priest's first confessant.[11] One can also come to the conclusion that the sentence 'If you see her, say hello' means what it means on the basis of reflection on the meaning of the words that compose the sentence. The former is a conclusion of inference, the latter a conclusion of reflection. What I am suggesting is that at least *some* propositions of common sense will, for many people, be conclusions of reflection. For many they require reflecting on if they are to be consciously believed.

I say this is true for *many* propositions of common sense. But it isn't true for all. Moore's (M1) through (M6), for example, for many of us won't be conclusions of reflection: they are so obviously true that no reflection is required in order to believe them. Staying with the examples offered earlier on, propositions like 'That is a red rose' and

'I was in Barcelona' are also propositions of common sense, but they aren't conclusions of reflection.

But the point of this section is that common-sense propositions, when believed, aren't believed on the basis of inference.

IMPRECISE

Nicholas Rescher has suggested that common-sense propositions are characterized by their imprecision, and that the fact that they are imprecise gives them their exalted epistemic status. In making this point he refers to a principle formulated by Pierre Duhem: 'There is a sort of balance between precision and certainty: the one cannot be increased except to the detriment of the other.'[12] Compare the following pairs of propositions:

- (a1) The Eiffel Tower is 317 metres tall.
- (a2) The Eiffel Tower is taller than 300 metres.
- (b1) We must strengthen the dykes to prevent future flooding.
- (b2) We must take steps to meet this threat.

Compared to proposition (a1), proposition (a2) is less precise, less definite. This is why, says Duhem's principle, (a2) is more secure than (a1): it is harder to prove it false than (a1). Likewise, (b2) is less precise than (b1), and therefore more secure than (b1). Duhem's general principle, then, is that the less precise a proposition is, the more secure it is, and the more precise, the less secure.

Now, Rescher's claim is that the propositions of common sense are so secure *because* they are imprecise, or vague.

I agree with Duhem's principle, but I don't think that all, or even most, of the common-sense propositions listed by Reid and Moore are imprecise. Suppose we think of imprecision, or lack of definiteness, as a property of propositions: a proposition *s* is imprecise provided it is lacking in definite detail in a way that involves hedging. The following propositions are fully precise and involve no hedging: 'The melting point of lead is 327.7 degrees Celsius' and 'The Eiffel Tower is 317 metres tall'. But the following propositions *are* lacking in definite detail in a way that involves hedging: 'Most dogs bark', 'In lower-pressure areas we normally don't see clear blue skies', and 'Mary and Jane are, by and large, equally good mathematicians'. Fully precise propositions have definite refutation conditions – imprecise propositions don't.

When we look at Reid's common-sense propositions, many don't seem to be imprecise. Take (C2), for instance: 'The thoughts of which I am conscious, are the thoughts of ... *myself*'; or (C3): 'Those things did really happen which I distinctly remember'; or (C4): 'Our own personal identity and ... existence [continues] as far back as we remember anything distinctly'. Nor are (C5) through (C9) imprecise. Likewise, many of Moore's propositions aren't imprecise: for example, (M1): 'There exists at present a living human body, which is *my* body'; (M2): 'This body was born at a certain time in the past, and has existed continuously ever since'; (M3): 'It has been either in contact with or not far from the surface of the earth'; (M4): 'At every moment since [this body] was born, there have also existed many other things, having shape and size in three dimensions, from which it has been *at various distances* ... and with which it was *in contact*.'

So not all the propositions listed by Moore and Reid are 'secure *because* they are imprecise', as Rescher has it. But this is not to deny that *some* of their propositions are, to a certain extent, imprecise. For instance, (C10): 'There is a certain regard due to human testimony in matters of fact, and even to human authority in matters of opinion'; and perhaps also (C11) and (C12). Also, since Reid and Moore didn't claim completeness for their lists, it is to be expected that there are common-sense propositions that *are* imprecise, and 'secure *because* imprecise'.

However, there will also be many propositions that are 'secure because imprecise' but that are not common-sense propositions – for example, 'The Eiffel Tower is taller than 300 metres'.

So, imprecision is not a feature of each and every common-sense proposition, even though there are common-sense propositions that are imprecise.

THE DELINEATION OF COMMON SENSE: AN INTERMEDIATE CONCLUSION

The discussion so far leads to the following conclusions. First, common-sense propositions cannot be delineated on the basis of content. Second, there is not *one* feature that marks out common-sense propositions. Rather, common-sense propositions lie in the area where a number of different groupings of propositions overlap. More specifically: common-sense propositions are to be found where the following groups of propositions overlap:

- A: propositions that are not based on scientific or scholarly research.
- B: propositions that are at least potentially widely believed.
- C: propositions whose denials are pragmatically incoherent.
- D: propositions that, if believed, are normally not believed on the basis of testimony.
- E: propositions that, if believed, are not believed on the basis of inference (although they may be conclusions of reflection).

It should be clear that none of these groupings fully overlaps with any of the other groupings. The propositions of common sense, as indicated, are located where these groupings overlap.

Third, and this is a point that so far has never been noted, common sense is a matter of degree: there are *degrees* to which propositions are propositions of common sense – in other words, one proposition can be more commonsensical that another.[13] The intuitive idea here is simple enough: when a proposition belongs to groups A, B, C, D, and E alike, its degree of commonsensicality is greater than that of a proposition belonging to groups A, D, and E only. And the degree of commonsensicality of the latter is greater than that of a proposition belonging to groups A and E only. This intuitive idea cries out for further elaboration. How shall we compare the commonsensicality of two propositions when the one belongs to groups A, B, and C and the other belongs to groups A, D, and E? These matters will have to await another occasion.

PROPOSITIONAL ATTITUDES TOWARDS COMMON-SENSE PROPOSITIONS

In the discussion so far I've talked mainly of common-sense propositions as objects of *belief*. This is surely in line with Reid, who repeatedly says that belief in common-sense propositions is psychologically irresistible. And if we assume that knowledge entails belief, this is also in line with Moore, who repeatedly said that he knew the propositions on his list 'with certainty to be true' – and hence implied that he believed them.

There is reason, however, for doubting that the propositions of common sense are each and every one *believed*. In this section I will canvass a number of propositional attitudes and suggest that the attitudes we take vis-à-vis common-sense propositions can be, and in fact are, of different kinds: vis-à-vis some we take a believing attitude, but vis-à-vis others we have other attitudes.

Many epistemologists distinguish between occurrent and non-occurrent (or 'dispositional') beliefs. One occurrently believes proposition p when one currently ('as we speak') assents to p. One can also believe the very same p while one is sound asleep or has one's mind on something other than p – then one believes p non-occurrently, or dispositionally. More precisely, one non-occurrently (or dispositionally) believes p provided (i) one once occurrently believed p, and (ii) one can remember p, and (iii) ever since having occurrently believed p, one hasn't come to believe that p is false.

It is surely possible to have a believing attitude vis-à-vis the common-sense propositions meant at (C1): vis-à-vis the proposition 'The pain in my ankle exists', we have the believing attitude (when we have pain there). Vis-à-vis Moore's propositions (M1)–(M14), when each is cut to one's own case, most of us will have the believing attitude. But vis-à-vis (C4), the proposition that personal identity and continued existence stretches back as far as we remember anything distinctly, this may not be the case. *Some* people, to be sure, have considered this proposition and believed it to be true. But no doubt others have *never* entertained the proposition – it never crossed their minds; the issue just never came up. And hence they never believed it. The same will be true of other propositions on Reid's list; for example, the logical axioms and Euclid's axioms.

But there are attitudes other than belief that we can take towards propositions. Next to the belief attitude there is also what has been called 'the disposition to believe that p'. One has a disposition to believe p provided (i) one has never occurrently believed p, and (ii) if p were to be brought to one's notice, one would believe it straightaway – that is, without further argument or reasoning. For example, you have probably never had the occurrent belief that you are shorter than 13 metres and 13 centimetres. But now that this proposition is brought to your attention, you believe it straightaway. We may presume that we have a disposition to believe numerous propositions that we, in fact, will never come to believe occurrently. Having a disposition to believe p isn't, perhaps, an attitude in the strict sense of the word, since the subject has never actually entertained or apprehended p. But in a loose sense it may be called an attitude towards p because p is obviously entailed by things the subject believes.

It seems uncontroversial that many common-sense propositions are such that we have a disposition to believe them. Many of them are so trivial and platitudinous that it just doesn't pay to form explicit beliefs about them. There is often no *need* to have the believing attitude towards them, no *occasion* to form them – unless, that is, someone (a sceptic perhaps, or an immaterialist) comes along who proposes a theory that entails the *denial* of common-sense propositions. In such circumstances, the disposition to form a believing attitude towards those propositions will be triggered, and the belief will be formed straightaway.

Well, perhaps not *always* straightaway. For, as suggested earlier on, it may well be that reflection on a proposition, perhaps even protracted reflection, is needed before one can believe it. Some beliefs are conclusions of reflection. The logical axioms are obvious examples, and so are the grammatical propositions in (N1), the first principles of morals in (N5), and the metaphysical principles in (N6).

But even if one's disposition to believe a particular common-sense proposition p is never triggered, and it never became the conclusion of reflection, one can still be said to have some kind of 'pro-attitude' towards p; for there is the taking-for-granted attitude, which is yet another propositional attitude, in a loose sense. Reid repeatedly says that propositions of common sense are *taken for granted*.[14] And as Wolterstorff (2001: 225) has rightly noted, one doesn't have to believe something in order to take it for granted. We take many things for granted that we never come to actually believe, even if we have a disposition to believe them. But what exactly is it to take a proposition for granted? I suggest it is to unreflectively (unwittingly, unconsciously, or subconsciously – i.e., without attending to it) presuppose it. Since there are several notions of presupposition, we should identify the one, or ones, involved in the taking-for-granted attitude.

First, proposition p presupposes q when the following is the case: if q is false, then p is false as well. For instance, 'John won the match' presupposes 'Somebody won the match', because if the latter statement is false, then so is the former. I call a presupposition of this sort a *propositional presupposition*. Propositions of common sense are not presuppositions in this sense. The proposition 'There is a computer in front of me' does *not* presuppose, for instance, (C5), which says that what we distinctly perceive really exists: even if the latter is false, the former may still be true.

This suggests another notion of presupposition: p presupposes q when the following is the case: if q is false, then one's belief in p will no longer be justified or warranted. My belief in the proposition 'There is a computer in front of me' *does* presuppose in this sense (C5). For the falsity of 'Those things do really exist which we distinctly perceive by our senses' would undermine my belief that there is a computer in front of me. I call a presupposition of this kind a *justification-conferring presupposition*. Reid's epistemological propositions (C1)–(C10) are, for many things we believe, presuppositions of just this kind. Some of Moore's propositions are also of this kind; for example, (M6): 'The earth has existed ... for many years before my [i.e., Moore's] body was born' is a presupposition in this sense of Moore's belief that the Battle of Hastings took place in 1066. For the latter belief would be undermined if (M6) were false. But we should not assume that *all* common-sense propositions are presuppositions of this kind.

We have already come across a third and final notion of presupposition: *pragmatic presuppositions*. A proposition *p* is a presupposition of a practice provided one cannot sensibly engage in the practice and deny *p*. I suggested earlier that many common-sense propositions are pragmatic presuppositions of practices. (C4), for example, is a pragmatic presupposition of the practice of promising; and (C7), the proposition that our faculties are not fallacious, is a pragmatic presupposition of practices of inquiry. No doubt some people *believe* (C4) and (C7). Others who don't, however, take them for granted in the sense that they presuppose (C4) and (C7): they are either pragmatic or justification-conferring presuppositions (or both).

What I have been arguing in this section can be summarized as follows. According to common-sense philosophers, humans have 'pro-attitudes' vis-à-vis common-sense propositions. But we don't all have the attitude of *belief* towards them; rather, we have attitudes from a *range* of pro-attitudes vis-à-vis common-sense propositions: we believe them, or we have a disposition to believe them, or we take them for granted in the sense that we presuppose them, either as pragmatic or as justification-conferring presuppositions.

SUMMARY

I have, thus, argued for the following points:

1. There is no *content* that groups the propositions of common sense together.

2. The common-sense grouping has a real purpose: it delineates propositions that we are at a very minimum justified in believing.

3. Common-sense propositions are to be found where the following groups of propositions overlap:

- A: propositions that are not based on scientific or scholarly research.
- B: propositions that are at least potentially widely believed.
- C: propositions whose denials are pragmatically incoherent.
- D: propositions that, if believed, are normally not believed on the basis of testimony.
- E: propositions that, if believed, are not believed on the basis of inference (although they may be conclusions of reflection).

4. This suggests a point that, I claimed, so far has never been noted, namely, that commonsensicality is a graded concept: there are *degrees* in which propositions are propositions of common sense.

5. Propositions of common sense are objects of at least one of the following attitudes: belief, disposition to believe, or taking for granted in the sense of presupposing them, either as a justification-conferring presupposition or as a pragmatic presupposition.

6. To complete the picture, it should be added that, although we *can* give up common-sense propositions, common-sense philosophers hold that we should only do so in the face of very weighty evidence. Whether or not science has given us such weighty reasons is a matter of intense debate (see Peels et al. 2020).

NOTES

1 The epistemic status of common-sense beliefs is discussed in Chapters 10 and 12 in this volume.

2 Reid's extensive discussion of first principles is in *Essays on the Intellectual Powers of Man* ((1785) 2002: 452–512).

3 As Van Cleve (2015: 304–7) has pointed out, (C1) is ambiguous. If we abbreviate 'conscious of *p*' as C*p*, it can mean (1) it is a first principle that,

for each p, $Cp{\rightarrow}p$, but also (2) for each p, $Cp{\rightarrow}$it is a first principle that p. I take it that Reid meant to endorse both (1) and (2).

4 I take it that (C4) has both an epistemological and a metaphysical side. The epistemological side is that it states or implies that memory is evidence of one's past existence; the metaphysical side is that one's past existence is *not constituted* by one's memories.

5 Van Woudenberg (2014a) is a discussion of the last of these principles.

6 For more on this, see Van Woudenberg (2014b).

7 I thus part ways with the suggestion that the proposition that the earth revolves around the sun has, by now, become a common-sense proposition.

8 Alston (1993) has argued that every argument for the conclusion that our basic belief-forming faculties are reliable is infected by what he calls epistemic circularity.

9 Moore too argued that the denial of common-sense propositions is contradictory – but he did not argue that it is *pragmatically* contradictory. Rather, he argued that it is *self*-contradictory (Moore (1925) 1993: 116–19).

10 Alston (1985) has argued that Reid used 'self-evident' in a capacious way, as encompassing both 'directly evident' and 'self-evident' in a narrower sense (i.e., the sense that understanding the words that express a proposition is sufficient for seeing that the proposition is true).

11 This example is due to A. C. Ewing.

12 Rescher (2005: 124). The quotation is taken from Duhem (1982: 179).

13 For how to think about degrees, see Van Woudenberg and Peels (2018).

14 'If there are certain principles ... which the constitution of our nature leads us to believe, and which we are under a necessity to take for granted in the common concerns of life, without being able to give a reason for them; these are what we call the principles of common sense' (Reid (1764) 1997: 33).

8   Common Sense in Metaphysics

Joanna Lawson

Metaphysics is rife with theories about the way the world really is that seem to fly in the face of common sense.[1] Theories like mereological nihilism, according to which there are, in reality, no tables (see van Inwagen 1990; Merricks 2001). Theories like panpsychism, according to which all fundamental particles are, in reality, endowed with minds (Goff et al. 2017). Theories like modal realism, according to which there are, in reality, a plethora of concrete possible worlds, as vast as, but completely isolated from, our own (Lewis 1986). It is tempting to respond with what David Lewis calls an 'incredulous stare' (Lewis 1986: 133). After all, such theories seem completely ridiculous, completely at odds with everything we typically take ourselves to know about the world.

Lewis himself acknowledges that 'my denial of common sense is severe, and I think it is entirely right and proper to count that as a serious cost' (Lewis 1986: 135). But why is denying common sense a cost? Why think that the world as it really is accords with how we take it to be in everyday life? What is the appropriate role for common sense in metaphysics?

In this chapter I argue that common sense ought to play an important, though defeasible, role in metaphysical theorizing. This claim, however, cannot be justified in a vacuum. Rather, in order to discern the appropriate role of common sense in metaphysics one must take for granted some particular metametaphysical stance. What one believes one is doing when one engages in metaphysics will determine whether (and if so, how much) one can and should rely on common sense in practising metaphysics.

In the first section, I explain what I mean by 'common sense'. Next I discuss the contexts in which we can justifiedly use common sense to guide our theorizing about fundamental reality. I maintain that reliance on common sense in metaphysics cannot be evaluated on its own, but only in the context of a particular understanding of metaphysics. In the third section I articulate the appropriate role of common sense in metaphysics for a particular metaphysical approach: metaphysics as modelling. In most cases the role of common sense in metaphysical theorizing will be importantly limited for the proponent of metaphysics as modelling. However, in some important cases, such as the investigation of the metaphysical structure of socially constructed entities, common sense will play a much more expansive role.

COMMON SENSE AND THE MANIFEST IMAGE

In this chapter, when I say that a metaphysical theory is commonsensical (or not), what I mean is that the theory in question matches up with the way things seem to be. It seems that there are tables and chairs. It seems that we causally affect the world. It seems that time passes. The sum total of these seemings amounts to the *manifest image* of reality.

The manifest image is to be contrasted with the scientific image.[2] Our best scientific theories describe the world at a scientific level. The scientific image includes oxygen, weak and strong forces, protons, cells, DNA, and the like. In our everyday lives, however, we don't interact with protons and DNA, at least not as such. We interact with co-workers, books, and breakfast. The level of co-workers, books, and breakfast is the level of the manifest image. Scientifically, the colour blue has to do with the refraction of a particular range of wavelengths of light. Manifestly, *blueness* has to do with a particularly coloured phenomenal quality – that is, with the colour as it appears in our ordinary experience. The commonsensical manifest image just is the world of ordinary experience.

I take common sense, understood as the manifest image, to be *quasi-perceptual* in nature. Things appear to us to be one way or another as we make ordinary judgments about the world of experience, as if we were simply perceiving them to be this way. And just as perceptual data are open to a certain amount of interpretation (is that a monster coming down the hill outside, or is it a fly on the windowpane?), so ordinary experience is open to a certain amount of interpretation (does time *really* seem to be A-Theoretic?). What seems to be the case is, in some instances, up for debate.

Furthermore, the manifest image, much like perception, is rooted in sensory experience. We come to the manifest image through what we see, touch, hear, smell, and taste. Raw sense-data are not all that is contained in the manifest image, however. Just as according to some views perception is richly contentful, I maintain that ordinary experience is laden with rich content. By this I mean that the manifest image presents us with more than just unprocessed sensory data.[3] When we experience the world we do experience raw seemings consisting of colours, shapes, feels, smells, etc. But most of what we experience is not raw in this way. Perhaps upon first waking, one blinks open one's eyes to see a brightly coloured, fluttering shape. After a few more blinks, the shape resolves itself into the image of a cardinal pecking at the birdfeeder outside the window. What we see, most of the time, is *the cardinal*, not just a brightly coloured fluttering shape. The world of ordinary experience is so readily intelligible to us because it is organized into conceptually accessible contentful chunks.[4]

The manifest image, then, is a quasi-perceptual, sensorily informed, richly contentful presentation of the everyday world of persons and objects. It is how the world appears to us, situated as we are in time and space, and equipped as we are with sensory capabilities and conceptual frameworks.

Understanding common sense as the manifest image presented to us in ordinary experience is helpful for understanding the constraints on what can appropriately be classified as 'common sense'. Not just anything a particular metaphysician finds intuitive ought to be included in the category. Rather, empirical data can and should constrain what we take to be part of the content of the manifest image.

These empirical data can come in many forms. Perhaps there are linguistic data which lead us to conclude that a supposedly commonsensical position is only attractive to people repeatedly exposed to a historically contingent metaphorical turn of phrase. Here we can assume that the right-soundingness of the position in question is due to the ubiquity of the metaphor, and not to the fact that the manifest image supports it.

Additionally, metaphysicians can benefit from the evidence provided by cognitive science. While armchair theorizing can be useful, a single philosopher's opinion can only go so far. By testing subjects' responses to perceptual stimuli it is possible to discern what appears (and what does not appear) to be the case to them.[5] This allows us to distinguish between the manifest image, considered as such, and mere intuition. Intuitions vary from person to person. The manifest image, on the other hand, is robust across individuals.[6]

I should emphasize that this does not mean that we should make use of science to revise the contents of common sense. Science cannot tell us that we ought to find dark matter commonsensical, even if it can tell us that we ought to believe there is such a thing. What I am suggesting instead is that it is not always obvious from mere reflection which plausible-sounding things are in fact part of common sense, construed as I have described it above. Cognitive science can help us understand what exactly is presented to us in experience, and what is not.

Finally, although the manifest image is content-laden, we should be careful not to pretend that it takes a stance on more metaphysical issues than it in fact does. That is, we should be careful not to unnecessarily foist a metaphysical theory on an experience which is in fact philosophically neutral. Perhaps it does seem (for instance) that time passes, but maybe this apparent 'passage' supports no metaphysical theory of time over any other.[7] This sort of care is needed in assessing cognitive science research just as much as in evaluating metaphysical arguments. It is possible to bake metaphysical assumptions into the scientific data, and so draw unwarranted conclusions from them. We should be careful to make arguments connecting the dots between what is presented to us in experience and the metaphysical question at hand. It is not feasible to assume without argument that the manifest image always takes a stand in a metaphysical debate.

So, when properly understood, common sense is not just mere intuition – our understanding of it is subject to correction, not least by empirical data. What sort of role common sense plays, however, will depend on what sort of thing one takes metaphysics to be.

METAMETAPHYSICS: JUSTIFYING THE USE OF COMMON SENSE IN METAPHYSICS

In the literature on common sense, it is often assumed that we ought to evaluate the evidential weight of common sense on its own.[8] However, the appropriate place of common sense in metaphysics depends not only on common sense, but on metaphysics itself. What are we doing when we do metaphysics? One's antecedent presuppositions about the nature of metaphysics as an enterprise are essential for determining the appropriate role of common sense in metaphysics. We cannot evaluate the viability of using common sense as a guide to metaphysics without knowing what metaphysics is attempting to do.

Taking even a cursory glance at the variety of stances towards common sense in metaphysics reveals the impact of one's metametaphysical approach. Take, for instance, deflationist ontologists of a Carnapian stripe, such as Amie Thomasson (2015). Thomasson maintains that ontological questions have 'easy answers'. All we have to do to find out whether tables exist is to look out into the world and see if there is anything that meets the application conditions for the term 'table'. Any competent language speaker, then, will be able to answer existence questions. This is because competent speakers know what terms mean and know how to make use of their access to the manifest image (common sense) to see if there are any (say) tables, or cardinals. So for the deflationist, common sense will play an enormous role. Aside from some technical scientific terms, common sense will be the deciding factor in the majority of existence questions.[9]

On the other end of the spectrum are extreme rationalist metaphysicians, who start with one or more general principles as epistemic starting points. The most extreme of them give common sense no weight at all. The job of metaphysicians is to cast aside intuitions and common-sense beliefs and 'train their gaze on reality itself' (Della Rocca 2013: 185). If we take common sense seriously as a guide to reality, we will be constrained to conservative metaphysical systems – systems that may have very little similarity to reality as it is in itself. We should take the manifest image into consideration in our metaphysical theorizing only if we can provide some reason to think that the manifest image is likely to get things right.

It is not my aim here to argue for or against any metametaphysical stance. I wish to point out that the use of common sense in metaphysics is vindicated only within the framework of a particular metametaphysical approach. Common sense is, among other things, a tool for the metaphysician. Whether it is the right tool for the job depends on what job the metaphysician wants to do. If the project is a deflationist one, then common sense will be indispensable. An extreme rationalist project, however, will require much more robust tools than common sense to accomplish its heavy-duty aims. It is in this way that a particular understanding of what metaphysics is and what it aims to do will impact how reasonable it is to rely on common sense.

In what remains of this section, I situate my own approach to common sense against the background of a particular metametaphysical stance: metaphysics as modelling. According to this approach, common sense serves as a defeasible theoretical virtue and a starting point for metaphysical theorizing.

Metaphysics as Modelling

According to a metaphysics-as-modelling approach, metaphysics is continuous with the sciences.[10] The subject matter under investigation differs, but the methods employed by the two disciplines are similar. In general, the questions that interest metaphysicians tend to be more general than, more fundamental than, and metaphysically antecedent to, the questions that are under the purview of science. For instance, evolutionary biologists may look at what causes the proliferation of certain biological features, while a metaphysician will be interested in the nature of causation itself.

The methods employed by metaphysicians and scientists in answering the questions they investigate, however, have some fundamental similarities. Both metaphysicians and scientists construct theories about ways the world might be. Both metaphysicians and scientists conduct experiments in order to test their theories. Scientists do this in the lab. Metaphysicians, too, are constrained by empirical adequacy. If their theories conflict with scientific research, they must be abandoned. But metaphysicians also work with thought experiments. These experiments are not conducted in a laboratory (or at least, they needn't be), but they can nevertheless be an important part of the process of determining which theories stand up to scrutiny, and which do not.

It is useful to conceive of this theory-building as *model construction*. A theoretician, in considering a particular way the world might be, builds (usually figuratively) a model of it, in order to demonstrate how such a situation would work. Models are fictions which free us to tinker with constraints however we would like. They allow room to idealize and to generalize in ways that can be revelatory even if the metaphysician or scientist doesn't for a second think they are accurate. In statistical mechanics, particles are not really massless, perfectly elastic points, but it can be helpful to consider them as such in order to construct a model. In metaphysics, thought experiments are helpful for smoothing over or abstracting away from messy real-life complications.

A metaphysical theory is a model or class of models that purports to be isomorphic with the real world in some way. The class of models according to which causation boils down to counterfactuals contains one model in which JFK would not have died if Lee Harvey Oswald had not shot him, another in which JFK would not have died if the FBI had not shot him. Both, notice, represent the causation in terms of counterfactuals, although the theory remains agnostic about who in fact did the shooting.

Both scientists and metaphysicians evaluate empirically adequate theories on the basis of theoretical virtues. A good theory does well with regard to virtues such as simplicity, fruitfulness, elegance, parsimony, and explanatory power. The exact list and weighting of virtues is up for debate, in both metaphysics and science.

The job of metaphysics, according to a metaphysics-as-modelling perspective, is to generate models of the way things might be. These models might be simplified or idealized in various ways. They may purport to represent some feature of the real world, or they may serve instead to demonstrate some hypothetical or logical point. Classes of models representing metaphysical theories are evaluated on the basis of empirical adequacy, as well as how well they exemplify various theoretical virtues.

Common Sense and Metaphysical Modelling

There are at least four reasons to think that common sense will play an integral role in metaphysics for the proponent of metaphysics as modelling. First, common sense plays a significant role in current scientific practice. Second, it provides data that any metaphysical model must account for to achieve empirical adequacy. Third, it serves as a base model fortified by theoretical inertia. Finally, alignment with the manifest image is itself a theoretical virtue that metaphysical models can exhibit to a greater or lesser extent. As such, alignment with the common-sense picture of the world is one of the things that metaphysicians (especially those interested in metaphysics as modelling) should strive to maximize when choosing a model.

An initial reason for thinking that common sense will be both important and defeasible on a metaphysics-as-modelling framework is that common sense plays such a role in science.[11] Nina Emery (2017) points out that there is a 'minimal-divergence norm' at work in the sciences. The norm is as follows:

> Insofar as you have two or more candidate theories, all of which are empirically and explanatorily adequate, you ought to choose the theory that diverges least from the manifest image.

This particular norm may seem scientifically controversial at first glance. Is it really a norm in scientific circles to prefer theories that cohere with the manifest image? However, as Emery points out, something like the minimal-divergence norm is the only thing that can explain certain features of scientific practice; namely, it explains why scientific practice rejects so-called sceptical hypotheses, including brain-in-vat, Boltzmann-brain, and Bostrom-simulation cases.[12] The best, and perhaps the only, reason to rule out these hypotheses is something like the minimal-divergence norm. So, given that these sceptical scenarios are largely ignored by the scientific community, such a norm must be in play.

This is a defeasible reason to think that something similar might be appropriate in the metaphysical sphere. Metaphysics, according to a metaphysics-as-modelling view, is continuous with science. If science is open to rejecting common sense while nevertheless deferring to it in many cases, then something similar might be right for metaphysics as well.

Second, the manifest image serves as an evidential starting point. An internally coherent model that has any hope of accurately representing the world we inhabit must make sense of the fact that we have the common-sense picture that we do. One way to do this is to maintain that reality itself resembles (or is isomorphic with) our common-sense picture of it. Another way to discharge the explanatory burden is to provide an error theory explaining why the manifest image is at odds with the reality. So at the very least, the metaphysician must engage with common sense in order to explain how it comes to be that we have the common-sense beliefs that we do. The manifest image serves as data that any empirically adequate theory must account for.

Third, common sense serves as a theoretical starting point. The manifest image provides us with a sort of ready-made starter model of the world. This model includes objects like cars and tables; it includes persons who have minds replete with experiences, beliefs, and intentions. The model is fairly coarse-grained: there are things it doesn't take a stance on, categories that are vague, and phenomena that need fleshing out in order to be made obviously consistent.

Just because common sense is a starting point doesn't mean that we must (or even should) end up there. But starting points do matter. Descartes insisted on starting with only his thoughts and ideas, and it is a wonder that he made it out of his head. Where you start will partially determine where you go. Furthermore, starting points matter because of what I call *theoretical inertia*. Theoretical inertia maintains that one ought not to abandon a theory without sufficient reason. This is not a particularly radical principle. Consider a sister-view: doxastic inertia.

> *Doxastic inertia*: it is irrational to change your doxastic attitudes without sufficient reason to do so.

Doxastic inertia is something of a truism. It is irrational, for instance, to go from believing p to believing not-p without having sufficient reason to make the switch. What counts as 'sufficient' will differ according to one's theory of best epistemic practice.[13] But the general principle is the same. And it certainly means that one should be steadfast in one's beliefs if there is no reason at all to change one's mind.

The following is a corresponding theoretical principle:

> *Theoretical inertia*: one ought not to adopt a new theory without sufficient reason to do so.

Theoretical inertia doesn't mean that one can never adopt a new theory. It does mean that, when considering alternative metaphysical models, a new model must be sufficiently attractive to lure us away from the old, 'default' model.[14] This principle holds as much for the sciences as for metaphysics. We would never have abandoned Newtonian physics unless Einstein (and others) provided us with good reason to do so. The same holds in metaphysics: if it ain't broke, don't fix it.

'Sufficient reason' to adopt a new metaphysical theory is cashed out, on a metaphysics-as-modelling view, in terms of theoretical virtue. A theory that runs counter to common sense must not only be empirically adequate but also offer a better combination of explanatory power, simplicity, elegance, theoretical fruitfulness, etc., than the manifest image offers. From a metaphysics-as-modelling perspective, it is completely respectable practice to generate models willy-nilly, just to explore unreached corners of logical space. But when it comes to actually adopting one of these theories as best, it is important to be choosy.

Common sense does not merely serve as an epistemic and theoretical starting point, however important these considerations might be. My fourth and final contention in this section is that accordance with common sense is something to strive for in its own right. This is because alignment with common sense is itself a theoretical virtue, alongside explanatory power, simplicity, fruitfulness, etc. A model which maintains that the manifest image of the world is largely right about the nature of reality is more virtuous along this dimension than a model which, although equally empirically and explanatorily adequate, maintains that the manifest image is largely misleading.

There are both epistemic and non-epistemic reasons to think that accordance with common sense (carefully depicted, with the help of empirical research) is a significant theoretical virtue. First the epistemic reasons: according with common sense may mean that a theory is more likely to be true.

The world of everyday experience is the world of action. The manifest image is our interface with the world; it enables us to act and interact effectively. Common sense is, therefore, incredibly *useful*. We need to ask why it is that common sense is so pragmatically efficacious. One plausible explanation of this fact is that the manifest image is truth-tracking, at least to a significant extent. We can draw an inference to the best explanation here. The reason that the manifest image is as useful in our everyday lives as it is, has to do with the fact that it latches on to reality.[15]

So there is reason to think that metaphysical models that accord with common sense are more likely to be true than those that do not. It is worth pointing out, however, that many time-honoured theoretical virtues do not have this feature. It is notoriously difficult to give any good reason for thinking that the simplicity of a theory (for instance, although this goes for parsimony, elegance, and fertility as well) is a good indicator of its truth (see Foley 1993). Nevertheless, the proponent of metaphysics as modelling has no trouble accepting simplicity as theoretically virtuous. So even if we think that convergence with the manifest image does not provide evidence of truth, we might still count such convergence as a virtue of the theory. This is especially the case if there are other, non-epistemic reasons to accept it as a theoretical virtue. And there are such reasons. Here are two.

First, it is easier to maintain consistent beliefs when one's preferred metaphysical model is commonsensical. This is because abandoning the common-sense picture of the world is difficult. Moore even maintains that:

> [A]ll philosophers, without exception, have agreed with me in holding [common-sense beliefs]: and that the real difference, which is commonly expressed this way, is only a difference between those philosophers, who have *also* held views inconsistent with these features in 'the Common Sense view of the world', and those who have not. (Moore (1925) 1993: 118–19)

The difficulty of giving up common sense may not provide evidence that common sense is right. But we may value, and wish to promote, intellectual consistency, independently of its truth-conduciveness. If we do, then common sense is something to be taken into account in our theorizing.

Furthermore, a metaphysical theory's being consistent with common sense might be advantageous because it allows for more robust interdisciplinary interactions. The manifest image can serve as a crucial point of connection, the nexus between different disciplines' ways of getting at reality. The way a neuroscientist understands the mind is very different from the way a psychologist understands the mind, which in turn is very different from the way a metaphysician understands the mind. But collaborations are nevertheless possible. They are possible in part because of the shared language of the manifest image. The neuroscientist, the psychologist, and the metaphysician are all (in common-sense terms) trying to figure out how people think, and what thought (as an umbrella term for conscious mental life) is. If the metaphysician departs too radically from common sense, she can undermine her ability to interact meaningfully with those outside her own field. So to the extent that one believes interdisciplinary collaboration and interaction are good things, common sense will be desirable in metaphysical theorizing.

By appealing to a particular metametaphysical stance – metaphysics as modelling – we can vindicate the important-but-defeasible role of common sense in metaphysics. The manifest image is important insofar as it is valued in the sciences (an enterprise continuous with metaphysics), and insofar as it provides epistemic and theoretical starting points for theorizing. Finally, the proponent of metaphysics as modelling has good epistemic and non-epistemic reasons to count alignment with common sense as a theoretical virtue when evaluating metaphysical models.

METAPHYSICS: COMMON SENSE, CONCEPTUAL ANALYSIS, AND SUBJECT MATTER

We have seen that, for the proponent of metaphysics as modelling, common sense plays an important role in the metaphysical process. But what exactly this looks like in practice requires more fleshing out. In this section, I first explore uses of common sense in combination with conceptual analysis. Second, I highlight the sensitivity of common sense's role to subject matter by considering the example of socially constructed entities.

Common sense is, first, a key resource in the metaphysically important process of conceptual analysis. For my purposes, conceptual analysis consists in the exploration of the features of our ordinary concepts, whatever these features might be.[16] Interesting features of concepts are discoverable through an appeal to the manifest image, or common sense. As was previously noted, concept deployment is a near-constant feature of everyday experience. That, there, is a cardinal; this is a book; *that* was an annoying thing to say. We are able to access facts about our concepts by appealing to common-sense uses of these concepts.

The metaphysician can use both the manifest image itself and her grasp of ordinary concepts strengthened by conceptual analysis to gain insight into the nature of reality. In what follows, I refer to the host of information contained in the manifest image as well as the conceptual schemes revealed through conceptual analysis as our 'ideas and concepts'. This should not mislead the reader, however. It is not just any ideas that are at issue here, but the common-sense ideas of everyday experience presented to us in the manifest image.

First, in order to have the ideas and concepts we have, there are perhaps necessary conditions on the nature of reality itself. What, in other words, are the metaphysical requirements for producing the sorts of concepts and ideas that we find ourselves with? Second, both common sense and our conceptual frameworks are useful for finding out what the world would have to be like in order to correspond to the manifest image. That is, what metaphysical features would the world need to have in order to align with our ideas and concepts? Third, we can make inferences to the best explanation about the origins of both our concepts and the manifest image, which may shed light on the nature of reality. How did these particular concepts and ideas arise?

Arguments that make use of our concepts and ideas in the first way are known as *transcendental arguments*. Such arguments start with the nature of our conceptual frameworks or a feature of the manifest image, and conclude with something that must be true about the nature of reality. In terms of modelling, it is an argument to the effect that all metaphysical models containing some common-sense feature X will also share some metaphysical feature Y. This would be one way of construing the *cogito*: Descartes's recognition that he thinks, that he has any concepts at all, leads him to conclude that he must exist.

Second, by figuring out what our ideas and conceptual structures are, we can take steps towards figuring out what the world would have to be like *if* they were 'carving at the joints'. Burge (1995) does something similar when he concludes that if we are critical reasoners (in the way that it seems we are), then it must be the case that we have privileged knowledge of the contents of our own minds. Or take an alternative example: perhaps by getting a better understanding of the way that time appears to pass, we can determine what the nature of reality would have to be like if this seeming were veridical.

Finally, by understanding the particular features of our ideas and concepts we can make inferences about the genesis of such concepts. Once we know the ins and outs of our concepts of, say, right and wrong, we can with greater accuracy determine whether the source of these concepts is some non-natural moral reality, or whether it is more likely to be a by-product of natural selection (Street 2006). Or perhaps the best explanation of the fact that time seems to pass is an irreducible directionality in the fabric of space-time. Our concepts and ideas are as they are for some reason or other. If the best explanation of a given concept is a particular metaphysical feature of the world, then we have some reason to posit such a feature.

The use of common sense as an aid in conceptual analysis and as providing resources for transcendental and conditional theorizing can therefore be very fruitful. But I must append several asterisks to this optimistic description. Despite its many uses, common sense is not indefeasible. I noted in the previous section that theoretical reasons may lead the careful metaphysician to abandon common sense, in spite of theoretical inertia.

Additionally, there may be good scientific reasons to depart from the manifest image. Perhaps the common-sense picture is inconsistent with our best scientific theories.[17] Or the evidence provided by the cognitive sciences might provide reasons for diverging from common sense. If it were demonstrated that a particular feature of the manifest image was a mere spandrel of our cognitive processes, this would significantly undercut the evidence of common sense (Paul 2016). Positing further features of the metaphysical landscape may well be superfluous if the features of experience in question are explicable in terms of a cognitive fluke. We may want to conclude, in light of such information, that some features of common sense are not themselves part of mind-independent reality, but a mere appearance caused by physiological or neurological processes.

Even given these caveats, there will still be a role for common sense in metaphysical theorizing. Not all appearances, presumably, are the mere result of evolutionary spandrels. As we come to understand our cognitive processes and our common-sense concepts better, it will become clearer which features of common sense we can rely on.

Common sense therefore plays a significant, although importantly limited, role in the metaphysical investigation of most subject matters. But for some subject matters of metaphysical investigation, a more expansive role for common sense is warranted. I conclude with an example of one such subject matter: socially constructed entities. By taking an in-depth look at a particular case, it becomes clear that the usefulness of common sense in metaphysics depends in part on what we are theorizing about.

Socially Constructed Entities

The manifest image contains things like women, lawyers, and money. Like cardinals, tables, and chairs, they are perceived (or quasi-perceived) features of our everyday existence. They are part of the manifest image. They are, additionally, social constructs. That is, they exist in part because of our social practices, conventions, and beliefs. Our thoughts shape (and are shaped by) our behaviours and practices, which in turn result in the construction of social entities. For the present purposes it doesn't matter exactly how this happens.[18] What does matter is that these social entities are particularly dependent on how we understand and treat them.

Because of this special relationship between minds and social constructs, common sense plays a more robust role in the metaphysical investigation of such entities. For many objects of study, we can hope that our common-sense beliefs are caused by, and so perhaps are likely to be approximately true of, the things the beliefs are about. When it comes to social constructs, however, the direction of fit goes the other way around. It is partly because we have the beliefs we do that the things themselves have the features that they do.[19]

All the typical uses of common sense apply to social constructs. We can use common sense as an evidential and theoretical starting point, make inferences to the best explanation of common sense, and use it to aid in conceptual analysis. However, there are some additional ways that common sense can help in understanding social constructs. Common sense is one of the things that makes socially constructed entities have the metaphysical features that they do. A widespread belief about, or practice involving, a social construct impacts what the construct is. It is therefore crucial for understanding such entities that we understand common-sense views of them.

Furthermore, some of the caveats and difficulties that applied to using common sense as a tool for understanding mind-independent entities don't apply here. The genesis of common-sense beliefs isn't relevant, for instance. Normally, finding out that some feature of the manifest image is a mere by-product of cognitive processing would undercut the evidence provided by common sense. For socially constructed entities, however, this doesn't matter in the same way. Maybe the male/female gender binary is a cognitive fluke, or a historical fluke, or maybe it is a product of evolutionary pressures to reproduce. It might be interesting to find out which, but it won't change the fact that gender, as it is constructed in contemporary Western society, *is* binary.[20]

This doesn't mean that metaphysical investigation of socially constructed entities is easy. As always, it is important to be careful that what we ascribe to common sense really is commonsensical. What seems obvious to one person may strike another as completely unintuitive. And especially when dealing with social constructs, this is of great significance. We *collectively* determine the existence and nature of social constructs. So an unshared intuition won't tell us much about the nature of reality, even for social constructs.

Furthermore, although collective attitudes impact the nature of social constructs, they aren't identical to the nature of social constructs. We can't read what gender is off of our collective attitudes towards gender. For one thing, our attitudes may be self-contradictory, or even incoherent. For another, it may not be obvious what our collective practices and beliefs, taken together, amount to. Marilyn Frye (1983) points out that door-opening rituals (in which gallant men insist on opening doors so that women may walk through unhindered) may be attributed to and consciously understood as an act of deference and subservience. However, taken together with a host of accompanying practices (including practices surrounding social education, physical activities, household labour, etc.) this practice may well take on a different character than it did considered in isolation.

Much philosophical work is therefore needed to figure out what exactly it is that we have constructed. And common sense will be a key resource in the process of completing this work. How we see socially constructed entities impacts what these entities are. It is important to recognize why this is. Socially constructed entities are *mind dependent.* Their metaphysical structure is dependent on us, on our behaviours and our psychology. So it perhaps should not be so surprising that common sense, a core feature of our understanding of the world, plays enough of a role in how we think and behave to impact these entities' metaphysical structure.

Social constructs are not the only mind-dependent entities. There are also experiences, motivations, beliefs, intentions, thoughts, and emotions, to name just a few. All of these things are philosophically interesting topics worthy of metaphysical investigation. Of course, social construction is a particularly clear-cut case. It is an open question whether and to what extent other mind-dependent entities are impacted by common sense. Nevertheless, the case of social constructs demonstrates that a one-size-fits-all approach is inappropriate. Especially for mind-dependent entities, we ought to carefully consider the nature of the entity at hand to determine how tentative we should be in making use of common sense. We shouldn't needlessly handicap ourselves in our investigations – metaphysics is hard enough as it is.

CONCLUSION

In order to determine the appropriate role of common sense in metaphysics, metametaphysics is indispensable. Without some particular stance on what metaphysics is, you cannot determine the appropriate place of common sense in metaphysical theorizing.

Against a background of metaphysics as modelling, common sense is an important, though defeasible, tool for the metaphysician. It serves as both an epistemic and a theoretical starting point. Furthermore, accordance with common sense is itself a theoretical virtue to be weighed against others, like simplicity, parsimony, and elegance.

In practice, common sense is often coupled with evidence provided by our conceptual frameworks. In order to determine the structure of these frameworks, common sense plays a key role in the process of conceptual analysis. By attending to our common-sense ideas and our conceptual frameworks, metaphysicians can construct transcendental arguments, appeal to interesting sets of conditional models, and make inferences to the best explanation of these ideas and concepts.

Most of the time, common sense must be handled with care. Our best scientific theories sometimes undercut the evidence provided by common sense. However, there are contexts in which we can safely disregard the warning label. In the case of socially constructed entities, for instance, common sense ought to play a more expansive role in descriptive metaphysics than it does elsewhere. This lesson may generalize to other domains of study, including various dimensions of the metaphysics of experience or the mind–world connection.

NOTES

1 I am grateful to the editors of this volume, as well as to Chris Blake-Turner, Bill Lycan, and Laurie Paul, for reading drafts, discussing ideas, and improving this chapter in other ways. Thanks also to the UNC Chapel Hill Works in Progress group for helping me think through this chapter at its earliest stages.

2 See Sellars (1962). The view I propose here is Sellarsian in spirit, though I don't aim to match Sellars's view in all its particularities. For a nuanced perspective on Sellars, see deVries (2016).

3 I take my understanding of rich content from Siegel (2010). My taking the manifest image to be richly contentful, however, does not commit me to a view about the contents of perception. It may be, as Siegel maintains, that rich content enters at the level of perception. Alternatively, it may be that perception is minimally contentful, and that the richness only enters the picture later, after being supplemented with conceptual resources.

4 I have left vague what exactly, beyond raw sensory data, is included in the manifest image. I find it plausible that our conceptual resources shape and constrain what is presented to us in experience. This, however, leaves plenty of room for debate about particulars. Does the manifest image take a stand on abstracta? On moral properties? On modal properties? This is a complex philosophical issue, and one there is not scope to delve into here.

5 For more on this, see Paul (2010).

6 At least for those individuals with comparable conceptual frameworks. The manifest image will be somewhat malleable when it comes to significant perceptually relevant conceptual alterations. For instance, a pre-literate child may see written language as mere squiggles or shapes, whereas a literate adult, by contrast, will see the words *as* words. Given that the manifest image is richly contentful, this conceptual difference may be enough to alter what is experienced.

7 See Deng (2013). Also relevant here are four-dimensionalist responses to the 'no change' objection (Sider 2001: 212–16; Sattig 2006: 108–9).

8 For some influential examples, see Reid ((1764) 1983); Moore ((1925) 1993); Ayer (1969); and Lycan (2001).

9 For an in-depth exploration of Thomasson's deflationism and its relationship to common sense, see Chapter 13 by Ranalli and De Ridder in this volume.

10 My characterization of metaphysics as modelling is drawn from Paul (2012).

11 For further defence of this, see Peels (2017a).

12 See Boltzmann (1895) (Albert 2000: chapter 4, for discussion); Putnam (1982); and Bostrom (2003).

13 The reason may be evidential – for instance, I may get some new evidence that favours not-*p*, and this is my reason for changing my belief. However, I don't wish to rule out theories according to which it can be rational to form beliefs on the basis of practical reasons (James 1897; Rinard 2017).

14 For an expansion on various versions of something like theoretical inertia as it applies to common sense, see Chapter 13 by Ranalli and De Ridder in this volume.

15 Kovacs (2019) argues that a metaphysician can, on the contrary, appeal to the usefulness of common-sense beliefs to excuse her departure from common sense. The thought is that the manifest image is the result of

evolutionary pressures which selected for the most pragmatic features to be highlighted in experience. Evolution and natural selection didn't care about truth, but about survival. So although *useful* common-sense beliefs may have been selected for, *true* common-sense beliefs probably were not. It may be that in some areas the manifest image opts for pragmatics over accuracy. But pointing out that something is useful hardly seems like reason to think that it *isn't* true. Quite the contrary – it seems like prima facie evidence for truth. What is needed is not only an explanation of the reason why the manifest image gets it wrong occasionally, but why we should think that it is wrong in *this* case, given that we have reason to think it is likely to be truth-tracking in general. Furthermore, as mentioned earlier, science itself seems to rely much of the time on common sense. We need some reason to think that evolutionary science is exempt from this general pattern, or that its reliance on common sense is restricted only to certain domains, or that it can in some other way undermine common sense without thereby undermining itself.

16 Conceptual analysis is traditionally taken to be the process of examining ordinary concepts in order to determine the necessary and sufficient conditions for membership in the target category (Margolis and Laurence 2019; Chalmers and Jackson 2001). However, as Strevens (2019) points out, there simply may not be any definitions containing necessary and sufficient conditions lurking deep in our consciousness to be found. But our ordinary concepts needn't be as fine-grained as all that to be interesting. So even granting Strevens's point, conceptual analysis (undertaken on the understanding that necessary and sufficient conditions may be an unrealistic goal) can be worthwhile and productive. (Strevens himself reserves the term 'conceptual analysis' for the traditional reading, and uses 'inductive analysis' to refer to something like the weakened version I use here. I take Strevens's point on board without changing terminology.)

17 These theories will have to be fairly robustly demonstrated to warrant a rejection of common sense. It might be that the Everett interpretation of quantum phenomena (say) is our 'best' theory of quantum mechanics. Nevertheless, this theory lacks sufficient confirmation to be worth so significant a departure from the manifest image, at least at this point (Emery 2017). (It is worth noting that McQueen and Vaidman (2020) maintain that the Everettian many-worlds view of quantum mechanics is

the one entailed by common sense. However, I take it that this is hardly a mainstream view.)

18 Though see Haslanger (2012) and Ásta (2018) for two accounts of social construction.

19 It is worth making explicit the link between our everyday beliefs and behaviours and the manifest image. Our everyday beliefs, behaviours, and practices are imbued with the kind of quasi-perceptual content (conceptual and non-conceptual) that constitutes the manifest image. Alterations to the manifest image may result in an alteration of these everyday attitudes, beliefs, and practices, and these in turn give rise to socially constructed entities. Thus the manifest image, mediated by our beliefs and practices, is causally relevant to the structure of socially constructed entities.

20 This may well be changing in some parts of the world, however (see, for instance, Dembroff 2019).

9 Common-Sense Realism

Nicholas Rescher

> Common sense is the best distributed thing in the world: for everyone
> thinks himself to be so well endowed with it, that even those who are
> hardest to please in everything else do not usually desire more of it than
> they already possess.

René Descartes, *Discourse on Method*

COMMON SENSE AND ITS NATURE

Common-sense convictions are obvious, inherently plausible, and 'self-evident'. They are the overtly plausible truths that people are naturally and invariably inclined to accept unless deflected by the artificial obstacles of sophisticated thought. (Cartesian demons that cast contrived doubt upon sensory reality are anathema to common-sense philosophers.) The crux of common-sense convictions is that they come with what the Germans call *gesunder Menschenverstand* – the plain man and woman's natural understanding of things.

Common sense is only operative in intelligent beings – that is, in creatures who use experience-developed thought in managing the affairs of their lives. Common-sense facts are indispensable factors in their thought, despite the fact that they require virtually no explicit attention. The reason they don't is that common-sense truths are not very interesting as such; they are trivial truisms. The information they convey does not come as news to anyone: 'There are human beings'; 'Trees can grow'; 'Some statements are false'; 'People sometimes make mistakes'. No one needs instruction in such matters, though of course the fact that they are not *interesting* does not mean that they are not *important*.

The common-sense school of philosophy started in eighteenth-century Scotland with the works of Thomas Reid (1710–96), Dugald

Stewart (1753–1828), James Beattie (1735–1803), and William Hamilton (1788–1856).[1] As they saw it, humans have an innate capacity for rational insight into fundamental ideas and principles of knowledge and action, an insight which impels them to the acceptance of various principles concerning cognition and morality.

Common sense is neither a cognitive faculty nor yet a method of production for beliefs in matters of thought and action. Rather, it is a status characterization of certain beliefs with regard to the qualifying conditions under which they obtain. To say of a belief that 'it is only a matter of common sense' is to classify it among the commonplace fundamental beliefs that generally prevail among normally competent adults.

Common sense is a matter of what the shared experience of the community has, over time, shown to be effective (i.e., productive, beneficial, advantageous, and the like) in meeting our personal and communal requirements. It embodies those convictions that the community generally accepts as a basis for dealing with matters of day-to-day existence.

Common-sense beliefs are pervasive among the members of a community on the basis of their shared experiences in managing their everyday affairs. Common-sense beliefs concern everyday things, run-of-the-mill matters. They do not concern remote eventualities; common sense does not encompass distinctions that are needed to address such eventualities.

Common sense is accordingly concerned with our everyday dealings with ordinary life matters and addresses the commonplace familiarities of ordinary life. It is not a merely a matter of widely held beliefs – superstitions about goblins and ghosts included – but it rather deals with the everyday commonplace of life. Accordingly, common sense is not merely general opinion as such.

There is, thus, a big difference between merely *common* beliefs that are very widespread (and perhaps even general) and specifically *common-sense* beliefs. The difference lies in the fact that common-sense beliefs are characterized not simply by the fact *that* they are widespread but rather by the additional explanatory rationale of *why* they are so widespread – namely, that such beliefs are so widespread because of their constructive role in enabling us to function effectively in the prevailing conditions. This sets the merely widespread belief (in certain circles) that you shouldn't go fishing after it has rained, apart from the common-sense belief that there is life and intelligence in the persons we converse with. For this latter belief enables us to function effectively in the social contexts we happen to find ourselves in. It is the essentially pragmatic grounding – that is, their facilitating the satisfaction of human needs – that defines common-sense beliefs. And the common-sense *principles of belief formation* are those that are pervasive because they are generally conducive to meeting our basic needs for such necessities as food, shelter, clothing, sociability, etc.

One of the mainstays of common-sense proceedings is the principle of economy of effort. For clearly 'it is only common sense' to manage things in the least burdensome, most cost-effective way. No sensible person would bring two large stones to do a job where a single medium-sized one will serve. No sensible person would write a long essay where a short note would do.

A common-sense belief is not a belief that is *produced* in a certain way but rather a particular sort of belief, namely, one that is available to people in general, on account of its triteness, its palpable obviousness. It is a non-discursive and non-reflective belief of which one is as certain – and as *reasonably* certain – as one can be of anything in the sense that it would be otiose to set out to find *reasons* for such a belief because the belief itself is just as – or even more – cogent and assured as would be the case with anything one might adduce on its behalf.

THE RIVALS OF COMMON SENSE

Common sense has three main rivals: scepticism, scientific sophistication, and utopian idealization. Scepticism can be either of the radical sort ('we know nothing whatsoever') or of the moderate variety ('we know nothing for certain – probability rules all'). Neither version has much traction – it is hard to cavil with G. E. Moore's common-sensical insistence, while he is pointing with one hand to his other hand, that he knows that 'this is a human hand' (Moore 1939).

Scientific sophistication is another matter. For to all viable appearances, when common sense and science clash, science has the upper hand. In every situation where scientific information is available, experience indicates that its authority outranks that of common sense. This is true for such areas as medicine, diet, and agriculture – here science will trump common sense.

On the other hand, the realism of common sense puts it into a position of dominance over utopian idealization, whose mindful thinking is at odds with the experiential wisdom of common sense. (The revolutionary who thinks that abolishing the prevailing system ensures an order of peaches and cream, and the young lady who envisions a postmarital reformation of her beau's bad habits, are posting mail orders for disappointment.)

Science is by nature progressive and therefore changeable. Its advice in human affairs is therefore changeable too. In such matters as medication and diet, science-based advice varies over the centuries. Common sense, by contrast, in its concern for fundamentals, tends to be stable. The moralist can still benefit from Aristotle, and the warrior can still read Clausewitz with profit. Common sense is advantageous by the fact that fundamentals tend to be stable.

In matters of common sense there is little room for specialized expertise. Common-sense information is the sort of knowledge that is at the disposal of everyone – it is available not only to the trained and knowledgeable but even to 'the meanest intellect'. For this very reason the proper range of common sense must be limited to the sorts of plain and unadorned facts that are readily apprehensible to anyone and everyone – such facts as that 'there are dogs in the world', for example. Facts that are to any degree complex and technical in nature are inaccessible to common sense. Complex and technical facts are matters of expertise, and getting to know them requires, to some extent or other, schooling, education, and training. Even if reasoning is involved so that intuition is not at issue, then the matter can still be one of common sense, provided that the reasoning is sufficiently obvious that its availability is effectively universal. There is thus nothing sophisticated, complicated, or technical about common-sense knowledge, and no special training or insight is needed for its realization. It relates to the sort of thing that anyone must realize who functions in the circumstances at hand.

THE THEMATIC TOPICALITY OF COMMON SENSE

Common sense is particularly suited to matters relating to the management of affairs in everyday life. It consists in the lessons of the general and commonplace experience of people – the general sum of the commonplace things they take themselves to have learned in the course of their everyday dealings with the world and with their fellows.

To be sure, the province of common sense certainly has limits. Common sense itself is clearly aware of this and makes no effort to stand in the way of innovation in the vast regions that it recognizes as beyond its reach. In fact, with respect to that enormous domain where expertise comes into play and where originality and creativity are needed, it is only commonsensical to endorse the need for novel resources beyond the range that common sense itself is able to afford.

No one does – or should – maintain that the *vox populi* invariably utters wisdom. But that in matters relating to the basics of the conduct of life a *vox populi* emerges from the course of experience *does* endow it with a certain credibility. Its very nature endows it with credentials that ventures into eccentric innovation generally lack.

Common sense has at its very foundation the democratic ethos that in matters affecting people's interest – and above all in matters affecting their economic interests – the general public is the best and most acceptable judge. The supposition of a commonsensical approach to problem policy matters is presupposed by democratic proceedings with their characteristic trust in majoritarian judgment.

THE SECURITY/DEFINITENESS BALANCE IN COMMON SENSE AND SCIENCE

There is nothing very novel or illuminating about matters of common sense. Its strictures are basic and elemental: 'When you are feeling ill, consult your physician about it', or 'Before using your umbrella on a rainy day, first open it up'. No one would buy a 'handbook of common sense'. Descartes was right: people think they already know it all – and they are by and large right about this.

For while most of our beliefs cry out for substantiation, common-sense beliefs do not. The evidence of our common-sense beliefs lies in their manifest obviousness. The answer to the question 'How is one to decide the acceptability of a common-sense belief?' is simple: one doesn't. There is no process of decision about it. Common-sense beliefs are self-evident in the sense of wearing their acceptability on their sleeves: they are acceptable not in virtue of the processes that engendered them, but simply in virtue of the obviousness of what they affirm. It is not that our common-sense beliefs do not *permit* evidentiation – it is just that they do not *require* it. For the most part, the considerations that could be adduced to substantiate a common-sense belief are less evident than those common-sense beliefs themselves. What speaks for those beliefs is just exactly their patent alignment to the general course of people's experience.

While both science and common sense provide us with instructive and acceptable representations of reality, they do so at very different levels of detail and precision. Moreover, they proceed in rather different ways and with decidedly different ends in view. And even as a geographic configuration – a city, say – looks very different on an inch-per-mile scale and on an inch-per-100-mile scale, so is this the case with the view of reality that we get at different positions of the security/definitiveness curve. The relationship between security and definitiveness was first clearly noticed by Pierre Duhem (1982: 179): 'There is a sort of balance between precision and certainty: one cannot be increased except to the detriment of the other.' Examples illustrate how this works. Compare the following two statements about the same tree: (1) that tree over there has a height of around 25 feet, and (2) that tree over there has a height between 1 inch and 100 yards. The first statement is more definite qua content than the second one; but, and for that reason, the first is less secure than the second one. Science aims at making very precise and definite statements – and this makes especially cutting-edge science vulnerable. The scientific statement that 'the melting point of lead is 327.7 degrees Celsius', for example, says that all pieces of pure lead melt at that temperature, not that many pieces are often inclined to do so. This degree of precision makes the statement vulnerable. Contrast this with the statements of common sense: these are very secure *because* they are *not* very precise and definite. Take, for example, the statement that 'peaches are delicious'. This statement says that most people will find the eating of suitably grown and duly matured peaches a rather pleasurable experience. This is not a very precise or definite statement since it contains various built-in safeguards and hedges, expressed in the words 'most', 'suitably grown', 'duly matured', and 'rather', that make the statement pretty invulnerable.

And so, while both science and common sense depict a common terrain, namely, the world we live in and its furnishings, they do this in such different ways that to all appearances they might as well be dealing with different terrains.

In areas where expertise is possible, which is the case in all the sciences – the natural and bio-medical sciences, and to some extent the social sciences – it is altogether reasonable to avail oneself of this. The questions that arise within these fields are best addressed via the methods and resources developed in these fields for dealing with them. Giving science the right of way within its own domain is itself 'only a matter of common sense'.

COMMON-SENSE PHILOSOPHY

There are in principle two modes of common-sense philosophy: the positive and the negative. The positive sees common sense as *sufficient* for philosophical adequacy. It takes the view that philosophical issues can be resolved on the basis of insight put at our disposal by common-sense considerations. The negative has it that our philosophical views must not contradict common sense: conjoinedness with common sense is an indispensable requisite of philosophical adequacy. Philosophers like Thomas Reid and G. E. Moore adopted the positive mode, in that they held that at least some philosophical issues can be resolved by reference to common sense. But they also adopted the negative mode, in that they held that a necessary requirement on any sound philosophy is its capability to accommodate common-sense beliefs.

The common-sense realism of the Scottish philosophers Thomas Reid and Dugald Stewart took the ontology of experiential objects at face value (see for this McDermid 2018). The things that people in general standardly perceive in ordinary circumstances are in fact as they appear to be. Perceptual objects are neither *inferences* from experience nor *constructs* from experiential data, but they are exactly what we experience them to be.

And these common-sense philosophers take the same sort of line in ethics. The principles of morality are not somehow conjectural excogitations by philosophical sophisticates, but inhere in the natural endowment of the generic normalcy of ordinary people. The basic ideas of morality are facts that do not require an introduction to rational support – they are 'self-evident' in the sense at work in America's Declaration of Independence: 'We hold these truths to be self-evident, that all men are created equal, that they are endowed by their creator with unalienable rights, that among these are life, liberty and the pursuit of happiness.'

One can of course ask why it should be in such matters that the general convictions of ordinary people are pretty much 'right on track' so to speak. Traditionally the agency of a benign creator was deemed adequate to explain why (as St Augustine put it) *securus iudicat omnia terrarum*, 'the verdict of the whole world is conclusive'. Later on the approach has been evolutionary rather than theological. The reasoning here is that moral convictions would not have survived in the evolutionary derby, would not have established themselves on a general and enduring basis in a society of rational agents, if they had negative survival value, that is, if they proved to be functionally inadequate when people put them into practice in different times, conditions, and circumstances. Now moral convictions have turned out to have staying power and this, it is urged, is best explained by saying that abiding by them is evolutionarily advantageous.[2]

One's view of common-sense philosophizing is bound to pivot crucially on one's conception of philosophy itself. Philosophy, after all, is from its start a matter of the pursuit of wisdom. Now if one sets the views of ordinary people at naught and looks for sagacity to the singular society of the hyper-gifted genius, then common-sense philosophizing will have precious little appeal. But if, on the other hand, one is prepared to acknowledge the collective 'wisdom of the group', one's view of the aficionados of common sense is bound to take on a more positive hue.

THE RELIABILITY OF COMMON SENSE

As G. E. Moore was wont to insist, any course of reasoning designed to invalidate such common-sense truisms as 'This [pointing] is a human hand' will have to proceed from premises a great deal more questionable than the theses whose invalidation is being sought.

In managing the commonplace dealings of ordinary life – prominently including resource allocation, goal seeking, and interpersonal affairs – we can do no better than to heed the voice of common sense.

But this means that common sense is bound to have very different degrees of credibility with regard to different issues. In particular, common sense is going to be very trustworthy when the course of experience with a particular range of phenomena is continuous, enduring, and stable, so that the ways of past experience are likely to continue into the present. Thus in areas of human experience that are substantially uniform throughout the ages – parent–child relations, for example, or road construction – the teachings of common sense are well worth heeding. On the other hand, in a sphere of substantial volatility – communication technology, for example – common sense is likely to prove of unreliable guidance. Still, in virtually every line of inquiry common sense is going to prove more useful in matters of general principle – which are mostly firmly stable – than in matters of operative detail, which generally change with the times and the occasions.

The credibility of common sense is bound up with the fact that its validity prevails only in the limited domain of the everyday-life circumstances of people in general. The crux of common sense is what ordinary people ordinarily think and do in response to the functional requirements of our world. The issues that can be decided on the basis of common-sense considerations are neither the technical issues of science and engineering nor the highly complex issues of economics or social planning. Rather they relate to what transpires within the sphere of our work-a-day affairs and the 'ordinary course of things' in everyday life. And precisely because common sense is based on the ordinary everyday experience of people in general, the bulk of whom are bound to be ordinary everyday individuals, it represents a domain from which expertise is excluded; a domain in which the learned enjoy no particular advantage over the vulgar – no doubt to the consternation of the former.

The real question is not 'Is common sense reliable?' but rather 'Is common sense reliable with respect to this or that particular family of issues?' For there simply is no thematic uniformity here.

The reliability of common sense in those areas where it appropriately functions is not one of theoretical general principles. It is itself subject to the same sort of empirical inquiry that is the essence of science. The reality of it is that science and common sense are deeply entangled and interconnected. And in fact, reliance on common sense has the backing of reason. The reliability of common sense in particular contexts can be evidentiated in various contexts (see, for example, Surowiecki 2003). And the appropriateness of scientific inquiry as a means of issue resolution is itself a matter of common sense.

With science and common sense alike, ample experience shows that with regard to the matters that are at issue in these respective domains, no better – that is, more trustworthy – recourse is at our disposal.

COMMON-SENSE REALISM AND APPEARANCES

It is sometimes suggested that the conceptual contrast between appearances and reality permanently emplaces mankind in a world of seeing. But this makes no sense at all. To conceive of reality in a way that precludes as a matter of principle the prospect that people should come to know reality is decidedly unreasonable. Reality, common sense tells us, is not to be construed as something inherently disjoint from the realm of the knowable.

'Appearance', as philosophers use the term, encompasses not just how things manifest themselves in sensory observation, but the much broader range of how we take matters to stand – how we take them to be not just in sense observation but in conceptual thought as well. On this basis it would be gravely fallacious to map the real/unreal distinction onto the real/apparent distinction. For this mixes the sheep and the goats in heaping veridical appearance together with mere (i.e., non-veridical) appearance, thereby subscribing to the paranoid delusion that things are never what they seem to be.

Reality is not a distinct realm of being that stands apart, and is separated, from that realm of being that is the manifold of appearances. 'Appearances', says the common-sense philosopher, will – insofar as they are correct – be appearances *of reality* that is represented in those appearances. And accordingly, says the common-sense philosopher, the contrast between reality and appearance is not an ontological contrast, not a contrast between different sorts of things. The realm of appearance is homogeneous with that of reality insofar as those appearances are correct, or veridical.

The fact of it is that things sometimes – perhaps even frequently – are substantially as they appear to be. Reality and its appearance just are not two separate realms: there is nothing to prevent matters actually being as they are perceived and/or thought to be.

Appearance can in principle be something self-contained and self-sufficient: there need not be *something* that appears. When it appears to me that there is a pink elephant in the corner, there need not be a *something* in that corner which appears as an elephant to me. Appearances may not only be deceiving: they may also be illusionary. In the sphere of appearance things can go seriously awry. And yet, while matters *can* go wrong here, they need not do so. Things can indeed *be* as they appear. Total paranoia is clearly unwarranted. There is no reason, that is, why appearance and reality cannot agree in this or that detail.

The conviction that we are dealing with a mind-independent reality plays a central and indispensable role in our everyday, common-sense thinking about cognition and communication. In both areas alike we seek to offer answers to questions about how matters stand in this 'objective realm', and the contrast between 'the real' and its 'merely phenomenal' appearances is crucial here. Moreover, the 'objective realm' is also seen as the target and *telos* of the truth-estimation processes at issue in inquiry; it provides a common focus in communication and communal inquiry. The 'real world' thus constitutes the 'object' of our cognitive endeavours in both senses of this term – the *objective* at which they are directed and the *purpose* for which they are exerted. And so the commitment to the existence of a pre-experiential reality becomes pivotal here, affording the existential matrix in which we move and have our being, and whose impact upon us is the prime mover for our cognitive efforts. All of these facets of the concept of reality are integrated and unified in the classical doctrine of truth as it corresponds to fact (*adaequatio ad rem*), a doctrine that only makes sense in the setting of a commitment to mind-independent reality. Common sense is committed to the classical *adaequatio* theory of truth.

But could reality possibly be *exactly* as it appears? It certainly could in this or that detail. When appearance puts the cat on the mat, there is no reason why reality cannot also do so. But reality could not be exactly as it appears *overall* and *in total*. For appearance has its imprecisions, its vagueness, and its blank specs of ignorance. Reality could not possibly be like that – it could not be imprecise, nor vague (nor non-existent where we are ignorant). There is always more to things than meets the eye of the appearances.

The paramount contrast for the appearance/reality distinction is that between how things are *correctly* thought to be and how they are *erroneously* thought to be. The salient distinction is accordingly not between mere belief and actual fact, but between belief that is true (correct) and belief that is not – a distinction of status that involves no separation of kinds. When we accept a belief as true, we have no alternative but to hold that that is how reality actually is. And realism thus emerges when we put these ideas together to arrive at the following principle: 'True claims about things can, and in suitably favourable circumstances will, characterize reality as it really is in some manner or respect.' This principle represents an indissoluble link between epistemology and ontology inherent in the medieval idea of truth as adequation to fact.

The crux of the matter, to say it again, is that things sometimes – perhaps even frequently – are exactly as they appear to be. For there is clearly nothing to prevent that things actually are as they are perceived and/or thought to be. In point of actual separation, the crucial contrast is that between how things are *correctly* thought to be and how they are *erroneously* thought to be, rather than that between what *is* and what *is thought to be*. There is no insuperable gap between the real and the knowable, no Kantian *Ding an sich*, everlastingly hidden away behind the impenetrable 'veil of appearance'.

A good deal of mischief has been done in philosophy by the idea of a 'veil of appearance' – an idea based on the distinction between the real and the unreal. This distinction cannot be identified with the epistemically more natural distinction between

appearance = how things are perceived/thought to be,

and

reality = how things actually are.

It is critically important, in the interests of clarity and agency, not to conflate these two distinctions.

Kant maintained – very problematically indeed – that appearance and reality are different forms of being: appearance is composed of 'mere phenomena' whose nature is irremediably mental, and reality is composed of 'things as they are in themselves' and thereby of a nature completely unknowable to us. Kant was convinced (for complex reasons) that something could not actually be as true thought about it represents it as being (which is, after all, what true thought is all about). But this view of the matter is deeply problematic. Reality and appearance are not two substantively different realms: rather, they involve two different thought perspectives upon one selfsame realm, that is, the realm of that which exists and thereby lays claim to authentic reality.

What happens all too commonly in this connection is that philosophers transmute such a *conceptual distinction* into a *substantial separation*. But it is a grave error to take the view that what is conceptually *distinct* is ipso facto also substantially *disjoint*. This idea is every bit as flawed as the idea that distinguishing between musicians and carpenters conceptually means that an item of the one type could not also be an item of the other type – that a carpenter could not possibly be a musician as well. Specifically, it is emphatically not the case that knowledge of reality is in principle infeasible because reality is somehow a *Ding an sich* hidden away behind the 'veil of appearance'. The fact of it is that much of reality stands in front of that 'veil' by encompassing that part of appearance which happens to be correct.

That those 'intuitive' beliefs of ours are the product of natural development is seen by evolutionists not as an objection to but as an index of reality. These beliefs would not live on to establish themselves in a society of rational agents if their ascriptions were not warranted by the reality of things. As Quine famously wrote in a discussion of induction: 'Creatures inveterately wrong in their inductions have a pathetic but praiseworthy tendency to die before reproducing their kind.'[3]

For the common-sense philosopher, appearance and reality are not different orders of being but are generally and normally one and the same. Appearances are subject to a presumption of authenticity: where and when they differ, special accounting is called for and always possible. Normally, ordinarily, and stand-ardly, people's cognitive resources are veridical: things are as they appear to be, and our instinctive trust in what we experience is in general warranted.

Science and common sense, to repeat, have different aims and therefore proceed in different ways. Science aims at precision and detail in matters of explanation in prediction, while common sense settles for enough accuracy to get by on. The scientist seeks to know the exact amount of lead contamination in the water, whereas for common-sense purposes it may well suffice to know whether there is any at all. We do not need to know exactly how much rain will fall to decide about taking an umbrella.

Science asks for precision and detail; common sense is content to settle for the inexactness that suffices 'for all practical purposes'. The practical concerns of common sense contrast with the theoretical concerns for science and address a situation where our limited senses of time, talent, and treasure mean that in many areas of life manage-ment it makes perfectly good sense to dispense with superfluous exactitudes. Bishop Butler may have been right in that probability is the guide of life. But even so, there is no need for scientific precision here: in many cases such rough distinctions as large/medium/small suffice for all practical purposes.

COMMON-SENSE MORALITY AND UTOPIANISM

Our beliefs can have many sorts of virtues: generality, evidentiation, precision, etc. But common sense refrains from ever asking for more in these regards than what is minimally required for meeting the situation at hand. Sufficing for the needs of the moment is a hallmark of common sense. This policy inclines common sense to form general principles over matters of sophisticated detail.

In every domain of thought and action, the fundamentals of the aims of the enterprise and the modalities of its effective management remain stably fixed in time. (However greatly medicine has changed over the years, its basic aims and modes of interaction have remained fixed since antiquity, and the oath of Hippocrates is still prevalent.) The fundamentals of morality – the basis of right and wrong – are and have to be matters of common sense. From here, the basics must be mastered at mother's knee – the child who does not have them at his or her command at age seven or eight will never learn them at all. And much the same holds for the basis of information management by linguistic means of the characteristic principles of social interaction.

It may well occasionally be advantageous to fly in the face of common sense. But such cases are few and far between – eccentric and surprising exceptions to the general rule. This pits common sense against utopianism. Most theorists – indeed most people – are utopian idealists about this or that, eager to change the world and fix its manifest defects. But it is hard to reform what you do not understand. And the crucial reality is that we do not fully understand what goes on in bits of physical matter, let alone in people and societies. It is all too easy to remedy defects by creating catastrophes – or replace the ills we see by greater ones we have not contemplated. No revolution has turned out as its inauguration imagined. The guidance of safety-first common sense is not very inspirational, but in nine cases out of ten it proves beneficial in the long run. For better or worse, common sense tends to what is unexciting but safe.

What remains, in the end, is the question of whether this or that specific belief qualifies for the accolade of common-sense endorsement. Establishing its claim would have to be in part a matter of the de facto difference of its acceptance. In part, it would be a matter of the more theoretical issue of how elaborate, contrived, and implausible an account that called common sense into question would have to be (e.g., a recourse to Descartes's 'evil deceiver').

What are we to say about people who set common sense at naught and proceed accordingly? Clearly insofar as they do injury to others – say, by hitting others with stones in order to cure their headaches – the usual preventive and primitive measures are called for. But otherwise they can be left to their own devices, leaving them to bear the risks they have created for themselves. All this would itself appear to be a matter of common sense.

In the end, the reliability of common-sense considerations within a given domain can and should of course be maintained by empirical inquiry. But this itself is simply a matter of common sense.

NOTES

1 Recent studies of the history of the Scottish school of common-sense philosophy are Broady (1990) and McDermid (2018).
2 Examples of explanations of this nature are Ruse (1986); Joyce (2006); and Churchland (2011). The explanations often take on the form of 'debunking' explanations: by pointing to the evolutionary origins of moral beliefs, those beliefs are argued to be false.
3 Quine (1969: 126). Quine's claim was challenged by Alvin Plantinga's evolutionary argument against naturalism, an early version of which appeared in Plantinga (1993: 216–237). This argument is inspired by doubts that Darwin himself harboured. Darwin wrote: 'With me the horrid doubt always arises whether the convictions of man's mind, which has developed from the mind of lower animals, are of any value or at all trustworthy.' Plantinga's argument has been scrutinized in Beilby (2002).

10 The Epistemic Authority of Common Sense

Rik Peels

INTRODUCTION

For centuries, common-sense beliefs and common-sense philosophy have been besieged by a wide variety of philosophical arguments, such as a priori reasoning to the effect that we cannot know that there is an external world.[1] During the last few decades, common sense has increasingly been criticized from another angle as well, namely, that of science. It is thought that science has shown that many of our common-sense beliefs are unreliably formed, false, or illusory: beliefs about the reasons for which we act, beliefs concerning free action, beliefs about the absoluteness of space and time, beliefs in alleged objective moral truths, and so forth.[2] Still others point out that common-sense beliefs are plagued by ambiguity, equivocation, and inconsistency (see Unger 1982). Many conclude that we should treat common sense with suspicion.

Adherents of common-sense philosophy, such as Thomas Reid, G. E. Moore, Roderick Chisholm, and Noah Lemos, think otherwise, of course. They take it that common sense has a certain epistemic authority that is only *on some occasions* defeated. Absent such relatively rare defeating conditions, common-sense beliefs are rational, epistemically justified, and instances of knowledge. I call this combination of alleged positive epistemic statuses the *epistemic authority* of common sense. The purpose of this chapter is to answer the question *in virtue of what*, if anything at all, common sense has such epistemic authority in the first place. After all, if it does not, then the fact that something is a common-sense belief does as such not count in favour of its truth.

This chapter is structured as follows. First, I lay out in more detail exactly what common sense and the supposed epistemic authority of common sense amount to. Next, I assess seven proposals that we find in the literature as to why common sense has epistemic authority. They say, respectively, that common-sense beliefs are irresistible; that there are no serious epistemic alternatives to thinking that common-sense beliefs have epistemic authority; that common-sense beliefs are certain, or at least more certain than any alternatives; that common-sense beliefs are instances of knowledge; that common-sense beliefs are vague and ambiguous and, therefore, likely to be true; that common-sense beliefs are the product of a reliable process of cultural evolution; and, finally, that God would not deceive us on such a large scale. I argue that the first five answers are not convincing, not even jointly, but that the sixth answer is, and that the seventh reply may well be combined with it.

EXACTLY WHAT IS THE QUESTION?

In order to clarify the question under consideration, I will answer three other questions in this section: (1) What is common sense? (2) What is epistemic authority? (3) Exactly what are we asking when we ask *in virtue of what* common sense has epistemic authority?

So, first, what is common sense? I take it, for the sake of the argument in this chapter, that 'common sense' denotes a class of beliefs: common-sense beliefs. I will not take a stance on whether there is such thing as a *common-sense faculty* or whether there are such things as *common-sense doxastic mechanisms*.[3] Thus, I focus on common-sense *beliefs*. Here are some examples of common-sense beliefs that I hold now:

1. The belief that I have hands.[4]
2. The belief that last week I flew to Denver, Colorado.
3. The belief that I feel no pain in my left leg.
4. The belief that I am worried about my friend's mental health.

5. The belief that most people have knowledge of the intentions of many other people.
6. The belief that our perception of mid-sized objects is, generally, reliable.
7. The belief that many species of plants and animals have lived on the earth.
8. The belief that one should not light a match in a gas-filled room.
9. The belief that torturing for the fun of it is morally wrong.

And, slightly more controversially, the following might also be a common-sense belief:

10. The belief that there are supernatural entities.

Some common-sense beliefs, such as (1), are based on *observational experience*. Others, such as (2), are based on *recollection and memory*. Still other common-sense beliefs, such as (3) and (4), are based on *self-awareness*, *introspection*, or *proprioception*. There are also beliefs in what seem *incontrovertibly obvious facts of common life*, such as (5), (6), and (7). Furthermore, there are *matters of prudence*, such as (8). Finally, there are beliefs that arise, at least partly, from a *moral sense*, such as (9), or a *religious sense*, such as (10). These are all beliefs that are often considered to be common-sense beliefs.[5] But what ties them together? What makes them *common-sense* beliefs?

I suggest that, roughly, there are two conditions and that all of these beliefs meet at least one of them. Meeting one of them is sufficient for a belief to count as a common-sense belief:

a. Being a belief in having a kind of property that almost everyone ascribes to himself or herself, at least when prompted.
b. Being a basic belief in a proposition that is deeply held by almost everyone.[6]

Thus, belief in (1)–(4) is belief in having some kind of property – a physical property, a property having to do with one's memory, a property concerning one's own mental state – that almost everyone has. I say 'a kind of property' rather than 'a property' because, obviously, only some people believe that they have no pain in their left leg – some people do believe that they feel pain in their left leg. The point is that this is the kind of belief that many people have. Belief in (5)–(9) is basic belief in a proposition that is deeply held in the sense of being fairly firmly believed by almost everyone: people are convinced, relatively certain of the truth of the propositions involved.[7] As I said above, belief in (10) is a slightly more controversial example. Yet, the majority of humanity believes in supernatural entities, as empirical research shows.[8] The issue for (10), then, is how many people ought to believe in it in order for it to count as a common-sense belief and to what degree people ought to be convinced of it. I will leave that for another occasion.

What is excluded by this disjunctive criterion? A lot: most beliefs based on scientific inquiry, most beliefs issuing from journalistic or criminal inquiry, moral and religious beliefs that only few people hold, beliefs based on complicated lines of philosophical reasoning, most beliefs based on technology, engineering, and social planning, beliefs based on economics and the law, and so on.

Second, what is it for common-sense beliefs to have *epistemic authority*? It is *not* for *each of them* to be rational, warranted, or to be an instance of knowledge. After all, even the boldest champions of common sense would not say that common-sense beliefs are *never* defeated by scientific inquiry or philosophical argument. The idea rather seems to be twofold. First, these beliefs are *usually* rational, warranted, and instances of knowledge, and they are only sometimes defeated. Second, these beliefs are not *easily* defeated: having *some* evidence to the contrary will not do. Even fairly strong evidence will sometimes not suffice. For example, G. E. Moore famously argued that he is more certain of the proposition that he knows he has hands than he is of the proposition that he does not know that he is dreaming or the victim of an evil demon (see Moore 1959b). The belief that he has hands and that he *knows* that he has hands are beliefs that are not easily overturned, not even by a challenging philosophical argument.[9]

I take it that this is what many authors have in mind when they talk about the 'epistemic authority', 'credibility', or 'probative authority' of common sense, when they say that common sense is 'reliable', that common-sense beliefs are 'rationally legitimate', or that 'we can rely on common sense'.[10]

Third, what are we asking when we ask *in virtue of what* these beliefs have epistemic authority? I suggest that what we are asking for is *non-question-begging reasons* to think that common-sense beliefs generally have a positive epistemic status and that they are not easily defeated. When I say these reasons should be non-question-begging, I mean that these reasons should not *assume* that common-sense beliefs are indeed epistemically justified, rational, instances of knowledge, and so on.

One might worry that this question is nonsensical, because common-sense beliefs have epistemic authority, but not in virtue of anything. Their epistemic authority is primitive or brute: it does not supervene on some other fact, in the same way as a particular elementary particle's being *that* particular elementary particle does not seem to supervene on some other fact. No non-question-begging reason for the epistemic authority of common sense can be given.

My reply is twofold. First, in the case of elementary particles there is good reason to think that it is a primitive fact that *that* elementary particle is *that* elementary particle, a fact that does not supervene on any other facts; it is hard to see what such facts would be. In the case of common sense, though, it is much harder to see why it would be a brute fact that common-sense beliefs have epistemic authority. Scientific and philosophical challenges even seem to provide *some* reason to doubt that common sense has epistemic authority. Of course, *some* scientific and philosophical arguments are meant to show merely that the epistemic authority is sometimes undermined. But, quite often, the lesson allegedly learned is much stronger: common sense does not have epistemic authority in the first place – we should not confer prima facie rationality to it that is not easily undermined. On the contrary, we should be highly sceptical of common-sense beliefs. According to British developmental biologist Lewis Wolpert, for instance, 'both the ideas that science generates and the way in which science is carried out are entirely counter-intuitive and against common sense – by which I mean that scientific ideas cannot be acquired by simple inspection of phenomena and that they are very often outside everyday experience ... I would almost contend that if something fits with common sense it almost certainly isn't science' (Wolpert 1992: 1, 11). Second and even more importantly, we should not lose sight of the dialectical situation: a wide variety of philosophers believe that common sense does *not* have any or not much epistemic authority. Claiming that it is a brute fact that it has such authority will not ameliorate the dialectical situation one bit, in the same way as claiming that it is a brute fact that some thesis *T* is true will not be helpful in any other debate (even though the claim may be justified).

I repeat the main question: in virtue of what does common sense have epistemic authority? The next sections explore seven different answers to this question.

FIRST ANSWER: IRRESISTIBILITY

A first line of defence appeals to the psychological irresistibility of common-sense beliefs: whether or not we like it, they are automatically and spontaneously formed in us and we, thus, cannot resist them. They are unavoidable for us. This seems to be the view of Thomas Reid:

> Methinks, therefore, it were better to make a virtue of necessity; and, since we cannot get rid of the vulgar notion and belief of an external world, to reconcile our reason to it as well as we can; for, if Reason should stomach and fret ever so much at this yoke, she cannot throw it off; if she will not be the servant of Common Sense, she must be her slave ... because it is not in my power; why then should I make a vain attempt ... My belief is carried along by perception, as irresistibly as my body by the earth. (Reid (1764) 1983: 4, 85)

Reid's idea seems to be this: since common-sense beliefs are psychologically unavoidable in the sense that there is nothing we can do to avoid having them, the best we can do is to take them for granted and reconcile reason to them as well as we can. It becomes clear from his work, such as his formulation of various common-sense principles that ought to guide our thinking, that, for Reid, this means that we need to assume that the common-sense beliefs we have are rational unless we have good reason to think otherwise.

For two reasons, this line of reasoning seems problematic to me. First, it might be a characteristic of common-sense beliefs that we cannot give up *all* of them, but it does *not* seem a characteristic of common-sense beliefs in general that for each of them, we cannot give them up. Take our moral beliefs. If we are convinced by evolutionary debunking arguments, we may give up our moral beliefs and continue to *assume* certain moral propositions or *accept* them rather than *believe them to be true*. If we think the arguments for atheism are convincing, we might give up all religious beliefs. If we accept certain conclusions drawn on the basis of social experiments regarding the motivations for our actions, we may come to think that we do not really know why we do the things we do. Consequently, we may decide, in a Humean fashion, to continue to lead our lives as we did but treat each claim about our motivations with a significant degree of scepticism, resulting in a suspension of judgment regarding the reasons for which we acted. Thus, even though *some* common-sense beliefs may well be irresistible, such as the belief that one exists, many of them are not. Irresistibility as such, therefore, cannot confer epistemic authority on common-sense beliefs.

Second, as Kant already noticed in his *Prolegomena to Any Future Metaphysics* (Preface: A259–60), we ought to distinguish between *psychological inevitability* and *rationality*, since the former does not entail the latter. Something can be psychologically inevitable and yet not rational, either because it is irrational or because it is beyond rationality. Imagine that Susie has survived a horrible elevator accident and is severely traumatized as a result. She goes through a long series of therapeutic sessions but unfortunately to no avail. Moreover, she delves into all the scientific research on elevator accidents and, thus, comes to know that there is strong evidence for thinking that elevator accidents are extremely rare. And yet, because of her traumatic experience, the belief that elevators are dangerous sticks with her. It is, thus, psychologically irresistible for her to believe that elevators are dangerous: there is nothing she can do to avoid it. In fact, she has done everything she could to get rid of the belief, but unsuccessfully so. However, it is clear that her belief is *irrational* and *unjustified*: it is unreliably formed, it conflicts with the evidence that she has (she has plenty of reason to think that accidents with elevators hardly ever occur), and so forth. Again, irresistibility as such cannot confer epistemic authority on common-sense beliefs.

One may reply that the elevator belief is irresistible *for Susie*, but that it is generally not irresistible for us, normal, healthy, and well-functioning human beings. However, there are beliefs that *many* people hold and that are clearly not rational. Take the belief that the Grand Canyon Skywalk (a glass bridge over the Grand Canyon) is not safe. There is plenty of evidence that it is safe, but many people, understandably, disbelieve that – at least in some sense of the word. Moreover, if irresistibility is not something that confers epistemic authority on a belief for Susie and a few others, then it is hard to see how that same irresistibility for more people (no matter what the number) does confer epistemic authority. The mere appeal to irresistibility will not do; one would have to explain why irresistibility is a good reason to think that common-sense beliefs have epistemic authority.

SECOND ANSWER: NO EPISTEMIC ALTERNATIVES

A second answer, suggested by Roderick Chisholm, is that there is no real epistemic alternative. He writes that in investigating the theory of knowledge from a philosophical point of view, we assume that what we know is pretty much that which, on reflection, we think we know. He goes on to say, 'This might seem like the wrong place to start. But where else could we start?' (Chisholm 1977: 16). Now, note that in saying this Chisholm implies that common sense has epistemic authority at least in the sense that, unless we have good reason to think that they are false or unreliably formed, we should continue to hold common-sense beliefs.

It is important to realize that this point is different from the previous argument for the epistemic authority of common sense. Here, the idea is not so much that it is *psychologically* impossible to start somewhere else because common-sense beliefs inevitably force themselves upon us. Rather, the suggestion is that, in forming beliefs, there is no serious *epistemic alternative* to starting with our common-sense beliefs.

Now, is Chisholm right that there is no epistemic alternative to common sense, at least when it comes to starting somewhere? I'm afraid he's mistaken about this. Let me give two examples.

First, it seems that there *are* epistemic alternatives to start with. Take Descartes's line of reasoning in favour of the reliability of our senses, that is, belief formation on the basis of sense perception (see Descartes 1988). He points out that we might be dreaming or deceived by an evil demon, so that all of our perceptual beliefs are false. Hence, our common-sense beliefs do *not* have epistemic authority. They gain such authority only if we can *show* that they are reliably formed. Needless to say here, Descartes offers a complicated argument for that, involving the idea that it is impossible to not exist if one notes that one thinks, the idea that God exists, and the idea that God would not deceive us by giving us unreliable perceptual cognitive faculties. In the course of his argument, he appeals to various controversial metaphysical principles that are clearly *not* common-sense beliefs. Whether or not this line of reasoning is actually convincing, the point is that this *is* an epistemic alternative to starting with common sense.

Or take scientism. Some of the stronger versions, such as that of Alex Rosenberg, say that only the natural sciences provide us with rational belief and knowledge.[11] Now, elsewhere I have argued that, in order for scientism to be true, at least *some* of our common-sense beliefs have to be rational and count as knowledge as well; we cannot discard *all* of our common-sense beliefs, because then science would never get off the ground (see Peels 2017a). Yet, clearly, not all of our common-sense beliefs are necessary for science. Many of our religious, moral, and introspective beliefs are irrelevant for science.[12] I presume one cannot do science without *some kinds of* common-sense belief, but one need not assume that all kinds of common-sense beliefs are generally reliably formed in order to do science.

Second, and most importantly, even if there is no alternative starting point, then that may confer practical or pragmatic authority on our common-sense beliefs: we have to start with them. Yet, it is not clear how that, as such, confers *epistemic* authority on our common-sense beliefs. Why should we think that if there is no alternative starting point, that very fact makes our common-sense beliefs epistemically rational unless there are defeaters for them?

Hence, whether or not they are viable, there are alternatives to assuming from the very start that our common-sense beliefs have epistemic authority.

THIRD ANSWER: RELATIVE CERTAINTY

A third answer one could give is that our common-sense beliefs are simply more certain than any of the other beliefs they might compete with – or, at least, that this is true for the vast majority of our common-sense beliefs, and that this confers epistemic authority on them. This might well be the view of G. E. Moore:

> But it seems to me a sufficient refutation of such views as these [i.e., sceptical views], simply to point to cases in which we do know such things. This, after all, you know, really is a finger: there is no doubt about it: I know it, and you all know it. And I think we may safely challenge any philosopher to bring forward any argument in favour either of the proposition that we do not know it, or of the proposition that it is not true, which does not at some point rest upon some premise which is, beyond comparison, *less certain*, than

is the proposition which it is designed to attack. (Moore 1960b: 228, my italics)

There is, in this quote, also the idea that common-sense beliefs constitute knowledge and have epistemic authority in virtue of that. I return to this idea in the next section. Here, I focus on another idea that we also find in this passage – an idea that I have made explicit by italicizing the words 'less certain'. The idea seems to be this: common-sense beliefs have prima facie epistemic authority because they have a high degree of *certainty*, very often a higher degree of certainty than some of the premises in the sceptical philosophical or scientific arguments that are levelled against common-sense beliefs. This raises at least two questions: (1) Is it *true* that quite often the relevant common-sense beliefs are more certain than some of the premises in the arguments raised against those beliefs? (2) If this is true, does that confer epistemic authority on common-sense beliefs? I answer these two questions in this order.

As many philosophers have pointed out, there are at least two different kinds of certainty: objective and subjective certainty. Objective certainty is the probability that a proposition is true given the evidence that one has. Subjective certainty is a person-dependent *feeling* of how convinced one is of the relevant belief. Objective certainty seems irrelevant here. After all, according to adherents of the common-sense tradition the very fact that something is a common-sense belief confers epistemic authority on it. Thus, it is at least prima facie rational, no matter what evidence there is in favour of it or against it (that evidence may defeat the common-sense belief so that ultima facie it is no longer rational to embrace; that leaves the prima facie rationality intact).

However, if subjective certainty is the relevant issue, then what we will have to say is that whether or not a particular common-sense proposition is more certain than each of the premises of the philosophical or scientific arguments levelled against it, depends on the person in question. Those who find, say, sceptical Brain-in-a-Vat arguments convincing are *not* more certain of the common-sense proposition that there is an external world than of each of the premises used in these arguments. And mutatis mutandis the same applies to those who embrace the results of experiments like those by Daniel Wegner and Thalia Wheatley,[13] which they take to demonstrate that we often do *not* know and even hold false beliefs about the reasons for which we act. So, whether or not a common-sense proposition is more certain for one than propositions that (jointly) conflict with it is person-dependent. Where does that leave us? Should we say that these common-sense propositions have epistemic authority for some people, but not for other people?

In order to answer this question, let us address the second question: if one believes the proposition p, does the fact that p is subjectively more certain for one than each of a set of alternative propositions $q_1, q_2, \ldots q_n$ confer epistemic authority on the belief that p? It is not clear that this is the case. People used to think that geocentrism is true until this was shown to be false by such scientists as Galileo Galilei and Johannes Kepler. What if people had replied that they were simply more certain of geocentrism than any of the premises in the scientific arguments against it? Would the common-sense view that geocentrism is true – at least, that was common sense *back then* – thereby have had epistemic authority? That seems questionable. Also, even if it had had epistemic authority *for them*, it certainly would not have had epistemic authority for the relevant scientists. That one is certain of something or more certain of it than of its rivals is hardly a reason to think that it is rational, justified, warranted, an instance of knowledge, or any such thing. Again, it seems that more is required than subjective certainty in order to explain why common sense has epistemic authority.

FOURTH ANSWER: COMMON-SENSE BELIEFS ARE INSTANCES OF KNOWLEDGE

As I pointed out in the previous section, in the writings of Moore we also find the idea that common-sense beliefs have epistemic authority because they are instances of *knowledge*. Knowledge seems epistemically at least as good as true belief, justified true belief, and so on, if not better. Surely, then, if we have good reason to think that common-sense beliefs are (usually) instances of knowledge, then common sense has a certain epistemic authority. A recent advocate and articulator of this idea is Noah Lemos. Says Lemos:

> Here, then, we have a reply to Ewing's question, why philosophers should be expected to pay so much respect to common sense. It is because some common sense beliefs are instances of knowledge and they are more reasonable than the philosophical principles that compete with them.[14]

One might wonder whether, in order for this line of reasoning to be convincing, the common-sense philosopher should give *arguments* for thinking that common-sense beliefs constitute knowledge. Lemos thinks that this is not the case: as long as common-sense beliefs do indeed constitute knowledge, it is perfectly fine to accept such beliefs – that is, to hold those beliefs and to endorse that one holds those beliefs. After all, if they constitute knowledge, common-sense beliefs have a wide variety of positive epistemic statuses, such as epistemic justification, being reliably formed, and so on.

What should we think of this approach? Well, undoubtedly, it would be a good thing if common-sense beliefs constitute knowledge. However, that is the very issue under consideration. The opponent of common sense doubts that common-sense beliefs constitute knowledge. To claim that common-sense beliefs *are* instances of rational belief, justified belief, knowledge, and so on, may well be true, but, clearly, doing so is *not* to provide a non-question-begging reason to take it that they have epistemic authority. The adherent of common-sense philosophy may of course very well be right that common-sense beliefs are justified and instances of knowledge, but merely claiming so is different from providing reasons or evidence for thinking that this is the case.

FIFTH ANSWER: COMMON SENSE IS VAGUE AND AMBIGUOUS

A fifth suggestion in reply to the question why we should think that common sense has epistemic authority is that common sense is vague and ambiguous (see Rescher 2005). It might sound somewhat paradoxical to say that vagueness and ambiguity can confer epistemic authority. Upon further consideration though, the idea is less implausible than one might initially think. The idea is that, since common-sense beliefs are fairly imprecise and ambiguous, there is likely to be some way in which they are true. For example, common sense tells us that human beings have free will or, in other words, that many of our actions are up to us. But it does not tell us exactly what such free will amounts to (thus also Haselager 2020). Since belief in free will is so ambiguous and imprecise, it may well still be true even if, say, determinism is true; for even if determinism is true, we are reason-responsive beings, and our deliberation makes a difference to what we do, so that our actions are at least *in some sense* up to us. Common-sense beliefs, then, are likely to be true and thus have epistemic authority.

The problem with this strategy is that it applies to relatively few common-sense beliefs. It applies to rather general metaphysical beliefs, such as the belief that we have free will, or general beliefs about the world, such as that the earth has existed for a very long time. However, take the common-sense beliefs mentioned at the outset of the chapter. There is nothing ambiguous or imprecise about perceptual beliefs, such as the belief that I have hands, beliefs based on memory, such as the belief that I was in Denver, Colorado, last week, beliefs based on proprioception, such as the belief that I feel no pain in my left leg, and many beliefs about one's own mental states, such as the belief that I am worried about my friend's mental health.

Thus, this reply may explain why *some* common-sense beliefs have epistemic authority, but it does not explain why common-sense beliefs *in general* have (defeasible) epistemic authority.

SIXTH ANSWER: COMMON SENSE IS THE PRODUCT OF EVOLUTION

The sixth answer to the question of what confers epistemic authority on common-sense beliefs is that they – or at least many of them – are the product of cultural (rather than biophysical) evolution and that cultural evolution selects for true beliefs, so that we have sufficient reason to trust the faculties that deliver common-sense beliefs. According to Nicholas Rescher (2005: 57),

> Man is a creature whose *modus operandi* evolves in the course of rational selection under the pressure of purposive efficacy. The validity of those established cognitive practices and customs is accordingly something that they wear on their sleeves: their appropriateness is manifested by the very fact of their being what they are – established customs and practices.

Cultural evolution can be seen as a rational process that, in the course of time, selects for true beliefs on issues that have to do with everyday affairs:

> They [i.e., common-sense beliefs] are the fruits of experience – the collective experience of people on a large scale and over a long time, having prevailed in the struggle for cultural survival through providing information that meets the needs of the group. Accordingly, they issue from principles rooted in human culture by means of rational selection ... And while even communal experience may not be an infallible and failproof resource, it is one that will (and given its rooting in a vastly extensive body of experience must) yield trustworthy results in the vast preponderance of cases relating to matters of everyday affairs. (Rescher 2005: 58)

In order to assess the claim that common-sense beliefs are the deliverances of a process of cultural evolution and the claim that this process has selected for true belief, we first need to know what 'cultural selection' amounts to. Presumably it is not the regular process of random mutation and natural selection, for then it would just be an instance of biophysical selection processes.[15] So what kind of process is it? Unfortunately, Rescher tells us little about this. What he does say raises significant worries, though. He talks about 'the struggle for cultural survival through providing information *that meets the needs of the group*' (my italics). This is worrisome, because information that meets the needs of the group need not be true or reliably formed – unless one takes it that the word 'information' is factive, but then this whole suggestion would beg the question, because what we need is an answer to the question of *why we should think* that common-sense beliefs constitute information or knowledge or understanding. Beliefs may be pragmatically useful or contribute to social cohesion without being true.

Fortunately, there are further ideas in the quote given above. Rescher speaks about 'rational selection', 'communal experience', 'trustworthy results in the vast preponderance of cases', and so on. More importantly, there is a whole field of research on the relation between biological and cultural evolution and the selection for true belief. Most participants in that debate agree that biological and cultural evolution jointly select for true belief. Someone with true beliefs is generally more likely to survive and reproduce than someone with false beliefs. Maybe for each common-sense belief an alternative can be concocted that has the same survival value, but it seems questionable whether this is also true for entire belief systems. It is more controversial whether this also applies to complex mathematical and other scientific beliefs, but it is widely taken to apply to beliefs from the senses, beliefs from memory, beliefs about macro material objects, such as tables and chairs, and so on.

I would also like to stress that the case for the epistemic authority of common-sense beliefs when it comes to the five senses and, say, memory and introspection is more likely to be convincing than it is for moral beliefs. Morality, after all, is concerned with the wrongness and permissibility of various actions, and those are abstract entities rather than physical characteristics we need to know in order to survive in this world. In fact, there is a whole separate literature on whether evolutionary theory provides debunking explanations of common-sense realist beliefs.[16]

One may object to this idea that in defending the epistemic authority of common sense, one will inevitably appeal to various common-sense beliefs and assume that *those* common-sense beliefs themselves have epistemic authority. Will an argument for the epistemic authority of common sense, therefore, not inevitably be circular? I think this is right. In fact, it seems to me this squares well with an important idea that we find in epistemology. The idea is that it is *impossible* to show or make plausible, without begging the question, that a large number of common-sense beliefs are epistemically justified, reliably formed, and so on. The idea is that this is impossible because, in order to show that they have these positive epistemic statuses, one will have to appeal to further common-sense beliefs and either assume that they have positive epistemic status or, in showing this, rely on even further common-sense beliefs (and so on). William Alston, for instance, has famously argued that we cannot show sense perception to be reliable.[17]

Thus, the argument for the epistemic authority of common sense will have to assume that common-sense beliefs have epistemic authority. I do not think that is a problem, though. The argument for the epistemic authority of common sense from the alethic orientation (truth-guidance) of evolutionary processes, for instance, is for an important part a *scientific* argument. Of course, science itself is built on a wide variety of common-sense beliefs. But there are few people who doubt not only common sense but also science. This is partly because science is thought to have filtered out many of the misleading common-sense beliefs. Since the appeal to common sense in this argument is very much indirect, it will convince many people, even though it is, strictly speaking, circular.

Note that for some kinds of common-sense beliefs, their epistemic authority cannot be defended by appealing to our evolutionary history.[18] Sharon Street (2006) has famously argued that evolution provides a debunking explanation of our moral realist common-sense beliefs, because true moral beliefs are in no way needed for survival or for increasing your chances at survival. Some philosophers have defended the position that the argument falls short (e.g., Copp 2008), but this just goes to show that we might need a different story to explain why moral common-sense beliefs have epistemic authority. In fact, various philosophers have tried exactly that, such as Jesse Prinz (2007) in defending sentimentalism and Terence Cuneo and Russ Shafer-Landau (2014) in arguing that moral truths are conceptual truths.

Does it follow that common-sense beliefs had no epistemic authority before Darwin developed evolutionary theory? Fortunately not. Common-sense beliefs may well have been rational, instances of knowledge, and so on before 1859. Of course, the fact that one had no argument for such common-sense beliefs before then does not imply that those beliefs were irrational; there are, according to many philosophers, properly basic beliefs after all. All I say is that since then we can formulate reasons of this kind to accept the epistemic authority of common sense.

SEVENTH ANSWER: GOD WOULD NOT DECEIVE US

A seventh and final proposal that I would like to consider is the idea that common-sense beliefs have epistemic authority, because humans use common sense on a large scale and God, being perfectly good, would not deceive us. Therefore, we can trust that common sense is largely reliable and that our common-sense beliefs are rational, instances of knowledge, and so on.

This line of reasoning – even though hardly ever *expressis verbis* cashed out in terms of common-sense beliefs – has, of course, a venerable pedigree. Descartes's appeal to the idea that God would not let us be deceived by our senses is a good example.

Another field from which one might derive theistic arguments for the reliability of common sense is the debate about the so-called argument from reason. The basic idea of the argument is that materialism and other varieties of naturalism cannot explain why we should trust logical and mathematical reasoning, whereas theism can (it provides a better explanation). The argument has received much attention ever since the well-known debate between C. S. Lewis and Elisabeth Anscombe. Recent literature provides detailed discussion of various objections against it (see, e.g., Reppert 2012).

There are various worries one can have with regard to this argument. Most importantly, one may not share the idea that there is a perfectly good God. Or one may not accept the idea that God has that kind of loving relationship with humans. But there are further worries apart from whether or not one accepts classical theism. One may also worry whether God's perfect goodness would entail that he ensures that our beliefs are by and large reliably formed. Clearly, the argument works only if premises along these lines hold water. Unfortunately, I cannot discuss the argument in much more detail here. Rather, I would like to stress that it may well be convincing for those who embrace theism, assuming that worries concerning various premises in the argument can be met.

I would like to stress here that the response from theism can be combined with other arguments, the response from evolution in particular. For, one might argue that God has equipped humans with reliable cognitive mechanisms *via a long evolutionary process*. As various philosophers of religion have argued, the randomness of neo-Darwinian evolution does not exclude theistic guidance (e.g., Plantinga 2011: 3–30). If this is true, then this response can well be combined with the previous one.

EPILOGUE

The central question of this chapter is why we should think that common-sense beliefs have epistemic authority. I have explored seven answers to this question that we find in the literature. I argued that only two of them are possibly convincing for a broad range of common-sense beliefs. Four of them either provide no *epistemic* (rather than practical or pragmatic) reason to think that common-sense beliefs are actually epistemically justified, rational, instances of knowledge, and so on, or they do so but beg the question in doing so. One of them provides *some* reason to think that common sense has epistemic authority, but the scope of the relevant common-sense beliefs is rather restricted. In order to explain why we should think that common-sense belief has epistemic authority, we should appeal to biological and cultural evolution or possibly, but more controversially, to theism. A particularly fascinating response would combine the two approaches. Such a response would have to address various questions in much more detail than I have been able to do in this chapter, such as the issue of whether evolution selects for true belief, exactly how cultural evolution works, how moral knowledge is possible, and why we should believe that God would ensure that common sense is by and large reliable.[19]

NOTES

1 Many claim that philosophy can overturn common sense. See, for instance, Ewing (1973) and Moser (1998: 364). Susanna Rinard (2013) even claims that philosophy can overturn common sense because science can do so, since those scientific arguments rely on philosophical assumptions.

2 See various essays in Peels et al. (2020).

3 Moore and Chisholm do not refer to a common-sense belief-forming faculty. Reid does do so (see Reid (1785) 2002), but it is not clear that he refers to a *sui generis* common-sense faculty.

4 This is a classic example of a common-sense belief, first provided by G. E. Moore. See also Rinard (2013: 186).

5 See Rescher (2005); Lemos (2004). See also their contributions to this volume, Chapters 9 and 12, respectively.

6 This strongly resembles Noah Lemos's definition of 'common sense'. See Lemos (2020: 20–21): 'Others may understand the notion of a common sense belief differently, but I shall take a common sense belief to be either (i)

a belief in a proposition that is deeply held by almost everyone or (ii) the self-attribution of a property that almost everyone attributes to himself.' One may wonder exactly who falls under 'everyone': everyone in history? Everyone in the past and now? Everyone in the West? For the purposes of this chapter, I take it to mean 'every healthy adult human being currently alive'.

7 Here I will not take a stance on whether that means that the belief is held *to a high degree* or whether the degree is held with a *high degree of conviction or certainty*, the difference between these boiling down to the issue of whether or not belief comes in degrees. Whether or not it does depends at least partly on what exactly it is for something to come in degrees. For more on that, see Van Woudenberg and Peels (2018).

8 See research by the Pew Research Center, e.g., www.pewforum.org/2012/ 12/18/global-religious-landscape-exec/.

9 Rinard (2013: 199–201) rightly points out that prima facie rationality or warrant is pretty weak. The second condition, which says that beliefs that have epistemic authority are not easily defeated, turns epistemic authority into a challenging property.

10 Thus, I do *not* take 'epistemic authority' to include *responsible belief* or *blameless belief*. This is not to deny that something's being a common-sense belief may well imply that it is responsibly or at least blamelessly held unless it is defeated. I explore this in more detail in Peels (2017b).

11 See Rosenberg (2011). See also various essays in De Ridder et al. (2018).

12 For an in-depth exploration of scientism, see De Ridder et al. (2018).

13 See Wegner and Wheatley (1999); Wegner (2002).

14 See Chapter 12 by Lemos in this volume; according to him, this is also William Lycan's view.

15 As to natural selection, philosophers like Alvin Plantinga have argued in detail that neo-Darwinian evolution does not select for true beliefs. That seems to be a minority position, though. See Beilby (2002).

16 See Street (2006) and all the literature in its wake.

17 See Alston (1993). The basic idea already plays a role in his argument for the rationality of religious belief; see Alston (1991).

18 For an argument along these lines, see Wilkins and Griffiths (2013).

19 For their helpful comments on earlier versions of this chapter I would like to thank Valentin Arts, Wout Bisschop, Lieven Decock, Jeroen de Ridder,

Chris Ranalli, Emanuel Rutten, René van Woudenberg, and Ruben Verhagen. This publication was made possible through the support of a grant from the Templeton World Charity Foundation. The opinions expressed in this publication are those of the author and do not necessarily reflect the views of the Templeton World Charity Foundation.

11 Scepticism and Certainty: Moore and Wittgenstein on Common Sense and Philosophy

Duncan Pritchard

INTRODUCTORY REMARKS

How should we conceive of the relationship between common sense and philosophy? This is a large question, but I want to suggest that we can get at least one interesting angle on this topic by considering a particular historical episode from early analytical philosophy. This concerns the problem of radical scepticism, at least in one of its (now, anyway) familiar guises.

In one corner we have G. E. Moore, who offers a distinctive account of how we should handle dialectical standoffs between philosophy and common sense, and who demonstrates the utility of his proposal by appealing to common-sense certainties in order to respond to philosophical concerns about our knowledge of an external world. In the other corner we have Wittgenstein, who rejects the Moorean account of common-sense certainties and their supposed philosophical import. But that's not because he wants to defend a traditional viewpoint of a kind that Moore was opposing with his common-sense philosophy. Wittgenstein instead offers a kind of inversion of the Moorean position, a position that accords our common-sense certainties a special role to play in our epistemic practices – and thus in our dealings with philosophical problems, such as radical scepticism – albeit in a very different manner to that envisaged by Moore.

As we will see, this debate is more than just of historical interest, since the two parties are outlining distinctive ways in which a common-sense epistemology might be developed.

MOORE ON COMMON SENSE AND CERTAINTY

Common sense is a recurring *motif* throughout Moore's philosophical corpus, but our interest here, for reasons that will become apparent, is specifically with Moore's treatment of certainty in the context of our knowledge of an external world. The thread that unites Moore's work in this regard is the idea that our common-sense certainties can be employed to push back against philosophical challenges to knowledge of this kind (from radical scepticism and idealism), and hence constitute legitimate dialectical stopping points in a philosophical debate.

In taking this general line, Moore is following in a philosophical tradition, as exemplified most notably by Thomas Reid.[1] Just as Reid countered the sceptical themes of his day, as represented especially in the work of Hume, by appealing to our common sense, so Moore does likewise in response to the prevailing scepticism about the external world of his day.[2] There were two sources of the scepticism that Moore was countering. The first was found in the idealism that was prominent in British philosophy at the turn of the twentieth century.[3] The second was the new forms of (indirect) realism regarding perceptual knowledge and experience that were being developed in the early twentieth century in response to such idealism, which make our knowledge/experience of the world essentially indirect and mediated by 'sense-data'. These latter views are not meant to be sceptical about the external world in the way that idealism is, but by making our knowledge of an external world indirect they inevitably generate sceptical worries of this kind regardless.[4]

Moore's response to these philosophical proposals that call our knowledge of the external world into question was to insist that since common sense tells us that we do have external-world knowledge, so it follows that there must be something amiss with the philosophical reasoning in play. When common sense and philosophy conflict, that is, the former always has priority. But what kind of priority did Moore have in mind?

The first thing to notice in this regard is that Moore doesn't hold that our common-sense beliefs are always true or that they are inherently epistemically justified, much less that they are immune to revision. It follows that we do not automatically have knowledge of these common-sense claims either. Nonetheless, what does seem clear is that Moore holds that common-sense claims have an intrinsic credibility that ensures that they are dialectically privileged relative to philosophical claims that oppose them.

Moreover, Moore also holds that the special status of these claims relates to the *certainty* with which we endorse them. In particular, our everyday common-sense convictions enjoy a certainty that philosophical theses lack. Accordingly, he maintains that where the two conflict it would be more reasonable to retain one's common-sense claims than to instead endorse the opposing philosophical position. Indeed, he also seems to want to say that the degree of certainty in play here is important, in that when it comes to those everyday common-sense claims of which we are optimally certain, it would be especially reasonable to retain one's conviction in the everyday claim rather than accede to the philosophical alternative.

In fact, it was these optimally certain everyday claims (in normal conditions anyway), and the special epistemic standing that they have as a result, that most interested Moore. Call these *Moorean certainties*. He presented a long list of Moorean certainties, the most famous of which was of course that one has hands, but which also included such claims as that one is not currently completely naked, and that the earth has existed for many years before one was born.[5] Presumably Moore holds that it is possible that we can be in error even here, though when it comes to these Moorean certainties he seems to want to claim that we simply cannot make sense of them being false (even though they might be). At the very least, the idea that philosophy might call them into question is rejected, as Moore maintains that it would always be more reasonable to maintain the Moorean certainty over any philosophical thesis that conflicted with it, given that the latter would inevitably be less certain. Here is

Moore, talking about philosophical views that challenge our knowledge of the external world:

> it seems to me a sufficient refutation of such views … simply to point to cases in which we do know such things. This, after all, you know, really is a finger: there is no doubt about it. I know it, and you all know it. And I think we may safely challenge any philosopher to bring forward any argument in favour either of the proposition that we do not know it, or of the proposition that it is not true, which does not at some point rest upon some premise which is, beyond comparison, less certain than is the proposition which it is designed to attack. (Moore 1918–19: 8)

Another crucial element to Moore's common-sense approach to these matters is to explicitly eschew the burden of explaining how one has knowledge of these Moorean certainties. That is, Moore holds that the foregoing demonstrates that it is more rational to endorse these Moorean certainties (and so regard them as known) than to be swayed by the opposing philosophical considerations (which purport to call such knowledge into question), even if one lacks an account of how these Moorean certainties amount to knowledge. Relatedly, one can legitimately reject these opposing philosophical claims even if one cannot explain exactly what is amiss with them. Indeed, Moore is even willing to grant that he finds the opposing philosophical claims credible. He famously contends that our situation with regard to scepticism about our knowledge of the external world is essentially a matter of one person's *modus ponens* being the other person's *modus tollens*, with plausible antecedents on either side (see especially Moore 1959a). But still he insists that it can be reasonable to reject these philosophical claims if they conflict with common sense, and hence embrace the antecedent of the conditional that goes along with our common-sense convictions.

Moore is effectively conceding here that his philosophical opponent has problematized the type of knowledge in question. There is, even by Moore's own lights, a standing challenge to explaining how our knowledge of the external world is possible. Moore is content to allow that he cannot meet this challenge, but he maintains that he doesn't need to meet it in order to reasonably insist that one has the knowledge in question. This is because he maintains that we can know things without being in a position to explain how we know them, much less being able to prove that we know them. Indeed, he even goes so far as to grant that we can legitimately maintain we have knowledge even if we cannot cite any specific evidence in support of the proposition in question, and even in the context of a philosophical challenge to that knowledge. In fact, Moore concedes that a lack of evidence of this kind is often the case when it comes to these Moorean certainties. Here he is talking about his knowledge of the common-sense claim that the earth has existed for many years before he was born:

> I certainly know this because I have known other things in the past which were evidence for it. And I certainly do not know exactly what the evidence was. Yet all this seems to me to be no good reason for doubting that I do know it. We are all, I think, in this strange position that we do know many things, with regard to which we know further that we must have had evidence for them, and yet we do not know how we know them, i.e., we do not know what the evidence was. (Moore 1925: 45)

Notice that Moore isn't saying that we lack evidence for these common-sense certainties. Instead, he maintains that we do have such evidence. And yet it is also the case, according to Moore, that we are unable to identify what this evidence is.

A further feature of Moore's treatment of these Moorean certainties, one that is often overlooked, is that he clearly thought that their certainty is completely unaffected by our engagement with the philosophical challenge that is posed to them. So discovering that there is a standing, and credible, philosophical puzzle about our knowledge of the external world, and coming to recognize that one cannot explain how one has this knowledge or even what specific evidence supports that knowledge, is compatible with one continuing to be, quite reasonably, just as certain of the truth of these propositions as before. Indeed, this much is clear from Moore's own reaction to the philosophical argument in play. His point is not just that those who haven't engaged with these challenges are entitled to their knowledge of these certainties even while lacking a grip on how this knowledge comes about or on what evidentially supports it. Rather, he further claims that even those who, like him, have engaged with these challenges and come to see their plausibility are nonetheless entitled to be no less certain that they have the knowledge in question. This is a quite remarkable stance, and goes well beyond the general idea behind a common-sense philosophical methodology such that common-sense claims should be privileged over philosophical challenges to them.

Moore's common-sense response to external-world scepticism is thus quite radical. It is not just that common sense is a kind of dialectical deal-breaker when it comes to a philosophical impasse, or even that common-sense claims have an inherent (albeit defeasible) epistemic pedigree on account of their certainty. Moore goes further to contend that we are entitled to these common-sense claims even if we recognize the force of the opposing philosophical argument and even if we recognize that we lack an account of how we can have the knowledge of these common-sense claims that we take ourselves to have. Indeed, even if we recognize that we cannot identify the evidential basis for this knowledge, it is nonetheless rational to continue to endorse them, and be no less certain of them.

WITTGENSTEIN ON CERTAINTY AND SCEPTICISM

Wittgenstein's final notebooks, published as *On Certainty*, are centrally concerned with the status of Moorean certainties.[6] Wittgenstein agrees that they play a special role in our practices, but he doesn't understand this role along the same lines that Moore did. In particular, while Moore holds that the optimal certainty that attaches to these propositions ensures that they have a special rational status, Wittgenstein holds that they have no rational standing at all.[7] Even so, he agrees with

Moore about the importance of these common-sense certainties when it comes to dealing with challenges to our knowledge of the external world. We thus have two very different conceptions of the role of common sense in philosophical methodology in play, with Moore representing a contemporary twist on the common-sense philosophical tradition and Wittgenstein presenting, in contrast, something much more iconoclastic.

The source of the divergence between Moore and Wittgenstein when it comes to these Moorean certainties is a radical difference in how they each take these certainties to relate to other, more mundane, everyday claims that we take ourselves to know. Right now, for example, I take myself to know that my car is parked outside my house. But while I take myself to know this, it is clearly not a proposition that is optimally certain, and much less is it the kind of claim that could play any kind of dispute-settling role in a philosophical debate. Interestingly, it is also something that I not only think that I know, but which I could easily tell you how I know (I remember parking the car there earlier, and have no reason for thinking that it has been moved since). Relatedly, I would have no problem articulating what evidence I had in support of this belief.

Moore effectively treats the relationship between the Moorean certainties and these mundane everyday claims as merely a matter of degree, where the former is simply more certain than the latter. We noted earlier that while Moore grants that we often can't identify the evidential basis of these Moorean certainties, he also held that one could not reasonably doubt that they were known, and thus that they did enjoy an adequate evidential basis. Moore seems to think that the fact that the evidential support for these Moorean certainties is not easily identifiable is merely a by-product of their common-sense status, in that they are so familiar and long-standing that it is understandable that their original evidential basis should now be long forgotten.

Wittgenstein takes a strikingly different line in this regard. He maintains that the optimal certainty that is associated with these

Moorean certainties means that we can make no sense of there being rational support in their favour (or against them, for that matter). In this regard they are very unlike our ordinary mundane claims to knowledge, where evidence for or against them can easily be marshalled. Wittgenstein focuses, in this regard, on the Moorean certainty that one has two hands. He writes:

> My having two hands is, in normal circumstances, as certain as anything that I could produce in evidence for it.
>
> That is why I am not in a position to take the sight of my hand as evidence for it. (Wittgenstein 1969: § 250)

The point is that the optimal certainty that applies to these Moorean certainties far outstrips any evidential basis that we could provide for them. Rather than this showing that there is something epistemically amiss with these certainties, however, Wittgenstein instead claims that it highlights the special role that they play in our epistemic practices, one that by its nature excludes them from rational evaluation altogether.

This point is further brought out by considering what doubt of a Moorean certainty would involve. Consider this passage:

> If a blind man were to ask me 'Have you got two hands?' I should not make sure by looking. If I were to have any doubt of it, then I don't know why I should trust my eyes. For why shouldn't I test my *eyes* by looking to find out whether I see my two hands? *What* is to be tested by *what*? (Wittgenstein 1969: § 125)

In normal circumstances, determining that one has two hands by looking would be simply bizarre. Having hands is not like having one's keys in one's pocket, where one might verify their existence by looking for them. Wittgenstein is again emphasizing the differences between Moorean certainties and our everyday knowledge claims, in that the former are nodes of a general backdrop of certainty against which our rational practices – and in particular our practices of offering reasons for and against propositions – take place.

This is why the Moorean certainties are characterized by Wittgenstein as having a 'hinge' status, and why the propositional attitude in play is often referred to as a *hinge commitment*. Consider this famous passage:

> [T]he *questions* that we raise and our *doubts* depend upon the fact that some propositions are exempt from doubt, are as it were like hinges on which those turn.
>
> That is to say, it belongs to the logic of our scientific investigations that certain things are *in deed* not doubted.
>
> But it isn't that the situation is like this: We just *can't* investigate everything, and for that reason we are forced to rest content with assumption. If I want the door to turn, the hinges must stay put. (Wittgenstein 1969: §§ 341–3)

Wittgenstein's point is that it is this backdrop of certainty that enables rational evaluation to take place. Rather than the optimal certainty associated with the Moorean certainties reflecting the fact that they enjoy a special level of rational support, it instead reveals how they are immune to rational evaluation since they constitute the framework relative to which rational evaluation occurs. As such they can be neither rational nor irrational (and hence are a-rational).

This last point is especially important to understanding Wittgenstein's account of hinge commitments. As he puts it in the passage just cited, it is not as if the hinge commitments are mere assumptions that we could rationally discharge. Indeed, they are not assumptions at all, since there is nothing remotely hypothetical about our commitment to them. On the contrary, Wittgenstein emphasizes how such certainty is rooted in our actions rather than being the result of ratiocination, how it is primitive, visceral, 'animal'.[8] Relatedly, it is not as if we could imagine a system of rational evaluation that lacked a-rational hinge commitments. Wittgenstein explains why by showing how the very idea of a universal rational evaluation – whether negative (sceptical) or positive (anti-sceptical) – is simply incoherent. As he remarks at one point (Wittgenstein 1969: § 450): 'A doubt that doubted everything would not be a doubt.' One needs somewhere to stand, from a rational point of view, in order to rationally doubt, and that constrains the scope of the doubt. Wittgenstein's insight was to recognize that what needs to be kept in place are our basic certainties, and that this is a point that cuts both ways. It is not just doubt that requires a backdrop of certainty, but belief too. That which cannot be rationally doubted cannot be rationally believed either. But the attempt to rationally doubt, or rationally support, a hinge commitment is tantamount to undertaking a universal rational evaluation. Although the propositions in play look mundane, their optimal certainty reflects the fact that they are codifying our fundamental relationship to the world. If, in normal conditions, I am wrong about whether I have hands, then everything is called into question (in contrast, for example, to being wrong about whether I have my keys in my pocket).

This is also why Wittgenstein is so keen to highlight the oddity of the way in which Moore enumerates these Moorean certainties (see, e.g., Wittgenstein 1969: § 6). Moore clearly thinks that in making these claims explicit he is simply highlighting some ordinary commitments that we hold which are especially certain. As noted above, he doesn't think there is any difference of kind in play when it comes to these Moorean certainties, in contrast to their more mundane counterpart everyday claims that are not optimally certain. But Wittgenstein shows us that the special status of these hinge commitments is revealed in our normal epistemic practices, and in particular in how these commitments are usually entirely tacit. Wittgenstein notes that we are not taught hinge commitments, but that we instead 'swallow them down' with the specific claims that we are taught (see Wittgenstein 1969: § 143). (For example, we are not taught that we have hands, but only how to do things with our hands.) Relatedly, we do not normally even notice these hinge commitments, as they 'lie apart from the route travelled by enquiry' (see Wittgenstein 1969: §

88). It takes an unusual philosophical context, such as the one that Moore is engaged in, in order to make these certainties explicit. In stating the Moorean certainties as he does, as if they are essentially no different from other empirical claims that he believes he knows, Moore is thus failing to recognize the distinctive role that they play in our epistemic practices.

WITTGENSTEIN ON COMMON SENSE

Wittgenstein thus offers a kind of 'inversion' of the Moorean picture. Whereas Moore holds that the optimal certainty enjoyed by the Moorean certainties means that they have a special rational status that enables them to be a dialectical stopping point in a philosophical dispute, Wittgenstein maintains that their optimal certainty in fact excludes them from having any rational status at all. Does that mean that Wittgenstein is an opponent of a common-sense philosophical methodology? I think that drawing this conclusion would be far too quick, for one could just as well regard Wittgenstein as developing a more refined version of a common-sense philosophical methodology.

In particular, Wittgenstein isn't disputing Moore's claim that these common-sense certainties play an important philosophical role. Rather, his point is that Moore has misunderstood their nature. Wittgenstein's criticism of Moore in this regard mirrors a broader critique that he offers of philosophy – a recurring theme in his earlier *Philosophical Investigations* – in terms of how it misuses our every-day language and, in the process, manufactures illusory philosophical puzzles that trade on this misuse of language (see Wittgenstein 1953). Moore misuses language by thinking that he can simply enumerate these Moorean certainties as if they were just like any other mundane empirical claim. In doing so, he fails to see their true significance.

Notice too how the conception of rational evaluation that Wittgenstein offers, which has hinge commitments at its heart, offers a much more powerful way of dealing with the sceptical problem than that proposed by Moore. One of the standard criticisms of a common-sense philosophical methodology like Moore's is why we should privilege common sense over philosophy, particularly when (as in Moore's case) we are offered no explanation for why the common-sense claim is true (and it is even granted that the opposing philosophical claim appears credible).[9] Wittgenstein's approach is not merely to accurately describe our epistemic practices and maintain that this correct description by itself should suffice to resolve the sceptical problem. Instead, he provides us with a compelling diagnosis of where the sceptical reasoning goes awry.

We can bring this point into sharper relief by comparing Wittgenstein's anti-scepticism with the kind of ordinary-language approach to the sceptical problem exemplified by J. L. Austin (another philosopher who could arguably lay claim to being part of the common-sense philosophical tradition). Like Wittgenstein, Austin also highlights how very different our everyday epistemic practices are when compared with the epistemic practices described by the radical sceptic (and also, for that matter, by philosophers attempting to deal with the sceptical problem; see, e.g., Austin 1961a). But as Barry Stroud (1984) powerfully argued, merely noting this difference is of dubious import to radical scepticism. This is because the radical sceptic can persuasively contend that what she is doing is presenting a *purified* version of our everyday epistemic practices – that is, once we strip away everything that is extraneous to those practices. After all, it is surely not contentious that in ordinary epistemic contexts our practices are influenced by all kinds of considerations – lack of imagination, lack of time, and so on – that have no bearing on the epistemic standing of our beliefs.[10] If that's true, however, then our 'purified' everyday epistemic practices might well be rather different to our actual everyday epistemic practices, and yet nonetheless be properly rooted in them. The radical sceptic could thus employ distinct epistemic practices while even so maintaining that she wasn't doing anything that wasn't licenced by our ordinary ways of conducting rational evaluations.

Wittgenstein's anti-scepticism blocks off even this style of response, however. For he demonstrates that the differences between the philosophical (i.e., sceptical/traditional anti-sceptical) description of our epistemic practices and our actual epistemic practices cannot be captured in this manner. This is because the former, far from being an extension (or purified version) of the latter, is in fact simply incoherent. We are not ignorant for lacking rational support for our hinge commitments, since there could be no such thing. To aspire for such would be to aspire for universal rational evaluations, and Wittgenstein has argued that this is impossible. We are consequently not lacking, from an epistemic point of view, in being unable to undertake them, any more than we are lacking, from an artistic point of view, in being unable to draw a realistic circle-square.[11]

The style of response that Wittgenstein is offering to the sceptical problem is thus very different to that attempted by Moore. In particular, Wittgenstein is showing how, by attending to the relevant features of our epistemic practices and characterizing them correctly, we can diagnose the philosophical confusion that is generating this puzzle. This is the sense in which what Wittgenstein is presenting is an *undercutting* anti-sceptical strategy, in that he is showing how what can seem like a genuine philosophical conundrum is in fact nothing of the kind. This is in contrast to the kind of *overriding* anti-sceptical strategy that Moore's style of common-sense line offers us. For remember that even while embracing the common-sense alternative, Moore nonetheless grants that he cannot explain where the sceptic(/idealist) goes awry or even explain how the contested knowledge is possible. Accordingly, he cannot possibly be in a position to offer an undercutting diagnosis of this problem.

This aspect of the Moorean line is apt to be overlooked because of how Moore presents the dialectic as being a clash between common sense and a philosophical *position*. This is in part because a significant element of what is driving his concern with our knowledge of the external world is the challenge to this knowledge posed by idealism, and that is of course a philosophical stance (indeed, a fairly popular one, in British philosophical circles at any rate, at the time he was writing). Radical scepticism, however, is best understood as a putative *paradox*, in the sense of a series of claims that look independently plausible – indeed, which seem to be rooted in our everyday practices – but which are collectively inconsistent. Radical scepticism as a position, after all, doesn't seem all that credible. Can we really make sense of someone who claims to doubt everything, and therefore doesn't know anything? (And why would we listen to the arguments offered by such a person?) But a paradox is a very different dialectical beast. In particular, in proposing a paradox one is not thereby committed to specifying which of the claims that make up the paradox should be rejected. So while radical scepticism as a position might be committed to maintaining that external-world knowledge is impossible, radical scepticism as a paradox can merely note how such knowledge is inconsistent with other independently plausible claims that we hold.[12]

Insofar as Moore is dealing with radical scepticism qua position, it seems perfectly reasonable to insist on common sense rather than embrace the radical sceptical conclusion, particularly if one grants that the two stances are in the dialectical impasse that Moore describes. With the debate so construed, it might not seem to be all that significant that Moore is unable to diagnose where the radical sceptic's reasoning goes awry or explain how external-world knowledge is possible after all. But this dialectical line is far less credible when cast against radical scepticism qua paradox. This is because Moore's common-sense response effectively leaves the paradox entirely intact, since he doesn't offer any theoretical diagnosis of what is amiss with it. But how then could the appeal to common sense possibly offer us any philosophical comfort in our dealings with this paradox? In effect, all it tells us is that there is a genuine paradox concerning our knowledge of the external world but that common sense assures us that we do have such knowledge. If anything, doesn't that simply exacerbate the mystery regarding our external-world knowledge, rather than do anything to remove it?[13]

CONCLUDING REMARKS

What does this contrast between Moore's and Wittgenstein's approaches to the problem of external-world knowledge tell us about appeals to common sense in philosophy? I think there are two broad conclusions that we can reach, which are intersecting in important ways. The first is that there are limits to the kind of philosophical satisfaction that we can achieve by simply appealing to common sense in the way that Moore did, without also at the same time offering an undercutting theoretical diagnosis of the philosophical puzzle in play. This is especially so when it comes to paradoxes (in contrast to challenges posed by philosophical *positions*), where mere appeals to common sense of this sort seem to offer no philosophical comfort whatsoever.

The second conclusion is that we cannot take common-sense claims at face value in the way that Moore supposes. In particular, the very articulation of common sense, far from being a straightforward task, requires philosophical acumen. Moore thought that his presentation of these Moorean certainties as articles of common sense was entirely unproblematic. But while he was right that they do tell us something about the fundamental nature of our everyday practices, their articulation in this manner in fact served to obscure their philosophical import. Far from being akin to ordinary empirical claims that happen to be optimally certain, they are in fact claims that play a distinctive role in our epistemic practices – one that is normally entirely tacit, and for good reason (as these claims provide the framework for these practices and hence are not themselves subject to that framework).

These two conclusions are intersecting because they each have a bearing on the other. Moore's failure to properly characterize our common-sense commitments lies at the source of his inability to diagnose where the radical sceptical puzzle goes awry. Conversely, any theoretical diagnosis of the sceptical problem of a kind that can undercut this puzzle will involve a philosophical account of what constitutes our common-sense commitments in this regard, and will not simply involve a bare endorsement of them.

Both Moore and Wittgenstein treat our everyday practices – and thus the everyday epistemic practices that presently concern us – as holding the key to resolving philosophical puzzles. In this broad sense they are both common-sense philosophers. But we have also seen that their approaches to dealing with philosophical puzzles are importantly different. Whereas the Moorean common-sense philosophical methodology holds that we can unproblematically identify common-sense claims and then straightforwardly employ them to resolve philosophical disputes, the Wittgensteinian philosophical methodology is much subtler. What might strike the philosopher as articles of common sense ought to be interrogated, and that requires philosophical acumen. In undertaking such an exercise, the philosopher is able to tease out the genuine features of our everyday practices from the theoretical claims that are imported into our descriptions of these practices by the philosopher. In doing so, she is able to unravel the problematic reasoning that led to the philosophical puzzle in hand.[14,15]

NOTES

1 In the last century the foremost exponent of this tradition, besides Moore himself, was probably Chisholm – see, for example, his famous defence of particularism as a response to the problem of the criterion in Chisholm (1977). For discussion of Chisholm's common-sense philosophical methodology, see Lemos (2004).

2 See Reid ((1764) 1997). For further discussion of Reid's common-sense philosophical methodology, and its particular application to Hume's writings, see Lemos (2004; 2020) and McAllister (2016).

3 For an overview of the main trends in so-called British idealism, see Brooks (2017). Of course, idealism is sometimes presented as a way of *responding* to scepticism about the external world.

4 See in particular Moore's (1918–19) discussion of Russell's account of perceptual experience and knowledge. Unhelpfully, Moore doesn't

specify which material by Russell he has in mind in this regard, but it is likely to be Russell (1914). Note that Moore (e.g., 1953b) himself endorses a kind of sense-datum theory, though he seems inclined to regard such a notion as picking out features of the world rather than one's perceptual experiences. Sense-datum theory, so construed, is obviously not committed to an indirect realism about perceptual experience (much less perceptual knowledge).

5 See, respectively, Moore (1939); Moore (1959a); and Moore (1925).

6 Published as Wittgenstein (1969). Note that granting that these notebooks are primarily concerned with Moorean certainties does not entail that Moore's work is the overarching focus of these writings as is often supposed. In fact, there are good reasons to think that Newman ((1870) 1979), which is also concerned with certainties of this kind, was also an important influence on these notebooks. For discussion of this point, see Kienzler (2006) and Pritchard (2015b).

7 Note that, following our two protagonists, I will be using the notions of evidence and reasons interchangeably. I think there are in fact crucial differences between these two notions, but since they are not relevant to our purposes here we can reasonably set them to one side.

8 Here is Wittgenstein (1969: § 359): 'I want to conceive [of this certainty] as something that lies beyond being justified or unjustified; as it were, as something animal.'

9 See Lemos (2008) for further discussion of this kind of criticism of Moore.

10 I am here setting aside the question of pragmatic encroachment in epistemology. For further discussion of this topic, see Fantl and McGrath (2010).

11 This is why it is misleading to simply describe us as lacking knowledge of Moorean certainties, as that implies that they are in the market for knowledge (and thus that we are ignorant of them), which is not the case. For some of the key interpretations of Wittgenstein's treatment of radical scepticism in On Certainty (where this includes works that offer epistemological theses broadly inspired by this work), see McGinn (1989); Williams (1991); Moyal-Sharrock (2004); Wright (2004b); Coliva (2010; 2015); and Schönbaumsfeld (2016). I offer my own interpretive line in this regard in Pritchard (2015a). For a recent survey of contemporary work on Wittgensteinian epistemology, see Pritchard (2017).

12 For further discussion of the idea of radical scepticism as a paradox as opposed to a position, and the dialectical important of this distinction, see Pritchard (2015a: part I).

13 The distinction between the problem of radical scepticism and idealism as two ways of calling our external-world knowledge into question is also important to understanding *On Certainty*. In particular, the first of the four notebooks that make up this work seems primarily devoted to the problem of idealism (and hence is mostly concerned with Moore's proof of an external world), with the other three notebooks primarily concerned with the sceptical problematic (and hence more concerned with the more general issue of the status of the Moorean certainties). Crucially, however, Wittgenstein's hinge epistemology seems to be directed at the latter rather than the former. This is because he treats attempts to even state idealism (or realism, for that matter, construed now as the rejection of idealism), such as a statement like 'There are physical objects', as being, unlike hinges, simply nonsense – see, for example, Wittgenstein (1969: § 35). For more on this point, see Williams (2004) and Pritchard (2015a: chapter 4).

14 Note that this is the sense in which a distinctively Wittgensteinian philosophical quietism is very different from a straightforward form of philosophical quietism that simply eschews philosophical puzzles, and thus philosophy, altogether. The conundrums that we are led into by faulty philosophical reasoning can only be unravelled by further philosophy. In this sense, philosophy is both the cause of, and the solution to, philosophical problems. For more on Wittgensteinian quietism, see McDowell (2009). For a contemporary discussion of varieties of philosophical quietism more generally, see Virvidakis (2006). See also Pritchard (2020), where I draw parallels between Wittgenstein's brand of quietism and Pyrrhonian scepticism (which is very different from the broadly Cartesian scepticism that has been our concern here).

15 Thanks to Rik Peels and René van Woudenberg for detailed comments on an earlier version of this chapter.

12 Morality and Common Sense

Noah Lemos

In the first section, I briefly describe what I take to be a central feature of the common-sense tradition in philosophy. I would say that it is characteristic of the common-sense tradition to hold that we do know, pretty much, what we ordinarily think we know and that it is reasonable for us to reject philosophical theories that imply that we do not. Among the things that we think we know are various 'common-sense' beliefs. Why give some common-sense beliefs more weight than various philosophical views? I suggest it is because some common-sense beliefs are things we know. The common-sense tradition holds that among the things we know are various facts about the external world and some epistemic facts; for example, that we know there are other people, people know their names, and we know that they know their names. In the second section I make two claims. First, that the common-sense tradition should include among the things known various common-sense moral claims as well as various particular moral claims that are no less evident. Second, that these claims are more reasonable to believe than any philosophical view that implies either that they are false or that we do not know them. In short, I suggest that the common-sense philosopher should treat some moral claims as having the same weight as some epistemic claims and claims about the external world. In the last three sections I consider some philosophical objections to this view. These include the objections that no evaluative claims are true or false, that we cannot know particular moral claims without knowing some general moral criterion, and that the appeal to our moral intuitions is illegitimate in philosophical inquiry.

SOME FEATURES OF THE COMMON-SENSE TRADITION

In his 1919 essay 'Some Judgments of Perception', G. E. Moore considers some views about perception and the possibility of perceptual knowledge. He rejects them because they imply that we cannot know various facts about the external world. He writes:

> But it seems to me a sufficient refutation of such views as these, simply to point to cases in which we do know such things. This, after all, you know, really is a finger; there is no doubt about it: I know it and you all know it. And I think we may safely challenge any philosopher to bring forward any argument in favour either of the proposition that we do not know it, or of the proposition that it is not true, which does not rest upon some premiss which is, beyond comparison, less certain, than is the proposition which it is designed to attack. (Moore 1960b: 228)

Elsewhere, Moore writes:

> There is no reason why we should not, in this respect, make our philosophical opinions agree with what we necessarily believe at other times. There is no reason why I should not confidently assert that I do really *know* some external facts, although I cannot prove the assertion except by simply assuming that I do. I am, in fact, as certain of this as of anything and as reasonably certain of it. (Moore 1960a: 163)

Moore holds that it is reasonable for us to reject various sceptical arguments because (1) they incorrectly imply that we do not know certain facts about this external world (e.g., that this is a finger) and (2) it is more reasonable for us to hold that we do know those facts than one or more of the premises of the sceptical argument.

A similar stance was taken by Roderick Chisholm concerning sceptical arguments about induction. Chisholm (1973: 232) writes: 'We reject the skeptical view according to which there is no good reason to believe that the premises of an inductive argument ever confer evidence upon the conclusion. If the skeptical view were true, then we would know next to nothing about the world around us.' Since we *do* know various facts about the external world, it is reasonable for us to reject the sceptical view.

Chisholm and Moore belong to the common-sense tradition in philosophy. We find a similar stance in the position of the eighteenth-century common-sense philosopher Thomas Reid. Reid writes,

> To what purpose is it for philosophy to decide against common sense in this or any other matter? The belief in a material world is older, and of more authority, than any of the principles of philosophy. It declines the tribunal of reason, and laughs at the artillery of the logician. It retains its sovereign authority in spite of all the edicts of philosophy, and reason itself must stoop to its orders. Even those philosophers who have disowned the authority of our notions of an external world, confess that they find themselves under a necessity of submitting to their power. (Reid (1764) 1983: 4)

Reid notes that the belief in a material world is older than the belief in various philosophical principles. He also points out that we cannot give up belief in a material world. It is irresistible for us. But what is most important, I suggest, is that Reid holds that the belief in the material world has more *authority* than the principles of philosophy. The concept of authority is a normative claim. He is not merely claiming that the belief in the material world is older and irresistible. He is claiming that it is more worthy of being believed than the principles of philosophy.

Philosophers in the common-sense tradition, such as Reid, Moore, and Chisholm, hold that they know various facts about the *external world*, for example, that this is a finger, there are other people, and we existed yesterday. They also hold that they know various *epistemic facts*, for example, that they *know* that this is a finger and others know it as well, and that almost everyone knows that there are other people. They hold that it is more reasonable to believe *some* propositions about the external world and about our knowledge of it than any philosophical principles or arguments that conflict with such claims, which imply either that such claims are false or that we do not know them. Philosophers in the common-sense tradition reject certain philosophical views because they conflict with and are less reasonable to believe than various other propositions that we know. Perhaps we might put this point by saying that some propositions about the external world and our knowledge of it have more weight for us than any philosophical principle or argument that conflicts with them.

Among the beliefs we ordinarily take to be instances of knowledge are a great many common-sense beliefs. Suppose we take a common-sense belief to be either (1) a belief in a proposition that is deeply held by almost everyone, or (2) the self-attribution of a property that almost everyone attributes to himself. If we understand a common-sense belief this way, then the beliefs that there are other people and that other people think and feel and have bodies will be common-sense beliefs since they are deeply held by almost everyone. Similarly, my beliefs that I think, I have a body, and I have been alive for several years, are common-sense beliefs since they are the self-attribution of properties, for example, thinking, having a body, and having been alive for several years, which almost everyone attributes to himself. Other examples of common-sense beliefs would be the beliefs that people are born, and that they existed yesterday, and my beliefs that I have hands, that I am alive, and that I was much smaller when I was born.[1]

In addition to the examples mentioned above, our common-sense beliefs include some epistemic beliefs. These would include the beliefs that people know their names, they know there are other people, and they know that others think and feel and have bodies. Moreover, there are common-sense beliefs about our faculties. These include the beliefs that our memories, under certain conditions, are reliable; that perception, under certain conditions, is reliable; and that introspection, under certain conditions, is reliable. These beliefs about our faculties might not be explicitly formulated, but they are accepted nonetheless. They guide our belief formation and the way we assess the testimony of others.

If this is how we understand a common-sense belief, then a great many common-sense beliefs are instances of knowledge. They are also instances of common knowledge. The fact that some common-sense beliefs are a matter of common knowledge is not without significance. If almost everyone knows that there are other people, that they think and feel and know things, then there must be some way of knowing these things that does not rest on philosophical arguments or considerations grasped only by a handful of philosophers, and this knowledge can't be the fruit of philosophical reasoning followed only by a philosophical elite. Whatever our account of knowledge, it must be adequate to the fact that such knowledge is widespread and common.

A. C. Ewing, who was sympathetic to the common-sense tradition in philosophy, asks why philosophers should be expected to pay so much respect to common sense. Why, he asks, should those who have studied philosophy alter their philosophical views because people who have never studied it think them wrong? What, he asks, would happen to the natural sciences if scientists had been forbidden to contradict the views which non-scientists held on scientific matters before they had studied science? He replies (Ewing 1973: 367): 'We should still be believing in a flat earth with the sun and all the stars going round it if people acted on those lines.'

In reply to Ewing, I would say that the *mere* fact that a philosophical view conflicts with a common-sense belief, in the sense suggested above, does not necessarily require philosophers to alter their views. But if a philosophical view is incompatible with those common-sense beliefs that are *known*, then the philosophical view is simply false. In this regard, there is no difference between philosophical or scientific views. Any view that denies what is known is simply mistaken.

What is important about some common-sense beliefs is that they are instances of knowledge and more reasonable to believe than various sceptical philosophical views or the premises that support those views. But, importantly, this feature is not unique to common-sense beliefs. There are *lots* of beliefs that share those features. Moore's belief that *this* is a finger is not a belief in a proposition that is deeply and widely held by almost everyone nor is it the attribution to oneself of a property that almost everyone attributes to himself. It is not, in the sense suggested above, a common-sense belief. Still, it is an instance of knowledge and more evident than one or more of the propositions to which the sceptic might appeal. The same is true of my beliefs that I had eggs for breakfast, I am presently typing, and I am thinking about Moore. Such particular beliefs are not deeply and widely held, but they are instances of knowledge and more reasonable for us to believe than any philosophical principle that implies that they are false or that they are not known.

THE COMMON-SENSE TRADITION AND MORAL BELIEFS

Philosophers in the common-sense tradition hold that they know various propositions about the external world and various epistemic propositions, and that these propositions are more reasonable for us to believe than one of more of the premises in philosophical arguments which imply that either such propositions are false or that they aren't known. But what about *moral* claims and propositions? Do any of them have the same status that philosophers in the common-sense tradition attribute to some propositions about the external world and some epistemic propositions? If we think that some claims about the external world and some epistemic claims have a special weight for the common-sense philosopher, do some moral claims have similar weight? I suggest they do. I suggest that our commonsensism should encompass some moral claims.

Are there any common-sense moral beliefs? I assume there are. There are, I believe, some moral propositions that are widely and deeply held. I assume, for example, that it is widely and deeply believed that some acts are wrong and others are right, that some ways of living are better or more desirable than others, that some actions are cruel or vicious and that others are generous or kind, that some actions are praiseworthy and that others are blameworthy, and that we sometimes ought to consider the consequences of our actions before deciding what to do.

In addition to these truisms, I think our common-sense beliefs include some general moral principles. These include the following: that we ought to show gratitude, to keep our promises, to make reparation to those we have injured, to help those who are in distress, not to lie, and not to steal. I assume further that almost everyone who accepts these principles views them as being at least prima facie principles, as claiming that the fact that an act has a certain character is at least some moral reason to do it or not to do it. So, the fact that an act would be the keeping of a promise or an instance of gratitude is at least some moral reason to do it, and the fact that an act would be a lie or a theft is some moral reason not to do it.

I assume, then, that there are some common-sense moral beliefs. But further I assume that some of them are instances of knowledge and they are more reasonable for us to believe than any philosophical principles that imply that they are false or that we do not know them. Indeed, I assume that this is true of the examples of common-sense moral beliefs stated above. Thus, I assume that I and others know that some acts are right and others are wrong and that some actions are cruel and others kind, that we ought to show gratitude and keep our promises.

Perhaps there are many other common-sense moral beliefs. Perhaps some of them are not worthy of belief and some of them are false. Perhaps some of them, to paraphrase Moore, 'deserve to be mentioned with contempt'. But I do not think the ones that I have stated above are false or unworthy of belief. On the contrary, I think that the ones I have stated are reasonable and among the things we know.

In addition to these common-sense moral beliefs, we know some particular moral propositions and these, too, are more reasonable for us to believe than any philosophical proposition that implies either that they are false or that we don't know them. Such propositions are not deeply and widely held because they concern particular acts which are not widely known. But like Moore's belief that *this* is a finger, they are instances of knowledge and more worthy of belief than any competing philosophical view.

For example, a few years ago, a man living in a town not far from mine had a dispute with his sister over some money he claimed she owed him. He went to his sister's apartment to collect the money he thought she owed him. She was not home, but her fourteen-year-old daughter and her two-year-old son were. The uncle slit the throat of his niece, took both children and drove them to a local bridge, and threw them in the creek below. His nephew drowned, but his niece survived. She wandered out to a highway where a passing couple found her and rushed her to a local hospital. Now, I would say (a) that it was wrong for that man to slit his niece's throat and to drown his nephew, and (b) that it was right for the passing couple to help the wounded niece. Moreover, I would say that I know both (a) and (b). Almost everyone familiar with the facts of this case also knows (a) and (b).

In addition to these particular moral claims, there are a great many other particular moral propositions that I also know. I know, for example, that it would be wrong for me now to kill my wife and my co-workers, to drive my car down a crowded sidewalk, to steal from the local stores, or to torture my students. I know that it is right for me now not to do such things. Other people know many similar things about themselves.

I would say, then, that we know many moral propositions, both general and particular. I know, for example, that it was wrong for the uncle to slit his niece's throat and to drown his nephew, and that it was right for the passing couple to help her. Again, many others know this, too. And, in the spirit of Moore, I would say we may safely challenge any philosopher to bring forward any argument in favour either of the proposition that we do not know them or of the proposition that they are not true which does not rest upon some premise which is, beyond comparison, less certain than the propositions which it is designed to attack.

But *how* do we know these moral propositions? That, of course, is an important epistemological question. Nevertheless, I would say that we need not know the answer to that philosophical question in order to have moral knowledge. In this respect, knowledge of moral propositions is no different from knowledge of propositions about the external world. In order to know that this is a hand or that is pencil, one does not need to have a philosophical theory that explains how such knowledge is possible. One does not need to be an epistemologist in order to have perceptual knowledge, and one need not be an epistemologist to have moral knowledge. Indeed, it seems that one could have perceptual knowledge and have *mistaken* epistemological views. Reid, Moore, and Chisholm, for example, have different, and in some respects conflicting, views about how they know the external world and how they know various epistemic facts. They can't all be right. Indeed, Moore seems to have thought at one time that his knowledge of some external facts – for example, that this is a pencil – was immediate knowledge, and, later in his career, he suggests that it is not.[2] Those views can't both be right. Still, Moore had perceptual knowledge even if he at some point held mistaken epistemological views. Knowledge of some external facts does not depend on knowing how one knows them, and the same is true of our knowledge of some moral facts.

COMMON SENSE AND NON-COGNITIVISM

Can there really be knowledge of moral propositions? There is, of course, a sophisticated body of non-cognitivist thought that holds that our ordinary moral language has no truth value, and thus there can be no such a thing as moral knowledge. Emotivism, in its simplest forms, holds that our moral utterances are mere expressions of our attitudes. Thus, when one says 'Murder is wrong', one means something like 'Murder! Boo!' Similarly, when one says 'Gratitude is good', one means something like 'Gratitude! Hurray!' Such emotional ejaculations express the speaker's attitude, but they lack truth value. Prescriptivism emphasizes the action-guiding role of moral language. According to prescriptivism, when one says 'Murder is wrong', one is attempting to guide people's conduct. Moral language, on this view, is best understood in terms of imperatives. So, when one says 'Murder is wrong', one means something like 'Do not murder!' and when one says 'Gratitude is good' one means something like 'Show gratitude!'[3]

In spite of the popularity of non-cognitivist analyses of our ordinary moral language, the view that some moral claims have a truth value has remained stubbornly persistent. There are various considerations against non-cognitivism, and it is well beyond the scope of this chapter to explore them in any depth. I shall, however, briefly mention a few.

First, we commonly take ourselves to be asserting something when we make a moral judgment, and the form of our judgment is typically declarative or assertive in form. When I judge, for example, that it was wrong for the uncle to slit his niece's throat and to drown his nephew, I am asserting something about his actions. I am judging that a certain proposition is true, namely, that his actions were wrong. Emotional attitudes, feelings, or sentiments might accompany moral judgments, but the ordinary user of moral language takes himself to be describing or characterizing the object of his judgment. In making a moral judgment, one is not merely expressing one's attitude the way one expresses disgust by uttering 'Ugh!' or joy by uttering 'Hurray!' If this is so, non-cognitivism fails to capture what the ordinary user of moral language means when she uses moral language.

The preceding points were made by Reid in his *Essays on the Active Powers of the Human Mind*. Reid notes that,

> Before the modern system of ideas and impressions was introduced, nothing would have appeared more absurd than to say, that when

I condemn a man for what he has done, I pass no judgment at all about the man, but only express some uneasy feeling in myself. (Reid 1969, essay 5, chapter 7: 457)

Every determination of the understanding, with regard to what is true or false, is judgment. That I ought not to steal, or to kill, or to bear false witness, are propositions, of the truth of which I am as well convinced as of any of the propositions of Euclid. I am conscious that I judge them to be true propositions; and my consciousness makes all other arguments unnecessary, with regard to the operations of my own mind. (Reid 1969, essay 5, chapter 7: 463–4)

For Reid, the suggestion that we do not make moral judgments that we take to be true or false contradicts that immediate testimony of consciousness (introspection). This is why he takes the view to be absurd.

Second, we think that some forms of moral argument are valid and others aren't. Consider for example the following argument: (1) if stealing is wrong, then it is wrong to encourage others to steal; (2) stealing is wrong; therefore (3) it is wrong to encourage others to steal. This is a deductively valid argument. Ordinarily, we take a deductively valid argument to be one in which the premises logically imply the conclusion. But if non-cognitivism is true, then neither the premises of the argument nor the conclusion have a truth value. But if they have no truth value, it is hard to see in what way they could logically imply the conclusion.

Third, moral sentences can meaningfully occur in the antecedents of conditionals such as (1). But it is far from clear that mere imperatives or prescriptions or the expressions of attitudes can meaningfully take the place of such antecedents. What would it mean to say 'If don't steal, then … ' or 'If boo to stealing, then … '? Moreover, suppose one accepts a conditional such as (1). One could accept (1) without having any particular attitude towards stealing, without having a pro or anti attitude towards stealing and without seeking to guide anyone's actions with regard to stealing. But if the meaning of the antecedent is either to express an attitude or to guide behaviour, then what does the antecedent of (1) mean in that case?

Fourth, our ordinary moral beliefs reflect a commitment to cognitivism. We believe that sometimes a person ought to have known better than to act as they did. We think in some cases a person should have known that what they did was wrong. We sometimes excuse people from moral blame when we believe that they lacked the capacity to know that what they did was wrong, or when they lack the capacity to know right from wrong. That we accept this excuse without excusing everyone reflects the ordinary view that people have the capacity to know what is right and what is wrong.

Finally, in considering the plausibility of non-cognitivism in ethics, we should also consider its plausibility in epistemology. Many epistemic concepts are evaluative. To say that a belief is an instance of knowledge, justified, or reasonable, is to evaluate it positively. To say that a belief is unjustified or unreasonable is to evaluate it negatively. If non-cognitivism about epistemic terms were true, then statements such as 'He knows he has hands' and 'She knows her name' would not be true, and statements such as 'He knows the earth is flat' and 'She knows $2 + 3 = 4$' would not be false. Furthermore, since knowing that p implies that p is true, one could never know that one knows something or know that one is justified in believing it. A non-cognitivist analysis would rule out knowing that one knows. Epistemically and morally evaluative claims are in the same boat, and since epistemic non-cognitivism is not plausible, we should also reject moral non-cognitivism. Indeed, given that the common-sense philosopher holds that he knows some epistemic claims, it seems that he ought to reject non-cognitivism in the moral sphere. Why, after all, should one treat the two forms of evaluation differently?[4]

PARTICULAR MORAL FACTS AND GENERAL PRINCIPLES

There is a second objection to the view that there is knowledge of particular moral facts, or, at least, to the view that such knowledge is as widespread as the common-sense philosopher might think. This objection presupposes a certain picture of what is necessary for such knowledge. It assumes that one's knowledge that some particular action is right or wrong depends epistemically on one's knowing some general criterion of right or wrong from which the rightness or wrongness of the particular action can be deduced.

One can find the view, I think, in John Stuart Mill's *Utilitarianism*. He writes in the first chapter of *Utilitarianism* (Mill 1979: 2): 'A test of right or wrong must be the means, one would think, of ascertaining what is right or wrong, and not a consequence of having already attained it.' Mill seems here to hold that our knowledge that some particular action is right or wrong depends upon our first knowing some general criterion of right or wrong. Perhaps we might take Mill to hold that in order for me to know that some particular action A is right (wrong), my belief that A is right (wrong) must be based on my knowing that A has some feature, F, and a general principle to the effect that whatever has F is right (wrong).

A similar view was suggested by William Alston concerning our knowledge of particular epistemic facts. Alston writes:

> In taking a belief to be justified, we are evaluating it in a certain way. And, like any evaluative property, epistemic justification is an evaluative property, the application of which is based on more fundamental properties ... Hence in order for me to be justified in believing that S's belief that p is justified, I must be justified in certain other beliefs, viz. that S's belief that p possesses a certain property, Q, and that Q renders its possessor justified. (Another way of formulating this last belief is: a belief that there is a valid epistemic principle to the effect that any belief that has Q is justified.) (Alston 1976: 170)

Alston is describing what is necessary for knowledge of particular epistemic facts, but his view would seem to apply more generally to our knowledge that any particular has an evaluative property, such as the properties of being right or wrong, good or bad. Others have held similar views.[5]

If these views are right, then it seems doubtful that knowledge of particular moral facts is widespread. This is because it seems doubtful that there is widespread knowledge of the relevant general principles. The plain man, not to mention the philosopher, might *believe*, for example, that it was wrong for the uncle to slit his niece's throat and to drown his nephew, but he might not *know* a general moral principle from which, with the aid of some non-moral premises, it deductively follows that the act was wrong.[6] He might know some prima facie moral principles, but the rightness or wrongness of particular actions does not logically follow from such principles. So, consider the following argument:

(1) You know that a particular action is wrong, A, only if you know both (i) that A has some non-moral property F, and (ii) that whatever has F is wrong.

(2) You do not know the relevant general principle concerning the uncle's attack on his niece and the drowning of his nephew.

(3) Therefore, you do not know that it was wrong for him to attack his niece and drown his nephew.

In reply to this argument, however, we might ask why we should assume that (1) is true. Indeed, which is more reasonable to believe: that (1) is true or that you *do* know that it was wrong for the uncle to attack his niece and kill his nephew? It seems to me that it is far more reasonable to believe the latter. Almost everyone who considers the matter knows it.

In any event, it is doubtful that this view about what is required for knowledge of particular evaluative facts is true. It certainly doesn't follow, as Alston suggests, from the supervenient character of evaluative properties. Even if evaluative properties supervene on more basic properties it does not follow that one has to know anything about those more basic properties in order to know that something has the evaluative property. Consider mental properties. It is plausible to suppose that mental properties supervene on brain states, but one doesn't have to know anything about one's brain states, much less some general principle connecting the possession of certain brain states to the exemplification of mental states, in order to know that one has a certain mental state. Moreover, there seem to be plausible cases of knowledge of evaluative properties that don't require knowledge of general principles or the beliefs in the relevant non-evaluative properties. Consider driving through the mountains and coming suddenly on some spectacular view. One thinks, 'That's beautiful!' One can know that the scene is beautiful, but one's knowledge that it is does not depend on one's having justified beliefs that the scene has some non-evaluative properties F and whatever has F is beautiful. This seems to require too much. One simply sees that it is beautiful.

None of this is intended to suggest that the search for general moral or epistemic principles is unimportant. Such principles would explain why actions or beliefs have the evaluative properties that they have. The point is simply that knowledge of such principles is not necessary for knowing, in at least some cases, that an act or belief has an evaluative feature.

REJECTING MORAL THEORIES ON THE BASIS OF COMMON-SENSE MORAL BELIEFS

Finally, I have suggested that it is characteristic of the common-sense tradition to reject various philosophical views when they conflict with those common-sense beliefs that we know. Many philosophers, however, have thought it mistaken or unsatisfactory to appeal to our ordinary moral beliefs or intuitions when engaged in moral philosophy. Consider the following passages, the first from Richard Brandt and the second by R. M. Hare:

> Various facts about the genesis of our moral beliefs militate against the mere appeal to intuition in ethics. Our normative beliefs are strongly affected by the particular cultural tradition which nurtured us, and would have been different if we had been in

a different learning situation with different parents, teachers or peers. Moreover, the moral convictions of some people derive, to use the words of Peter Singer, 'From discarded religious systems, from warped views of sex and bodily functions, or from customs necessary for survival of the group in social and economic circumstances that now lie in the distant past.' What we should aim to do is to step outside our own tradition somehow, see it from the outside, and evaluate it, separating what is only a vestige of a possibly once useful moral tradition from what is justifiable at present. The method of intuitions in principle prevents us from doing this. It is only an internal test of coherence, what may be no more than a reshuffling of prejudices. (Brandt 1979: 21–2)

The intuitions that give rise to the conflict are the product of our upbringings and past experiences of decision-making. They are not self-justifying: we can always ask whether the upbringing was the best we could have, or whether the past decisions were the right ones, or even if so, whether the principles then formed should be applied to a new situation, or if they cannot be applied, *which* should be applied. To use intuition itself to answer such questions is a viciously circular procedure; if the dispositions formed by our upbringing are called into question, we cannot appeal to them to settle the question. (Hare 1981: 12)

Do these passages provide good reason to eschew appeals to those common-sense moral beliefs which we take ourselves to know when we are evaluating moral theories or moral principles?

One problem that Brandt and Hare seem to be pointing to is the problem of epistemic circularity. Let us say that a way of supporting the reliability of a source, F, is epistemically circular just in case one uses the testimony of F to support that F is reliable. An argument that a source F is reliable is epistemically circular if one or more of the premises is based on the testimony of F. Many philosophers hold that an epistemically circular argument for the reliability of F cannot justify a belief that F is reliable.[7] They would tell us that one cannot use the testimony of memory to support the reliability of memory or use the testimony of perception to support the reliability of perception. It would be like using other copies of a newspaper to support what was said in one of them. Or taking a man's word for his own veracity.

Perhaps Brandt and Hare think that using one's moral intuitions or one's moral beliefs to support the reliability of one's ways of forming moral beliefs would be epistemically circular. To use our own moral beliefs to support the view that our ways of forming moral beliefs is reliable is, according to Hare, 'viciously circular', and to use or own moral beliefs to support a set of moral principles, even one that coheres with our deepest moral beliefs, may be, according to Brandt, 'no more than a reshuffling of prejudices'. For both Brandt and Hare, the remedy is to 'get outside' our own moral beliefs by appealing to non-moral beliefs to support an independent criterion, a criterion of right action that is independent of our moral beliefs for its support. Thus, Brandt appeals to beliefs about 'rational' action and desire and Hare to beliefs about various logical principles, including principles about the logic of moral terms, and various empirical, non-moral premises. Once we find such a criterion, we can use it to assess our dispositions to form moral beliefs.

It is unclear, however, that the strategy of getting outside our moral beliefs and turning to some new domain of beliefs will solve the problem of epistemic circularity. One could, after all, raise similar questions about the reliability of those beliefs formed in the new domain. Indeed, one could ask whether Brandt's beliefs about 'rational' action and Hare's beliefs about the logic of moral terms, as well as their beliefs about various empirical facts, are reliably formed. If one thinks that the only legitimate strategy for dealing with challenges to the reliability of beliefs in a particular domain is an 'exit strategy', to get outside the domain of beliefs called into question, where does one then turn once beliefs in the new domain are called into question?

Still, many philosophers have discussed the problem of epistemic circularity, and it is far from clear that one cannot support the belief that a source is reliable by making use of beliefs from that source. Indeed, there are reasons to believe that epistemic circularity need not be vicious.[8] But, what is more, since the problem of epistemic circularity is not unique to our moral beliefs but a pervasive issue for *all* of our ways of forming beliefs, it is not clear why we should forego the appeal to our moral beliefs and our moral intuitions in our philosophical inquiries, including the search for moral criteria. Since the issue of epistemic circularity concerns *all* of our ways of forming beliefs, not just our moral beliefs, it seems to be no good reason to treat our moral beliefs differently.

A different objection to the use of moral beliefs in philosophical inquiry is suggested by Brandt. Brandt cites Singer's remark that some moral beliefs derive from discarded religious systems, warped views of bodily functions, and customs that are no longer necessary for the survival of the group. But even if this is so, it is not true of the common-sense moral beliefs I mentioned above. It is also not true of some particular moral beliefs, such as the beliefs that it was wrong for the uncle to attack his niece and drown his nephew and that it was right for the passing couple to come to the niece's aid. It is not true of the beliefs that it would be wrong for me now to kill my wife and co-workers or drive my car down a crowded sidewalk.

No doubt many of our moral beliefs are influenced by our culture and upbringing. Many of them reflect our moral training, and, no doubt, some of them would have been different had we been raised in a different culture with different teachers. But this is also true of many of our non-moral beliefs about history and science. Had I been raised in Presocratic Greece my beliefs about history and science would have been very different. But that hardly supports the view that my current beliefs about history and science are not instances of knowledge, or that I should not rely upon them in intellectual inquiry.

Our moral beliefs have different degrees of justification. Some are evident and sufficiently justified for knowledge, and some enjoy weaker degrees of justification. Still, some of our moral beliefs, such as those mentioned above, are more evident and more reasonable to believe than some of the propositions to which philosophers such as Brandt and Hare would appeal in an attempt to offer an independent justification for a moral criterion. For example, Hare asks us to consider the following two propositions: (i) I now prefer with strength S that if I were in that situation x should happen rather than not, and (ii) if I were in that situation, I would prefer with strength S that x should happen rather than not. Hare claims that it is a conceptual truth that to know (ii), (i) must be true. But which is more evident, this alleged conceptual truth *or* the propositions that it was wrong for the uncle to slit his niece's throat, it was wrong for him to drown his nephew, and it was right for the passing couple to help the niece? Is it *really* a close call?

Moreover, suppose someone argued for a moral criterion from premises including no moral propositions. Would it really be reasonable for us to accept such an independently supported criterion if it did not imply, or even rejected, various common-sense beliefs that we know? Suppose, for example, that some proposed criterion implied that it was not wrong for the uncle to attack his niece and drown his nephew or that it was not right for the passing couple to help the niece. Would it not be reasonable for us to reject that criterion because it conflicts with what we know?

Finally, as Hare points out, if philosophers appeal to different and conflicting intuitions about particular cases it is difficult, if not impossible, to settle their disagreements about which ways of forming moral beliefs are reliable or which moral criterion is true. If someone denied that it was wrong for the uncle to attack his niece and nephew, it might indeed be hard to reach an agreement with him about fundamental moral principles.

But how important a goal is reaching agreement or settling disputes? One could always reach agreement simply by changing one's view and acquiescing to the views of others, or, alternatively, offering them hemlock. Suppose instead one wants to get to the truth and, even more, to know the truth about what makes right acts right. In that case, *not* to make use of what one knows in philosophical inquiries seems poor intellectual procedure and intellectually irresponsible. In trying to get to the truth in philosophical inquiry one should use *all* one's evidence. One's evidence includes those things that we know and this includes a great many common-sense moral beliefs and beliefs about particular cases. The common-sense philosopher's procedure in rejecting various arguments because they conflict with what he knows is good intellectual procedure even if it begs the question against some philosophical views.[9]

Of course, one *might* engage in philosophical inquiry by confining one's evidence to that which is certain and infallible. Perhaps such a restriction might be justified if one seeks truth and is especially averse to error. But we have seen how well that works out. Or, perhaps, one wants to pursue inquiry reasoning only from mutually accepted premises. Such a restriction might be justified on *some* ground, perhaps a moral ground of conviviality or even mutual respect. What is admissible for evidence in inquiry can certainly be limited by moral or practical considerations, as in a trial where certain types of evidence are inadmissible. But it is not clear that there are any moral or practical reasons for not appealing to what we know in philosophical inquiries. One should search for the truth with both eyes open.

The common-sense tradition in philosophy holds that it is reasonable to accept various beliefs about the external world and various epistemic claims, and that it is more reasonable to accept them than to accept various philosophical arguments that imply that such beliefs are false or not instances of knowledge. There is, I think, no good reason not to take the same stance with regard to some of our moral beliefs.

NOTES

1 I do not assume that Reid, Moore, and Chisholm all understand common sense in the way suggested here. John Greco, for example, takes Reid to hold that common sense in the primary sense of the expression refers to a faculty or set of faculties that all normally functioning human beings possess. The 'first principles' of common sense are the immediate, non-inferential judgments or content of those judgments that issue from those faculties. These would include the immediate, non-inferential judgments of perception, memory, reason, and consciousness (introspection). Whether this is the best way to understand Reid is perhaps a matter of debate best left for another occasion. In any event, it is not clear that this is how Moore and Chisholm understand what it is for something to be a common-sense belief. See Greco (2011: 144).

2 For example, in 'Hume's Theory Examined', Moore (1953a: 142) claims that he knows the proposition that the pencil exists immediately. But in 'Four Forms of Skepticism', he claims that he does not know it immediately (Moore 1959c: 226).

3 Classic statements of emotivism include Barnes (1933); Stevenson (1944); and Ayer (1952). Classic statements of prescriptivism include Carnap (1937) and Hare (1952; 1963).

4 The same would apply of course to other sorts of evaluative or normative knowledge, such as prudential or aesthetic knowledge.

5 Cf. also the following remark by R. M. Hare (1952: 111): 'If we knew all the descriptive properties which a particular strawberry had ... and if we knew also the meaning of the word "good", then what else should we require to know, in order to be able to tell whether a strawberry was a good one? Once the question is put in this way, the answer should be apparent. We should require to know, what are the criteria in virtue of which a strawberry is to be called a good one, or what are the characteristics that make a strawberry a good one, or what is the standard of goodness in strawberries. We should require to be given the major premiss.'

6 Perhaps it will be suggested that the relevant general principle is 'All killing is wrong', and that from this general principle one deduces that it was wrong for the uncle to kill his nephew. But is this general principle true, much less known? What about killing animals or plants for food or killing deadly bacteria? What about killing in self-defence or in a just war? I am not

sure what the relevant general principle would be from which it *deduct-ively* follows that the uncle's action was wrong. I do not think one needs to know such a general principle from which it deductively follows that the uncle's action was wrong in order to know that it was wrong. Moreover, I would say that any proposed general principle would be less evident than that the uncle's action was wrong.

7 Richard Fumerton writes (1995: 177): 'You cannot *use* perception to justify the reliability of perception! You cannot *use* memory to justify the reliability of memory! You cannot *use* induction to justify the reliability of induction! Such attempts to respond to the skeptic's concerns involve blatant, indeed pathetic, circularity.' A similar objection is raised by Laurence BonJour (1985: 10): 'Since what is at issue here is the metajustification of an overall standard of empirical knowledge, rather than merely an account of some particular region of empirical knowledge, it seems clear that no empirical premises can be employed. Any empirical premise employed in such an argument would have to be either (1) unjustified, (2) justified by an obviously circular appeal to the very standard in question, or (3) justified by some other standard of empirical justification (thereby implicitly abandoning the claim that the standard in question is the correct overall account of epistemic justification for empirical beliefs). Thus, the argument will apparently have to be purely *a priori* in character, and it is certainly far from obvious how such an *a priori* argument might go.' I will simply note here that Fumerton treats direct acquaintance as a reliable way of forming beliefs and BonJour treats a priori insight as reliable, yet both of those sources would also confront the problem of epistemic circularity. See Lemos (2004: chapters 2 and 3).

8 One of the best defences of the view that epistemic circularity is not vicious can be found in Sosa (1994).

9 For an excellent discussion of these issues, see Kelly (2008). See also Lemos (2004: chapter 1).

13 Common Sense and Ontological Commitment

Chris Ranalli and Jeroen de Ridder

[Wittgenstein] once greeted me with the question: 'Why do people say that it was natural to think that the sun went round the earth rather than that the earth turned on its axis?' I replied: 'I suppose, because it looked as if the sun went round the earth.' 'Well,' he asked, 'what would it have looked like if it had looked as if the earth turned on its axis?' This question brought it out that I had hitherto given no relevant meaning to 'it looks as if' in 'it looks as if the sun goes round the earth'. My reply was to hold out my hands with the palms upward, and raise them from my knees in a circular sweep, at the same time leaning backwards and assuming a dizzy expression. 'Exactly!' he said.

G. E. M. Anscombe, *An Introduction to Wittgenstein's 'Tractatus'*

INTRODUCTION

How ontologically committal is common sense? Is the common-sense philosopher beholden to a florid ontology in which all manner of objects, substances, and processes exist and are as they appear to be to common sense, or can she remain neutral on questions about the existence and nature of many things because common sense is largely non-committal? The task of this chapter is to sketch different answers to this question and to offer a provisional assessment of their strengths and weaknesses.

The question is important for a number of reasons. First, common sense is often considered to be a central touchstone for philosophical theorizing, especially in metaphysics (cf. Nolan 2016). To show that a proposed metaphysical theory violates common sense is typically considered a strike against it. Although philosophers differ in their assessment of exactly how bad it is for a theory to go against common sense, most agree that it is strongly preferable for theories to respect common sense.[1] In fact, philosophers proposing metaphysical theories that appear to violate common sense often go to great lengths to show that, contrary to appearances, their theory is compatible with common sense after all, or else that it violates common sense only in minor and insignificant ways.[2] But of course, in order to determine whether a metaphysical theory goes against common sense, it needs to be clear what exactly common sense is committed to. If a theory is committed to the existence of objects constituted by random mereological sums such as this volume and the leaning tower of Pisa, that surely seems to go against common sense, but as long as it's unclear whether common sense is committed to the non-existence of such objects, we can't really tell whether there is a conflict.

Second, the ontological commitments of common sense are also important for claims about (alleged) conflicts between science and common sense. Science has been claimed to debunk common-sense convictions about ordinary physical objects. Sir Arthur Eddington's famous discussion of the two tables eloquently expresses the thought:

> Yes; there are duplicates of every object about me – two tables, two chairs, two pens ... One of them has been familiar to me from earliest years. It is a commonplace object of that environment which I call the world ... It has extension; it is comparatively permanent; it is colored; above all it is substantial ...
>
> Table No. 2 is my scientific table. It is a more recent acquaintance and I do not feel so familiar with it. It does not belong to the world previously mentioned ... My scientific table is mostly emptiness. Sparsely scattered in that emptiness are numerous electric charges rushing about with great speed; but their combined bulk amounts to less than a billionth of the bulk of the table itself. (Eddington 1928: ix–x)

More recently it has also been maintained that science undermines common-sense convictions about the nature of human beings, free will, rationality, and morality (cf. Peels et al. 2020). Assessing the merits of these debunking claims requires a clear view of what common sense is committed to.

Third, getting clear about the ontological commitments of common sense is important for common-sense philosophy itself. It is, quite simply, a part of its self-understanding. And while much has been said about the epistemological commitments and implications of common-sense philosophy (see several other contributions to this volume, especially Chapters 9, 11, 12, 14, and 15), it appears that its ontology has received significantly less attention.

TAKING COMMON SENSE AT FACE VALUE

We introduce two initially plausible lines of thought about the ontological commitments of common sense. The first, explored in this section, naturally leads to the conclusion that common sense is substantially ontologically committed; the other, discussed in the next section, to the opposite conclusion, namely, that common sense bears very little ontological commitment.

The first line of thought starts from the idea that common sense is a container for the collective wisdom of ages. It has been shaped and moulded by human biological and cultural evolution and by the collective experience of many people over long periods of time. Even though common sense isn't the outcome of sustained systematic scientific inquiry, it has been tried and tested over time through everyday experience and hence there is extensive confirmation and broad evidence for its correctness. Hence, we ought to put a lot of stock in what common sense affirms and denies.[3] Moreover, we don't have anywhere else to start – it's not as if we can just decide to put common sense aside, assume nothing, and begin with a blank slate. If common sense tells us that an external world exists, that tables and chairs exist, that people have free will, that you are the same person you were ten years ago, etc., then we should take those claims at face value and conclude that common sense is ontologically committed to an external world, to tables and chairs, to free will, to identity over time, etc. When philosophy or science clash with common sense, this is a strike against them. Occasionally, when the scientific evidence is overwhelming or the force of the philosophical argument irresistible, there might be ultima facie reason to revise our commonsensical commitments, but we shouldn't do so easily. In short:

> *Common-sense commitment principle*: if common sense says that there are entities E or things or events of kind K, then one is prima facie entitled to believe that there are Es/Ks.

By 'prima facie entitled to believe that there are Es/Ks' if common sense says that there are Es/Ks, we mean that one can reasonably accept that there are Es/Ks independently of having a justifying argument in favour of believing that there are Es/Ks. As long as one lacks reasons to believe there are no Es/Ks, one is thereby prima facie entitled to accept that there are Es/Ks if common sense says that there are Es/Ks. For example, if common sense says that people have free will, one can reasonably accept that there are some actions which are free even if one lacks a good argument for believing it. All one needs is to lack justification for believing that there are no such actions. This common-sense principle is a restricted form of epistemic conservatism and is thus far more moderate than unrestricted varieties of epistemic conservatism. Epistemic conservatism says that if you believe that p and there are no salient defeaters for your belief, then you are prima facie justified in retaining your belief that p. In this case, the principle is restricted to the ontological commitment claims of common sense.[4]

To explore this first line of thought further, suppose we accept that common sense bears significant epistemic weight and that its ontological commitments should not easily be put aside. What, then, are its ontological commitments? And how do we find out?

The literature contains a number of proposals. Let's begin by looking at three key ideas about what ontological commitment is. Our first stop is the quantifier account of ontological commitment, as famously defended by Quine (1953):

Quantifier account: a theory T is ontologically committed to all and only those entities to which the variables of the quantified sentences of T range over if T is to be true.

The quantifier account looks to the values of the variables of the sentences that compose the theory to tell us what its ontological commitments are. For example, consider the following statement:

(1) The hydrogen failed to bond with the oxygen.

We can state this sentence in first-order predicate logic as follows:

(2) $\exists x \exists y$ Hydrogen(x) & Oxygen(y) & ~Bonded(x, y).

From (2) it follows that:

(3) $\exists x$ Hydrogen(x).

According to the quantifier account of ontological commitment, (3) is ontologically committed to hydrogen because the variable in (3) ranges over hydrogen. The quantifier account implies that a sentence like (3) is ontologically committed to *only* what the bound variable x ranges over in order for that sentence to be true. Since (3) doesn't have any variable which explicitly ranges over *electron*s or even *physical objects*, (3) is not ontologically committed to an electron or a physical object. For (3) to be ontologically committed to an electron or a physical object, the broader theory which embeds or implies (3) would need to contain other sentences which explicitly quantify over electrons or physical objects.

Indeed, one challenge for the quantifier account is that theories often have implicit ontological commitments. For example, while (3) explicitly quantifies over hydrogen, hydrogen is a physical object with one proton and one electron, so one might naturally think that any theory which includes (3) ought to be committed to the existence of at least one proton and at least one electron. The quantifier account, however, doesn't predict this. For the theory which includes (3) might not explicitly mention protons or electrons and thus will fail to explicitly state $\exists z$ Proton(z) and $\exists v$ Electron(v) as sentences of the theory. This challenge is perhaps most pronounced in the case of atomic predicates which convey extrinsic properties, such as *child*. Consider a theory which contains (4) $\exists f$ Child(f). Since there are no (absolutely) parentless children, the truth of (4) requires that the world contain parents. Yet parents don't need to be counted among the values of the bound variables of (4) for (4) to be true.[5] So one unintuitive consequence for the quantifier account with respect to (4) is that it would turn out to be *not* ontologically committed to parents. Since this sort of problem will arise for any theory which contains atomic predicates expressing extrinsic properties, the proponent of the quantifier account will need to explain why the appearance of additional ontological commitment in cases like (4) are misleading or else explain how we can account for implicit ontological commitments using the quantifier account.[6]

Our next stop is the entailment account of ontological commitment. The entailment accounts says that the ontological commitment of a theory consists in what the theory entails exists. For example, if atomic theory entails that there are protons, then atomic theory is ontologically committed to protons. It needn't be that protons are explicitly bound to the variables of the quantified sentences of the theory. It is enough that the sentences which compose the theory *entail* that there are protons. We can summarize the account as follows:

> *Entailment account*: a theory T is ontologically committed to an entity E or entities of kind K if and only if T entails that there are Es/Ks.[7]

The entailment account allows one to distinguish between the sentences which compose a theory – some of which might explicitly feature quantified sentences ranging over certain objects – and the ontological commitments of those sentences. For example, intuitively the sentence 'There is a birch tree' is ontologically committed not just to a birch tree simpliciter, but also to organic entities, to physical objects, to bark, and so forth.

One upshot of the entailment account is that implicit ontological commitments of a theory are made visible, for it will count these entities as ontological commitments insofar as the theory entails that they exist. The ontological commitments of the theory don't need to be those which are bound to variables of the quantified statements of the theory. For example, if every cell must have ribosomes, then even if cell theory doesn't explicitly contain a quantification sentence which binds *ribosomes* to a variable, it would still be among the ontological commitments of the theory. Likewise with extrinsic properties such as *being a child*. Suppose there is a single sentence theory consisting of $\exists x$ daughter(x). Since the existence of children is entailed by the existence of parents, a theory which is ontologically committed to parents would thereby be ontologically committed to children as well.

While the entailment account does much better on implicit ontological commitments than the quantifier account, it seems to overgenerate ontological commitments. Consider some traditionally metaphysically problematic entities, such as God, or numbers, or universals. These sorts of entities are taken to exist necessarily if they exist at all. Now consider two theories which disagree over the existence of God – theism and atheism. If theism is true, then God necessarily exists. By the entailment account of ontological commitment, however, God will be among the ontological commitments of atheism as well. After all, necessary truths are entailed by any statement, and since 'God exists' would be a necessarily true statement if theism is true, it would be an entailment of atheism as well. But that God might turn out to be an *ontological commitment* of atheism is absurd. The problem naturally extends to other cases as well. For it would be absurd to think that, if Platonism turned out to be correct, numbers (considered as non-spatiotemporal abstracta) would be an ontological commitment of fictionalism, or that, if realism about universals turned out to be correct, universals would be an ontological commitment of nominalism.[8]

The final stop on our tour is the truthmaker account of ontological commitment. According to the truthmaker account, the ontological commitments of a theory are the truthmakers of the theory:

> *Truthmaker account*: a theory T is ontologically committed to an entity E or entities of kind K if and only if Es/Ks are among the truthmakers of T.[9]

For example, consider the theory that there are other minds. The authors of this chapter – being two people – are truthmakers for this theory. The readers of this chapter are also truthmakers for this theory, as well as the editors of this volume. In this way, the truthmaker account of ontological commitment predicts that the theory that there are other minds is ontologically committed to (among other candidates) the authors, the editors, and the readers as truthmakers.

One virtue of the truthmaker account of ontological commitment is that, like the entailment account, it can explain the implicit ontological commitments of a theory. For example, recall that one problem facing the quantifier account was that a theory can have implicit ontological commitments in the sense that the existence of some entity might be necessary for the explicit quantified statements of the theory to be true but there is no explicit quantification over the relevant entity by any sentence of the theory. This is so in the case of extrinsic properties, such as *daughter* or *grandfather*, as well as for parts of objects which are themselves objects, such as protons and electrons for hydrogen in the case of 'There is hydrogen'. But unlike the entailment account, it doesn't seem liable to the charge of overgenerating ontological commitments. To see this, consider the theist and atheist dispute again. Theists accept the existence of God as a part of their theory whereas atheists deny the existence of God as a part of their theory. The truthmaker account rightly predicts both that God is an ontological commitment of theism and that God is not an ontological commitment of atheism, because God is needed to make theism true but God is not needed to make atheism true. If theism turned out to be true so that 'God exists' is necessarily true, it would be an entailment of any theory – including atheism – that God exists, but, crucially, it wouldn't be an *ontological commitment* of those theories.

A worry for each of these accounts is that they saddle common sense with plenty of heavyweight ontological commitments. This is most clearly so for entailment and truthmaker accounts, but quantifier accounts, too, cannot easily escape commitment to whatever is needed for existentially quantified sentences to come out as true. To see this, consider the following set of propositions:

(1) Common sense is ontologically committed to free actions.
(2) Necessarily, free actions are undetermined agent-caused events.
(3) Common sense is not ontologically committed to undetermined agent-caused events.

Consider (1) first. Free action certainly seems to be part of common sense's ontological commitments. It also seems to be the case that common sense is *not* ontologically committed to undetermined agent-caused events. Common sense just doesn't say anything about these types of events. So (3) seems to be true as well. If the entailment account of ontological commitment is correct, however, then common sense is ontologically committed to whatever is entailed by the sentences which compose common-sense theory. For example, since 'There are free actions' is part of common sense – and thereby common sense is ontologically committed to free actions – it follows that if free actions are essentially undetermined agent-caused events, as (2) suggests, then it is entailed by 'There are free actions' that there are undetermined agent-caused actions. Likewise for the truthmaker account. For if free actions are essentially undetermined agent-caused events, then a truthmaker for 'There are free actions' would be that there are undetermined agent-caused events. Hence, it would follow that undetermined agent-caused actions are ontological commitments of common sense. But that seems absurd.

The puzzle also arises for the quantifier account, although matters are less straightforward here. On one reading of the quantifier account, a theory is ontologically committed to only what is bound to the variables of the quantified sentences of the theory. Since 'There are undetermined agent-caused events' is *not* plausibly a sentence that is part of common sense, undetermined agent-caused events won't be referred to by any sentence of common sense. However, there are other readings of the quantifier account on which it may well turn out to be within the range of the quantified sentences that are part of common sense. For example, one version of the quantifier account is the so-called modal criterion:

> *Modal quantifier account*: a theory T is ontologically committed to entities E or entities of kind K if and only if for every world W, T is true at W only if the domain of W contains at least one E or entity of kind K.

For example, common sense says that ordinary objects like tables and chairs exist. So, common sense is ontologically committed to ordinary objects if and only if for every world W, common sense – or this part of common sense, anyway – is true at W only if the domain of W contains at least one ordinary object, like a chair or table. If to be an ordinary object just is to be a composite material object, then any world at which there is at least one ordinary object will be a world at which there is at least one composite material object. Hence, common sense would also be ontologically committed to composite material objects by virtue of its commitment to ordinary objects. The same holds for free actions. Common sense is ontologically committed to the type of action *free action* if and only if for every world W, common sense is true at W only if the domain of W contains at least one event type falling under *free action*. If free actions are essentially undetermined agent-caused events, then every world at which there is a free action is a world at which there is an agent-caused event. Indeed, since we are supposing that free actions are identical to undetermined agent-caused events, there are no worlds at which there is the former but not the latter and vice versa. So here, too, common sense's ontological commitment to free action would carry an ontological commitment to undetermined agent-caused events if the two are identical, for then W will be the same world at which common sense is true whether or not it explicitly stated 'There are free actions' versus 'There are undetermined agent-caused events'.

Of course, (2) is a philosophically controversial view. But the point is that *whatever* theory of free action turns out to be the correct one, it's hard to see how common sense could be said to be ontologically committed to the type of event which the target philosophical theory requires in order for that theory to be true. Even if one believes that common-sense ontological commitments carry significant evidential weight in disputes within science and philosophy, it seems like overreach to maintain that common sense can straightforwardly adjudicate between sophisticated competing metaphysical theories. Recalling the second line of thought discussed above, common sense didn't evolve to capture the underlying reality behind everyday appearances, so using it to settle heavyweight metaphysical controversies seems misguided. The problem here is that common sense, since it has certain philosophically controversial ontological commitments – namely, free actions, beliefs, knowledge, and persons and their persistence over time – would be able to lay claim to whichever philosophical theory of the nature of these actions, entities, or events turned out to be true since it would be ontologically committed to whatever would need to exist for common-sense ontology to be true. This provides motivation to look for alternative ways of thinking about the ontological commitments of common sense, which is what we'll do in the next section.

THE SUPERFICIALITY AND LOCALITY OF COMMON SENSE

The second line of thought we wish to explore also grants that common sense receives extensive support from collective experience and history, but qualifies the import of this in two significant ways. First, strong and extensive confirmation of common sense only extends to *superficial claims;* that is, claims about surface-level appearances and everyday functioning and operation of the entities, things, and events we encounter. The experience crystallized in common sense is, after all, everyday experience and doesn't include systematic scrutiny of underlying natures, microstructures, macrodevelopments, controlled interventions, and all the other deep and non-obvious phenomena that science and philosophy try to unearth. What common sense is committed to, then, is nothing more than things looking and behaving in certain ways on the outside. For example, common sense appears to be ontologically committed to certain objects, kinds, and events, such as trees, parents, air, ageing, and so on. That these sorts of things exist or occur is uncontroversial. But common sense doesn't tell us anything about the underlying *nature* or the *essence* of trees or of air. This attitude is captured nicely in the Wittgenstein anecdote Elizabeth Anscombe recounts, which we cited at the beginning of the chapter.

Second, common sense consists of a *patchwork of local claims* which function in specific contexts and circumstances. Commonsense claims don't aspire to universal validity and absolute objectivity; they aren't couched in scientifically or philosophically rigorous and regimented language that aims to cut nature at the joints. Rather, they help people in their practical and theoretical endeavours as they live their daily lives. Folk psychology, for instance, which ascribes beliefs, desires, and other mental states to people, has proven to be tremendously successful in helping people make sense of each other's actions, but was never meant to lay bare the internal workings and inventory of the brain, which may well be radically different. The commitments of common sense, then, are not only superficial, but also typically localized and relativized to various practical, social, or theoretical contexts.[10] The upshot of this line of thought is that common sense is to a large extent neutral between different scientific or metaphysical accounts of the underlying natures of objects, processes, and persons as long as they predict the same surface-level appearances and behaviour in the relevant local contexts. We can summarize these ideas as follows:

Superficiality and locality of common-sense ontology principle: common sense is ontologically committed to surface-level claims about the objects or kinds affirmed by our ordinary beliefs, and not to facts about their essences or underlying natures. These commitments are, moreover, localized to specific contexts and don't necessarily hold universally, regardless of context.[11]

Here's a worry about this principle: common sense also seems to have ontological commitments to entities or events the very *existence* of which (not just their nature or essence) is already philosophically controversial. After all, common sense appears committed to beliefs, persons, and free actions, while some philosophers have denied the existence of exactly these things. Hence, you might think that common sense in fact does have non-superficial ontological commitments by being committed to philosophically controversial entities. There are two ways to alleviate this worry. First, observe that what we mean by the superficiality of common sense's ontological commitments is that its ontological commitments do not extend beyond the *existence of something or other* that looks, behaves, or operates as the relevant entities, kinds, or events do. That is, common sense does not say much, if anything, about the nature or essence of these things. It doesn't say, for instance, that beliefs *are* mental representations and that there are mental representations; nor that persons *are* souls and that there are souls; nor that free actions *are* undetermined agent-caused events and that there are undetermined agent-caused events. Second, one might understand claims about the existence of philosophically controversial entities as relativized to local contexts. When someone says that Sue freely chose in what programme to enrol, this is a local 'folk-psychological' explanation of her behaviour in the context of our everyday interactions with other people, and not an attempt to state something scientifically or metaphysically universally true about the existence of free actions.

Of course, some common-sense philosophers, such as Thomas Reid, have argued that freedom of the will is undetermined agent-causation. Likewise, G. E. Moore argued that ordinary objects exist unperceived. So one might think that the views of card-carrying common-sense philosophers contradict the superficiality and locality principle. Indeed, one might worry that, since Reid and Moore are exemplary of common-sense philosophy and their views are *not* only about what exists but also about the nature of what exists (e.g., regarding freedom and ordinary objects), this makes it hard to see how the principle could be correct. Someone who buys into the superficiality and locality principle can respond, however, by claiming that Reid's account of freedom of the will, for example, is not born out of the idea that it's just common sense that free actions are undetermined agent-caused events. Rather, Reid offers first-order philosophical arguments for why we should think that free actions have that nature. It is never assumed or taken as part of the manifest image of reality that free action has that nature.

Moore is a trickier case. In 'A Defence of Common Sense', Moore begins with a list of 'obvious truisms', some of which are philosophically controversial ((1925) 1993: 106). He argues that some of them cannot be true 'unless some *material things* have existed' ((1925) 1993: 112). This seems like a claim about the nature of some of the things on his list. If one accepts the superficiality and locality principle, however, one can claim that Moore is in fact going beyond common sense here. His starting point is common sense – the 'obvious truisms' on his list – but he then makes controversial metaphysical claims about what's necessary for them to be true. That they are *true* is philosophically controversial *and* yet consistent with the principle concerning the superficiality and locality of common sense. What is *not* consistent with that principle is the view 'That there are material objects must be true if the propositions on Moore's list are to be true' in the sense intended by Moore (e.g., there need to be mind-independent spatiotemporal objects for the propositions on his list to be true). That sort of view goes beyond the principle, and in any case doesn't seem to be part of what Moore strictly means by 'common sense'.

After seeing where it leads, a friend of common sense might feel uneasy about the superficiality and locality of the common-sense ontology principle. Emphasizing that common sense is only committed to superficial claims in specific local contexts might seem like a blanket strategy for avoiding any sort of serious onto-logical commitment. As long as the (superficial, local) phenomena are saved, common sense would be compatible with even the most abstruse and counter-intuitive underlying metaphysics. And that, the common-sense philosopher might insist, is a bridge too far.

REVISITING ONTOLOGICAL COMMITMENT

Both lines of thought we've explored so far lead to unattractive conse-quences. What if there was a way of giving serious weight to the apparent ontological commitments of common sense, while avoiding heavyweight ontological commitments that seem to stretch common sense beyond its intuitive limits? One thing one might do is recon-sider what is at stake with ontological commitment as such. In the present section, we discuss accounts of quantifier variance and onto-logical deflationism. Each in their own way, they maintain that onto-logical commitment is cheap and that very little is at stake.

Quantifier Variance

So far we've been implicitly assuming that the existential quantifier has a single meaning, or at least that it has a single meaning when it is used in ontology.[12] Because of this, the thought went, it is possible to read off ontological commitment of (suitably cleaned-up and regi-mented) uses of the existential quantifier. But this claim – that the existential quantifier has a single meaning – is exactly what is denied by those who propose quantifier variance. Eli Hirsch has defended this idea at great length (Hirsch (2011) collects his central papers on the topic). The basic view is that the meaning of the existential quantifier, and hence that of 'existence', varies between different languages, where different languages include variants of English articulating different ontological theories. When an adherent of ontological nihilism asserts 'There are no tables', she's speaking a different language than the common-sense metaphysician who claims 'There are tables'. Since, Hirsch takes it, they probably mean the same thing by 'table', they must mean something different by 'there are'. It follows that the disputants are asserting different propositions and hence aren't in genuine disagreement. Their dispute is merely verbal. Similarly for other ontological disputes about the existence of fusions, numbers, statues, etc.

The mere fact that the existential quantifier can mean different things doesn't yet show that there is no uniquely correct way of determining ontological commitment. It might be that, when it comes to ontological commitment, we ought to look at one particular use of 'existence'. But another component of Hirsch's view denies that this is so: no single language is privileged. We don't have reason to prefer the language of the ontological nihilist over that of the common-sense philosopher or that of any other metaphysical theory. This is because, for Hirsch, reality itself is unstructured and there are many, equally good languages that can be used to describe it (Bricker 2016). Hence, no language is metaphysically privileged because it makes for a better fit with the objective structure of reality than another.

This has rather surprising consequences for ontological commitment. Even though different languages may appear to have very different ontological commitments – one is committed to the existence of tables, another isn't, etc. – they are all really only committed to one and the same unstructured underlying reality. So while quantifier variance initially seems to offer a way of salvaging the ontological commitments of common sense by making commonsensical claims about what exists come out as true, on closer inspection it does have counter-intuitive consequences in terms of what it says about underlying reality. Common sense might not be committed to any very specific claims about the structure of reality, but it certainly does seem to run counter to common sense that reality is wholly unstructured.[13]

Deflationism

Amie Thomasson's deflationist 'easy approach to ontology' (Thomasson 2007; 2015) presents another way of accepting common-sense ontological commitments while rejecting the idea that they are metaphysically deep. Common sense seems ontologically committed to tables, statues, lumps of clay, symphonies, holes, mental states, persons, numbers, and what have you, but that is no big deal, since ontological commitment is 'cheap'. On Thomasson's view, onto-logical questions typically either have easy answers or are unanswer-able. Answering ontological questions takes conceptual and empirical work, but no sophisticated metaphysical theorizing. Questions about whether Xs exist can be answered by getting clear about the application conditions of the concept of X and then doing some empirical work to verify whether these application conditions have indeed been satisfied in the actual world. For instance, when we want to know whether tables exist, all we need to do is get clear on the application conditions of our concept of table – an easy task for competent speakers – and look around us to see whether these condi-tions are satisfied. In this case, as in most others, the answer is an easy yes. When it comes to witches or phlogiston, on the other hand, the application conditions for these concepts are also relatively clear, but they aren't satisfied. Hence, they do not exist.

In other cases, however, particularly when very general or abstract terms such as 'object', 'thing', or 'entity' are used, existence questions and questions about quantity may be ill-formed or ambigu-ous because 'object' or similarly general terms are used with unclear application conditions. Thomasson (2007: chapter 6; 2015: 218–19) points out that 'object' can be used in a covering sense, so that whenever a more concrete sortal term with clear application conditions applies ('table', 'kangaroo', 'symphony', etc.), 'object' automatically applies too. In such cases, we can give easy answers again. Alternatively, 'object' can be used as a sortal term with application conditions of its own, the satisfaction of which can be checked without referring to more concrete sortal terms. On this usage, Thomasson takes nihilists and universalists about material composition to disagree about the application conditions of 'object'. Whereas the nihilist denies that there is an object composed of particles arranged tablewise, the universalist affirms this (and many other existence claims besides). For Thomasson, however, this shows that the disagreement between universalists and nihilists is a merely verbal dispute: they just employ different senses of 'object'. Once the application conditions are made fully explicit, we can again give easy answers. When 'object' isn't used in its covering or sortal senses, it's unclear how it is used, and questions about the existence or quantity of objects become unanswerable.[14]

Thomasson's easy approach to ontology results in a wide variety of ontological commitments to the entities, events, and kinds of common sense. For most of the concepts used to refer to commonsensical entities, events, and kinds, it will be true and easily verifiable that their application conditions are satisfied. Thus they all exist and common sense is ontologically committed to them.[15] Is this bad? Some metaphysicians have thought so (Sidelle 2008; Schaffer 2009; Sider 2009): a plenitudinous metaphysics violates parsimony and runs into well-known problems about co-location, double-counting, ubiquitous overdetermination, etc. Thomasson's basic line of response is the same in all cases: the aforementioned problems are illusory because, on her approach, being ontologically committed is nothing more than just granting that the application conditions of certain concepts are satisfied. It doesn't introduce any additional metaphysical 'stuff' into the world. So even though both tables and particles arranged table-wise exist (as do table legs and a table top), nothing of any deep metaphysical import is at stake. Whenever there are particles arranged table-wise it follows analytically that the application conditions for 'table' are also satisfied, so that we can conclude that a table exists. But the table doesn't take up additional space, doesn't have extra causal powers 'over and above' the particles, and doesn't instantiate some mysterious composition relation not instantiated by the relevant collection of particles.[16]

On Thomasson's approach, then, determining the ontological commitments of common sense is easy. We just need to attend to the application conditions of our common-sense concepts – something competent speakers of a language are able to do – and check whether they are satisfied. Moreover, ontological commitment and existence aren't weighty affairs; the mere fact that an ontology contains many items isn't as such a reason to reject that ontology, as long as there are analytical entailments between claims about co-located objects and objects composing one another.

Thomasson's view appears to have considerable appeal in light of the two lines of thought we explored above. It grants serious authority to common sense and its commitments, without running the risk of making common sense do deep metaphysical work it was never meant to do (because there simply is no such work). As always, however, the view comes at a cost. One needs to be willing to reject neo-Quinean metaphysical orthodoxy of several decades, according to which metaphysics is in the business of discovering deep truths about the world by employing broadly scientific methods – that is, by developing theories that strike an optimal balance between the traditional criteria for theory choice, such as simplicity and explanatory scope.[17] In other words, one needs to be willing to discard much of the contemporary literature in metaphysics as being deeply misguided – engaged in verbal disputes or employing the wrong methods to settle easy questions – and, basically, a waste of time. Determining whether this cost is ultimately worth it falls outside the scope of our chapter.

CONCLUSION

Common sense takes a stand on ontology – that claim itself seems part of common sense. This gives rise to a puzzle when combined with mainstream theories of ontological commitment. On these theories, accepting relatively innocuous ontological commonsensical commitments – medium-sized dry goods, but also free action, knowledge, persons, and beliefs, as well as rightness and wrongness – leads to the conclusion that common sense is ontologically committed to much more than innocuous entities, events, properties, and phenomena. It appears to be ontologically committed to whatever the final philosophical analysis will tell us is identical with those events, states, objects, or properties. That common sense would really carry such metaphysically deep ontological commitments seems highly counter-intuitive.

An alternative approach, however, on which the ontological commitments of common sense are limited to surface-level and local phenomenology, seems unbearably lightweight. On this approach, it looks like common sense can be made compatible with any ontology whatsoever, no matter how abstruse, austere, or florid. Any apparent commonsensical ontological commitments can always be explained away by emphasizing its superficiality or locality. This, too, seems wrong.

This motivated looking for a third way. If ontological commitment isn't a weighty affair – as Amie Thomasson's easy approach to ontology tells us – there is no harm in granting whatever entities, events, phenomena, etc. one's favourite theory of ontological commitment predicts common sense is committed to. On this approach, then, we can happily embrace most commonsensical ontological commitments. At the same time, common sense isn't implausibly made to do metaphysical heavy lifting, simply because there is no need for it. Settling metaphysical disputes is easy and typically requires nothing more than verifying whether the application conditions for our concepts are satisfied. The attractions of Thomasson's view come at a cost, however, for it requires a radical rejection of much work in contemporary analytic metaphysics.[18] We leave it to readers to decide whether such a rejection would or would not be in line with common sense.

NOTES

1 Lewis famously thought that we are ontologically committed to the entities quantified over by the best total theory, where the best total theory includes what common sense says exists. Indeed, textbooks in metaphysics often note how common sense constrains the explanatory demands on a metaphysical theory. Consider, for example, how Loux (2006: 240) takes it that perdurantists need to explain why their ontology exceeds what common sense says exists: 'What gives this task the philosophical urgency it has for perdurantists is the fact that common sense recognizes only a handful of the material objects perdurantists tell us there are; and perdurantists owe us an account of why this is so.'

2 For example, van Inwagen (1990) argues that ordinary assertions about material objects, such as 'There are three chairs in the room', can be true consistently with the thesis that there are no composite material objects.

3 One way to resist this line of argument is to argue that common sense has only developed to give us beliefs that are *useful* for various purposes, not beliefs that are *true*. Korman (2014) explores such debunking arguments against ordinary perceptual beliefs.

4 The common-sense commitment principle doesn't prevent philosophical arguments from undermining common sense. A view which is much stronger than ours is offered by Kit Fine (2001: 2): 'In this age of post-Moorean modesty, many of us are inclined to doubt that philosophy is in possession of arguments that might genuinely serve to undermine what we ordinarily believe.' Adapting this to ontological issues, Fine's principle would be: if the existence of Es/Ks is part of common sense and you believe that there are Es/Ks, then a philosophical argument for the view that there are no Es/Ks rationally should not undermine your belief that there are Es/Ks. This is much stronger than our principle, which only says that we are prima facie entitled to believe what common sense says exists. It could be that especially strong philosophical arguments against the existence of Es/Ks should *undermine* our beliefs. For further discussion of this issue, see Kelly (2008) and Rinard (2013).

5 See Rayo (2007: § 2.1) for this challenge.

6 See Bricker (2016: § 1.7.4) for further discussion.

7 This view is defended by Peacock (2011) as 'implicit' ontological commitment. A variation of this theory is explicitly modal: a theory T is ontologically committed to an entity E or entities of kind K if and only if

T *necessarily* entails that there are Es/Ks. See Bricker (2016: § 2.2) for discussion.

8   See Jackson (1989) for this general worry.

9   This view is suggested by Armstrong (2004). See Cameron (2008) and Rettler (2016) for explicit defences.

10   This feature may not be unique to common sense. John Dupré (1993) and Nancy Cartwright (1999) have argued that the same holds for science: scientific theories and explanations, too, give us a patchwork of claims and not a grand unified account of reality.

11   One way of thinking about this principle is that common sense is only committed to whatever is part of the manifest image of reality: with the way that reality appears to us to be. See Sellars (1962) for the distinction between the manifest and scientific images of reality, and Lawson's chapter in this volume for the idea of a commonsensical metaphysical theory as one which 'matches up' with the manifest image of reality.

12   It might be that we use it in different senses outside philosophy, but that wouldn't undercut the idea that there is a privileged univocal use within the discipline of ontology (cf. Sider 2009: 397).

13   This concern is also behind Ted Sider's central objection to quantifier variance. For Sider, as for many others, it is a given that reality does have its own structure. The point of ontology, and of quantification specifically, is to carve reality at the joints. The meaning of the existential quantifier that does this best is the uniquely privileged one (cf. Sider 2011).

14   For an argument to think Thomasson is wrong that there are only two uses of 'object', see Korman (2019).

15   Note, however, that Thomasson's view must be distinguished from radical conventionalism, according to which there are no mind-independent constraints on what objects there are. Determining what objects exists and where their boundaries are is all a matter of conventions, and there are no natural mind-independent boundaries that must be recognized – see Varzi (2011) and Tahko (2016: 76–83) for discussion of such a view. Thomasson is perfectly happy to grant mind-independent structure in reality to which our concepts and quantifiers are supposed to latch on, even though she might deny that there is any one privileged way in which they can do so (see Thomasson 2015: chapter 10).

16   Space is lacking here to attend to her treatment of all these and other problems, but see Thomasson (2007: chapters 3–7) for this.

17 See van Inwagen (2009); Sider (2009; 2011) for defences of this approach to metaphysics.

18 Such a radical rejection wouldn't be entirely unique. Ladyman and Ross (2007) also argue that most contemporary analytic metaphysics is pointless, albeit on very different grounds than Thomasson's.

14 The Tension between Scientific Knowledge and Common-Sense Philosophy

Massimo Pigliucci

Werner Heisenberg, one of the creators of the theory of quantum mechanics, adopted what by today's standards would be a rather unusual position for a scientist, especially a physicist. In *Physics and Philosophy: The Revolution in Modern Science*, he wrote:

> The concepts of classical physics form the language by which we describe the arrangements of our experiments and state the results. We cannot and should not replace these concepts by any others ... The concepts of classical physics are just a refinement of the concepts of daily life and are an essential part of the language which forms the basis of all natural science. There is no use in discussing what could be done if we were other beings than we are. At this point we have to realize, as von Weizsacker has put it, that 'Nature is earlier than man, but man is earlier than natural science.' The first part of the sentence justifies classical physics, with its ideal of complete objectivity. The second part tells us why we cannot escape the paradox of quantum theory, namely, the necessity of using the classical concepts. (Heisenberg 1958: 46–56)

In these days when science in general, and physics in particular, have gotten even weirder than in Heisenberg's time, such talk feels strange and perhaps outmoded. What could it possibly mean to remind ourselves that 'nature is earlier than man, but man is earlier than natural science', if natural science speaks to us of cosmic superstrings (Vachaspati et al. 2015), parallel universes (Linde 2017), and the illusory nature of time itself (Elmahalawy et al. 2015)? The picture of the world that science pushes on us is getting farther and farther away from our common-sense view of that same world. The desk on which I'm typing this is not 'really' a solid thing, according to fundamental physics, but rather a dynamic entity made possible by close-quarters interactions among tiny particles (Amoroso et al. 2013). My decision to accept to write this chapter for the book you are reading wasn't 'really' mine, because according to some neuroscientists we don't have anything remotely comparable to the sort of will that we sense, intuitively, we do have (Roskies 2012). Examples could be multiplied easily. Just open any graduate-level textbook, or even popular science book, in biology, neuroscience, or physics, and you'll immediately get the picture.

And yet, science, as Heisenberg was directly hinting at, is an irreducibly human activity. I do not mean that it is (entirely) a social construction of the kind sometimes fantasized about by extreme postmodernist authors (see discussion in Hacking 1999). I mean the more straightforward, and yet still crucial, insight that science is a particular type of human social enterprise (Longino 1990). Yes, its results are certainly constrained by the way the world 'out there' really is, but that is true only insofar as we have the powers to empirically investigate, and theoretically understand, said world. And those powers are, ultimately, rooted in ordinary human cognitive and sensorial abilities, the very same source of common-sense understanding.

'Common sense', of course, is a notoriously slippery term. My desktop dictionary defines it as 'good sense and sound judgment in practical matters', which is hardly helpful. More technically, 'common-sense philosophy' refers to a family of positions developed by a number of exponents of the Scottish Enlightenment, and particularly Thomas Reid (1915). Reid famously emphasized the human ability to perceive some common notions (e.g., the existence of the self and the existence of real objects) and thought that this kind of 'common sense' is the foundation of philosophical inquiry. His was a rebuttal of Humean scepticism, among other things. The degree to which Reid was correct is very much a question of open debate in philosophy, and the challenge presented by decidedly anti-commonsensical ideas originating from science is what I am concerned with here.

In this essay I briefly discuss two examples of contrast between scientific understanding and philosophically relevant common-sense beliefs and notions. I then explore pertinent aspects of Wilfrid Sellars's philosophy (Sellars 1962), in particular his distinction between the manifest and the scientific images of the world, in order to make sense of my two examples and of pertinent others that could be brought into this discussion. Sellars's views have been used by his own students in highly diverging fashions: on the one hand, so-called right-wing Sellarsians (e.g., Patricia and Paul Churchland, Ruth Millikan, Jay Rosenberg) deploy the distinction between the two images to argue for the elimination of common-sense views and their replacement with a strictly scientific approach; I take this to be a quintessentially scientistic, and not particularly useful, view of the world, where scientism is the attitude that science is by definition the only source of knowledge and understanding (Pigliucci 2018a; De Ridder et al. 2018). On the other hand, left-wing Sellarsians (e.g., Robert Brandom, John McDowell, Richard Rorty) use the same distinction to demarcate limits to scientific understanding and to advocate for the irreducibility of, for instance, social rules and moral norms (deVries 2016), a position that Reid would have probably felt comfortable with. I will come down somewhere on the centre-left of this debate, suggesting that Sellars's approach can be useful not just within the context of the common-sense tradition in philosophy, but more generally to structure a constructive relationship between philosophy and science. Indeed, as originally suggested by Sellars, to articulate such a constructive relationship should be considered the major task of modern philosophy. It should be noted that my project may not, in the end, 'save' common-sense philosophy as understood by Reid and his intellectual heirs, but rather carve out some important ground for a modified form of common-sense philosophy and develop a more constructive relationship of philosophy with science.

SCIENCE VS COMMON SENSE: TWO EXAMPLES

In this section I explore two examples of tension between scientific and common-sense understanding. In the first case, about a particular conception of free will, I argue that the scientific image – contra popular (mis)understanding – does not trump the manifest one (or at least, one of the available manifest ones), and that instead the two complement each other, depending on which level of description one is interested in or finds most useful for a particular purpose. In the second instance, about the nature of time, we encounter a situation in which common sense at the very least indicates that there is something missing – if not downright wrong – in the scientific image.

Free Will, Stoic Style

Free will, we keep hearing these days, does not exist. And yet, it seems to me that it was my decision to write these words, as well as to accept the invitation to compose this chapter. Ah, but that, some say, is because free will is an 'illusion' (e.g., Heisenberg 2009; Nahmias 2014). This is not at all a novel debate, as in the Western tradition it can be traced back twenty-four centuries into the past, at least to the atomists Democritus and Leucippus (Taylor 2010). As I argue below, new discoveries in science – as interesting as they are – have not actually changed the terms of the discussion, even though they have enriched it somewhat. As such, the philosophy vs science debate about free will is a prime, and very relatable for us all, example of the contrast and potentially fruitful interaction between the scientific perspective and the common-sense one. Since the topic is now characterized by an enormous literature which would require a book-length treatment to adequately address, I will focus my remarks by adopting the specific framework provided by a single philosophical tradition: the Stoic one initiated by Zeno of Citium around 300 BCE (Pigliucci 2018b). I will do so in part for the simple reason that I am intimately familiar with that tradition, and in part because I think that, by and large, the Stoics actually got it about right.

Within the context of Stoic philosophy, the problem of free will can be understood as one of reconciling the idea that we can work to improve our character – a basic assumption shared by all virtue ethical traditions (Hursthouse and Pettigrove 2016) – and the contention that we live in a universe determined by a universal web of cause and effect, a contention consistent with modern science and accepted by the ancient Stoics. These are still pretty much the terms of the modern debate, except that the emphasis is usually on our individual decisions and not the broad goal of improving one's character.

The Stoics employed two useful terms within the context of this discussion: *prohairesis* and *hêgemonikon*. The first one refers to our ability to arrive at judgments about things; for instance, whether to go to the gym is better or worse, for me, than to stay home and watch television. The second term refers to whatever area of the human mind (or brain) is in charge of such judgments. Roughly, then, prohairesis is an ability, and the hêgemonikon is whatever makes that ability possible.

Modern neuroscience has managed to essentially identify the hêgemonikon: the frontal lobes are areas of the brain that are particularly developed in both humans and other great apes (but, interestingly, not so in lesser apes and monkeys: Semendeferi et al. 2002). The frontal lobes (one per hemisphere) are also the largest of the four lobes of the mammalian brain, and experimental research has associated them with the following functions: reward, attention, short-term memory tasks, planning, and motivation (Kimberg and Farah 1993). They also allow us to project the future consequences of our intended actions, to choose between what seem to us good or bad actions, to override and suppress socially unacceptable responses, and to assess similarities and differences between things and events. That sounds to me very much like what the Stoics were talking about whenever they used the term 'hêgemonikon', usually translated as 'ruling faculty'. Here is Marcus Aurelius, for instance:

> Things stand outside of us, themselves by themselves, neither knowing anything of themselves nor expressing any judgment.

> What is it, then, that passes judgment on them? The ruling faculty.
> (*Meditations* 9.15)

Modern science tells us that the frontal lobes do not fully mature in human beings until our late twenties, and of course a variety of situations can impair their proper function, from accidents such as the famous one that occurred in 1848 to the American railroad construction foreman Phineas Gage to strokes, Alzheimer's disease, and various forms of dementia.

Still, in the light of modern discoveries in neuroscience we can do justice to one of the most famous passages in Epictetus' *Discourses*:

> For a start, don't be carried away by [the impression's] vividness, but say: Wait for me a bit, impression; let me take a look at you and what you are about, let me test you. Next, don't let it lead you on by painting a picture of what comes next. Otherwise, it is off and away, taking you wherever it wishes. Instead, confront it with another impression, a fine and noble impression, and dismiss this foul one.
> (*Discourses* 2.18)

It is the hêgemonikon that both presents us with the 'impression' (say, of an attractive member of the other sex) and with memories to draw from (of pleasurable previous sexual encounters). But it is our prohairesis that applies reason to the situation and denies assent to the impression (I am in a committed relationship, and I will therefore not pursue sex on the side with another person). Free will, then, for the Stoics, is at least in part about the ability to veto certain impulses that otherwise come naturally to the human animal.

Anthony Long (2002) provides a very good analysis of why he ends up translating 'prohairesis' with 'volition', which happens to be the preferred term in modern psychology. Consider this next passage, also from Epictetus:

> And who told you; it is your function to walk unimpeded? What I was telling you is that the only unimpeded thing is the impulse.

> Wherever there is a need for the body and the body's cooperation, you have long ago heard that nothing is your own. (*Discourses* 4.1.72–3)

What Epictetus is reminding his student of here is that even our bodily actions are not entirely up to us: we may decide to start walking, but we could be paralysed by disease, or chained to a wall by a tyrant. So the action is not (entirely) up to us, only the impulse to perform the action. That's why volition, and not, say, 'agency', is a better translation of 'prohairesis'. In modern psychology, volition is the cognitive process by which an individual decides on and commits to a particular course of action. It is defined as purposive striving and is one of the primary human psychological functions.

Now, as Long (2002, 220) correctly points out, volition is not contradictory to a physicalist view of the world as determined by cause and effect: 'We take people to have volitions irrespective of whether these are predetermined or independent of antecedent causation.' Moreover, modern psychological science considers volition to be a process of conscious action control which becomes automatized. But wait a minute! Isn't it a fact of modern science that free will, however one wishes to call it, is an 'illusion'? Specifically, didn't the famous experiments by Benjamin Libet back in the 1980s (Libet et al. 1983) conclusively show that to be the case? Does that not mean, therefore, that the entire Stoic philosophy of mind in particular and any modern hope for a similar account crumble under the pounding of modern science, an example of the scientific image trumping the manifest one? No, not at all. On the contrary, Libet's experiments, and subsequent others carried out since, spectacularly confirm the ancient Stoic intuition about prohairesis, which was their 'common-sense' version of compatibilism about free will (though nowadays contemporary philosophers seem to be divided on what, exactly, counts as the common-sense view on this topic: Bourget and Chalmers 2014).

Libet performed some fascinating experiments on conscious vs unconscious decision-making, beginning back in 1983. Briefly, he asked subjects to follow the movements of a dot on the screen of an oscilloscope. The dot moved like the hands of a clock, but faster. Libet told his subjects to move a finger at a moment of their choice during the experiment, noting the position of the dot when they became aware of their decision to act. The experiment seemed to show that the decision to move the finger entered conscious awareness about 200 milliseconds before the actual movement. But, stunningly, there was a rise in the so-called readiness potential, which was thought to be associated with the preparation for action, about 550 milliseconds before movement. So the subjects appeared to be getting ready to move the finger a full 350 milliseconds before they became conscious of their decision to do so. (Indeed, in later experiments the readiness potential has been shown to build up even as long as 1.5 seconds before movement.)

Taken at face value, Libet's results seem to show that we decide our actions unconsciously, and that what we call consciousness is simply a (late) awareness of a decision that has already been made. Could there be a more stunning case of science defeating common sense? And yet, there are several well-known criticisms of such a conclusion, beginning with the obvious one, that the experimental conditions have precious little to do with the recursive, complex behaviour that we normally label 'conscious decision-making', and which is understood as a continuous feedback loop between what Daniel Kahneman (2011) calls System 1 (fast, subconscious) and System 2 (slow, deliberate) brain processing systems. And in fact it was Libet himself who rejected the facile 'free will is an illusion' interpretation of his own research. Here is part of his commentary:

> The finding that the volitional process is initiated unconsciously leads to the question: is there then any role for conscious will in the performance of a voluntary act? The conscious will does appear 150 msec before the motor act, even though it follows the onset of the cerebral action by at least 400 msec. That allows it, potentially, to affect or control the final outcome of the volitional process. An

interval msec before a muscle is activated is the time for the primary motor cortex to activate the spinal motor nerve cells, and through them, the muscles. During this final 50 msec, the act goes to completion with no possibility of its being stopped by the rest of the cerebral cortex. The conscious will could decide to allow the volitional process to go to completion, resulting in the motor act itself. Or, the conscious will could block or 'veto' the process, so that no motor act occurs. (Libet 2004: 137)

Note that the motor cortex in question is part of the frontal lobes (specifically, part of the posterior border of the lobe, called the pre-central gyrus), which I have suggested is the anatomical counterpart of the Stoic hêgemonikon, which in turn enables the faculty of prohairesis.

Also, more recent research (Schultze-Kraft et al. 2016) has led to a reinterpretation of Libet's original findings that aligns them even more with the common-sense philosophy of the Stoics. For instance, a group of researchers in Germany has modified the original protocol to test Libet's idea of a veto power exercised by conscious thought. Subjects were asked to hit a foot pedal as quickly as possible after seeing a green light on a screen, but also to stop themselves from doing so (i.e., cancel their own movements) whenever a red light appeared. Researchers then put the red light under the control of a computer monitoring the participants' brain waves. The twist was that whenever the computer detected the above-mentioned readiness potential building up, it would make a red light appear. In agreement with Libet's veto hypothesis, participants were, in fact, able to stop themselves from pushing the pedal, reversing the build-up of the action potential. This was possible up until a point of no return: if the red light was too close after the green one (about 0.25 seconds), then the foot movement could not be completely inhibited.

And there is more. A French team of neuroscientists published a paper (Schurger et al. 2012) in which they argue for a different interpretation of Libet's original experiments. They suggest that the readiness potential does not, in fact, signal the brain's preparation for a specific action. Rather, the potential goes up and down randomly, but movement can only occur when a certain threshold in the potential is reached. Sure enough, they conducted an experiment in which they asked subjects to press a button, either at moments of their own choosing or when they heard a random click. The results show that the responses to the random clicks were much faster when they happened to coincide with a (random) surge in the readiness potential than when the potential happened to be low. So the potential is not really a sign of an already-made unconscious decision, but rather one of a number of co-occurring causes that facilitate the movement.

All of the above seems to me eminently compatible with the Stoic take on volition. Please understand that I am not suggesting that the ancient Stoics somehow anticipated modern neuroscience. That would be preposterous. They knew nothing about action potentials and the like. They even located the hêgemonikon in the heart, until they were corrected by Galen. But their philosophical common-sense understanding of human psychology (volition) and of physics (cause and effect) – on which they built their entire moral philosophy of action – were right on target, which makes their philosophy compatible with modern cognitive science. There is no magic here; the Stoics were simply astute observers of human nature, and very good philosophers.

Time, Causality, and the Laws of Nature

A few years ago, philosopher Roberto Mangabeira Unger and physicist Lee Smolin wrote a book entitled *The Singular Universe and the Reality of Time: A Proposal in Natural Philosophy* (Unger and Smolin 2014). Although they did not use the term, they sought to bring what can only be referred to as a bit of common-sense philosophy into the increasingly esoteric (some would say unhinged: Baggott 2013; Hossenfelder 2018) world of modern fundamental physics.

Unger and Smolin present three key ideas for the consideration of their readers:

> The first idea is the singular existence of the universe ... There is only one universe at a time, with the qualifications that we discuss. The most important thing about the natural world is that it is what it is and not something else. This idea contradicts the notion of a multiverse – of a plurality of simultaneously existing universes – which has sometimes been used to disguise certain explanatory failures of contemporary physics as explanatory successes. (Unger and Smolin 2014: x)

The authors explain that there is no particular scientific reason to believe in the multiverse, that the idea is empirically untestable and therefore not scientific, and that the whole concept is a metaphysical (in the bad sense of the word) cover-up for what they see as the current failure of cosmological models. To believe in things for which there is no empirical evidence whatsoever goes, shall we say, against the common-sense foundations of science.

> The second idea is the inclusive reality of time. Time is real. Indeed, it is the most real feature of the world, by which we mean that it is the aspect of nature of which we have most reason to say that it does not emerge from any other aspect. Time does not emerge from space, although space may emerge from time. (Unger and Smolin 2014: x)

They go on to explain that this conviction comes out of taking seriously what they consider (rightly, I think) cosmology's most fundamental discovery of the twentieth century: that the universe has an age. This discovery, they argue, is incompatible with the oft-repeated idea that time is relative and that there is no privileged absolute measure of it. Before you throw general relativity at them (or me), keep in mind that Unger and Smolin are perfectly aware of Einstein's theory, and they deal with it accordingly, philosophically in the first part of their book (written by Unger) and scientifically in the second part (written by Smolin). They do not reject general relativity, they simply reject what they think are unwarranted metaphysical extrapolations of it that many physicists have taken for granted but that can be challenged in light of the empirical data coming out of cosmology. Again, they call for the return of some common sense in fundamental physics.

> The third idea is the selective realism of mathematics. (We use realism here in the sense of relation to the one real natural world, in opposition to what is often described as mathematical Platonism: a belief in the real existence, apart from nature, of mathematical entities.) Now dominant conceptions of what the most basic natural science is and can become have been formed in the context of beliefs about mathematics and of its relation to both science and nature. The laws of nature, the discerning of which has been the supreme object of science, are supposed to be written in the language of mathematics. (Unger and Smolin 2014: xii)

But they are not, the authors argue, because there are no 'laws' and because mathematics is a (very useful) human invention, not a mysterious sixth sense capable of probing a deeper reality beyond the empirical, as Pythagoras and Plato thought. This needs some unpacking, of course, but it will be immediately clear that, even in this third claim, Unger and Smolin are arguing for a philosophically commonsensical approach to the interpretation of scientific findings.

Let me start with mathematics, then move to the issue of natural laws. Mathematical Platonism is a compelling idea, which makes sense of the 'unreasonable effectiveness of mathematics' as Eugene Wigner (1960) famously put it. It is a position shared by a good number of mathematicians and philosophers of mathematics. It is based on the strong gut feeling that mathematicians have that they don't invent mathematical formalisms, they 'discover' them, in a way analogous to what empirical scientists do with features of the outside world. It is also supported by an argument analogous to the defence of realism about scientific theories and advanced by Hilary Putnam

(Linnebo 2018): it would be nothing short of miraculous, it is suggested, if mathematics were an arbitrary creation of the human mind, and yet time and again it turns out to be spectacularly helpful to scientists.

But there are, of course, equally (more?) powerful counterarguments (French 2000). To begin with, the whole thing smells a bit too uncomfortably of mysticism (and goes, therefore, against common sense): where, exactly, is this realm of mathematical objects? What is its ontological status? Moreover, and relatedly, how is it that human beings have somehow developed the uncanny ability to access such a realm? We know how we can access, however imperfectly and indirectly, the physical world: we evolved a battery of sensorial capabilities to navigate that world in order to survive and reproduce, and science has been a continuous quest for expanding the power of our senses by way of more and more sophisticated instrumentation, to gain access to more and more (and increasingly less relevant to our biological fitness!) aspects of the world.

Indeed, it is precisely this analogy with science that powerfully hints to an alternative, naturalistic interpretation of the effectiveness of mathematics. Maths too started out as a way to do useful things in the world, mostly to count (arithmetic) and to measure up the world and divide it into manageable chunks (geometry). Mathematicians then developed their own (conceptual, as opposed to empirical) tools to understand more and more sophisticated and less immediate aspects of the world, in the process eventually abstracting entirely from such a world in pursuit of internally generated questions (what we today call 'pure' mathematics).

Unger and Smolin do not by any means deny the power and effectiveness of mathematics. But they also remind us that precisely what makes it so useful and general – its abstraction from the particularities of the world, and specifically its inability to deal with temporal asymmetries (mathematical equations in fundamental physics are time-symmetric, and asymmetries have to be imported as externally imposed boundary conditions) – also makes it subordinate to empirical science when it comes to understanding the one real world.

Perhaps the best example of this tension is provided by the backward extension of the field equations of general relativity, which is the basis for the claim – rejected by Unger and Smolin – that the universe began with a 'singularity' characterized by infinite mass and energy. They flip things around, asserting that the logical impossibility, as well as the complete dearth of empirical evidence, of any infinite quantities in nature must take precedence instead. Applying common sense to advanced science, if the theory of general relativity predicts physical infinities then too bad for general relativity: it simply means that that particular theory, like all scientific theories, has a specific domain of application (admittedly, fairly large: most of the known universe, for most of its history), beyond which it breaks down. Some physicists, according to Unger and Smolin, commit instead the same mistake as the (fictional) authors of *The Hitchhiker's Guide to the Galaxy*, warning their readers that in case of conflict between the guide and reality (or, here, metaphysical speculation and common sense), it is reality that is at fault.

And finally to the issue of laws of nature, where it turns out that a common-sense approach could potentially overturn a three-century-old way of thinking within the physics community. The whole idea of laws of nature has a controversial history and is of surprisingly recent vintage. Among the early natural philosophers, Descartes and then Newton were enthusiastic supporters of the notion, which of course they directly ascribed to the existence of a creator God: after all, if there are laws, we need a law-giver of some sort. Hobbes and Galileo, by contrast, were distinctly unexcited by it, preferring instead to talk about empirical approximations and generalizations. While the Cartesian-Newtonian camp holds sway in modern physics, a number of philosophers have pointed out that this is likely a mistake, introducing an enigma (where do the laws come from?) in order to explain a mystery (some observed general regularities in the way the universe works).

Two such philosophers are Nancy Cartwright and Ian Hacking. They independently published two seminal books on the topic: *How the Laws of Physics Lie* (Cartwright 1983) and *Representing and Intervening* (Hacking 1983). According to Cartwright in particular, laws of nature are not true generalized descriptions of the behaviour of particles, say, but rather statements about how particles would behave according to idealized models, her crucial point being that theories are to be reinterpreted as (empirical), idealized models of reality, not as more or less isomorphic (true) maps of the world. Cartwright distinguishes between fundamental and phenomenological laws: fundamental laws are those postulated by realists, and they (supposedly) describe the true deep structure of the universe; phenomenological laws, conversely, can be used to make predictions – they work well enough, but they are, strictly speaking, false.

Newtonian mechanics is then interpreted as a phenomenological law: it is an idealization that works well for certain practical purposes. Crucially, for Cartwright, all laws are like that (so she is an anti-realist about laws), which means that in physics, instead of looking for a fundamental 'theory of everything', we should be working on putting together a coherent patchwork of local (phenomenological) theories and laws, each characterized by a limited domain of application. Here is how she summarizes it (Cartwright 1983: 194): 'Neither quantum nor classical theories are sufficient on their own for providing accurate descriptions of the phenomena in their domain. Some situations require quantum descriptions, some classical and some a mix of both.' To say something along the lines of 'yes, but in principle we could use quantum mechanics for everything' is, according to Cartwright, to go beyond the empirical and wade into shaky metaphysical ground.

While Unger and Smolin don't quite go that far, the spirit of their criticism is similar. Interestingly, however, they derive it from an analysis of physical laws that begins with another staple of philosophical discourse: causality (Dowe 2007). The basic idea is simple, profound, and eminently commonsensical: we usually explain causal processes and interactions by invoking laws. But in fact, the authors argue, it is more plausible to think that it is the (appearance of) laws that emerge from causal interactions. That is, causal processes are primary, and when they happen with predictable regularity we call the resulting pattern a law. This, in turn, stems from their treatment of time as not emergent, as referred to above: if there is anything that defines causality it is precisely temporal asymmetry, and in fact time itself can be defined in terms of causality:

> If time were not real, there could be no causal relations for the reason that there would be no before (the cause) and after (the effect) . . . Nothing would distinguish causal connections, which are time-bound, from logical or mathematical relations of implication, which stand outside time. (Unger and Smolin 2014: 7)

And also:

> Within this view, time is intimately and internally connected with change. Change is causal. Time is change. In the spirit of these propositions, we should take inspiration, not discouragement, from Mach's remark: 'It is utterly beyond our power to measure the change of things by time. Quite the contrary, time is an abstraction at which we arrive by the changes of things.' (Unger and Smolin 2014: 222)

But wait, is it not the case that we have lots of empirical evidence that time changes depending on local conditions, such as the speed at which we move, or gravitational effects? Unger and Smolin have obviously considered this (2014: 232): 'No necessary, one-to-one relation exists between the Einsteinian-Riemannian ontology and the hard empirical content of general relativity. We can keep the empirical residue while dispensing with the ontology.' The commonsensical solution here is to conceive of absolute time not in terms of standard units, such as seconds, oscillations of reference atoms, and the like. Time is, if I understand them correctly, simply the succession of causal connections between events. This succession can locally take place at a different pace, but this does not invalidate the universally true fact that certain things (like, most obviously, the Big Bang) happened before (meaning that they were causally antecedent to) others.

There are two crucial consequences of this attempt to reinsert some common sense into modern physics: to begin with, that the laws of nature themselves may, potentially, change over 'time'. Indeed, they already have. Unger and Smolin think that the universe has gone through at least two phases, and possibly many more before those. One phase was the Big Bang and what happened immediately before and after. During this sequence of causal events (i.e., 'time'), things were happening that did not abide by anything like the predictable regularity we see operating today, because the causal processes themselves were changing. The second phase is the one of the cooled-down universe, which has gone on for billions of years now and which can (to a good approximation, as Cartwright would say) be described as law-abiding, because the nature of the causal interactions that characterize it is either not changing or not changing appreciably. But this state of affairs may not last forever, and the universe may go through yet another period of upheaval, and so on and so forth, indefinitely.

The second crucial consequence is that physicists should take cosmology seriously as a fundamentally historical science, to be modelled after some of the 'special' sciences like geology and biology, not in the increasingly singular way in which fundamental physics proceeds. Indeed, the idea that the very regularities governing the universe change with the causal conditions appears odd only in fundamental physics, because it has been so influenced by abstract (and necessarily time-invariant!) mathematics. All other sciences have long recognized the emergence of new patterns of behaviour (i.e., new regularities) triggered by changed causal conditions. For instance, major transitions in biological evolution (e.g., from unicellular to multicellular life) have made possible entirely new modes of evolutionary change (a concept known as 'evolvability': Pigliucci 2008) that were simply not instantiated before. The appearance of sentient beings capable of reasoning has triggered novel types of causal interactions described by the social sciences (psychology, sociology, history, economics), again following patterns that were simply not accessible to the universe before a certain point. This yields an appealing picture of open possibilities, where the future is not fixed by the past but depends on how causality will change and on what novel forms it will take.

I cannot say whether Unger and Smolin's view, or the allied one articulated by Cartwright and Hacking, will win the day, in either physics or philosophy. Indeed, at the moment they seem to be minoritarian positions in both fields. But at the very least they represent refreshing examples of how a return to common sense even in science can be fruitful. And given that the current extremely messy state of fundamental physics (Baggott 2013; Hossenfelder 2018) is largely to be imputed to a massive flight from common sense, we could certainly use some rethinking in that department.

WILFRID SELLARS AND THE STEREOSCOPIC VIEW

Wilfrid Sellars is arguably one of the least recognized major philosophers of the twentieth century, although this is hopefully changing. He did nothing less than propose a refocusing of the entire field of philosophy in terms of his notion of a 'stereoscopic view' encompassing the scientific and manifest images of the world. Sellars introduced the distinction between the two images in 'Philosophy and the Scientific Image of Man' (Sellars 1962). The scientific image is, of course, the ever-changing view of the world that comes out of the best science of the moment. Its fundamental elements, to which everything else is at least in theory reducible, are things like quarks and other particles, or whatever fundamental physics says lies at the foundational bottom of the cosmos (Ladyman and Ross 2007). The manifest image is concerned with how human beings operate within their social world, which means that 'the conceptual framework of persons is the framework in which we think of one another as sharing the community intentions which provide the ambience of principles and standards (above all, those which make meaningful discourse and rationality itself possible) within which we live our own individual lives' (Sellars 1962: 40). That is, things like persons and values are the 'atoms', if you will, of the manifest image. While the manifest image is 'commonsensical', we should recognize that what counts as common sense, and hence what the common-sense approach in philosophy maintains, itself changes over time, in part precisely because it is in constant dialogue with the scientific image. This in and of itself means that to defend either the scientific approach or the common-sense approach is profoundly misguided. What's interesting is how they inform each other. In this context, I do accept Peels's (2017a) contention that science is, ultimately, based on common sense, since scientists are bound to use human reasoning and to rely on human senses. That said, scientific methods and instruments have obviously allowed us to transcend, in part, such limitations, through the use of tools ranging from supercomputers to powerful telescopes or particle accelerators. What we ought to be seeking, then, just like Sellars put forth, is a dynamic equilibrium between the two images, not the prevalence of one to the exclusion of the other.

The scientific image has been within the purview of philosophy, and specifically of natural philosophy, ever since the Presocratics (Waterfield 2000), but with the advent of the Scientific Revolution of the seventeenth through the nineteenth centuries, it has become the exclusive domain of a number of disciplinary spin-offs that emerged from philosophy and became the special sciences: first physics, with Galileo and Newton; then chemistry, with Boyle; then biology, with Darwin; and finally economics (Smith) and psychology (James). This process of budding from the philosophical core continues today, as we see the study of consciousness gradually migrating from philosophy of mind to the cognitive sciences (Margolis et al. 2012).

Yet, for every field that moves from the conceptual to the empirical – and thus from the domain of philosophy to that of science – we immediately see the articulation of a related 'philosophy of' (e.g., of physics, of biology, of economics, of the social sciences), the partial aim of which is to deploy common-sense philosophy to analyse, and sometimes criticize, the new scientific fields. This analysis (and, sometimes, criticism) is carried out both in epistemic terms (e.g., what is the structure of scientific theories? What is the connection between theory and empirical evidence in, say, biology?), and also in ethical terms (e.g., how should we use advances in human molecular genetics? What sort of priorities should be given to different scientific projects, in terms of their human impact?). In both cases – epistemic and ethical – the typical components of Sellars's manifest image, like persons and values, play a dominant role, which in turn means that common-sense philosophy deploys its approach to the descriptive as well as pre-scriptive study of both what the sciences are and what they ought to be doing.

It would seem like philosophy would be well-positioned, then, to carry out the comprehensive task that Sellars wants to assign to her: neither reducing the manifest image to the scientific one (because things like persons, values, and so forth are not found anywhere in the conceptual arsenal of the natural sciences), nor certainly some kind of subordination of the natural sciences to common sense, which would be a form of denial of the spectacular advances of the sciences since Galileo. Hence Sellars's idea of a philosophical stereoscopic vision, through which the philosopher can make sense of the discoveries of science and yet continue to operate qua human being in a world that makes sense to human beings. As Sellars put it (1962: 15): 'The so-called "analytic" tradition in recent British and American philosophy, particularly under the influence of the later Wittgenstein, has done increasing justice to the manifest image, and has increasingly succeeded in isolating it in something like its pure form, and has made clear the folly of attempting to replace it piecemeal by fragments of the scientific image.' And moreover:

> The conceptual framework of persons is not something that needs to be reconciled with the scientific image, but rather something to be joined to it. Thus, to complete the scientific image we need to enrich it not with more ways of saying what is the case, but with the language of community and individual intentions, so that by construing the actions we intend to do and the circumstances in which we intend to do them in scientific terms, we directly relate the world as conceived by scientific theory to our purposes, and make it our world and no longer an alien appendage to the world in which we do our living. (Sellars 1962: 40)

Except, of course, that beginning with some of Sellars's own students, analytic philosophy has become increasingly a parroting of the natural sciences, and it is nowadays very easy to find talk of the 'illusion' of free will, consciousness, and the like, an attitude that dissenter John Searle has famously referred to as 'denying the phenomenon' (referring to consciousness; Searle 1999: 47). This attitude of analytic philosophy should surprise no one, considering that it is rooted in the declared programme of the early analytics, beginning of course with Bertrand Russell (1914), who wished to pattern philosophy after science. As deVries (2016) notes in his in-depth commentary on Sellars, the latter's philosophy has given rise to two diverging branches of thought, what he calls right-wing and left-wing Sellarsians. As we saw in the beginning, the first group takes the position that whenever a conflict arises between the two images, the scientific one trumps the manifest one, while the second group thinks that certain differences between the two images actually point to some of the limits of science, especially, but not only, when it comes to social categories and phenomena, such as value judgments, moral prescriptions, and the like, as clearly stated by Sellars himself. Scientific results often surely run counter to common sense, but it's normally endowed human beings who arrive at them and have to understand them.

The two examples I discussed in the central part of this chapter – which could easily be multiplied at will – clearly show why philosophers should work on developing Sellars's stereoscopic view in the sense intended by the left-wing Sellarsians and reject the reductive approach of the right wing. It is indubitable that science has arrived at conceptions of free will and time that are in stark contrast with the common-sense ones. Two things, however, are not at all clear: (1) whether the scientists have not actually run away into a direction that has led them to deny (or at the very least drastically redefine) the phenomena, rather than actually explaining them; and (2) what we, as human beings, are supposed to do with the developing scientific image in those two cases.

In terms of (1), physicists have not even attempted to give us an account of how, exactly, the alleged illusion of time arises in the world that we experience. Without such an account, the scientific image itself is clearly incomplete. And that's setting aside that some physicists, like Lee Smolin, think that it is physics that is wrong or incomplete, and that there is in fact nothing amiss with our common-sense conception of time. Regarding free will, its alleged illusory status is based on rather tentative metaphysics (extreme reductionism), and on even more questionable science (as I have briefly discussed, Libet-style experiments do not prove what a lot of scientists and philosophers seem to think they prove).

But it is (2) that is of most concern to everyone except a few theoretical physicists and neuroscientists. Let us assume for the sake of argument that free will and time are in some sense illusory, or at least are to be characterized – scientifically speaking – in a radically different fashion from what we are used to. So what? How do we live a life in which we still have to make decisions, and that seems to be marked by the inexorable passing of time? This is where the modern common-sense philosopher finds her natural arena: in the construction, development, and testing of those Sellarsian binoculars that allow us to see the world, and act in it, by intelligently integrating the scientific and the manifest images. It's the commonsensical thing to do.

15 A Scientific-Realist Account of Common Sense

Orly Shenker

THE PROBLEM

There are good reasons to endorse scientific realism and good reasons to endorse common-sense realism. However, it has sometimes been suggested that there is tension between the two, which makes it difficult to endorse both (Russell 1940: 15): 'Naïve realism leads to physics, and physics, if true, shows that naïve realism is false. Therefore, naïve realism, if true, is false; therefore, it is false.' In this chapter I propose a way to solve this tension and to retain both.

SCIENTIFIC REALISM

'It is perhaps only a slight exaggeration to say that scientific realism is characterized differently by every author who discusses it, and this presents a challenge to anyone hoping to learn what it is. Fortunately, underlying the many idiosyncratic qualifications and variants of the position, there exists a common core of ideas, typified by an epistemically positive attitude towards the outputs of scientific investigation, regarding both observable and unobservable aspects of the world' (Chakravartti 2015). This positive attitude consists of three theses: *'The Metaphysical Thesis*: The world has a definite and mind-independent structure. *The Semantic Thesis*: Scientific theories should be taken at face value. They are truth-conditioned descriptions of their intended domain, both observable and unobservable. Hence, they are capable of being true or false. The theoretical terms featuring in theories have putative factual reference. So, if scientific theories are true, the unobservable entities they posit populate the world. *The Epistemic Thesis*: Mature and predictively successful scientific

333

theories are well confirmed and approximately true of the world. So, the entities posited by them, or, at any rate, entities very similar to those posited, inhabit the world' (Psillos 2009: 4).[1]

Scientific realism famously faces a variety of challenges, which I will not address here (for an overview see Chakravartti 2015). In this chapter I focus only on the problem described briefly above and in more detail throughout this chapter concerning the relation between scientific realism and common sense.

COMMON SENSE

'Common-sense realists about the world hold that there exist ordinary everyday objects, such as trees, water, rocks and cats, with properties such as hardness, wetness, impenetrability and furriness; and these also stand in relations to one another (e.g. the cat is in the tree). All of these objects, properties and relations exist mind-independently of human beings; that is, if we were not to perceive any of these items, or think about them, or form theories of them or use language to refer to them, then they would still exist' (Nola and Sankey 2007: 338).

'Common-sense is not a theory towards which we can have a stance of strict and literal belief', because 'many terms and predicates we use in our commonsensical description of the world are vague and imprecise' (Psillos 2009: 79). In the literature (including this volume), common-sense beliefs are characterized by a variety of criteria (as can be seen from the variety of accounts in this volume). For the present discussion it is useful to distinguish between three kinds of such criteria:

(1) *Psychological*: here, the idea is that our psychological making is such that we find common-sense beliefs irresistible. Below I distinguish between two kinds of such psychological irresistibility: (i) cases in which the feeling of irresistibility is a result of our (temporary) failure to imagine an alternative, but when it is presented to us we can entertain it and even change

belief; (ii) cases in which beliefs are imposed on us by our making, and because of that they cannot be eschewed, regardless of arguments. (See especially the section 'The Psychological Characterization of Common Sense and Its Reconciliation with Scientific Realism'.)

(2) *Epistemological*: here, the idea is that at least some of the common-sense beliefs are true (or, are instances of knowledge) and endorsing them is justified. (See detailed discussion of the epistemic authority of common sense in Chapter 10 in this volume.)

(3) *Denotational*: finally, an important way of characterizing common-sense beliefs is by denotation, that is, by providing a list of examples, with the implicit suggestion that this list can be extended by the reader. Some try to generalize or abstract from these examples.

For example, all three kinds of characterization are present in G. E. Moore's (1925) paper 'A Defence of Common Sense'; whether or not they are independent of each other in his view is a matter I shall not discuss here.[2] Moore (1925) replies to some of the criticisms mounted against the first two characterizations, but he apparently accepts that their combination is not definitive of common sense, and therefore he also provides a denotational characterization and supplies a list of examples of common-sense beliefs. Moore's list is (I think) by and large uncontroversial: its propositions are easily recognizable as common sense, despite the lack of an explicit criterion for this judgment. (Other examples are brought below.)

These characterizations have been criticized in the literature;[3] in this chapter I address those common-sense beliefs that do fall under them. A main point that I make here is that the key to restoring compatibility between those common-sense beliefs and scientific realism is focusing on the *psychological* characteristics of common-sense beliefs. As common-sense beliefs – like all beliefs – are, first and foremost, mental states, I will bring in a naturalistic understanding of mental states as (supervening on) brain states, and claim that a scientific explanation of how these particular mental states come about will also explain why certain beliefs and not others are included in the *denotational* characterization of common sense, and provide a new meaning to its *epistemological* characterization.

THE EPISTEMOLOGICAL CHARACTERIZATION OF COMMON SENSE

The justification of common-sense beliefs has been studied extensively in the literature (see Chapter 10 in this volume). On one extreme we find Thomas Reid's ((1764) 1997: 175) view which, on a standard reading, says that these beliefs are self-justified (but Nichols and Yaffe (2015) think that for him this was only a mere matter of burden of proof, for which the symmetry breaker is the psychological fact that we in fact entertain common-sense beliefs and not sceptical ones). For G. E. Moore (1925; 1939), some justification for endorsing common-sense beliefs is required, although this justification needn't be explicitly remembered by us; and therefore we are sometimes justified in rejecting common-sense beliefs on scientific grounds – namely, when those grounds undermine the original justification we had for endorsing them. What sorts of justifications can there be for *initially* endorsing the common-sense beliefs? Possibly, the justifications might be that the common-sense beliefs are 'put to critical test on countless occasions each and every day. Our practical interaction with the world vindicates a common-sense view of the world every day of our lives … [C]ommon-sense beliefs are among the most highly confirmed beliefs in our belief system precisely because they are subjected to critical scrutiny on a regular basis' (Sankey 2014: 17). And it is because of this that 'common-sense has a prior claim on our belief. Beliefs based on common-sense … are only to be rejected after less pivotal beliefs have been considered for rejection. Given their privileged status, any challenge to common-sense is to be met with suspicion' (Sankey 2014: 16).

These justifications may suggest that there need not always be a clash between science and common sense. Can they indeed be compatible, despite the prima facie impression to the contrary, as explained in the first section? Let us now briefly describe two attempts at making them compatible, and then focus on a new line enabling peaceful coexistence.

Do Common Sense and Science Address Different 'Levels'?

One proposal to allow common-sense beliefs and scientific beliefs to coexist peacefully is that they are about (so-called) different 'levels'. 'Facts of a more fundamental level are suitably connected with facts of a less fundamental level, without thereby denying the reality of the less fundamental facts ... [R]ealism is about what is real and not about what is fundamentally real' (Psillos 2009: 38). The idea of ontological 'levels' is built on ideas such as 'multiple realizability' (Putnam 1967; Fodor 1974; Polger and Shapiro 2016) or 'strong emergence' (O'Conner and Wong 2015) or other metaphysical relations (such as 'grounding' – see Bliss and Trogdon 2016) that are problematic in their own right.[4] To use this line of thinking one needs to treat common sense as a 'theory' that is at either a higher level or a lower level relative to the relevant scientific theories.

One the one hand, as far as the *ontology* is concerned, it is by and large non-controversial that the fundamental theories of physics describe the fundamental *reality*,[5] and then it would be natural to take common-sense beliefs to pertain to higher-level matters of fact.

On the other hand, as far as *explanation* or *justification* is concerned, the order may be the reverse: common-sense beliefs may be more fundamental, especially if they are taken to stand in some confirmatory relations to scientific theories rather than be theories in their own right (Psillos 2009: 79).

The proposal made later in this chapter puts these two kinds of relations in one framework.

Are Common Sense and Science Different Perspectives on the Same Thing?

Another proposal to allow common-sense beliefs and scientific beliefs to coexist peacefully is that they are different perspectives on the same thing or differ only in degree of precision. 'The perspectival difference at issue is substantially analogous to the perspectival difference at issue when one and the same landscape is described by the agriculturist, the landscape painter, and the military engineer' (Rescher 2005: 135). 'While both science and common-sense depict a common terrain – the world we live in and its furnishings – they do this in so different a manner that to all appearance – to all visible intents and purposes they might as well be dealing with different terrains' (Rescher 2005: 157). Since, notwithstanding the apparent differences, these are descriptions of the same thing, there needn't be a fundamental incompatibility between the common-sense picture and the scientific picture.

Additionally, the scientific account of reality, Rescher argues, is simply more exact than its common-sense account. 'From the angle of precision, frontier science is in good shape ... Common sense, on the other hand, ... is so untidy conceptually that it lacks the precision required by detailed informativeness' (Rescher 2005: 150). This gives good reason to *accept* common-sense beliefs, since 'it is a basic principle of epistemology that increased confidence in the correctness of our estimates can always be purchased at the price of decreased accuracy' (Rescher 2005: 137), and therefore 'from the angle of truth [science's] condition is rather problematic. Common sense, on the other hand, stands on firmer ground in relation to security' (Rescher 2005: 150).

However, not all examples can be explained in these ways. One example is the common-sense belief that the sun moves in the sky, which I discuss in detail below, since it is used as an illustration by Sankey. (This belief may be a common-sense one in certain places and cultures but not for others; I do not address in this chapter the variability of common-sense beliefs.) For now, consider another kind of example, taken from recent results of studies in cognitive psychology and brain research. These fields address not the external world itself but the way we perceive it. And it turns out that here, too, there is a discrepancy between science and common sense, so that it may be that this discrepancy is the rule rather than the exception and is unavoidable. Here are two examples.

(1) One discovery, based on understanding the physiology of the visual system, is the so-called blind spot. A region in the retina is taken by the beginning of the optic nerve and is therefore not covered with photoreceptor cells; and so the corresponding part of the visual field is invisible. A mechanism in the brain processes the information obtained from the visual field surrounding the blind spot and creates this part of the visual field by extrapolation (see Dainton 2018).

(2) Another discovery in contemporary cognitive psychology is that the picture of the 'now' in which all the sensory modalities are integrated and merged to form one whole is a highly edited 'video clip' built from a-synchronous inputs, belonging to the so-called specious present. (The scientific research on this topic was strongly influenced by Dennett and Kinsbourne (1992); see also Dainton (2018).) These and other discoveries reveal that our common-sense view of reality is distorted even in the most mundane circumstances.[6] I discuss this example further below.

These examples suggest that there is substantial incompatibility between the world pictures of scientific realism and common sense, which is not merely a matter of difference between two compatible perspectives on the same thing or a matter of degree of precision. Reconciling the contents of science and common sense is a more complex matter, one that I address in the next sections.

The next attempts at reconciling common sense with scientific realism focus not on the epistemological characterization of common sense but on the psychological one.

THE PSYCHOLOGICAL CHARACTERIZATION OF COMMON SENSE AND ITS RECONCILIATION WITH SCIENTIFIC REALISM

Let us now leave for a moment the epistemological discussion (concerning the truth of the common-sense propositions) and return to the psychological fact concerning the irresistibility of the common-sense beliefs – for example, those that appear in the denotational descriptions of Moore (1925) and Eddington (1928). Reid (quoted in Rosenfeld 2011: 72) noticed early on that 'there are certain principles ... which the constitution of our nature leads us to believe, and which we are under a necessity to take for granted in the common concerns of life, without being able to give a reason for them'. Elsewhere he writes: 'My belief is carried along by perception, as irresistibly as my body by the earth' (quoted in Lemos 2020).

Of course, as Lemos (2020) emphasizes, the psychological fact of *irresistibility* does not entail the epistemic characteristic of *truth*. Moreover, since the irresistibility of common-sense beliefs is a mere psychological fact, it may have exceptions: some common-sense beliefs may be more compelling than others, or they may be more compelling for some people than for others; and – perhaps more important for us here – it may change with time and culture.

An example that is important for the discussion that follows is the belief that all the celestial objects revolve around the earth; that is, a geocentric picture rather than a heliocentric one. For many people a geocentric picture felt – and for many it still feels – compelling; but not for all, as we know from the history of science. Despite the change in the beliefs of astronomers, the geocentric picture is taken to be part of common sense by, for example, Sankey (see below), and (I think) for good reason. Let me explain why and elucidate and illustrate the notion of irresistibility that is involved here.

Consider, for example, the story by Hanson (1958; 1969) concerning the astronomers Tycho Brahe, who held a geocentric theory of the earth/sun relation, and Johannes Kepler, who held a heliocentric theory. Hanson invites us to imagine them at dawn and claims that, while Brahe saw a mobile sun that rises above the horizon, Kepler saw a static sun and a dropping horizon. Hanson concludes that 'seeing is a "theory-laden" undertaking' (Hanson 1958: 19) and that 'we usually *see* through spectacles made of our past experience [and] our knowledge' (Hanson 1969: 149). Proctor and Capaldi (2012: 290–1) suggest that non-professional astronomers, even if they accept the *heliocentric theory*, would, in fact, have a *geocentric perception*. Using this example, we can distinguish between two senses in which the geocentric belief is (ir)resistible or compelling.

Case (1): a belief may seem to us compelling just because we cannot think, at that time, 'outside the box'. In this case, when an alternative view is offered to us, our beliefs may change. (Few people can open their own boxes: a relevant example here is Copernicus.) Once our beliefs change in this way, they lose their aura of irresistibility and cease to be part of common sense.

Case (2): another sense in which the geocentric belief might be irresistible or compelling is this – regardless of what we believe to be theoretically true, we find ourselves having *experiences* that match the common sense that we take to be *false*. For example, some philosophers object to Hanson's picture, insisting that Kepler, despite endorsing a heliocentric theory, would have the same geocentric-like experience as Brahe (see Proctor and Capaldi 2012). Importantly, this debate is about *a matter of psychological fact*, and the way to settle it is, therefore, by scientific psychological research rather than by philosophical intuitions.

Case (2) is puzzling, and Sankey's (2014) solution is this: 'Science does not lead to the overthrow of common sense. Rather, science explains why common-sense objects appear as they do. It explains why in some cases the common-sense appearance of things is misleading' (Sankey 2014: 23). He illustrates this idea using the astronomical example. The theory of geocentric astronomy is that the bodies *in fact* revolve; the support for it is that the sun *appears to us* to cross the sky. According to heliocentric astronomy, the *appearance* that the sun crosses the sky is misleading since the sun does not *in fact* move; rather, the earth revolves about its own axis. When the geocentric astronomy is replaced by the heliocentric astronomy, 'the appearances do not change. Neither does commonsense experience. What changes is what we think happens. Our understanding of what takes place is altered' (Sankey 2014: 19). (Since common sense, as explained above, comprises beliefs – not experiences – I take it that the phrase 'common-sense experience' refers to interpreting the experience as reflecting the state of affairs in the world that obtains according to the common-sense beliefs.)

In what sense does science explain common sense in this picture? Let me add here the following observation, which I would like to emphasize. The geocentric astronomy and the heliocentric astronomy are *both theories* (or models, or something else like this; I will not make these distinctions since they don't matter at this point). Both theories are (presumably) compatible with the *observations* that ordinary people make in their normal (non-scientific) course of life, although arguably, when it comes to more precise observations, the heliocentric theory fares better than the geocentric one. (I will not challenge any of this here and will take all of it as given.) So we have here three elements: two *theories* and, in addition, the fact that 'it *appears* to us that the sun crosses the sky each day'. What is the status of this latter fact? This statement describes an everyday experience which supports the *geocentric theory* in a straightforward way. But – importantly – this same everyday experience *also* supports the *heliocentric theory*, for otherwise the heliocentric theory would be *refuted* by our everyday experience. Why, then, does Sankey (correctly) say that 'geocentric astronomy has a basis in common-sense experience', instead of saying that *both* astronomical theories have a basis in common-sense experience? (Recall that the phrase 'common-sense experience' refers to interpreting the experience as reflecting the state of affairs in the world that obtains according to the common-sense beliefs.)

Consider the case of Brahe and Kepler and the way in which Hanson interprets it, as described above. Hanson makes a psychological conjecture, and whether it is true or not is a matter of fact to be determined by experimental psychology. In our context, according to Hanson there are four possible cases:

(a) The case of 'Hanson's Brahe': an observer experiences (feels, perceives) that the sun moves, and believes in geocentrism.

(b) The case of a contemporary lay person: an observer experiences that the sun moves, and believes in heliocentrism.

(c) The case of 'Hanson's Kepler': an observer experiences that the sun does *not* move (and the earth revolves about its axis), and believes in heliocentrism.

(d) The fourth logical option is, interestingly, missing in Hanson's account: it is the case of an observer who experiences that the sun does not move, and yet believes in geocentrism. We shall add this fourth case to our picture, because it provides a hint on the way to understanding the relations between common-sense realism and scientific realism.

To understand the differences between these four cases, let us distinguish between the *geometrical relations* between the sun and the earth and the *absolute movement* of either of them. The geometrical relations are compatible with all four options. But whereas (a) and (b) are compatible with the claim that the sun absolutely moves and the earth is at absolute rest (call this the 'sun moves'), (c) and (d) are compatible with the claim that the sun is at absolute rest and the earth revolves about its axis (call this the 'earth moves' option). Geocentrism takes the 'sun moves' option at face value and includes it in the astronomical theory, whereas heliocentrism says that the 'earth moves' option is true.

According to Sankey, the 'sun moves' option is part of common sense. Given this common-sense belief, option (a), the case of 'Hanson's Brahe', seems the easiest: the 'sun moves' feeling is explained by the geocentric theory according to which the sun indeed moves. Option (b) is a bit less easy, because it involves a prima facie incompatibility between the 'sun moves' common-sense belief and the heliocentric theory.

Importantly, the common-sense belief of 'sun moves' is *not* enforced on us by experience: our experience is compatible with the *geometrical relations*, and those are compatible with *both possible experiences*. Why, then, aren't we all 'Hansonian Keplers'? Why, despite believing as we do in heliocentrism, don't we change our common-sense belief in such a way that it would fit our theoretical beliefs in the most natural way, endorsing 'earth moves' beliefs? Option (c) of 'Hanson's Kepler' is structurally as simple as option (a) of 'Hanson's Brahe' and as compatible with the experienced geometrical relations. Why, then, is it not prevalent? The key to understanding this is noticing that, even for Hanson, case (d) is absent. If an 'earth moves' feeling would be possible for us, we would not rule out case (d).

Of course, we could say that we are born with 'sun moves' beliefs as a default which is changeable, or that it so happens to be the case that the 'sun moves' belief just happens to be common to all known cultures. In any case, the main point is that whether or not cases (c) and (d) are psychologically possible is a question of fact, not of logical possibility or conceptual precedence; the fact that (a) and (b) are prevalent while (c) and (d) are not has nothing to do with the contents of these beliefs. What, then, explains this fact?

If the *observed* (the sun, the earth, and their geometrical relations) and the *theory* (either geocentrism or heliocentrism) cannot explain our preference for the 'sun moves' option over the 'earth moves' option, then perhaps the explanation for this preference lies in us – in the *observer*. This is the line we shall take in the next section.

RESTORING THE COHERENCE OF SCIENTIFIC REALISM BY FOCUSING ON THE RIGHT EXPLANANDUM: COMMON SENSE AS A PSYCHOLOGICAL FACT

One way to look at the preference for 'sun moves' beliefs over 'earth moves' beliefs – that is, for the fact that the former is part of our common sense but the latter is not – is to return to the distinction between the three kinds of characterizations of common-sense beliefs. This preference is, first and foremost, a *psychological fact*. As such, there are two naturalistic (families of) ways to explain it.

Route (I) is to assume that the content of our common-sense beliefs reflects *correctly* something about the external world, and to explain the route from the external world via our sense organs to our brains in such a way that this psychological fact comes about.

Route (II) is to accept that it may be the case that the content of our common-sense beliefs does *not* reflect correctly the external world but that this content is (nevertheless) created in a way that science can explain; for example, by describing the interactions between our sense organs and the environment and then a causal chain that ends up in a certain brain state.

Sankey (2014) took route (I); this leads to the problems described in the previous section – and so I propose to take route (II).[7] This line of thinking will solve the dilemma and add to the strength of scientific realism, as I show momentarily. Here are some more details, beginning with an analysis of some examples mentioned above.

Start with the case of astronomy. As we saw in the previous section, the contents of the common-sense belief that the 'sun moves' has two relevant aspects. One (the geometrical relations between the positions of the sun and earth) is compatible with both geocentrism and heliocentrism, and the other (the absolute motion of the sun) is compatible only with geocentrism. Why is the 'sun moves' belief so irresistible despite the fact that it is false according to heliocentrism, a theory that we accept as true? Why isn't our common sense heliocentric? Why do cases (a) and (b) seem reasonable and cases (c) and (d) not, as presented in the previous section? This calls for explanation.

The explanans that is suitable to this explanandum consists of science as a whole, including in particular the science of the sensory system and of mental states.[8] What science must explain is how our common-sense beliefs come about, given that the world is as science tells us it is. The explanation must not stop at describing the external world (for instance, it cannot stop by saying that the world is heliocentric and not geocentric): it must include an account of why it is that we come to have certain *mental* pictures and not others, given that the world is as science describes it (e.g., why we are compelled to experience the data in a geocentric way and not in a heliocentric way). If brains are the seat of the mental experience, then the explanation must include an account of the workings of our brains.[9] It is still true that upon replacing geocentric astronomy with heliocentric astronomy 'the appearances do not change. Neither does common-sense experience. What changes is what we think happens. Our understanding of what takes place is altered' (Sankey 2014: 19). But it is *not* true – more precisely, it is not the whole story – that 'heliocentrism explains why common-sense experience is the way that it is' (Sankey 2014: 19). It is the entire body of science, including in particular the science pertaining to our mentality, that must take part in this endeavour. Our understanding of what takes place in our heads, not (only) outside, should be altered if we are to give a scientific account of common sense.[10]

This account is reductionist, but it does not have to be eliminativist. For example, Eddington's (1928) account is not eliminativist: for him the common-sense table does not disappear. Instead, it ceases to be a description of the table; it becomes a description of Mr Eddington's mental state. Therefore, in this account, Mr Eddington is not mistaken in describing the table in the terms of common sense, if we understand common sense correctly, as pertaining to mental states (which are brain states, in a fully psychophysical reductionist view). In our context, we should understand Mr Eddington's uttering 'My table is substantial' as Mr Eddington saying 'I entertain the belief that my table is substantial', where the latter is a correct description of his own mental state. This mental state should – in turn – be accounted for by science. Science should account for the very fact of his state of belief; but this need does not entail that the content of this belief is true of the world, in this case, of the table itself.

Above I presented the psychological criterion for beliefs to form part of common sense as the feeling that these beliefs are irresistible. I distinguished between two notions of irresistibility. Case (1) was such that the feeling of irresistibility is essentially temporary and depends on the circumstances; it may disappear as alternative ideas are presented to us. In case (2), by contrast, regardless of the beliefs that one holds (and expresses) following scientific research, one is compelled to feel the same; for example, to feel – and act accordingly, verbally and otherwise – that the earth is static and the sun revolves around it. Here I would like to focus on this latter case. I will assume for the sake of this discussion that this is in fact the case concerning the geocentric picture (a point that is subject to scientific investigation). Sankey seems to take this picture to be part of common sense, in the sense that even a person who, like Kepler, is convinced that the heliocentric picture is a more accurate account of reality than the geocentric picture, is psychologically compelled, when watching the sun set, to experience the sun descending rather than the earth revolving. Whether or not this is the case is a matter of psychological fact about human beings, about our brain and the way that it brings about our mental states. I leave the determination of this matter of fact to scientific psychological research. My aim here is clarification, and so I distinguish between two cases and focus on one of them. The two cases – distinguished above – are (1) the set of beliefs that initially seem compelling just because we couldn't think 'outside of the box', but once a new perspective is offered to us these beliefs are no longer compelling and we can change them; and (2) a set of beliefs such that due to our making we are physiologically-psychologically compelled to hold them. As I said, while the very existence of the second set is to be determined by scientific psychological research, I will here conjecture that they might exist, and the cases that prompt me to do so are the new findings in cognitive and brain science concerning our conceptions regarding the very way in which we experience the world. Whether Sankey's astronomical example belongs to case (1) or to case (2) is a question of fact; here, for the sake of discussion, I will take it to belong to case (2). I will assume, that is, that such beliefs are *wired* into our cognitive system so that we can't help but experience the world in this way. We continue experiencing the environment in a certain way even if we are convinced by scientific arguments that the mind-independent environment is not at all like this. And the task that science must undertake – if it is to explain common sense and restore the coherence of scientific realism – is to provide a scientific explanation of why it is that we find it irresistible to continue holding beliefs that according to our convictions are false.

'A doctrine of common-sense that cannot reconcile itself to science ... would be a doctrine not worth having' (Rescher 2005: 156). But what does reconciling a doctrine of beliefs with science amount to? Rescher writes, 'we can indeed call upon science to look at common-sense at large – at the wholesale rather than retail level, so to speak – and to explain at the physiological, psychological, and sociological levels: how it is that a creature such as Homo sapiens, placed in the world as we indeed are, should have effectively universal beliefs of the common-sense type' (Rescher 2005: 130). So far, I concur: a belief is reconciled with science if science as a whole can explain how the psychological fact of entertaining it came to be. However, in the approach that I propose here, this is all there is to reconciling common sense with science. In particular, the scientific explanation of entertaining a belief need not entail that the content of this belief is true of the world. In fact, with respect to common sense it is quite the opposite: since the pictures of science and of common sense are radically different, if science is correct then the contents of (at least some of) the common-sense beliefs are *not* correct, and therefore (*pace* Rescher) we should *not* aim to show (and we will *not* succeed in showing) 'why it is that such [common-sense] beliefs will be substantially correct' (Rescher 2005: 130). Those common-sense beliefs are not true, and science will explain both why they are false, and why we nevertheless entertain them.

To sum up, in a nutshell, I propose the following doctrine of common sense. Suppose that we are testing empirically a given scientific theory. In testing it we make observations, and we describe these in sentences that are common-sense-laden. Then, after the theory is confirmed, we take it to be true, according to scientific realism. And then we challenge our theory to explain how we came to have the common-sense beliefs that formed part of the confirming statements. This psychological fact is the explanandum. The explanans consists of all the relevant scientific theories: it can involve both claims about the external world and claims about the way in which our experiences come about. The explanation need not entail that the contents of our common-sense beliefs are true, since these contents may be false and remain so after the scientific explanation. The challenge will be to explain how we came to entertain these contents, regardless of whether they are true or false: the truth value of our common-sense beliefs plays no important role in the scientific explanation of common sense.[11]

On the proposed account, science explains two sorts of facts and, according to scientific realism, makes true statements about them. One sort of facts is about, for example, Eddington's scientific table – facts independent of the existence of Mr Eddington. The other sort of facts is about Mr Eddington's mental states, including his beliefs with the contents of a common-sense table. These latter facts are not about the table, but about Mr Eddington's mental state, and possibly also about the causal (or other) chain that brought it about, which may include some aspects of the scientific table. There is no contradiction between the two kinds of facts, even if the *contents* of Mr Eddington's beliefs contradict the *contents* of the scientific statements about the table. Since there is no contradiction, coherence of scientific realism is restored.

Since in this picture scientific realism is coherent, it is also strengthened. Suppose that science delivers the goods and explains how we come to have our common-sense experience. In this case we complete a cycle, thereby establishing that our overall scientific world picture is *coherent*. Moreover, because of this coherence science is the best explanation of our common-sense experiences; and as such we have good reason to accept it as (approximately) *true* about the world, including about ourselves.

The so-called common-sense philosophers, such as Reid and Moore, sought to provide knowledge claims with a *foundation*, and they found it in common sense.[12] Presumably, for them coherence would not suffice. However, foundationalism based on common sense is incompatible with scientific realism. And so, if one thinks that there are good reasons to endorse scientific realism, then one needs to eschew common-sense realism. A viable option is the above proposal: achieve coherence between scientific realism and common sense by providing a scientific account of the psychological fact of common-sense beliefs, and take this coherence as the best support of scientific realism from inference to the best explanation.

This account is naturalistic. Part of it is the idea that we and everything about us are part of nature, and are thus within the intended domain of science. In 'everything' here I include the mental phenomena: the mental is not supernatural nor extrascientific. Needless to say, I do not claim that we know how to go about accounting for the mental in contemporary scientific terms. I think we have no clue whatsoever about this, despite all the advancement in brain science. The claim is one of principle and part of a general naturalistic outlook. It is fair to say that the account of the mental is the main challenge for contemporary science, and extending naturalism to the mental domain is (at present) a commitment, supported by the success of the naturalistic project so far[13] – not more than that.[14]

NOTES

1 Importantly, as Psillos (2009: chapter 2) emphasizes, scientific realism as such is not necessarily reductive, in that it can be, and sometimes is, taken to be about all the facts that are stated by the sciences, not only those of so-called 'fundamental' science. Here, non-fundamental science should be distinguished from common sense; for the non-reductivism of scientific realism does not imply supporting the reality of non-scientific common-sense entities.

2 It seems to me that Moore does not commit the fallacy of deriving the epistemological characterization from the psychological one. By contrast, Thomas Reid is sometimes charged with this fallacy, but Nichols and Yaffe (2015) think this charge is mistaken.

3 For challenging the psychological characterization see, for example, Sankey's 'Science, Common-Sense and Reality' (unpublished manuscript). For challenging the epistemological characterization see, for example, Eddington (1928).

4 For the flat-physicalist view, see Shenker (2017) and Hemmo and Shenker's 'On Why Functionalism Is a Form of "Token-Dualism"' (unpublished manuscript).

5 There are non-foundationalist metaphysical views, but they are not specifically relevant for our present discussion.

6 Some say that this distortion has evolutionary advantages; for example, McKay and Dennett (2009). But this is only as good as evolutionary arguments get, and in any case this is not relevant to my point here.

7 According to (II), scientific realism does not entail common-sense realism and this, in turn, entails that one should argue for scientific realism on grounds other than expanding or generalizing common-sense realism. Since Sankey (2008) argues for scientific realism on such grounds, route (II) is in tension with his overall project, and so it is natural for him to take route (I).

8 Here and everywhere in this chapter I assume, of course, that science can explain the mental. I do not argue for this assumption here.

9 By the way, for those who endorse the thesis of multiple realization of the mental by the physical or the physiological, non-brain systems 'made of Swiss cheese' (Putnam 1967) can have the same mental images. It is not clear that, for them, the claim that 'brains are the seat of mental experience' is in fact part of contemporary science.

10 This may suggest that meanings are in the head. If the reader endorses externalism, then she needs to refer to the environment in addition to the brain. I reject externalism, but I will not argue for this here.

11 This may be suggestive of the principles of the so-called strong programme in the sociology of scientific knowledge (Bloor 1991). But my claim here, while certainly naturalistic, is not sociological. If anything, it is physicalist.

12 See Rescher (2005: especially chapter 5).

13 See Papineau (2001) on this.

14 I am very grateful to Howard Sankey for his perceptive, careful, and extremely helpful comments on this chapter, and to the editors of this volume for comments that helped to greatly clarify and improve this chapter.

References

Albert, D. 2000. *Time and Change*. Cambridge, MA: Harvard University Press.

Alston, W. P. 1976. 'Two Types of Foundationalism'. *The Journal of Philosophy* 73: 165–85.

Alston, W. P. 1985. 'Thomas Reid on Epistemic Principles'. *History of Philosophy Quarterly* 2: 435–52.

Alston, W. P. 1991. *Perceiving God: The Epistemology of Religious Experience*. Ithaca, NY: Cornell University Press.

Alston, W. P. 1993. *The Reliability of Sense Perception*. Ithaca, NY: Cornell University Press.

Amoroso, R. L., Kauffman, L. H., and Rowlands, P. 2013. *The Physics of Reality: Space, Time, Matter, Cosmos*. Singapore: World Scientific.

Anscombe, G. E. M. 1963. *An Introduction to Wittgenstein's 'Tractatus'*. 2nd rev. edn. New York: Harper & Row.

Armstrong, D. 2004. *Truth and Truthmakers*. Cambridge: Cambridge University Press.

Ásta. 2018. *Categories We Live By: The Construction of Sex, Gender, Race, and Other Social Categories*. Oxford: Oxford University Press.

Audi, R. 1999. 'Moral Knowledge and Ethical Pluralism'. In J. Greco and E. Sosa (eds), *The Blackwell Guide to Epistemology*, London: Blackwell, 271–302.

Austin, J. L. 1961a. 'Other Minds'. In J. O. Urmson and G. J. Warnock (eds), *Philosophical Papers*, Oxford: Clarendon, 44–84.

Austin, J. L. 1961b. *Philosophical Papers*. Edited by J. O. Urmson and G. J. Warnock. Oxford: Clarendon.

Austin, J. L. 1961c. 'A Plea for Excuses'. In J. O. Urmson and G. J. Warnock (eds), *Philosophical Papers*, Oxford: Clarendon, 175–204.

Austin, J. L. 1962. *Sense and Sensibilia*. Edited by G. J. Warnock. 2nd edn. Oxford: Oxford University Press.

Avenarius, R. 1891. *Der menschliche Weltbegriff*. Leipzig: O. R. Reisland.

Avramides, A. 2017. 'Wittgenstein and Ordinary Language Philosophy'. In H. Glock and J. Hyman (eds), *A Companion to Wittgenstein*, Hoboken: John Wiley and Sons, 718–30.

Ayer, A. J. 1952. *Language, Truth, and Logic*. New York: Dover.

Ayer, A. J. 1969. *Metaphysics and Common Sense*. New York: Macmillan.

Baggott, J. 2013. *Farewell to Reality: How Modern Physics Has Betrayed the Search for Scientific Truth*. New York: Pegasus Books.

Baker, G. 2002. 'Wittgenstein on Metaphysical/Everyday Use'. *The Philosophical Quarterly* 52 (208): 289–302.

Baldwin, T. 2011. 'Wittgenstein and Moore'. In M. McGinn (ed.), *The Oxford Handbook of Wittgenstein*, Oxford: Oxford University Press, 550–69.

Barnes, W. H. F. 1933. 'A Suggestion about Value'. *Analysis* 1: 45 6.

Baz, A. 2012. *When Words Are Called For: A Defense of Ordinary Language Philosophy*. Cambridge, MA: Harvard University Press.

Beattie, J. 1770. *An Essay on the Nature and Immutability of Truth; in Opposition to Sophistry and Scepticism*. Edinburgh: A. Kincaid, J. Bell, and E. and C. Dilly.

Beattie, J. 1774. *An Essay on the Nature and Immutability of Truth, in Opposition to Sophistry and Scepticism*. 5th edn. London: Edward and Charles Dilly and William Creech.

Beattie, J. 1775–6. 'Hints for an Answer to Dr Priestley's Remarks on the Essay on Truth'. MS 30/46, Aberdeen University Library.

Beattie, J. 1777. *An Essay on the Nature and Immutability of Truth, in Opposition to Sophistry and Scepticism*. 6th edn. Edinburgh: William Creech et al.

Beilby, J. (ed.) 2002. *Naturalism Defeated? Essays on Plantinga's Evolutionary Argument against Naturalism*. Ithaca, NY: Cornell University Press.

Bergmann, G. 1957. *Philosophy of Science*. Madison: University of Wisconsin Press.

Berington, J. 1776. *Letters on Materialism and Hartley's Theory of the Human Mind, Addressed to Dr. Priestley, F.R.S.* London: G. Robinson.

Berkeley, G. 1964. *The Works of George Berkeley: Bishop of Cloyne*. Edited by A. A. Luce and T. E. Jessop. London: Thomas Nelson and Sons.

Bermes, C. 2004. *'Welt' als Thema der Philosophie*. Hamburg: Felix Meiner.

Blankenburg, W. 2012. *Der Verlust der natürlichen Selbstverständlichkeit: Eine Beitrag zur Psychopathologie symptomarmer Schizophrenien*. Berlin: Parados Verlag.

Bliss, R., and Trogdon, K. 2016. 'Metaphysical Grounding'. In E. N. Zalta (ed.), *The Stanford Encyclopedia of Philosophy* (Winter 2016). https://plato .stanford.edu/archives/win2016/entries/grounding/.

Bloor, D. 1991. *Knowledge and Social Imagery*. Chicago: Chicago University Press.

Boltzmann, L. 1895. 'On Certain Questions of the Theory of Gases'. *Nature* 51: 413–15.

BonJour, L. 1985. *The Structure of Empirical Knowledge*. Cambridge, MA: Harvard University Press.

Bostrom, N. 2003. 'Are We Living in a Computer Simulation?' *The Philosophical Quarterly* 53 (211): 243–55.

Boudry, M., and Pigliucci, M. (eds) 2017. *Science Unlimited? The Challenges of Scientism*. Chicago: University of Chicago Press.

Bourget, D., and Chalmers, D. J. 2014. 'What Do Philosophers Believe?' *Philosophical Studies* 170 (3): 465–500.

Brandt, R. 1979. *A Theory of the Good and the Right*. Oxford: Oxford University Press.

Bricker, P. 2016. 'Ontological Commitment'. In E. N. Zalta (ed.), *The Stanford Encyclopedia of Philosophy* (Winter 2016). https://plato.stanford.edu/arch ives/win2016/entries/ontological-commitment/.

Broady, A. 1990. *The Tradition of Scottish Common Sense Philosophy*. Edinburgh: Polygon.

Brooks, T. 2017. 'British Idealism'. *Oxford Bibliographies: Philosophy*. www .oxfordbibliographies.com/view/document/obo-9780195396577/ob o-9780195396577-0015.xml.

Brown, T. 1824. *Lectures on the Philosophy of the Human Mind*. 4 vols. 2nd edn. Edinburgh: W. and C. Tait.

Buffier, C. 1724. *Traité des premières véritez et de la source de nos jugements, où l'on examine le sentiment des philosophes de ce temps, sur les premières notions des choses*. Paris: François Didot.

Burge, T. 1995. 'Our Entitlement to Self-Knowledge'. *Proceedings of the Aristotelian Society, Supplementary Volumes* 69 (1): 91–116.

Cameron, R. 2008. 'Truthmakers and Ontological Commitment: Or, How to Deal with Complex Objects and Mathematical Ontology without Getting into Trouble'. *Philosophical Studies* 140: 1–18.

Campbell, G. 1762. *A Dissertation on Miracles: Containing an Examination of the Principles Advanced by David Hume, Esq; in an Essay on Miracles*. Edinburgh: A. Kincaid and J. Bell.

Campbell, G. 1776. *The Philosophy of Rhetoric*. 2 vols. London: W. Strahan and T. Cadell.

Campbell, K. 1988. 'Philosophy and Common Sense'. *Philosophy* 63: 161–74.

Carnap, R. 1937. *Philosophy and Logical Syntax*. London: Kegan Paul, Trench, Trubner.

Cartwright, N. 1983. *How the Laws of Physics Lie*. Oxford: Oxford University Press.

Cartwright, N. 1999. *The Dappled World*. Cambridge: Cambridge University Press.

Chakravartti, A. 2015. 'Scientific Realism'. In E. N. Zalta (ed.), *The Stanford Encyclopedia of Philosophy* (Fall 2015). http://plato.stanford.edu/arch ives/fall2015/entries/scientific-realism/.

Chalmers, D., and Jackson, F. 2001. 'Conceptual Analysis and Reductive Explanation'. *Philosophical Review* 110: 315–61.

Child, W. 2011. *Wittgenstein*. London: Routledge.

Chisholm, R. M. 1973. 'On the Nature of Empirical Evidence'. In R. M. Chisholm and R. J. Swartz (eds), *Empirical Knowledge*, Englewood Cliffs: Prentice–Hall, 224–49.

Chisholm, R. M. 1977. *Theory of Knowledge*. 2nd edn. Englewood Cliffs: Prentice-Hall.

Churchland, P. S. 1986. *Neurophilosophy: Toward a Unified Science of the Mind-Brain*. Cambridge, MA: MIT Press.

Churchland, P. S. 2002. *Brain-Wise: Studies in Neurophilosophy*. Cambridge, MA: MIT Press.

Churchland, P. S. 2011. *Braintrust: What Neuroscience Tells Us about Morality*. Princeton, NJ: Princeton University Press.

Coady, C. A. J. 2007. 'Moore's Common Sense'. In S. Nuccetelli and G. Seay (eds), *Themes from G. E. Moore: New Essays in Epistemology and Ethics*, Oxford: Oxford University Press, 100–18.

Coliva, A. 2010. *Moore and Wittgenstein: Scepticism, Certainty, and Common Sense*. London: Palgrave Macmillan.

Coliva, A. 2015. *Extended Rationality: A Hinge Epistemology*. London: Palgrave Macmillan.

Coliva, A., and Moyal-Sharrock, D. 2016. *Hinge Epistemology*. Leiden: Brill.

Copp, D. 2008. 'Darwinian Skepticism about Moral Realism'. *Philosophical Issues* 18 (1): 186–206.

Cowley, S. 2015. *Rational Piety and Social Reform in Glasgow: The Life, Philosophy and Political Economy of James Mylne (1757–1839)*. Eugene: Wipf and Stock.

Crary, A. 2002. 'The Happy Truth: J. L. Austin's How to Do Things with Words'. *Inquiry: An Interdisciplinary Journal of Philosophy* 45 (1): 59–80.

Cuneo, T., and Shafer-Landau, R. 2014. 'The Moral Fixed Points: New Directions for Moral Nonnaturalism'. *Philosophical Studies* 171 (3): 399–443.

Curd, P. 1998. *The Legacy of Parmenides: Eleatic Monism and Later Presocratic Thought*. Princeton, NJ: Princeton University Press.

Dainton, B. 2018. 'Temporal Consciousness'. In E. N. Zalta (ed.), *The Stanford Encyclopedia of Philosophy* (Winter 2018). https://plato.stanford.edu/arch ives/win2018/entries/consciousness-temporal/.

Daley, C. 2010. *An Introduction to Philosophical Methods*. Peterborough: Broadview Press.

Davia, C. 2017. 'Aristotle and the Endoxic Method'. *Journal of the History of Philosophy* 55 (3): 383–405.

Della Rocca, M. 2013. 'The Taming of Philosophy'. In M. Laerke, J. E. H. Smith, and E. Schliesser (eds), *Philosophy and Its History: Aims and Methods of Early Modern Philosophy*, Oxford: Oxford University Press, 178–208.

Dembroff, R. 2019. 'Beyond Binary: Genderqueer as Critical Gender Kind'. http://philsci-archive.pitt.edu/16317/1/Beyond%20Binary%20Final.pdf.

Deng, N. 2013. 'On Explaining Why Time Seems to Pass'. *The Southern Journal of Philosophy* 51 (3): 367–82.

Dennett, D., and Kinsbourne, M. 1992. 'Time and the Observer: The Where and When of Consciousness in the Brain'. *Behavioral and Brain Sciences* 15: 183–201.

De Ridder, J., Peels, R., and van Woudenberg, R. (eds) 2018. *Scientism: Prospects and Problems*. New York: Oxford University Press.

Descartes, R. 1964. *Oeuvres de Descartes*. Edited by C. Adam and P. Tannery. Paris: Vrin.

Descartes, R. 1984–5. *The Philosophical Writings of Descartes*. Translated by J. Cottingham, R. Stoothoff, and D. Murdoch. Cambridge: Cambridge University Press.

Descartes, R. 1988. *Descartes: Selected Philosophical Writings*. Cambridge: Cambridge University Press.

DeVries, W. 2016. 'Wilfrid Sellars'. In E. N. Zalta (ed.), *The Stanford Encyclopedia of Philosophy* (Winter 2016). https://plato.stanford.edu/archives/win2016/entries/sellars/.

Diels, H., and Kranz, W. 1951. *Fragmente der Vorsokratiker*. 6th edn. Berlin: Weidmann.

Dowe, P. 2007. 'Causal Processes'. In E. N. Zalta (ed.), *The Stanford Encyclopedia of Philosophy* (Summer 2018). https://plato.stanford.edu/entries/causation-process/.

Downing, L. 2005. 'Berkeley's Natural Philosophy and Philosophy of Science'. In K. P. Winkler (ed.), *The Cambridge Companion to Berkeley*, Cambridge: Cambridge University Press, 231–65.

Duhem, P. 1982. *The Aim and Structure of Physical Theory*. Translated by P. Wiener. Princeton, NJ: Princeton University Press.

Dupré, J. 1993. *The Disorder of Things: Metaphysical Foundations of the Disunity of Science*. Cambridge, MA: Harvard University Press.

Eddington, A. S., Sir. 1928. *The Nature of the Physical World*. New York: Macmillan; Cambridge: Cambridge University Press.

Elmahalawy, Y., Hellaby, C., and Ellis, G. F. R. 2015. 'Ricci Time in the Lemaître–Tolman Model and the Block Universe'. *General Relativity and Gravitation* 47: 113.

Emery, N. 2017. 'Against Radical Quantum Ontologies'. *Philosophy and Phenomenological Research* 95 (3): 564–91.

Ewing, A. C. 1973. 'Common Sense Propositions'. *Philosophy* 48: 363–79.

Fantl, J., and McGrath, M. 2010. 'Pragmatic Encroachment'. In S. Bernecker and D. Pritchard (eds), *Routledge Companion to Epistemology*, London: Routledge, 558–68.

Ferguson, A. 1785. *Institutes of Moral Philosophy*. 3rd edn. Edinburgh: John Bell and William Creech.

Fine, K. 2001. 'The Question of Realism'. *Philosophers' Imprint* 2: 1–30.

Fischer, E. 2005. 'Austin on Sense-Data: Ordinary Language Analysis as "Therapy"'. *Grazer Philosophische Studien* 70: 67–99.

Fish, S. 1980. *Is There a Text in This Class? The Authority of Interpretive Communities*. Cambridge, MA: Harvard University Press.

Fodor, J. 1974. 'Special Sciences: Or the Disunity of Science as a Working Hypothesis'. *Synthese* 28: 97–115.

Fogelin, R. J. 1996. 'Wittgenstein's Critique of Philosophy'. In H. D. Sluga and D. G. Stern (eds), *The Cambridge Companion to Wittgenstein*, Cambridge: Cambridge University Press, 34–58.

Fogelin, R. J. 2009. *Taking Wittgenstein at His Word: A Textual Study*. Princeton, NJ: Princeton University Press.

Foley, R. 1993. 'What's to Be Said for Simplicity?' *Philosophical Issues* 3: 209–24.

Forbes, W., Sir. 1807. *An Account of the Life and Writings of James Beattie, LL.D. Late Professor of Moral Philosophy and Logic in the Marischal College and University of Aberdeen*. 3 vols. 2nd edn. Edinburgh: Archibald Constable et al.

Fordyce, D. 1735. 'David Fordyce to William Craig, 23 December 1735'. MS 2670, fo. 158v, National Library of Scotland.

Fordyce, D. 1748. 'David Fordyce to John Canton, 30 April 1748'. Canton Papers, vol. II, fo. 15r, Royal Society of London.

Forguson, L. 1989. *Common Sense*. London: Routledge.

Frankfurt, H. 1969. 'Alternate Possibilities and Moral Responsibility'. *Journal of Philosophy* 66: 828–39.

Frede, D. 2012. 'The Endoxon Mystique: What Endoxa Are and What They Are Not'. *Oxford Studies in Ancient Philosophy* 43: 185–215.

French, S. 2000. 'The Reasonable Effectiveness of Mathematics: Partial Structures and the Application of Group Theory to Physics'. *Synthese* 125: 103–20.

Frye, M. 1983. *The Politics of Reality: Essays in Feminist Theory*. Berkeley: The Crossing Press.

Fumerton, R. 1995. *Metaepistemology and Skepticism*. Lanham, MD: Rowman and Littlefield.

Garvey, B. (ed.) 2014. *J. L. Austin on Language*. London: Palgrave-Macmillan.

Gaskin, R. 2013. *Language, Truth, and Literature: A Defence of Literary Humanism*. Oxford: Oxford University Press.

Gerard, A. 1760. *The Influence of the Pastoral Office on the Character Examined; with a View, Especially, to Mr. Hume's Representation of the Spirit of that Office*. Aberdeen: James Chalmers.

Gettier, E. 1963. 'Is Justified True Belief Knowledge?' *Analysis* 23 (6): 121–3.

Glasgow Literary Society. 1764–79. 'Minutes of the Glasgow College Literary Society, 1764–1779'. MS Murray 505, Glasgow University Library.

Goff, P., Seager, W., and Allen-Hermanson, S. 2017. 'Panpsychism'. In E. N. Zalta (ed.), *The Stanford Encyclopedia of Philosophy* (Winter 2017). https://plato.stanford.edu/archives/win2017/entries/panpsychism/.

Grayling, A. C. 2005. 'Berkeley's Argument for Immaterialism'. In K. P. Winkler (ed.), *The Cambridge Companion to Berkeley*, Cambridge: Cambridge University Press, 166–89.

Greco, J. 2011. 'Common Sense in Thomas Reid'. *The Canadian Journal of Philosophy* 41: 142–55.

Grice, P. 1989. *Studies in the Way of Words*. Cambridge, MA: Harvard University Press.

Gustafsson, M., and Sorli, R. (eds) 2011. *The Philosophy of J. L. Austin*. Oxford: Oxford University Press.

Haack, S. 2007. *Defending Science – Within Reason*. New York: Prometheus.

Hacking, I. 1983. *Representing and Intervening: Introductory Topics in the Philosophy of Natural Science*. Cambridge: Cambridge University Press.

Hacking, I. 1999. *The Social Construction of What?* Cambridge, MA: Harvard University Press.

Hankinson, R. J. 2003. 'Stoic Epistemology'. In B. Inwood (ed.), *The Cambridge Companion to the Stoics*, Cambridge: Cambridge University Press, 59–84.

Hanson, N. R. 1958. *Patterns of Discovery: An Inquiry into the Conceptual Foundations of Science*. Cambridge: Cambridge University Press.

Hanson, N. R. 1969. *Perception and Discovery: An Introduction to Scientific Inquiry*. Belmont: Wadsworth.

Hardie, P. 1719. *Dissertatio philosophica de immaterialitate animæ*. Aberdeen: James Nicol.

Hare, R. M. 1952. *The Language of Morals*. Oxford: Clarendon.

Hare, R. M. 1963. *Freedom and Reason*. Oxford: Clarendon.

Hare, R. M. 1981. *Moral Thinking*. Oxford: Oxford University Press.

Harris, J. A 2015. *Hume: An Intellectual Biography*. Cambridge: Cambridge University Press.

Haselager, P. 2020. 'Conceptual Revisions: Intentions and Free Will in the Light of Cognitive Neuroscience'. In R. Peels, J. de Ridder, and R. van Woudenberg (eds), *Scientific Challenges to Common Sense Philosophy*, London: Routledge, 104–20.

Haslanger, S. 2012. *Resisting Reality: Social Construction and Social Critique*. Oxford: Oxford University Press.

Heisenberg, M. 2009. 'Is Free Will an Illusion?' *Nature* 459: 164–5.

Heisenberg, W. K. 1958. *Physics and Philosophy: The Revolution in Modern Science*. London: George Allen & Unwin.

Hirsch, E. 2011. *Quantifier Variance and Realism: Essays in Metaontology*. New York: Oxford University Press.

Horwich, P. 2011. *Wittgenstein's Metaphilosophy*. Oxford: Oxford University Press.

Hossenfelder, S. 2018. *Lost in Math: How Beauty Leads Physics Astray*. New York: Basic Books.

Hume, D. (1739–40) 2007. *A Treatise of Human Nature*. Edited by D. F. Norton and M. J. Norton. 2 vols. Oxford: Clarendon.

Hume, D. (1740) 2007. *An Abstract of a Book Lately Published, Entitled, A Treatise of Human Nature, &c. Wherein the Chief Argument of that Book Is Farther Illustrated and Explained*. In D. Hume, *A Treatise of Human Nature*. Edited by D. F. Norton and M. J. Norton. 2 vols. Oxford: Clarendon, 403–17.

Hume, D. (1745) 2007. *A Letter from a Gentleman to His Friend in Edinburgh*. In D. Hume, *A Treatise of Human Nature*. Edited by D. F. Norton and M. J. Norton. 2 vols. Oxford: Clarendon, 419–31.

Hume, D. (1748) 2000. *An Enquiry Concerning Human Understanding*. Edited by T. L. Beauchamp. Oxford: Clarendon.

Hume, D. 1777. *Essays and Treatises on Several Subjects*. 2 vols. New edn. London: T. Cadell, A. Donaldson and W. Creech.

Hume, D. 1932. *The Letters of David Hume*. Edited by J. Y. T. Greig. 2 vols. Oxford: Clarendon.

Hursthouse, R., and Pettigrove, G. 2016. 'Virtue Ethics'. In E. N. Zalta (ed.), *The Stanford Encyclopedia of Philosophy* (Summer 2018). https://plato .stanford.edu/entries/ethics-virtue/.

Husserl, E. 1950a. *Die Idee der Phänomenologie*. The Hague: Martinus Nijhoff.

Husserl, E. 1950b. *Ideen I*. The Hague: Martinus Nijhoff.

Husserl, E. 1952. *Ideen II*. The Hague: Martinus Nijhoff.

Husserl, E. 1992. *Grundprobleme der Phänomenologie 1910/1911*. Hamburg: Felix Meiner.

Inwood, B., and Donini, P. 1999. 'Stoic Ethics'. In K. Algra, J. Barnes, J. Mansfeld, and M. Schofield (eds), *The Cambridge History of Hellenistic Philosophy*, Cambridge: Cambridge University Press, 675–738.

Jackson, F. 1989. 'A Puzzle about Ontological Commitment'. In J. Heil (ed.), *Cause, Mind, and Reality*, Dordrecht: Kluwer, 191–200.

James, W. 1897. *The Will to Believe and Other Essays in Popular Philosophy*. Cambridge, MA: Harvard University Press.

Jeffrey, F. 1803–4. 'Review of D. Stewart, *Account of the Life and Writings of Thomas Reid, D.D.F.R.S. Edin. Late Professor of Moral Philosophy in the University of Glasgow*'. *Edinburgh Review* 3: 269–87.

Jenkins, J. J. 1983. *Understanding Locke*. Edinburgh: Edinburgh University Press.

Jensen, H. 1979. 'Reid and Wittgenstein on Philosophy and Language'. *Philosophical Studies* 36 (4): 359–76.

Jessop, T. E. 1953. *Berkeley: Philosophical Writings*. Austin: University of Texas Press.

Johansen, T. K. 2016. 'Parmenides' Likely Story'. *Oxford Studies in Ancient Philosophy* 50: 1–29.

Joyce, R. 2006. *The Evolution of Morality*. Cambridge, MA: MIT Press.

Kahneman, D. 2011. *Thinking, Fast and Slow*. New York: Farrar, Straus and Giroux.

Kant, I. (1783) 1950. *Prolegomena to Any Future Metaphysics*. Translated by L. W. Beck. Indianapolis: Bobbs-Merrill.

Kant, I. (1783) 1971. *Prolegomena to Any Future Metaphysics*. Translated by P. G. Lucas. Manchester: Manchester University Press.

Kaplan, M. 2000. 'To What Must an Epistemology Be True?' *Philosophy and Phenomenological Research* 61 (2): 279–304.

Kelly, T. 2008. 'Common Sense as Evidence: Against Revisionary Ontology and Skepticism'. *Midwest Studies in Philosophy* 32 (1): 53–78.

Kienzler, W. 2006. 'Wittgenstein and John Henry Newman on Certainty'. *Grazer Philosophische Studien* 71: 117–38.

Kimberg, D. Y., and Farah, M. J. 1993. 'A Unified Account of Cognitive Impairments Following Frontal Lobe Damage: The Role of Working Memory in Complex, Organized Behavior'. *Journal of Experimental Psychology* 122: 411–28.

Kline, A. D. 1987. 'Berkeley's Theory of Common Sense'. *International Studies in Philosophy* 19 (3): 21–31.

Korman, D. 2014. 'Debunking Perceptual Beliefs about Ordinary Objects'. *Philosophers' Imprint* 14: 1–21.

Korman, D. 2019. 'Easy Ontology without Deflationary Metaontology'. *Philosophy and Phenomenological Research* 99 (1): 236–43.

Kovacs, D. M. 2019. 'How to Be an Uncompromising Revisionary Ontologist'. *Synthese*: 1–24.

Ladyman, J., and Ross, D. 2007. *Every Thing Must Go: Metaphysics Naturalized*. Oxford: Oxford University Press.

Lawlor, K. 2013. *Assurance: An Austinian View of Knowledge and Knowledge Claims*. Oxford: Oxford University Press.

Lawlor, K. 2017. 'Austin on Perception, Knowledge, and Meaning'. In S. L. Tsohatzidis (ed.), *Interpreting Austin: Critical Essays*, Cambridge: Cambridge University Press, 165–85.

Lawlor, K. 2018. 'Ordinary Language Philosophy Needs Situation Semantics (or, Why Grice Needs Austin)'. In E. Marchesan and D. Zapero (eds), *Context, Truth and Objectivity: Essays on Radical Contextualism*, London: Routledge.

Leite, A. 2012. 'Austin, Dreams, and Scepticism'. In M. Gustafsson and R. Sorli (eds), *The Philosophy of J. L. Austin*, Oxford: Oxford University Press, 78–113.

Lemos, N. 2004. *Common Sense: A Contemporary Defense*. Cambridge: Cambridge University Press.

Lemos, N. 2008. 'Moore and Skepticism'. In J. Greco (ed.), *Oxford Handbook of Skepticism*, Oxford: Oxford University Press, 330–47.

Lemos, N. 2020. 'Common Sense, Philosophy, and Science'. In R. Peels, J. de Ridder, and R. van Woudenberg (eds), *Scientific Challenges to Common Sense Philosophy*, London: Routledge, 20–39.

Lesher, J. H. 1991. 'Xenophanes on Inquiry and Discovery: An Alternative to the 'Hymn to Progress' Reading of Fr.18'. *Ancient Philosophy* 11: 229–48.

Lesher, J. H. (ed.) 1992. *Xenophanes of Colophon, Fragments: A Text and Translation with a Commentary*. Toronto: University of Toronto Press.

Lewis, D. 1986. *On the Plurality of Worlds*. Oxford: Blackwell.

Libet, B. 2004. *Mind Time: The Temporal Factor in Consciousness*. Cambridge, MA: Harvard University Press.

Libet, B., Gleason, C. A., Wright, E. W., and Pearl, D. K. 1983. 'Time of Conscious Intention to Act in Relation to Onset of Cerebral Activity (Readiness-Potential): The Unconscious Initiation of a Freely Voluntary Act'. *Brain* 106: 623–42.

Linde, A. 2017. 'A Brief History of the Multiverse'. *Reports on Progress in Physics* 80 (2). https://doi.org/10.1088/1361-6633/aa50e4.

Linnebo, Ø. 2018. 'Platonism in the Philosophy of Mathematics'. In E. N. Zalta (ed.), *The Stanford Encyclopedia of Philosophy* (Summer 2018). https://plato.stanford.edu/entries/platonism-mathematics/.

Locke, J. (1690) 1990. *An Essay Concerning Human Understanding*. Edited by P. H. Nidditch. Oxford: Clarendon.

Locke, J. 1975. *An Essay Concerning Human Understanding*. Edited by P. H. Nidditch. Oxford: Oxford University Press.

Locke, J. 1997. *An Essay Concerning Human Understanding*. Edited by R. Woolhouse. New York: Penguin Books.

Long, A. A. 2002. *Epictetus: A Stoic and Socratic Guide to Life*. Oxford: Oxford University Press.

Long, A. A., and Sedley, D. N. 1987. *The Hellenistic Philosophers*. Cambridge: Cambridge University Press.

Longino, H. 1990. *Science as Social Knowledge: Values and Objectivity in Scientific Inquiry*. Princeton, NJ: Princeton University Press.

Longworth, G. 2015. 'John Langshaw Austin'. In E. N. Zalta (ed.), *The Stanford Encyclopedia of Philosophy* (Summer 2015). https://plato.stanford.edu/archives/sum2015/entries/austin-jl/.

Loux, M. J. 2006. *Metaphysics: A Contemporary Introduction*. 3rd edn. New York: Routledge.

Luce, A. A. 1963. *The Dialectic of Immaterialism*. London: Hodder & Stoughton.

Lycan, W. 2001. 'Moore against the New Skeptics'. *Philosophical Studies* 103 (1): 35–53.

Marcil-Lacoste, L. 1982. *Claude Buffier and Thomas Reid: Two Common-Sense Philosophers*. Kingston and Montreal: McGill-Queen's University Press.

Margolis, E., and Laurence, S. 2019. 'Concepts'. In E. N. Zalta (ed.), *The Stanford Encyclopedia of Philosophy* (Summer 2019). https://plato.stanford.edu/archives/sum2019/entries/concepts/.

Margolis, E., Samuels, R., and Stich, S. P. (eds) 2012. *The Oxford Handbook of Philosophy of Cognitive Science*. Oxford: Oxford University Press.

McAllister, B. 2016. 'Re-Evaluating Reid's Response to Skepticism'. *Journal of Scottish Philosophy* 14: 317–39.

McDermid, D. 2018. *The Rise and Fall of Scottish Common Sense Realism*. Oxford: Oxford University Press.

McDowell, J. 2009. 'Wittgenstein's "Quietism"'. *Common Knowledge* 15: 365–72.

McGinn, M. 1989. *Sense and Certainty: A Dissolution of Scepticism*. Oxford: Blackwell.

McKay, R. T., and Dennett, D. 2009. 'The Evolution of Misbelief'. *Behavioral and Brain Sciences* 32: 493–561.

McQueen, K., and Vaidman, L. 2020. 'How the Many Worlds Interpretation Brings Common Sense to Paradoxical Quantum Experiments'. In R. Peels, J. de Ridder, and R. van Woudenberg (eds), *Scientific Challenges to Common Sense Philosophy*, London: Routledge, 40–61.

Merricks, T. 2001. *Objects and Persons*. Oxford: Oxford University Press.

Mill, J. S. 1979. *Utilitarianism*. Indianapolis: Hackett.

Moore, G. E. 1903. *Principia Ethica*. Cambridge: Cambridge University Press.

Moore, G. E. 1914. 'The Status of Sense-Data'. *Proceedings of the Aristotelian Society* 14: 355–80.

Moore, G. E. 1917. 'The Conception of Reality'. *Proceedings of the Aristotelian Society* 18: 101–22.

Moore, G. E. 1918–19. 'Some Judgements of Perception'. *Proceedings of the Aristotelian Society* 19: 1–29.

Moore, G. E. 1922. *Philosophical Studies*. London: Kegan Paul, Trench, Trubner.

Moore, G. E. 1925. 'A Defence of Common Sense'. In J. H. Muirhead (ed.), *Contemporary British Philosophy* (second series), London: George Allen & Unwin, 193–223.

Moore, G. E. (1925) 1993. 'A Defence of Common Sense'. In T. Baldwin (ed.), *G. E. Moore: Selected Writings*, London: Routledge, 106–33.

Moore, G. E. 1939. 'Proof of an External World'. *Proceedings of the British Academy* 25 (5): 273–300.

Moore, G. E. 1942. 'A Reply to My Critics'. In P. A. Schilpp (ed.), *The Philosophy of G. E. Moore*, La Salle: Open Court, 533–687.

Moore, G. E. 1953a. 'Hume's Theory Examined'. In G. E. Moore, *Some Main Problems of Philosophy*, New York: Macmillan, 124–43.

Moore, G. E. 1953b. 'Sense-Data.' In G. E. Moore, *Some Main Problems of Philosophy*, London: George Allen & Unwin, 28–40.

Moore, G. E. 1953c. *Some Main Problems of Philosophy*. London: George Allen & Unwin.

Moore, G. E. 1959a. 'Certainty'. In G. E. Moore, *Philosophical Papers*, London: George Allen & Unwin, 226–51.

Moore, G. E. 1959b. 'A Defence of Common Sense'. In G. E. Moore, *Philosophical Papers*, London: Allen & Unwin, 32–59.

Moore, G. E. 1959c. 'Four Forms of Skepticism'. In G. E. Moore, *Philosophical Papers*, London: George Allen & Unwin, 196–226.

Moore, G. E. 1959d. *Philosophical Papers*. London: George Allen & Unwin.

Moore, G. E. 1960a. 'Hume's Philosophy'. In G. E. Moore, *Philosophical Studies*, London: Routledge & Kegan Paul, 147–67.

Moore, G. E. 1960b. 'Some Judgements of Perception'. In G. E. Moore, *Philosophical Studies*, London: Routledge & Kegan Paul, 220–52.

Moore, G. E. 1966. *Lectures on Philosophy*. London: George Allen & Unwin.

Moser, P. 1998. 'Epistemological Fission'. *The Monist* 81 (3): 353–70.

Mossner, E. C. 1948. 'Beattie's "The Castle of Scepticism": An Unpublished Allegory against Hume, Voltaire and Hobbes'. *University of Texas Studies in English* 27: 108–45.

Moyal-Sharrock, D. 2004. *Understanding Wittgenstein's 'On Certainty'*. London: Palgrave Macmillan.

Muirhead, J. H. 1924. 'Editor's Preface'. In J. H. Muirhead (ed.), *Contemporary British Philosophy: Personal Statements*, London: George Allen & Unwin, 9–12.

Nahmias, E. 2014. 'Is Free Will an Illusion? Confronting Challenges from the Modern Mind Sciences'. In W. Sinnott-Armstrong (ed.), *Moral Psychology. Vol. IV: Freedom and Responsibility*, Cambridge, MA: MIT Press, 1–26.

Newman, J. H. (1870) 1979. *An Essay in Aid of a Grammar of Assent*. Notre Dame, IN: University of Notre Dame Press.

Nichols, R., and Yaffe, G. 2015. 'Thomas Reid'. In E. N. Zalta (ed.), *The Stanford Encyclopedia of Philosophy* (Summer 2015). http://plato.stanford.edu/arch ives/sum2015/entries/reid/.

Nola, R., and Sankey, H. 2007. *Theories of Scientific Method*. Durham: Acumen.

Nolan, D. 2016. 'Method in Analytic Metaphysics'. In H. Cappelen, T. S. Gendler, and J. Hawthorne (eds), *The Oxford Handbook of Philosophical Methodology*, New York: Oxford University Press, 159–78.

Norton, D. F. 1982. *David Hume: Common-Sense Moralist, Sceptical Metaphysician*. Princeton, NJ: Princeton University Press.

O'Connor, T., and Wong, H. Y. 2015. 'Emergent Properties'. In E. N. Zalta (ed.), *The Stanford Encyclopedia of Philosophy* (Summer 2015). http://plato .stanford.edu/archives/sum2015/entries/properties-emergent/.

Oswald, J. 1766–72. *An Appeal to Common Sense in Behalf of Religion*. 2 vols. Edinburgh: A. Kincaid, J. Bell, et al.

Papineau, D. 2001. 'The Rise of Physicalism'. In C. Gillette and B. Loewer (eds), *Physicalism and Its Discontents*, Cambridge: Cambridge University Press, 1–36.

Pappas, G. S. 1991. 'Berkeley and Common Sense Realism'. *History of Philosophy Quarterly* 8 (1): 27–42.

Pappas, G. S. 2000. *Berkeley's Thought*. Ithaca, NY: Cornell University Press.

Paul, L. A. 2010. 'A New Role for Experimental Work in Metaphysics'. *Review of Philosophy and Psychology* 1: 461–76.

Paul, L. A. 2012. 'Metaphysics as Modeling: The Handmaiden's Tale'. *Philosophical Studies* 160 (1): 1–29.

Paul, L. A. 2016. 'Experience, Metaphysics, and Cognitive Science'. In J. Sytsma and W. Buckwalter (eds), *A Companion to Experimental Philosophy*, Hoboken: Wiley Blackwell, 419–33.

Peacock, H. 2011. 'Two Kinds of Ontological Commitment'. *Philosophical Quarterly* 61 (242): 79–104.

Peels, R. 2017a. 'The Fundamental Argument against Scientism'. In M. Boudry and M. Pigliucci (eds), *Science Unlimited? The Challenges of Scientism*, Chicago: Chicago University Press, 165–84.

Peels, R. 2017b. *Responsible Belief: A Theory in Ethics and Epistemology*. New York: Oxford University Press.

Peels, R., de Ridder, J., and van Woudenberg, R. (eds) 2020. *Scientific Challenges to Common Sense Philosophy*. London: Routledge.

Perkins, P. 2016. 'The Philosophical Relation between Husserl and Avenarius in "The Basic Problems of Phenomenology"'. *Ideas y Valores* 65 (162): 409–11.

Pigliucci, M. 2008. 'Is Evolvability Evolvable?' *Nature Reviews Genetics* 9: 75–82.

Pigliucci, M. 2018a. 'Scientism and Pseudoscience: In Defense of Demarcation Projects'. In M. Boudry and M. Pigliucci (eds), *Science Unlimited? The Challenges of Scientism*, Chicago: University of Chicago Press, 185–201.

Pigliucci, M. 2018b. 'Stoicism'. In J. Fiesner (ed.), *Internet Encyclopedia of Philosophy* (Summer 2018). http://www.iep.utm.edu/stoicism/.

Pitcher, G. 1984. *Berkeley*. London: Routledge.

Plantinga, A. 1993. *Warrant and Proper Function*. Oxford: Oxford University Press.

Plantinga, A. 2011. *Where the Conflict Really Lies: Science, Religion, and Naturalism*. Oxford: Oxford University Press.

Polger, T., and Shapiro, L. 2016. *The Multiple Realization Book*. Oxford: Oxford University Press.

Pomeroy, R. 1974. 'Moore as an Ordinary-Language Philosopher'. *Metaphilosophy* 5 (2): 76–105.

Priestley, J. 1774. *An Examination of Dr. Reid's Inquiry into the Human Mind on the Principles of Common Sense, Dr Beattie's Essay on the Nature and Immutability of Truth, and Dr. Oswald's Appeal to Common Sense in Behalf of Religion*. London: J. Johnson.

Priestley, J. 1775. *Hartley's Theory of the Human Mind, on the Principles of the Association of Ideas; with Essays Relating to the Subject of It.* London: J. Johnson.

Prinz, J. 2007. *The Emotional Construction of Morals.* Oxford: Oxford University Press.

Pritchard, D. 2015a. *Epistemic Angst: Radical Skepticism and the Groundlessness of Our Believing.* Princeton, NJ: Princeton University Press.

Pritchard, D. 2015b. 'Wittgenstein on Faith and Reason: The Influence of Newman'. In M. Szatkowski (ed.), *God, Truth and Other Enigmas*, Berlin: Walter de Gruyter, 141–64.

Pritchard, D. 2017. 'Wittgenstein on Hinge Commitments and Radical Scepticism in *On Certainty'*. In H. Glock and J. Hyman (eds), *Blackwell Companion to Wittgenstein*, Oxford: Blackwell, 563–75.

Pritchard, D. 2020. 'Wittgensteinian Epistemology, Epistemic Vertigo, and Pyrrhonian Scepticism'. In K. M. Vogt and J. Vlasits (eds), *Epistemology after Sextus Empiricus*, Oxford: Oxford University Press, 173–92.

Proctor, R. W., and Capaldi, E. J. 2012. *Psychology of Science: Implicit and Explicit Processes.* Oxford: Oxford University Press.

Pryor, J. 2004. 'What's Wrong with Moore's Argument?' *Philosophical Issues* 14 (Epistemology): 349–78.

Psillos, S. 2009. *Knowing the Structure of Nature.* London: Macmillan.

Putnam, H. 1967. 'Psychological Predicates'. In W. H. Capitan and D. D. Merrill (eds), *Art, Mind, and Religion*, Pittsburgh: University of Pittsburgh Press, 37–46.

Putnam, H. 1982. *Reason, Truth and History.* Cambridge: Cambridge University Press.

Quine, W. V. 1953. 'On What There Is'. In W. V. Quine, *From a Logical Point of View*, New York: Harper, 1–19.

Quine, W. V. 1969. 'Natural Kinds'. In W. V. Quine, *Ontological Relativity and Other Essays*, New York: Columbia University Press, 114–38.

Rae, M. (ed.) 1997. *Material Constitution: A Reader.* Boulder, CO: Rowman and Littlefield.

Rawls, J. 1999. *A Theory of Justice.* 2nd edn. Oxford: Oxford University Press.

Rayo, A. 2007. 'Ontological Commitment'. *Philosophy Compass* 2 (3): 428–44.

Recanati, F. 2004. *Literal Meaning.* Cambridge: Cambridge University Press.

Reid, T. (1764) 1983. *Inquiry and Essays.* Edited by R. E. Beanblossom and K. Lehrer. Indianapolis: Hackett.

Reid, T. (1764) 1997. *An Inquiry into the Human Mind on the Principles of Common Sense.* Edited by D. Brookes. Edinburgh: Edinburgh University Press.

Reid, T. 1769. 'Of Common Sense Curâ primâ'. MS 2131/2/III/7, Aberdeen University Library.

Reid, T. 1770. '[Untitled Discourse on Common Sense]'. MS 2131/2/III/8, Aberdeen University Library.

Reid, T. 1775. 'Review of J. Priestley, *Hartley's Theory of the Human Mind, on the Principles of the Association of Ideas; with Essays Relating to the Subject of It*'. *Monthly Review* 53: 380–90.

Reid, T. 1775? 'Of Constitution'. MS 3061/8, Aberdeen University Library.

Reid, T. 1776. 'Review of J. Priestley, *Hartley's Theory of the Human Mind, on the Principles of the Association of Ideas; with Essays Relating to the Subject of It*'. *Monthly Review* 54: 41–7.

Reid, T. (1785) 2002. *Essays on the Intellectual Powers of Man*. Edited by D. Brookes. Edinburgh: Edinburgh University Press.

Reid, T. 1915. *Selections from the Scottish Philosophy of Common Sense*. Chicago: Open Court Publishing. https://oll.libertyfund.org/titles/reid-selections-from-the-scottish-philosophy-of-common-sense.

Reid, T. 1969. *Essays on the Active Powers of the Human Mind*. Cambridge, MA: MIT Press.

Reid, T. 1989. *The Philosophical Orations of Thomas Reid Delivered at Graduation Ceremonies in King's College, Aberdeen, 1753, 1756, 1759, 1762*. Edited by D. D. Todd. Translated by S. D. Sullivan. Carbondale and Edwardsville: Southern Illinois University Press.

Reid, T. 2002. *The Correspondence of Thomas Reid*. Edited by P. Wood. Edinburgh: Edinburgh University Press.

Reppert, V. 2012. 'The Argument from Reason'. In W. L. Craig and J. P. Moreland (eds), *The Blackwell Companion to Natural Theology*, Oxford: Blackwell, 344–90.

Rescher, N. 2005. *Common-Sense: A New Look at an Old Philosophical Tradition*. Milwaukee: Marquette University Press.

Rettler, B. 2016. 'The General Truthmaker View of Ontological Commitment'. *Philosophical Studies* 143: 1405–25.

Rinard, S. 2013. 'Why Philosophy Can Overturn Common Sense'. In T. S. Gendler and J. Hawthorne (eds), *Oxford Studies in Epistemology, Vol. IV*, Oxford: Oxford University Press, 185–213.

Rinard, S. 2017. 'No Exception for Belief'. *Philosophy and Phenomenological Research* 94 (1): 121–43.

Roberts, J. R. 2007. *A Metaphysics for the Mob: The Philosophy of George Berkeley*. Oxford: Oxford University Press.

Rosen, S. 2002. *The Elusiveness of the Ordinary*. New Haven, CT: Yale University Press.

Rosenberg, A. 2011. *The Atheist's Guide to Reality: Enjoying Life without Illusions*. New York: W. W. Norton.

Rosenfeld, S. 2011. *Common Sense: A Political History*. Cambridge, MA: Harvard University Press.

Roskies, A. L. 2012. 'How Does the Neuroscience of Decision Making Bear on Our Understanding of Moral Responsibility and Free Will?' *Current Opinion in Neurobiology* 22: 1022–6.

Ross, D., Ladyman, J., and Spurrett, D. 2007. 'In Defence of Scientism'. In J. Ladyman and D. Ross, *Every Thing Must Go: Metaphysics Naturalized*, Oxford: Oxford University Press, 1–65.

Ruse, M. 1986. *Taking Darwin Seriously*. Oxford: Blackwell.

Russell, B. 1912. *The Problems of Philosophy*. Oxford: Oxford University Press.

Russell, B. 1914. *Our Knowledge of the External World as a Field for Scientific Method in Philosophy*. London: George Allen & Unwin.

Russell, B. 1940. *An Inquiry into Meaning and Truth*. London: Allen & Unwin.

Russell, B. 1948. *Human Knowledge: Its Scope and Limits*. London: Allen & Unwin.

Sankey, H. 2008. *Scientific Realism and the Rationality of Science*. London: Ashgate.

Sankey, H. 2014. 'Common-Sense and Realism'. *Kairos: Revista de Filosofia & Ciencia* 10: 11–24.

Sattig, T. 2006. *The Language and Reality of Time*. Oxford: Oxford University Press.

Schaffer, J. 2009. 'The Deflationary Meta-ontology of Thomasson's *Ordinary Objects*'. *Philosophical Books* 50 (3): 142–57.

Schönbaumsfeld, G. 2016. *The Illusion of Doubt*. Oxford: Oxford University Press.

Schultze-Kraft, M., Birman, D., Rusconi, M., Allefeld, C., Görgen, K., Dähne, S., Blankertz, B., and Haynes, J. D. 2016. 'The Point of No Return in Vetoing Self-Initiated Movements'. *Proceedings of the National Academy of Sciences* 113: 1080–5.

Schurger, A., Sitt, J. D., and Dehaene, S. 2012. 'An Accumulator Model for Spontaneous Neural Activity Prior to Self-Initiated Movement'. *Proceedings of the National Academy of Sciences* 109: E2904–13.

Scott, R. E. 1810. *Inquiry into the Limits and Peculiar Objects of Physical and Metaphysical Science, Tending Principally to Illustrate the Opinions of Philosophers, Ancient and Modern, concerning That Relation*. London: Longman et al.

Searle, J. 1999. *Mind, Language and Society*. London: Weidenfield and Nicolson.

Sellars, W. 1962. 'Philosophy and the Scientific Image of Man'. In R. Colodny (ed.), *Frontiers of Science and Philosophy*, Pittsburgh: University of Pittsburgh Press, 35–78.

Sellars, W. 1963. *Empiricism and the Philosophy of Mind*. London: Routledge & Kegan Paul.

Semendeferi, K., Lu, A., Schenker, N., and Damasio, H. 2002. 'Humans and Great Apes Share a Large Frontal Cortex'. *Nature Neuroscience* 5: 272–6.

Shafer Landau, R. 2012. *The Fundamentals of Ethics*. 2nd edn. New York: Oxford University Press.

Shenker, O. 2017. 'Flat Physicalism: Some Implications'. *Iyyun: The Jerusalem Philosophical Quarterly* 66: 211–25.

Sidelle, A. 2008. 'Review of Amie L. Thomasson, *Ordinary Objects*'. *Philosophical Quarterly* 58 (230): 172–6.

Sider, T. 2001. *Four-Dimensionalism: An Ontology of Persistence and Time*. Oxford: Oxford University Press.

Sider, T. 2009. 'Ontological Realism'. In D. Chalmers, R. Wasserman, and D. Manley (eds), *Metametaphysics: New Essays on the Foundations of Ontology*, New York: Oxford University Press, 384–423.

Sider, T. 2011. *Writing the Book of the World*. Oxford: Oxford University Press.

Siegel, S. 2010. *The Contents of Visual Perception*. Oxford: Oxford University Press.

Smith, B. 1995. 'Common Sense'. In B. Smith (ed.), *The Cambridge Companion to Husserl*, Cambridge: Cambridge University Press, 394–437.

Soldinger, E. 2010. 'Husserls Auseinandersetzung mit Avenarius und Mach und ihr Verhältnis zur Lebensweltproblematik'. In P. Merz, A. Staiti, and F. Steffen (eds), *Geist – Person – Gemeinschaft: Freiburger Beiträge zur Aktualität Husserls*, Würzburg: Ergon Verlag, 189–217.

Sommer, M. 1985. *Husserl und der frühe Positivismus*. Frankfurt: Vittorio Klostermann.

Sosa, E. 1994. 'Philosophical Scepticism and Epistemic Circularity'. *Proceedings of the Aristotelian Society, Supplement* 68: 263–90.

Stevenson, C. L. 1944. *Ethics and Language*. New Haven, CT: Yale University Press.

Stewart, D. 1793. *Outlines of Moral Philosophy*. Edinburgh: William Creech.

Stewart, D. 1803. *Account of the Life and Writings of Thomas Reid, D.D.F.R.S. Edin. Late Professor of Moral Philosophy in the University of Glasgow*. 2nd edn. Edinburgh: William Creech, and Longman and Rees.

Stewart, D. (1815–21) 1854–60. *Dissertation: Exhibiting the Progress of Metaphysical, Ethical and Political Philosophy, since the Revival of*

Letters in Europe. In Sir W. Hamilton (ed.), *The Collected Works of Dugald Stewart, Esq., F.R.S.S.* 11 vols. Edinburgh: T. Constable, vol. I.

Street, S. 2006. 'A Darwinian Dilemma for Realist Theories of Value'. *Philosophical Studies* 127 (1): 109–66.

Strevens, M. 2019. *Thinking Off Your Feet: How Empirical Psychology Vindicates Armchair Philosophy.* Cambridge, MA: Harvard University Press.

Stroud, B. 1984. *The Significance of Philosophical Scepticism.* Oxford: Clarendon.

Suderman, J. M. 2001. *Orthodoxy and Enlightenment: George Campbell in the Eighteenth Century.* Montreal, Kingston, London, and Ithaca, NY: McGill-Queen's University Press.

Surowiecki, J. 2003. *The Wisdom of Crowds.* New York: Doubleday.

Tahko, T. 2016. *Introduction to Metametaphysics.* Cambridge: Cambridge University Press.

Taylor, C. C. W. 2010. *The Atomists: Leucippus and Democritus; Fragments.* Toronto: University of Toronto Press.

Thomasson, A. L. 2007. *Ordinary Objects.* New York: Oxford University Press.

Thomasson, A. L. 2015. *Ontology Made Easy.* New York: Oxford University Press.

Tipton, I. C. 1974. *Berkeley: The Philosophy of Immaterialism.* London: Methuen.

Tomeček, M. 2015. *Berkeley's Common Sense and Science.* New York: Peter Lang.

Traill, R. 1755. *The Qualifications and Decorum of a Teacher of Christianity Considered; with a View to the Temper of the Present Age Respecting Religion, and to Some Late Attacks Which Have Been Made upon It.* Aberdeen: James Chalmers.

Travis, C. 2008. *Occasion-Sensitivity: Selected Essays.* Oxford: Oxford University Press.

Tsohatzidis, S. L. (ed.) 2018. *Interpreting J. L. Austin: Critical Essays.* Cambridge: Cambridge University Press.

Turnbull, G. (1726) 2014. 'On the Most Beautiful Structure of the Material and the Rational World'. In G. Turnbull, *Education for Life: Correspondence and Writings on Religion and Practical Philosophy.* Edited by M. A. Stewart and P. Wood. Indianapolis: Liberty Fund, 59–74.

Ulman, H. L. (ed.) 1990. *The Minutes of the Aberdeen Philosophical Society, 1758–1773.* Aberdeen: Aberdeen University Press.

Unger, P. 1982. 'Toward a Psychology of Common Sense'. *American Philosophical Quarterly* 19: 117–29.

Unger, R. M., and Smolin, L. 2014. *The Singular Universe and the Reality of Time: A Proposal in Natural Philosophy.* Cambridge: Cambridge University Press.

Vachaspati, T., Pogosian, L., and Steer, D. A. 2015. 'Cosmic Strings'. *Scholarpedia* 10 (2): 316–82.

Van Cleve, J. 2015. *Problems from Reid*. Oxford: Oxford University Press.

Van Inwagen, P. 1990. *Material Beings*. Ithaca, NY: Cornell University Press.

Van Inwagen, P. 1997. 'Foreword'. In M. Rae (ed.), *Material Constitution: A Reader*, Boulder, CO: Rowman and Littlefield, ix–xii.

Van Inwagen, P. 2009. 'Being, Existence, and Ontological Commitment'. In D. Chalmers, R. Wasserman, and D. Manley (eds), *Metametaphysics: New Essays on the Foundations of Ontology*, New York: Oxford University Press, 472–506.

Van Woudenberg, R. 2006. 'Conceivability and Modal Knowledge'. *Metaphilosophy* 37: 210–21.

Van Woudenberg, R. 2014a. 'Disagreement, Design, and Thomas Reid'. *Canadian Journal of Philosophy* 41: 224–39.

Van Woudenberg, R. 2014b. 'True Qualifiers for Qualified Truths'. *The Review of Metaphysics* 68: 3–36.

Van Woudenberg, R. 2018. 'Reading as a Source of Knowledge'. *Synthese*. https://doi.org/10.1007/s11229-018-02056-x.

Van Woudenberg, R. 2021. *The Epistemology of Reading and Interpretation*. Cambridge: Cambridge University Press.

Van Woudenberg, R., and Peels, R. 2018. 'The Metaphysics of Degrees'. *European Journal of Philosophy* 26 (1): 46–65.

Varzi, A. 2011. 'Boundaries, Conventions, and Realism'. In J. K. Campbell, M. O'Rourke, and M. Slater (eds), *Carving Nature at Its Joints: Natural Kinds in Metaphysics and Science*, Cambridge, MA: MIT Press, 129–53.

Virvidakis, S. 2006. 'Varieties of Quietism'. *Philosophical Inquiry* 30: 157–75.

Wagner, S. 2014. *Squaring the Circle in Descartes' Meditations: The Strong Validation of Reason*. Cambridge: Cambridge University Press.

Waterfield, R. 2000. *The First Philosophers: The Presocratics and the Sophists*. Oxford: Oxford University Press.

Wegner, D. M. 2002. *The Illusion of Conscious Will*. Cambridge, MA: MIT Press.

Wegner, D. M., and Wheatley, T. 1999. 'Apparent Mental Causation'. *American Psychologist* 54: 480–92.

White, A. 1986. 'Common Sense: Moore and Wittgenstein'. *Revue Internationale de Philosophie* 40 (158): 313–30.

Wigner, E. 1960. 'The Unreasonable Effectiveness of Mathematics in the Natural Sciences'. *Communications in Pure and Applied Mathematics* 13 (1): 1–14.

Wilkins, J. S., and Griffiths, E. P. 2013. 'Evolutionary Debunking Arguments in Three Domains: Fact, Value, and Religion'. In J. M. G. Dawes (ed.), *A New Science of Religion*, New York: Routledge, 133–46.

Williams, M. 1991. *Unnatural Doubts: Epistemological Realism and the Basis of Scepticism*. Oxford: Blackwell.

Williams, M. 2004. 'Wittgenstein's Refutation of Idealism'. In D. McManus (ed.), *Wittgenstein and Scepticism*, London: Routledge, 76–96.

Williamson, T. 2000. *Knowledge and Its Limits*. Oxford: Oxford University Press.

Wisdom, J. 1942. 'Moore's Technique'. In P. A. Schilpp (ed.), *The Philosophy of G. E. Moore*, La Salle: Open Court, 421–50.

Wittgenstein, L. 1953. *Philosophical Investigations*. New York: Macmillan Company.

Wittgenstein, L. 1969. *On Certainty*. Edited by G. E. M. Anscombe and G. H. von Wright. Translated by D. Paul and G. E. M. Anscombe. Oxford: Blackwell.

Wolpert, L. 1992. *The Unnatural Nature of Science*. Cambridge, MA: Harvard University Press.

Wolterstorff, N. 2001. *Thomas Reid and the Story of Epistemology*. Cambridge: Cambridge University Press.

Wood, P. 1993. *The Aberdeen Enlightenment: The Arts Curriculum in the Eighteenth Century*. Aberdeen: Aberdeen University Press.

Wood, P. 2012. 'Dugald Stewart's Original Letter on James Beattie's *Essay on Truth*, 1805–1806'. *History of European Ideas* 38: 103–21.

Wood, P. 2018. 'The "New Empire of Common Sense": The Reception of Common Sense Philosophy in Britain, 1764–1793'. In C. B. Bow (ed.), *Common Sense in the Scottish Enlightenment*, Oxford: Oxford University Press, 165–99.

Wright, C. 1985. 'Facts and Certainty'. *Proceedings of the British Academy* 71: 429–72.

Wright, C. 2004a. 'Scepticism, Certainty, Moore and Wittgenstein'. In M. Köbel and B. Weiss (eds), *Wittgenstein's Lasting Significance*, London: Routledge, 228–48.

Wright, C. 2004b. 'Warrant for Nothing (and Foundations for Free)?' *Proceedings of the Aristotelian Society* 78: 167–212.

Wright, C. 2014. 'On Epistemic Entitlement (II): Welfare State Epistemology'. In D. Dodd and E. Zardini (eds), *Scepticism and Perceptual Justification*, Oxford: Oxford University Press, 211–47.

Wright, J. P. 1987. 'Hume vs. Reid on Ideas: The New Hume Letter'. *Mind* 96: 392–8.

Zagzebski, L. T. 2012. *Epistemic Authority: A Theory of Trust, Authority, and Autonomy in Belief*. Cambridge: Cambridge University Press.

Index

Other Volumes in the Series of Cambridge Companions